A VERY
STABLE
GENIUS

A VERY STABLE GENIUS

DONALD J. TRUMP'S
TESTING OF AMERICA

PHILIP RUCKER AND
CAROL LEONNIG

BLOOMSBURY PUBLISHING
LONDON · OXFORD · NEW YORK · NEW DELHI · SYDNEY

BLOOMSBURY PUBLISHING
Bloomsbury Publishing Plc
50 Bedford Square, London, WC1B 3DP, UK

BLOOMSBURY, BLOOMSBURY PUBLISHING and the Diana logo are
trademarks of Bloomsbury Publishing Plc

First published in Great Britain 2020

A catalogue record for this book is available from the British Library

ISBN: HB: 978-1-5266-0907-6; TPB: 978-1-5266-0908-3;
eBook: 978-1-5266-0905-2

4 6 8 10 9 7 5 3

4 6 8 10 9 7 5

Printed and bound in Great Britain by CPI Group (UK) Ltd, Croydon CR0 4YY

MIX
Paper from
responsible sources
FSC® C020471

To find out more about our authors and books visit
www.bloomsbury.com and sign up for our newsletters

To John, Elise, and Molly—you are my everything.

To Naomi and Clara Rucker

CONTENTS

———

AUTHORS' NOTE

Reporting on Donald Trump's presidency has been a dizzying journey. Stories fly by every hour, every day. With each momentous event we chronicled, we realized history was unfolding in front of our eyes and we had little chance to take stock. There was always something next. So we decided to hit the pause button. We wanted to drill down deeper than our daily news reporting allowed, to truly understand what was happening behind the scenes, and to assess the reverberations for the country.

This book is based on hundreds of hours of interviews with more than two hundred sources, including Trump administration officials, friends, and outside advisers to the president, as well as other witnesses to the events described herein. Most of the people who cooperated with our project agreed to speak candidly only on the condition of anonymity, either to protect their careers in the government or because they feared retaliation from the president or his allies. Many of our sources recounted their experiences in a background capacity, meaning we were permitted to use the information they shared so long as we protected their identities and did not attribute details to them by name. We recorded many of our interviews.

We are objective journalists who seek to share the truth with the public. In this book, we aimed to provide the closest version of the truth that we could determine based on rigorous reporting. We carefully reconstructed scenes to reveal President Trump unfiltered, showing him in action rather than telling readers what to think of him. These scenes are based on firsthand accounts and, whenever possible, corroborated by multiple sources and buttressed by our review of calendars, diary entries, internal memos, and other correspondence among principals, as well as private video recordings. Dialogue cannot always be exact but is based here on multiple people's memories of events and, in many cases, contemporaneous notes taken by witnesses. In a few instances, sources disagreed substantively about the facts in an episode, and when necessary we note that in these pages, recognizing that different narrators sometimes remember events differently.

This book is an outgrowth of our reporting for *The Washington Post*. As such, some of the details in our narrative first appeared in stories we authored for the newspaper, some of them in collaboration with other colleagues. However, the vast majority of the scenes, dialogue, and quotations are original to our book and based on the extensive reporting we conducted exclusively for this project.

To reconstruct episodes that played out in public, we relied upon video of events, such as presidential speeches, many of which are archived on C-SPAN's website. We also relied on contemporaneous news reports in an array of publications. We have also drawn from the government record, including the report produced by special counsel Robert S. Mueller III, and in most instances built upon the published record with our own original reporting. Material gleaned from such accounts is properly attributed, with a direct reference either in the text or in the endnotes.

We sought to interview President Trump for this project and first approached him in the early stages of our reporting. In a phone call, Trump told Philip Rucker he would like to sit for an interview. "Come in. You'll do a fair one," Trump said. The president added, "I'll do it. I'll do it. I'll do it. I'd like to have a proper book done. You're a serious person. So that's good." In later months, as Trump escalated his war with the media, he declined through an aide the opportunity to sit for an interview and to provide his own recollection and context for events described in this book. After several weeks of back-and-forth discussions, Trump's spokespeople were unable to substantively answer questions about those events or to provide the president's responses before the deadline for publication.

PROLOGUE

I alone can fix it."

On July 21, 2016, as he accepted the Republican presidential nomination in Cleveland, Donald John Trump spoke more than four thousand words, but these five would soon become the tenet by which he would lead the nation.

That night, Trump stood by himself at the center of Quicken Loans Arena on an elevated stage, which he had helped to design. A massive screen framed in gold soared behind him, projecting a magnified picture of himself along with thirty-six American flags. This was a masculine, LED manifestation of his own self-image. His speech was dark and dystopian. He offered himself to the American people as their sole hope for renewal and redemption. Past presidential nominees had expressed humility, extolled shared values, and summoned their countrymen to unite to accomplish what they could only achieve together. But Trump spoke instead of "I."

"I am your voice."

"I will be a champion—your champion."

"Nobody knows the system better than me, which is why I alone can fix it."

It would be all too easy to mistake Trump's first term for pure, uninhibited chaos. His presidency would be powered by solipsism. From the moment Trump swore an oath to defend the Constitution and commit to serve the nation, he governed largely to protect and promote himself. Yet while he lived day to day, struggling to survive, surfing news cycles to stay afloat, there was a pattern and meaning to the disorder. Trump's North Star was the perpetuation of his own power, even when it meant imperiling our shaky democracy. Public trust in American government, already weakened through years of polarizing political dysfunction, took a body blow.

Tens of millions of Americans were angry, feeling forgotten by bureaucrats in Washington, derided by liberal elites, and humiliated by a global economy that had sped ahead of their skills and consigned their children to be the first American generation to fare less well than their parents. Trump crowned himself their champion. He promised them he would "make America great again," a brilliant, one-size-fits-all mantra through which this segment of the country could channel their frustrations. They envisioned an America in which regulations didn't strangle the family business, taxes weren't so onerous, and good-paying jobs were plentiful and secure. Some of them also harked back to the 1950s, envisioning a simpler, halcyon America in which white male patriarchs ruled the roost, decorous women kept home and hearth, and minorities were silent or subservient.

President Trump was the indefatigable pugilist for MAGA nation. He did not bother with carefully selecting a group of leaders to help him govern. The flashy promoter and reality-television star believed he could run the U.S. government the way he led his real estate development company from a corner suite on the twenty-sixth floor of Trump Tower—on his own gut instincts to seize opportunities and to size up and cut down competitors.

Yet Trump's own recklessness hampered his ability to accomplish the very pledges on which he campaigned. From the start, government novices and yes-men made up much of his inner circle, a collective inexperience that exacerbated the troubles, wasted political capital, and demoralized committed public servants. The universal value of the Trump administration was loyalty—loyalty not to the country but to the president himself. Some of his aides believed his demand for blind fealty—

and his retaliation against those who denied it—was slowly corrupting public service and testing democracy itself.

Two kinds of people went to work for the administration: those who thought Trump was saving the world and those who thought the world needed to be saved from Trump. The latter, who at times were drawn in by Trump's charm, were seasoned and capable professionals who felt a duty to lend him their erudition and expertise. Yet as the months clicked by, the president wore down these "adults in the room" with what they considered the inanity, impropriety, and illegality of his ideas and directives. One by one, these men and women either resigned in frustration or were summarily dismissed by Trump. He engaged in a constant cycle of betrayal, rupturing and repairing relationships anew to constantly keep his government aides off balance to ensure the continuity of his supremacy. Some of them now sigh from a distance at a president they hoped to guide and the realization that fewer voices of wisdom remain to temper his impulses. They lament a president who nursed petty grievances, was addicted to watching cable television news coverage of himself, elevated sycophants, and lied with abandon.

Trump has delivered in part on his promise to be a human hand grenade, to raze and remake Washington. He has weakened the regulatory state, toughened border enforcement, and refashioned the federal judiciary, including with two nominations to the Supreme Court—all priorities for his conservative political base.

Trump also transformed America's trade posture, weakening multilateral agreements, which he believed allowed smaller countries to take advantage of the United States, and forging new bilateral accords on more favorable terms. He inherited a growing economy from President Obama and kept it humming, even as economists in mid-2019 predicted an eventual downturn.

As Trump often reminded his critics, he has been a president like no other. He has challenged the rule of law and jolted foreign alliances, disregarding seventy years of relations with other democracies while encouraging dictators and despots. He questioned the nation's very identity as a diverse haven for people of all races and creeds by not silencing the white supremacists and bigots among his followers—and, occasionally, by employing racist rhetoric of his own. He treated subordinates and military officers with malice and detained migrant families. He broke boundaries for reasons significant and picayune, nefarious and innocuous. For this president, all that mattered was winning.

Trump's ego prevented him from making sound, well-informed judgments. He stepped into the presidency so certain that his knowledge was the most complete and his facts supreme that he turned away the expertise of career professionals upon whom previous presidents had relied. This amounted to a wholesale rejection of America's model of governing, which some of his advisers concluded was born of a deep insecurity. "Instead of his pride being built on making a good decision, it's built on knowing the right answer from the onset," a senior administration official said.

When Trump's own intelligence analysts presented him with facts, the president at times claimed conspiracies. He refused to fully acknowledge that Russia had tried to help him win the 2016 election, despite conclusive evidence. He sought to thwart the Justice Department's investigation of Russia's election interference—and, after Robert Mueller was appointed special counsel, tried to have him removed. Yet Trump escaped being accused of a crime, despite scores of federal prosecutors who believed he would have faced criminal charges if he were anyone other than a sitting president.

These are conclusions drawn from nearly three years of reporting about Trump's presidency. They reflect the experiences and opinions of several of the most senior principals who served in his administration, lived its dysfunction, and now fear the damage it is inflicting on the country they served. They took us for the first time inside some of the most controversial and defining moments of Trump's presidency.

In a way, never before has an American president been as accessible and transparent as Trump. He telegraphed his moods and aired his disagreements in daily, sometimes hourly posts on Twitter. Behind-the-scenes revelations of tumult and lawlessness spilled forth daily. Whistleblowers stood up in dark corners of the federal bureaucracy to bring light to corruption and malfeasance. The president's state of mind was obvious to anyone. But the greater and perhaps more shocking meaning of the events of Trump's first term, beyond the daily news cycle, has not yet been made clear.

"I've served the man for two years. I think he's a long-term and immediate danger to the country," a senior national security official told us.

Another senior administration official said, "The guy is completely crazy. The story of Trump: a president with horrible instincts and a senior-level cabinet playing Whac-A-Mole."

Most of the officials who spoke with us did so on the condition of anonymity to avoid retribution from Trump and his team or because they felt honor-bound not to publicly criticize a sitting president. Sometimes government officials decide to cooperate with book authors to settle scores or generate a political outcome, and certainly some of our sources fall into this category. However, we found that many of them were motivated to tell the truth for the benefit of history. Some wanted to accurately explain moments that had been contorted by the president and his handlers' spin, easily forgotten, or, in some cases, kept entirely secret until now.

Trump's defenders said those who fear his presidency have it all wrong. What others saw as recklessness, they saw as the courage to make decisions. They pointed out that every night on television the president's critics decried the end of democracy as we know it but the sun still rose the next morning.

There are no perfect heroes in our book. Robert Mueller, perhaps Trump's greatest antagonist, was a faultless paragon of integrity from his days as a platoon commander in Vietnam to his directorship of the FBI, but emerged from two years of shadowboxing with Trump with scratches. In the estimation of many fellow prosecutors, he got outfoxed.

World leaders, meanwhile, were ever adjusting to react to Trump's whims. Allies had little faith in what U.S. diplomats said because they could be overruled by a presidential tweet at a moment's notice. Foreign presidents and prime ministers were terrified about what Trump might plunge into in the name of "America First."

"This guy is the most powerful man on earth," said Gérard Araud,

France's ambassador to the United States for the first two years of Trump's presidency. "Everything he does and decides may have very, very dire consequences on us, so we are all in a mode of damage control." Ahead of Trump's first major summit with foreign counterparts, the May 2017 Group of Seven gathering in Taormina, Sicily, Trump's advisers offered the other governments damage-control tips: don't be patronizing to Trump, and sprinkle in compliments of him. "It was all advice on how to handle a difficult teenager—a very sensitive, touchy teenager," Araud recalled. "So you have six adults trying not to excite him, and they are facing somebody who has no restraint and no limits. To be the adult in the room is to suffer the tantrum of the kid and not to take it seriously."

The title of this book borrows Trump's own words. In January 2018, as Trump neared the end of his first year in office, a national discussion was under way about the president's fitness for office—specifically, his mental acuity and psychological health. Just before sunrise on January 6, Trump tweeted that the media were "taking out the old Ronald Reagan playbook and screaming mental stability and intelligence."

"Actually, throughout my life, my two greatest assets have been mental stability and being, like, really smart," he continued. "Crooked Hillary Clinton also played these cards very hard and, as everyone knows, went down in flames. I went from VERY successful businessman, to top T.V. Star to President of the United States (on my first try). I think that would qualify as not smart, but genius . . . and a very stable genius at that!"

Trump invoked the "stable genius" phrase at least four additional times. At a NATO summit in July 2018, he labeled himself "a very stable genius" as he tried to dismiss a reporter's question about whether he would reverse his support for NATO after leaving the Brussels meeting. In a July 2019 morning tweetstorm that covered everything from the Democratic presidential primaries to the Pledge of Allegiance, Trump wrote of himself, "What you have now, so great looking and smart, a true Stable Genius!" On a Saturday morning in September 2019, Trump quoted himself on Twitter by writing: "'A Very Stable Genius!' Thank you." And in October 2019, as he defended his conduct on a phone call with his Ukrainian counterpart, Trump remarked, "There are those that think I'm a very stable genius, okay? I watch my words very, very closely."

Critics mockingly concluded that any man who feels compelled to announce to the world that he is a stable genius is neither stable nor a genius; however, Trump's intimates offered a different interpretation. "He truly has genius characteristics," said Thomas Barrack, a longtime Trump friend and business associate who chaired his presidential inaugural. "Like all these savants, he has edges that at times people wish weren't there. He may not have the trained or staged elegance of an Obama or the ambassadorial restraint of a Kennedy or the soft regal-ness of a Reagan, but he has a kind of brilliance and charisma that is unique, rare, and captivating, although at times misunderstood. When he speaks one-on-one or to a crowd, you believe that you are the only star in his galaxy. . . . He is a genius warrior."

Many close observers of Trump saw his so-called genius as far more destabilizing. One of them was Peter Wehner, who served in the Ronald Reagan, George H. W. Bush, and George W. Bush administrations. An early and outspoken critic of Trump's, Wehner was one of the first Republicans to warn publicly about his psychological unfitness to be president. By the spring of 2019, Wehner had become truly distraught by what he was witnessing.

"He is a transgressive personality, so he likes to attack and destroy and unsettle people," Wehner said. "If he sees an institution that he thinks is not doing his bidding, not protecting him like he wants or is a threat to him, he'll go after it. The intelligence community because they didn't tell him what he wanted to hear. The Justice Department because it wasn't doing what he wanted to do. The North Atlantic Treaty Organization because he doesn't think they pay enough. . . . The press is 'the enemy of the people.' So he doesn't have any regard for institutions, the role they play, why they're important, and he delights in tearing them down."

Wehner pointed to the British philosopher and statesman Edmund Burke, who wrote in his 1790 pamphlet, *Reflections on the Revolution in France*, that "the rudest hand" of any mob could annihilate an institution but rebuilding one from the rubble would be far more difficult. "Rage and phrenzy will pull down more in half an hour than prudence, deliberation, and foresight can build up in a hundred years."

What follows is a chronological account of Trump's vainglorious pursuit of power in his first term, one that seeks to make meaning by finding patterns in the seeming chaos. There are rages and frenzies but also moments of courage and perseverance. The narrative is intended to reveal Trump at his most unvarnished and expose how decision making in his administration has been driven by one man's self-centered and unthinking logic—but a logic nonetheless. This is the story of how Trump and his advisers have scrambled to survive and tested the strength of America's democracy and its common heart as a nation.

PART
ONE

BUILDING BLOCKS

O n November 9, 2016, President-elect Donald Trump began to staff his administration. Because he never truly expected to win, he was unprepared. Trump prioritized loyalty above all, and so, instinctively, he and his family knew whom to knight first: Michael Flynn.

Flynn was a retired lieutenant general and had been a respected intelligence officer. Yet his former colleagues had shunned him for a bill of particulars that included Islamophobic rhetoric, coziness with Russia and other foreign adversaries, and a reliance on flimsy facts and dubious assertions. None of that mattered to Trump.

During the campaign, Flynn was one of the few men who had ever worn stars on their shoulders willing to promote Trump. His allegiance was so intense that he had led an anti–Hillary Clinton chant of "Lock her up" at the Republican National Convention, which mortified his military and intelligence brethren, who believed he was leveraging his status as a decorated former military officer to fuel society's more dangerous elements. Yet this endeared him to Trump. Flynn made himself indispensable to Trump, whispering in his ear that he couldn't trust most intelligence officials but could trust Flynn. He was crafty enough to ingratiate himself with Trump's family, too—including Jared Kushner, the candidate's ambitious son-in-law who had no experience in politics or

foreign affairs, yet styled himself as Trump's political strategist and interlocutor with foreign governments.

The day after the election, the flattering consigliere got his reward at
a transition meeting on the twenty-sixth floor of Trump Tower. Ivanka
Trump, the president-elect's elder daughter, and her husband, Kushner,
who together helped oversee some of the high-level appointments in the
new administration, made clear to Flynn that he could choose any job he
wanted.

"Oh, General Flynn, how loyal you've been to my father," Ivanka said
in her distinctive breathy voice, adding something to the effect of "What
do you want to do?"

Don McGahn frowned with some surprise. He had been the Trump
campaign's lawyer and was now in line to become White House counsel.
He had nothing personal against Flynn. He didn't really know him. But
others in the room noticed McGahn's displeasure, which seemed to say,
"Is this really how we're going to do this?"

Some in the room could hardly believe people were being appointed
to key jobs so indiscriminately and irresponsibly. As Steve Bannon, the
campaign's chief executive officer who also was joining the administration, saw it, Ivanka was the princess with the sword, just tapping Flynn
on the shoulder. McGahn and Bannon, hardly allies, shared the belief
that this was a recipe for missteps and, quite possibly, disaster.

The haphazard and dysfunctional transition was a harbinger for the
administration. Trump placed a premium on branding and image at the
expense of fundamental competence. He and many of his advisers had no
experience with public service, and therefore little regard for its ethics or
norms. Rather than hewing to an ideological agenda, the entire operation was guided by Trump's instincts and whims.

Flynn's dream was to be national security adviser. Kushner, who was
envisioning for himself a West Wing role as a shadow secretary of state—
interacting with foreign leaders, negotiating Middle East peace, and
running point on such key relationships as China and Mexico—calculated
that installing Flynn as national security adviser would create for himself
the freedom to maneuver as he pleased. Just like that, Flynn's wish was

granted. It would take another eight days for his appointment to be announced, but everything was set in motion on November 9.

Nobody bothered to vet Flynn. There was no review of his tenure as a U.S. military intelligence chief in Afghanistan, which had been the subject of a misconduct investigation. Nor of his time as director of the Defense Intelligence Agency, which President Obama had cut short. Nor of his international consulting firm and his contracts with Kremlin-aligned companies. Nor of his attendance at a 2015 Moscow gala as a guest of Russia, seated at the table of President Vladimir Putin.

Flynn had used the Trump campaign as a gravy train, hoping to better his lifestyle after thirty-three years of relatively low military wages. At the same time he was advising candidate Trump, Flynn was working for the Turkish government and, according to federal investigators, concealing the nature of that arrangement. On Election Day, Flynn published an op-ed in *The Hill* in which he trumpeted Turkish president Recep Tayyip Erdogan's cause by comparing his political opponent, Fethullah Gulen, who was living in exile in the United States, to Osama bin Laden. Flynn called for the United States to force Gulen out of the country, stunning his former colleagues in the intelligence and national security communities.

Chris Christie, the New Jersey governor who had endorsed Trump and was the chairman of the presidential transition, was flabbergasted when the president-elect told him he would name Flynn his national security adviser.

"You can't do that," said Christie. "First, you have to have a chief of staff in place and let your chief of staff have input on that because the security adviser's going to be reporting to the chief of staff. And Flynn's just the wrong choice. He's just a horrific choice."

"You just don't like him," Trump replied.

"Well, you're right," Christie said. "I don't like him. Do you want to know why?"

"Yeah," Trump said.

"Because he's going to get you in trouble," Christie replied. "Take my word for it."

Trump didn't want to hear anything else about Flynn. He told Christie to go downstairs to the fourteenth floor, where the campaign headquarters had morphed overnight into a transition command center. Christie had a government to assemble.

Later that week, Christie was canned by Trump. Technically, he was fired by Bannon, who told Christie he was acting on orders from Kushner, but Trump had allowed the termination. He was replaced as transition chairman by Vice President-elect Mike Pence. Eleven years earlier, Christie had been U.S. attorney in New Jersey and had put Kushner's father, Charles, head of the family's real estate business, behind bars for tax evasion, witness tampering, and illegal campaign contributions. The case humiliated the Kushner family and left a lasting impression on young Jared.

On November 10, Trump was 230 miles south in Washington, visiting Obama at the White House. Obama was unsettled by Trump's victory, but less than forty-eight hours after the election, in accordance with America's tradition of peaceful transfers of power, he welcomed his successor into the Oval Office and offered him some advice. Two things the forty-fourth president said stuck with the forty-fifth: one, that North Korea was the biggest foreign policy challenge and security threat, and, two, that he should not hire Flynn.

Obama personally warned Trump against hiring Flynn because he found his judgment dubious and his motives untrustworthy. Obama had fired Flynn in 2014 from the Defense Intelligence Agency amid complaints in the agency that he lacked focus and an even temperament. Trump later recounted to aides that Obama had called Flynn a "flake" and a "bad guy," a critique Trump dismissed.

The president-elect approached the ten-week transition as a casting call for a new season of *The Apprentice*, the NBC reality show that had made him a household name. Day after day, Trump Tower's golden-framed revolving door on Fifth Avenue delivered politicians, business leaders, and celebrities, who paraded through the lobby for their appointed visits. They came to pitch themselves for jobs in the administration or to curry favor with the president-elect or simply to get a piece of the action. "It was like walking into the Jabba the Hutt bar in *Star Wars*," one Trump adviser said dismissively. "You never knew who was going to crawl in." The president-elect loved to gin up the ratings, and was quick to seize on how the presidency could benefit his personal brand and his businesses. He held job interviews and transition meetings not inside the federal office building in Washington that was provided for this purpose but at Trump Tower, Trump National Golf Club in Bedminster, New Jersey, and Mar-a-Lago in Palm Beach, Florida.

In the helter-skelter, unstructured rhythms of the transition, a trio of campaign power players jockeyed for influence: Kushner, Bannon, and Reince Priebus. Kushner had exalted status as Trump's son-in-law, while Priebus and Bannon were appointed early on as White House chief of staff and White House chief strategist—a unique arrangement in which they had coequal footing atop the organizational chart.

Trump tapped Priebus, who had been the Republican National Committee chairman, partly as a thank-you present for the foot soldiers and state-by-state organization that the RNC built for Trump to compensate for his campaign's almost-nonexistent ground game. Well connected in Washington, Priebus was considered by GOP leaders to have the most capable set of hands among Trump's aides.

Bannon, meanwhile, was impolitic, gruff, and unkempt. He had proven his loyalty in the trenches with Trump during the toughest stretch of the campaign. Bannon had previously run the conservative website Breitbart and pitched himself to Trump as the essential conduit to his indispensable base, which he affectionately referred to as "the deplorables," a reference to Clinton's infamous gaffe about Trump's "basket of deplorables. . . . The racist, sexist, homophobic, xenophobic, Islamophobic—you name it."

Priebus set about installing former RNC staffers and other trusted figures in key West Wing roles, while he, Bannon, and Pence focused on cabinet positions. They paid special attention early on to national security roles and had their eyes on Mike Pompeo to lead the CIA. Pompeo had been elected to Congress as a Kansas Republican in the Tea Party wave of 2010, and when he arrived in Washington, he quickly established himself as a hard-line conservative and a sharp partisan. From his perch on the House Permanent Select Committee on Intelligence, Pompeo had hounded Clinton over Benghazi, making him a Breitbart favorite.

Though he had known Priebus, Bannon, and Pence for years, Pompeo was an outsider to Trump's world. In fact, he had campaigned vigorously against Trump in the primaries as a Marco Rubio surrogate. During the March 5 Kansas caucuses, Pompeo had warned that Trump would be "an authoritarian president who ignored our Constitution," and he urged his fellow Kansans to "turn down the lights on the circus."

But Pompeo was eager to join the circus now. Bannon knew that it would be hard to sell a small-state congressman he regarded as "a warrior's warrior" as a potential CIA director to the elites he dubbed "the *Morning Joe* crowd," given Pompeo's Benghazi bludgeoning. But Pompeo wanted the job.

On November 16, Pompeo traveled to New York to meet with the president-elect. Priebus had prepped Trump on Pompeo's credentials, and Bannon had given Pompeo a pep talk, telling him something along the lines of "We're just going to go in, I'm going to reiterate you're number one in your class at West Point, number one in your class at Harvard Law School, you're the best guy intelligence ever had. I'm going to tee you up—and don't wait for him to say anything. You just rip. Do not wait for a question, because there won't be a question. He doesn't even know what intelligence is. Just rip."

The meeting went off without a hitch. After others fluffed him up before the boss, Pompeo talked about restructuring the CIA. He and Trump chewed over problems with the Iran nuclear deal. As a West Point and Harvard Law graduate, Pompeo easily checked the credentials box. The former army captain, beefy and hulking as he works a room, also had the imposing, tough-guy image Trump desired.

Before the meeting concluded, Pompeo had the job. Trump shook his hand, turned to Bannon and Priebus, and said, "I love it. Let's do it."

Two days later, Pompeo was formally announced as Trump's nominee for CIA director. Pompeo would become one of the more respected members of the administration, but Trump offered him the CIA directorship based on a single interview.

Trump approached staffing the administration like a casting call and sought "the look," a fixation in keeping with the beauty pageants he had once run. For national security positions, he gravitated toward generals. For public-facing communications roles, he wanted attractive women. At the United Nations, he picked as his ambassador Nikki Haley, whom he typecast for the UN in part because she was a daughter of Indian American immigrants. To Trump, one of the most important attributes for any job candidate was the ability to present well on television.

"Don't forget, he's a showbiz guy," Christopher Ruddy, a Trump friend and the chief executive of Newsmax, remarked. "He likes people who present themselves very well, and he's very impressed when somebody has a background of being good on television because he thinks it's a very important medium for public policy." Ruddy added, "The look might not necessarily be somebody who should be on the cover of *GQ* magazine or *Vanity Fair*. It's more about the look and the demeanor and the swagger."

On December 6, Trump formally announced the retired Marine Corps general James Mattis as his nominee for defense secretary, playing up his rugged appearance and combat history. He told aides he was especially enamored with the nickname that Mattis privately disliked. "Mad Dog plays no games, right?" Trump told a roaring crowd as he announced Mattis's nomination at a rally in Fayetteville, North Carolina. He called a reluctant Mattis onto the stage and lauded him as "the closest thing to General George Patton that we have," referring to the legendary World War II commander played by the late George C. Scott in the 1970 biopic, one of Trump's favorite films.

While Trump was taken with Mattis's physical appearance and his macho moniker, his nomination was very reassuring to the national security establishment. At least there would be a seasoned and steady set of hands at the Pentagon. When Mattis later interviewed candidates for senior staff positions at the Pentagon, he would ask, "Can you ride the brand?" What he really meant was, can you support Trump, warts and all? He knew this would be a controversial presidency.

The transition's official vetting process varied from minimal to nonexistent, depending on the candidate. Most important in researching one's background was a review of news articles and social media accounts to see whether he or she had ever said anything derogatory about Trump. One senior Trump adviser recalled, "People filled in paperwork on the airplane on their way down to the inauguration. . . . Well, they might as well have. They didn't think about transition until literally the day they started the job.

"In hockey," this official added, "you can lose a knee playing with a lot of inexperienced people. That's how this has felt."

Behind the scenes, Rick Gates, who had worked on the campaign as chairman Paul Manafort's deputy, was putting together the inauguration. Gates and Manafort were longtime lobbying partners, specializing in representing foreign governments in shady plots, and when Manafort was fired from the campaign in August 2016, Trump figured his No. 2 would leave with him. Trump strongly disliked and distrusted Gates, due in part to a toxic reaction he had to a poll Gates had commissioned. Trump didn't like the survey's results, which rated his popularity as low, and felt Gates was cheating the campaign by paying the pollster for such junk. "Gates gives me the creeps," Trump told some associates.

But Gates had a powerful champion in Thomas Barrack, who chaired the Presidential Inaugural Committee. Trump had no idea Gates was quietly helping Barrack direct the inaugural festivities until one night sometime in the middle of the transition when the president-elect overheard his wife, Melania, talking about him. At the same time, Johnny McEntee, twenty-six, Trump's personal assistant and body man, had arrived at the Trumps' penthouse to bring the president-elect a sub sandwich for dinner. In the living room, Melania and Stephanie Winston Wolkoff, a friend of the incoming first lady's who was helping plan inaugural events, were sitting on a sofa talking about inauguration plans. Trump walked into the room to get his sandwich from McEntee just as he heard Melania say the name Rick.

"Rick? Rick who?" Trump asked his wife.

"Rick Gates," she said.

Trump lost it. He started yelling.

"What the fuck are you doing?" he asked.

Trump decided to fire Gates on the spot and turned to McEntee and said, "Johnny, get with Melania. You're the executive director."

By all accounts, McEntee was an excellent body man. Since joining the campaign before the primaries, he had spent most of his waking hours at Trump's side. He looked up to the boss, was loyal to the family, and did not leak to reporters. McEntee had Hollywood good looks, just the kind of image Trump sought to project. He was athletic, too, having played quarterback for the University of Connecticut Huskies and even becoming something of a YouTube sensation for a viral video of football trick shots.

McEntee, however, had precisely zero experience in running a presidential inaugural. This was a $107 million operation, not merely a grand celebration of Trump's election, but also a projection to the nation of the new president's values and goals for governing. Within a few hours, after Barrack persuaded Trump to reverse his snap decision and simply put up with Gates for a little longer, McEntee was back to being the body guy and would move with Trump to Washington.

The president-elect completely disregarded government ethics and the law. Ivanka and Kushner were eager to leave their mark on Washington and to serve in the West Wing, a role they thought would burnish the personal brands they had so carefully cultivated back in New York. Some Trump advisers saw this as a risky proposition, certain to invite cries of nepotism and create an untenable working environment. Yet even before the inauguration, no one felt they could tell the kids—among some West Wing colleagues, Ivanka and Kushner were called just that, the kids—no.

"There's some things in life, when you shoot, you better kill. I knew that this was not a winning effort to stop the kids from coming into the

West Wing," recalled one of their colleagues. "They were dead set on coming, and there was nothing anyone was going to do about it. And I think everyone understood that."

White House lawyers were concerned that Ivanka's business interests created potentially huge ethical quagmires. In addition to her clothing company, she was involved in the Trump International Hotel in Washington, which could easily become a direct conflict with her White House role.

The president had the broad authority to name his relatives to join the White House staff. Antinepotism laws barred a president only from appointing family members to agency jobs, according to a ruling from the Justice Department's Office of Legal Counsel. Ivanka was envisioning a norm-breaking role for herself. She wanted special treatment and sought to be immune from all of the cumbersome rules for government jobs, which she thought she could achieve by becoming an informal "volunteer" adviser.

Even Trump had mixed feelings about whether it was a good idea for his daughter and son-in-law to follow him into the city he derided as a swamp. "Why would you want to kill yourself and come to Washington, D.C., and get shot up by all these media killers?" Trump wondered aloud to some of his advisers. But Trump couldn't say no to the kids, either. He wanted family around.

As the inauguration neared, Trump did not fully trust all of the aides he was hiring. He did not know whether they were coming to work for him as Trump devotees or whether he was simply their means to a job in the White House, the ultimate résumé line for any political operative. His suspicions regularly burst into the open, including one evening shortly before Christmas at Mar-a-Lago, Trump's private club in Palm Beach. On December 19, the day the Electoral College electors were certified, officially affirming Trump's victory, the president-elect celebrated over dinner with seven of his top aides: Priebus, Bannon, deputy campaign manager Dave Bossie, communications adviser Hope Hicks, senior policy adviser Stephen Miller, social media director Dan Scavino, and Priebus's deputy, Katie Walsh. The eight of them sat around the table, and when the conversation turned to personnel matters, Trump impressed upon his team the importance of loyalty. As they ticked through candidates for various jobs, the president-elect repeatedly asked, "Is he loyal?" "Is she loyal?"

Trump spent the week between Christmas and New Year's at Mar-a-Lago, accompanied by a slimmed-down cadre of aides. The morning of December 29, as the president-elect enjoyed some golf at one of his nearby courses, CNN turned to a breaking story: "White House announces retaliation against Russia." The Obama administration had decided to punish Russia for interfering in the 2016 election, shuttering two Russian compounds in the United States and ejecting thirty-five diplomats suspected of spying.

Trump was angry when he learned the news. He felt it was one thing for Clinton's advisers and allies to accuse Russia of meddling in the election; he could just accuse the Democrats of sour grapes. But retaliatory action against Russia by the U.S. government effectively confirmed that Russia had actually interfered in the election—and that, Trump believed, raised doubts about his own victory.

"They're trying to delegitimize your presidency right now," Bannon told the president.

Trump was piqued that the Obama administration was sticking his incoming team with an aggressive slap at Russia—a significant foreign policy move—without so much as consulting him.

The day before in Washington, Obama had signed the sanctions order with plans to announce it the next day, but a few news outlets reported on the evening of December 28 that some retaliation against Russia was expected soon. Also that evening, Russian ambassador Sergei Kislyak was given a heads-up on the sanctions by the State Department. Flustered and upset, he reached out to the Trump team. Kislyak texted Flynn on December 28, "Can you kindly call me back at your convenience?"

Flynn was spending the holiday week with his wife at a resort in the Dominican Republic. Reception there was spotty, so he did not see the ambassador's text until the next day, around the time the Obama administration had announced the sanctions. Before Flynn called Kislyak back, he wanted to check with the transition team in Mar-a-Lago. He talked for about twenty minutes with his deputy, K. T. McFarland, who was at Trump's Palm Beach club with the president-elect. Flynn and McFarland went over the Obama administration's punitive shot and agreed it could hurt Trump's intended goals of cultivating a better relationship with Putin. McFarland shared with Flynn the consensus among the team at Mar-a-Lago: they hoped Russia would not ratchet up the aggression in responding to Obama's move.

Immediately after hanging up with McFarland, Flynn dialed Kislyak and asked that the Kremlin not get into a "tit for tat." Flynn assured the ambassador that the incoming administration would likely revisit sanctions and possibly rescind them. He raised the possibility that he could arrange a meeting with Trump later on, once they were all in the White House.

By communicating about U.S. policy with Kislyak before Trump took office, Flynn was undermining the current administration and breaking the standards of diplomacy. His communications were instantly picked up and stored by the massive listening apparatus of the National Security Agency, which routinely surveils prominent government officials and helps the FBI monitor suspected spies who work for hostile foreign powers.

Despite the high drama of the Russian compounds' being evacuated, Putin's reaction the next day, December 30, was unexpectedly calm. "We will not create any problems for U.S. diplomats," Putin said. "It is regrettable that the Obama Administration is ending its term in this manner. Nevertheless, I offer my New Year greetings to President Obama and his family," he said. "My season's greetings also to President-elect Donald Trump and the American people."

Putin's tone surprised CIA director John Brennan and Director of National Intelligence James R. Clapper. At that time neither of them knew about Flynn's secret assurances to and request of Kislyak. Some U.S. officials wondered if Putin was just toying with the Americans. Yet he never pounced. That same afternoon, Trump startled the outgoing Obama team with this tweet: "Great move on delay (by V. Putin)—I always knew he was very smart!"

On January 6, Brennan, Clapper, FBI director James Comey, and National Security Agency director Michael Rogers traveled to New York to brief Trump, Pence, and their top advisers about the extensive Russian campaign to influence the 2016 election in Trump's favor and sow discord through cyberattacks and social media infiltration. During this infamous briefing at Trump Tower, the president-elect rejected what did not confirm his view. This was not how an incoming commander in chief was meant to act.

As the ninety-minute meeting wrapped up, Comey and Trump cleared the room to speak alone. The FBI director brought up a salacious dossier, a widely circulated collection of intelligence reports written by the former British spy Christopher Steele. Comey noted that it alleged that Russians had filmed Trump interacting with prostitutes in Moscow in 2013. Trump immediately denied the allegations, snorting, "There were no prostitutes," and arguing that he wasn't the kind of man who needed to "go there." Trump had praised Comey for having reopened the Hillary Clinton email investigation in the final stretch of the 2016 campaign but now wondered whose team Comey was really on. Trump's distrust of the intelligence community only grew when, shortly after the Trump Tower meeting, the agencies published their report detailing Russia's election interference campaign. This infuriated Trump. He concluded that the national security establishment would never respect him and was determined to sabotage his presidency.

There were three core questions facing U.S. intelligence officials about Russia's role in the 2016 election. First, did the Russian government itself interfere? The overwhelming evidence said yes. Next, did Russia try to help Trump win? Much of the evidence suggested yes. Finally, did Russia's efforts change the election result? Intelligence leaders argued they lacked the ability to say definitively. But Trump believed that acknowledging Russian intervention effectively tainted his victory.

In the days following the January 6 intelligence briefing, Priebus,

Kushner, and other advisers pleaded with Trump to publicly acknowledge the unanimous conclusion the spy chiefs had presented to him. They held impromptu interventions in his twenty-sixth-floor office in which they tried to convince him that he could affirm the validity of the intelligence without invalidating or even diminishing his win. "This was part of the normalization process," one adviser explained. "There was a big effort to get him to be a standard president."

But Trump dug in. Each time his advisers pushed him to accept the intelligence, he grew more agitated. He railed that the intelligence community's leaders were deceitful and could not be trusted. "I can't trust anybody," the president-elect said. On that point, he was seconded by Bannon, who said of the Russia report, "It's all gobbledygook." The president-elect said he believed admitting that the Kremlin had hacked Democratic emails would be a "trap."

On January 11, just nine days before the inauguration, Trump held a news conference in the pink-marbled lobby of Trump Tower. His advisers pleaded with him once more to accept the intelligence community's assessment, and he begrudgingly complied. "As far as hacking, I think it was Russia," Trump told reporters. "But I think we also get hacked by other countries and other people." Yet Trump also accused the intelligence agencies, without evidence, of leaking the Steele dossier to Buzz-Feed, which had published the salacious material on January 10. "That's something that Nazi Germany would have done and did do," he said. "I think it's a disgrace that information that was false and fake and never happened got released to the public."

Soon after the news conference ended, however, Trump told his aides that he regretted accepting the findings about Russian hacking. "It's not me," he told his aides. "It wasn't right."

Two

PARANOIA AND
PANDEMONIUM

Before his inauguration, President-elect Trump did not know that the FBI was secretly conducting a counterintelligence investigation of Michael Flynn, but once he did, it would plant seeds of paranoia that would germinate and take root during his presidency. Investigators were examining whether Flynn had betrayed the United States by acting as an agent of the Russian government. Intelligence officials learned from an intercepted communication that Flynn had made a secret call to Russian ambassador Sergei Kislyak on December 29, 2016, to consult with him about the Obama sanctions, one he would later lie about.

FBI deputy director Andrew McCabe alerted acting assistant attorney general Mary McCord to the call on January 3, 2017. He stressed the obvious: Flynn's conversations were especially disturbing given his role on the incoming White House team. "Trump's about to become the president, and this is his announced national security adviser," McCabe said. Now their bosses, James Comey and acting attorney general Sally Yates, had to consider how much to share with the president-to-be about Flynn's secret outreach, but as they debated, intervening events got the jump on them.

On January 12, the fact that Flynn had secretly called Kislyak on December 29 appeared in a *Washington Post* column by David Ignatius, though Ignatius did not report the topic of the conversation. One top U.S. official described the stunned reaction inside the Justice Department: "Everybody is like, 'What the fuck? How has this already leaked?'"

Hours later, the Trump team—clueless still about the intercept in the FBI's hands—repeated Flynn's lie. On the evening of January 12, the transition's spokesman Sean Spicer insisted Flynn didn't talk with Kislyak about sanctions. "The call centered around the logistics of setting up a call with the president of Russia and the president-elect after he was sworn in," Spicer said. Then, on January 15, Vice President-elect Pence flatly denied that Flynn and Kislyak discussed sanctions. "It was strictly coincidental that they had a conversation," Pence said in an interview on CBS's *Face the Nation*. "They did not discuss anything having to do with the United States' decision to expel diplomats or impose censure against Russia."

Yates was alarmed. If Pence was telling what he thought was the truth, she knew that meant the vice president-elect had been lied to—and that the Russians knew, too. Flynn's lying led to a tug-of-war between Yates and Comey. She wanted to alert Trump that his national security adviser was compromised, but Comey said he didn't want to reveal concern about Flynn until they had more facts. In keeping with how he had handled the Hillary Clinton email investigation, Comey would ultimately decide he knew best.

Yates believed it was well past time to alert Trump to Flynn's lie, but Comey was trying to convince intelligence leaders that doing so would jeopardize the investigation. On January 19, the evening before Trump's swearing in, the clock had run out. "They're in their tuxedos by now," one of Yates's deputies complained as the Trump team gathered to celebrate at Washington's iconic train station. "I just don't see how you drop this turd on him tonight. It's not like one more day is going to change anything."

On January 20, Trump was sworn in to office and uneasily tried to settle into his new life as president. He was apprehensive about moving to Washington, a city in which he had many adversaries, far fewer allies, and no true friends. Despite his extroverted personality, Trump was a homebody and a creature of comfort. Having campaigned on the idea that the nation had been betrayed by its political class, Trump, now the most powerful man in Washington, did not know whom he could trust. He and his advisers feared from the moment they seized power that the capital's entrenched interests would scheme to undermine the administration. The night of January 23, the first Monday of his presidency, Trump came face-to-face with House and Senate leaders from both parties at a White House reception with his top administration officials. At a long table in the State Dining Room, Steve Bannon, one of the inspirations of Trump's "American carnage" address, could not stop looking at Nancy Pelosi. In the Democratic House leader, he saw Katharine Hepburn from *The Lion in Winter*—who looks up and down the table and thinks to herself, "These men are all clowns," and plots her return to power.

Pelosi assumed Trump would open the conversation on a unifying note, such as by quoting the Founding Fathers or the Bible. Instead, the new president began with a lie: "You know, I won the popular vote." He claimed that there had been widespread fraud, with three to five million illegal votes for Clinton. Pelosi interjected. "Well, Mr. President, that's not true," she said. "There's no evidence to support what you just said, and if we're going to work together, we have to stipulate to a certain set of facts." Watching Pelosi challenge Trump, Bannon whispered to colleagues, "She's going to get us. Total assassin. She's an assassin."

On January 24, as Yates debated with her staff who best to contact at the White House about Flynn, she got a call from Comey, who delivered an annoying surprise: FBI agents were at the White House to interview Flynn. Yates was furious. Comey, who had repeatedly insisted he needed to keep this probe under wraps, had neglected to notify the Justice Department. Yates said something to the effect of "How could you make this decision unilaterally?" Comey told her it was just a normal investigative step.

At the Justice Department, one senior official recalled, "The reaction that we all had is they're going to try to get a false statement . . . and we're going to look terrible, like we set him up," the official said. "Like we've known about this for a week, haven't told anybody, and now it looks like a setup of the national security adviser, like we backed him into a corner."

Finally, on January 26, Yates asked Don McGahn if she could meet with him in his West Wing office that day. She laid out the intercept and explained that Flynn had lied to Pence and that FBI agents had interviewed him about his Kislyak communications. McGahn listened, then asked some questions. Mostly he wanted to know why one person lying to another in the White House worried the Justice Department. Yates explained that Flynn was compromised because the Russians knew the truth and could use the fact of the national security adviser's lie to manipulate him.

When Yates departed, McGahn went to Reince Priebus's office and found the chief of staff and Bannon there. "Did Flynn tell you guys that the FBI was here talking to him earlier in the week?" he asked.

Priebus and Bannon looked at each other with surprise, then back at McGahn.

"What are you fucking talking about?" Bannon said.

"You've got to be kidding me," Priebus said. "Is this some kind of joke?"

"Well, the FBI was here in that office on Tuesday," McGahn said, referring to the national security adviser's suite down the hall.

"We haven't even been here a week," Bannon said.

McGahn then went to the Oval Office to alert Trump. The president was largely nonplussed. Flynn hadn't told the senior Trump leadership team that he had been interviewed by the FBI about his calls with the

Russian ambassador, but Trump expressed no concern about Flynn's lying to Pence. Rather, he was bothered that Yates was questioning Flynn's motives—and by extension Trump's personnel decisions. The president said something to the effect of "We've only been here for four days, and they're already questioning our guy?"

On January 27, without consulting his Justice Department or fully briefing his homeland security secretary, Trump issued a travel ban barring citizens and refugees from seven majority-Muslim countries from entering the United States. Chaos reigned at large international airports, and immigration lawyers filed emergency petitions asking federal courts to intervene to halt enforcement of the ban, arguing that it was unconstitutional.

The ban was drafted in secret by Bannon and Stephen Miller, Trump's thirty-one-year-old senior policy adviser and a hard-line opponent of illegal immigration. They didn't consult McGahn or Yates about its legal framework. Secretary of Homeland Security John Kelly, whose department had to enforce the ban, never got to see the final version until after Trump delivered his executive order. Kelly was on a plane when the ban went into effect, which meant his deputy had to arrange an emergency conference call to explain to top department officials how it would be enforced, and didn't have a copy of the document itself. Customs and Border Protection agents, wholly confused by the order's language, inconsistently enforced a part of the ban that was later found to be illegal: barring people who had green cards from returning to their homes in the United States. Even Trump's allies acknowledged the unmitigated disaster.

At the White House, staffers working through the weekend were shocked by the footage of dark-skinned people being rounded up in foreign airports and escorted away from the boarding line for planes bound for the United States. The saga played out on television screens hanging throughout the building. "It was like running a meeting in a Buffalo Wild Wings. There are TV screens everywhere," one senior administration official recalled. "Nobody really seemed to realize that the government roundup was being done by people who are in the administration, this administration. People are rubbing their heads and going, 'Huh? Why is this happening?'"

Trump's aides blamed each other for the chaos. Some argued that Priebus and his deputies should have better coordinated with various departments and taken charge more robustly of public relations. Others placed the responsibility squarely on Miller.

Amid the mayhem, some of Trump's new appointees donned black tie and evening gowns to attend the Alfalfa Club dinner, an annual gathering of business and political elites. It was a Saturday night, January 28, and the Trumpers mixed with the likes of Bill Gates, Warren Buffett, and Jeff Bezos, to name a few. As French ambassador Gérard Araud watched the masters of the universe line up to shake hands with Kellyanne Conway, Trump's omnipresent campaign manager turned White House counselor, he whispered to her, "That's the sweet fragrance of power."

But these elites were never to be trusted by Trump. Miller shared this mind-set and would later explain to Araud over dinner at the ambassador's residence that the president had been elected for the explicit purpose of creating unease for the establishment. "This president is revolutionary, so he has to break China," Miller said. "The scope and scale of change we're seeking to implement by definition will involve disruption." He added, "If we follow the normal procedures, we work into the hands of our enemies."

By Monday, January 30, Flynn and White House aides wanted to hear his intercepted call with Kislyak. Yates called McGahn to tell him White House lawyers could come over to listen to the tape in one of their sensitive compartmented information facilities. Separately, Yates issued a memo instructing Justice Department employees not to defend the travel ban because she had concerns it was unconstitutional. Trump and his allies considered this an abuse of her office and fired Yates that afternoon. The White House said Yates had "betrayed the Department of Justice by refusing to enforce a legal order designed to protect the citizens of the United States." The Flynn investigation continued without Yates.

On February 2, *The Washington Post* reported a cantankerous phone call the president had had five days earlier with Australian prime minister Malcolm Turnbull. Trump badgered Turnbull over an existing refugee agreement and accused him of seeking to export "the next Boston bombers." Trump fumed, "This is the worst deal ever." The Associated Press reported on the same day that Trump had a similarly blunt conversation with Mexican president Enrique Peña Nieto in which he threatened to deploy U.S. troops to stop "bad hombres down there."

Trump was furious. He demanded that his aides root out the sources for the leaks and suggested that reporters needed to go to jail. Trump hated all leaks and made no distinction between West Wing infighting and sensitive national security decisions. Despite repeated efforts by his lawyers to explain, Trump did not understand that leaks of unflattering details of his constant television watching or limited understanding of government were not punishable crimes.

By February 7, a team of *Washington Post* reporters had confirmed that Flynn had indeed discussed sanctions in his December 29 call with Kislyak. With that story, Pence learned Flynn had lied to him. Neither Trump nor McGahn had felt it important to alert him earlier. Flynn continued in his job, flying that weekend with Trump to Florida for a summit with Japanese prime minister Shinzo Abe at Mar-a-Lago.

On February 13, with everyone back at the White House, the Trump team debated Flynn's fate. Pence said he was willing to let bygones be bygones and wouldn't oppose Flynn staying on. But Priebus, still smarting from having repeated Flynn's lie early on, insisted he had to go. Flynn told Trump that he would go quietly, no whining. He submitted his resignation late that night, and Trump accepted. Flynn's lie was not the only reason for his dismissal. Trump had had growing doubts about Flynn's fitness for the job and had found Flynn's briefings discursive and lacking precision.

The day after Flynn's ouster was Valentine's Day. Chris Christie and his wife, Mary Pat, traveled to Washington to have lunch with Trump. Jared Kushner joined them.

"I fired Flynn, so the whole Russia thing is over," Trump said, referring to the FBI's ongoing investigation of Russia's election interference.

"Mr. President, we're going to be sitting here a year from now talking about Russia," Christie said.

Kushner said that was crazy, because there was nothing to any of the Russia nonsense. Christie replied that he's the only one among them who had both conducted federal investigations, when he was U.S. attorney in New Jersey, and been the subject of one, the Bridgegate scandal.

"There's absolutely no way you can make this shorter, but there's lots of ways you can make it longer, so keep quiet, listen to your lawyers, and that's the way it will go the shortest," Christie told the president.

At that very moment, Spicer was holding his press briefing, and it played on the television in Trump's private dining room. The president, Christie, and Kushner watched as Spicer threw Flynn under the bus. He told reporters that Trump asked for Flynn's resignation on account of an "evolving and eroding level of trust as a result of this situation and a series of other questionable instances."

As Spicer kept parrying questions, Kushner's phone rang.

"It's Flynn! It's Flynn!" Kushner mouthed to Trump and Christie.

Flynn was pissed. He had thought if he left quietly he would not be disparaged.

"Make nice," Trump instructed Kushner. "Make nice."

Kushner told Flynn, "You know the president respects you. The president cares about you. I'll get the president to send out a positive tweet about you later."

The call ended. "We should try to help him out. He's a good guy," Kushner said to Trump and Christie.

"Bad people are like gum on the bottom of your shoe," Christie replied. "Very hard to make them go away."

Trump had some sympathy for Flynn. The two men had developed a genuine friendship as they hopscotched the battleground states together. That afternoon in the Oval Office, as a homeland security meeting wrapped up, Trump asked the FBI director to stay behind so they could speak alone. Trump told Comey that he did not believe Flynn had done anything wrong but explained that he still had to let him go. Then he pleaded for leniency, evincing no hesitation as he sought to use his power to let a loyalist off the hook. "I hope you can see your way clear to letting this go, to letting Flynn go," Trump told Comey, according to the FBI director's contemporaneous notes. "He is a good guy. I hope you can let this go."

Spicer had been holding the dual roles of press secretary and communications director and was drowning—and not only because of Melissa McCarthy's devastating portrayal of him on *Saturday Night Live*. A stout five feet six inches, Spicer did not have "the look" that Trump envisioned representing him on television, nor did the former Republican National Committee spokesman have the renegade pedigree that would have made him a natural representative of the "Make America Great Again" insurgency. Trump dissed Spicer's briefing performances behind his back. "Sean can't even complete a sentence," Trump told other aides. "We've got a spokesperson who can't speak."

Spicer needed help, so he reached out to Michael Dubke, a veteran operative who ran a public relations firm, and asked him to interview for the communications director job. On February 10, Dubke came to the White House to meet with Spicer. The Flynn story was still hot. Spicer was too busy to talk with Dubke, so for hours the job candidate hung around outside his office, next to the copy machine in the "upper press" area. Nobody paid much attention to Dubke except for the NBC correspondent Peter Alexander.

"So who are you?" Alexander asked.

Not wanting to blow his cover, Dubke said, "I'm a friend of Sean's . . . and just wanted to see how things work around here."

Finally, Spicer brought Dubke in. They talked for maybe twenty minutes about the job, and Spicer asked Dubke to come back Saturday to meet with Priebus. This time the three men talked for forty-five minutes, and Priebus asked Dubke if he had anything on social media trashing Trump. Dubke was a low-profile operative who mostly kept his opinions to himself. "No, you won't find anything from me," he assured Priebus.

On February 16, Dubke came back for an Oval Office interview with Trump. He was just a few minutes into telling the president about the company he founded and his philosophy on branding when Trump had an idea. "What do you think about a press conference?" he asked.

"Well, I would decide what the three messages are that you want to talk about, and I'd bring the expert in from each of the agencies, have this conversation," Dubke said.

"No, no, no, no, no," Trump said. "Today. What if we do it today?"

Dubke thought he was joking. Trump was serious. Spicer turned tail out of the Oval to start setting things into motion. In any normal government, this kind of knee-jerk decision would be madness. But in the Trump White House, this was just another Thursday.

"Sean!" Trump yells out to Spicer. "We've got to get the East Room ready."

Within minutes, White House tours were canceled for the remainder of the day to clear the residence. A lectern and camera risers were assembled within three hours. Soon, administration policy experts filed into the Oval Office to brief Trump, and Dubke hovered on the edge of the room, his visitor badge dangling from his neck.

"I'm Mike Pence," the vice president said, introducing himself.

"Yes, sir, I know who you are. I'm Mike Dubke," he said.

"So what's going on?" Pence asked.

"Well, I think they're preparing for a press conference right now," Dubke said.

"What's your role here?" Pence inquired.

"Well," Dubke said, "this was my interview for communications director."

Pence laughed, a momentary acknowledgment of the absurdity.

"How's that going?" he asked Dubke.

There was no thematic purpose for Trump's press conference. The president simply wanted to have one. Trump stepped out to his lectern and for one hour and seventeen minutes delivered to a live television audience a fiery, stream-of-consciousness screed.

"I turn on the TV, open the newspapers, and I see stories of chaos—chaos," Trump said. "Yet it is the exact opposite. This administration is running like a fine-tuned machine."

This was the twenty-seventh full day of his presidency, and Trump was unscripted. The president denied dysfunction in an administration plainly defined by it. The next day, Dubke was officially hired, but as he began work as communications director, he knew he could not direct Trump. The ineptitude came from the very top. Trump cared more about putting on a show than about the more mundane task of governing. There would be no restraining the grievances Trump felt nor curbing the chaos he created. They could only be managed.

On February 23, two highly regarded cabinet members, Secretary of State Rex Tillerson and Kelly, ran into the Trump buzz saw when they traveled to Mexico City seeking to fix a problem their boss had created. Tillerson, sixty-four, a former chief executive of ExxonMobil, and Kelly, sixty-six, a retired four-star Marine Corps general, were both men of substance and gravitas. They saw their jobs as capstones on their already decorated careers and had agreed to join the administration out of a patriotic call to duty to help a neophyte president navigate a complicated world. Yet their experience and knowledge mattered little in Trump's cabinet.

Tillerson and Kelly had been trying to smooth over the hurt, defensive feelings of America's long-standing ally after Trump threatened huge tariffs on Mexican goods if the country did not agree to pay for construction of the border wall, his signature campaign promise. A planned meeting in Washington between Trump and Mexican president Enrique Peña Nieto was hastily called off on January 26.

Compounding the challenges Tillerson and Kelly confronted was the fact that Kushner was operating as an interlocutor with Mexico outside the boundaries of the State Department or the National Security Council. This arrangement not only smacked of nepotism but also undermined lines of authority, creating confusion for other officials in the government as well as for foreign diplomats. Mexican foreign minister Luis Videgaray, however, cultivated a friendship with Kushner during the campaign, and in the fraught early months of Trump's presidency Videgaray would lean on Kushner as a troubleshooter.

In Mexico City on February 26, as Tillerson and Kelly believed they had reached a kumbaya moment in face-to-face meetings with their counterparts, Trump let the world know who was in charge. In what had become a startling new trend in the White House, the president let the cameras roll as he spoke off the cuff in meetings. At his 10:30 a.m. meeting with two dozen U.S. manufacturing executives in the State Dining Room, Trump applauded his administration's decision to launch a "military operation" to deport criminals who had snuck illegally into the country and Kelly's work to stop "really bad dudes" from crossing the border. "All of a sudden, for the first time, we're getting gang members out, we're getting drug lords out, we're getting really bad dudes out of this country—and at a rate that nobody's ever seen before," Trump said. "And it's a military operation."

Though the White House and Kelly's office had both denied they would deploy the military, nobody was entirely sure what the fledgling administration might ultimately do. After all, the travel ban had been launched without any warning. The president's remarks became breaking news bulletins.

At this very moment, Tillerson and Kelly were at their hotel preparing to leave by motorcade for the official meetings with their Mexican hosts. Tillerson, who had been alerted to the news in Washington by his staff, ran into Kelly in the hotel hallway. "You're never going to believe what the president just did," Tillerson said. "He said he's sending troops to the border." They both knew the disaster rolling over them. The Mexican leaders were sure to be infuriated. Kelly closed his eyes and cursed.

"Oh, fuck," he said. Trump had just cut them off at the knees for the sake of the show, to look tough on television.

Tillerson and Kelly had about an hour before they were scheduled to give a joint press conference with Videgaray and Mexican interior secretary Miguel Ángel Osorio Chong. When they arrived at the ministry for their meetings, the Americans found the Mexicans stunned. Videgaray asked, "Was this a setup? Were Tillerson and Kelly in on this joke?" "Videgaray was saying, 'What the hell? What are we going to do now?'" said one U.S. official present for the meetings. "It was very hard for them to believe this was not planned."

Tillerson and Kelly both insisted they knew nothing about it. Kelly was firm, telling the Mexican officials that the United States was not sending any troops. Still, Osorio Chong was stone-faced as he cited chapter and verse of the Mexican Constitution. "Let me explain to you why this is never going to happen," the interior secretary said, assuring the Americans his country's laws prohibit U.S. troops from coming onto Mexican soil.

The Mexicans kept their composure, which Kelly and Tillerson considered a gift. Setting aside the craziness from Trump, the Mexican leaders appeared to be working overtime to keep their eyes on the bigger prize: a productive working relationship with the United States, almost in spite of its president. When Kelly and Tillerson were done assuring the Mexicans in private, Kelly went to clean up the public mess. "Give me my binder," he told David Lapan, his communications director. He wanted the folder where he kept his prepared remarks. "I need to make some changes."

Kelly's instincts were to try to correct the record and ensure both the Mexican officials and the international media that the U.S. military would not actually be deployed as troops to guard the border. The press conference started about twenty minutes late. Kelly was the last of the four principals to speak. He began by celebrating Mexico as a critical U.S. ally in combating trafficking and criminal gangs. Then he lifted up his head and stared over the room, where the local press and traveling

U.S. press corps sat with microphones running. "Now this is something I would really like you all to pay attention to because it is frequently misrepresented or misreported in the press," Kelly said. "Let me be very, very clear. There will be no—repeat no—mass deportations. Everything we do at DHS will be done legally, according to human rights and the legal justice system of the United States."

Kelly explained that deportations would be focused on criminals and stressed the "interaction and friendship" between Mexico and the United States. Then he returned to his earlier point: "Again, listen to this, no, repeat no use of military force in immigration operations. None. I repeat: There will be no use of military in this. . . . At least half of you try to get that right, because it continues to come up in your reporting."

Kelly had gotten out the message but found a clever way to correct the president: scolding the press, even though they were merely reporting the president's own words. The moment was a forerunner for the rash actions he would confront again and again from Trump.

Kelly had a deep, nuanced, and personal understanding of the desperation that fueled the migration from Central America northward from his years as commander of the military's U.S. Southern Command. Though Trump was fixated on erecting a wall, Kelly believed a sea-to-sea physical barrier was not the solution to illegal border crossings. In the secure confines of the Department of Homeland Security's Washington headquarters, Kelly would snort at Trump's public pronouncements about a wall with his top deputies. "Oh, come on, it's bullshit. We're not building any wall," Kelly would tell them. He would really get a chuckle out of Trump's promise to force Mexico to pay for the wall. Confiding in his aides, the secretary would say of his boss, "He doesn't know what he's talking about."

Three

THE ROAD TO OBSTRUCTION

On March 1, 2017, nearly six weeks after President Trump had raised his right hand and swore to preserve, protect, and defend the Constitution of the United States, he struggled to read aloud the words of the founding document. A film crew had come to the White House to record the new president reading a section of the Constitution. Trump chose to participate in the HBO production because he did not want to forgo the chance to be filmed for history, and he knew that as the sitting president he would be the documentary's most important character.

The documentary, titled *The Words That Built America*, was directed by Alexandra Pelosi, a daughter of House Democratic leader Nancy Pelosi. Her conceit was that the country was starkly divided after the ugliness of the 2016 campaign but the founding documents remained a unifying force for the nation's factions. Pelosi and her team had a novel and distinctly bipartisan hook: all six living presidents, as well as six vice presidents, would join in reading the Constitution on camera, while other political figures and actors would read portions of the Bill of Rights and the Declaration of Independence. Each performance would be edited to create a lively, unabridged reading of the treasured documents that have united the nation for more than two centuries.

On March 1, Pelosi and her crew arrived at the White House, and as they were getting ready in the Blue Room, Trump entered the opulent parlor, which sits at the center of the residence's first floor and opens onto the South Portico. The Blue Room, distinguished by its French blue draperies and gold wallpaper, is steeped in history. It was where President Grover Cleveland and his wife exchanged wedding vows in 1886, and every December the White House's primary Christmas tree is erected at the center of the oval-shaped room.

On this day, Trump seemed stiff and uncomfortable. Though he was technically in his own home, he did not greet his guests. Rather, he stood waiting for someone to approach him. Pelosi moved in to thank Trump for participating in this special history project, but he appeared to have no idea who she was, apparently not briefed on her political lineage or her role as the director. The president asked for some water, and with no staff bringing any to him, Pelosi handed him a bottle of Aquafina from her purse. "I've been into the White House," Pelosi later said of visits to see previous presidents. "There are always protocols. Here there were no rules, no protocol." She added, "There's so much wrong with the whole thing. I'm thinking, isn't there someone who's supposed to guard what he's eating and drinking?"

Meanwhile, a White House staffer gave the other crew members instructions about what they could and could not do with the president. The very first rule was for the makeup artist: Do not touch the president's hair. On his face, light powder only. The next instruction was for the technical crew: Could they make the lighting a little more orange? The president preferred a warm glow on camera. The mention of "orange" struck some in the room as an odd choice. Outside the bubble of the White House, late night TV show hosts and cartoonists had been mocking the perpetually orange hue of Trump's skin.

Pelosi had let presidents and vice presidents choose the portion of the Constitution they wanted to read. Many were wary of reading the section on the rules for impeachment or foreign emoluments. Trump had selected the opening of Article II, the part of the Constitution that addresses a president's election and the scope of his or her power. It would normally have been the perfect selection for a president—but was an ironic one for Trump, who had spoken of his desire to exercise his executive power as much as possible, including by threatening Congress and challenging the judiciary.

With LED lights on stilts in front of him, Trump took his seat. "You're lucky you got the easy part," Pelosi told him cheerfully. "It gets complicated after this." But the president stumbled, trying to get out the words in the arcane, stilted form the Founding Fathers had written. Trump grew irritated. "It's very hard to do because of the language here," Trump told the crew. "It's very hard to get through that whole thing without a stumble." He added, "It's like a different language, right?" The cameraman tried to calm Trump, telling him it was no big deal, to take a moment and start over. Trump tried again, but again remarked, "It's like a foreign language."

The section, like many parts of the Constitution, was slightly awkward—an anachronistic arrangement of words that don't naturally trip off the tongue. Members of the crew exchanged looks, trying not to be obvious. Some believed Trump would eventually get it, but others were more concerned. The president, already bristling about his missteps, was getting angry. He chided the crew, accusing them of distracting him. "You know, your paper was making a lot of noise. It's tough enough," Trump said.

"Every time he stumbled, he manufactured something to blame people," another person in the room recalled. "He never said, 'Sorry, I'm messing this up.' [Other] people would screw up and say, 'Ohhhh, I'm sorry.' They would be self-effacing. He was making up excuses and saying there were distracting sounds. . . . He was definitely blaming everyone for his inability to get through it. That was prickly, or childish." Though stiff, he eventually made it through without any errors.

Trump presented a stark contrast to many other readers, including the Supreme Court associate justice Stephen Breyer, who read as if he knew the full text by heart, and Senator Ted Cruz, who "knew it from beginning to end" as a result of performing dramatic readings of the Constitution as a high school student, according to Pelosi. "Donald Trump is a celebrity and he came to perform," she said. "He had not practiced it beforehand. I don't think anyone would show up to read the Constitution without practicing it first."

Whatever the reason for Trump's discomfort with the reading, several watching agreed on this much: he behaved like a brooding child, short-tempered, brittle, and quick to blame mystery distractions for the mistakes. "I didn't expect this, but I felt sorry for him," another witness said. "When [Vice President] Pence is reading it, when [former vice president Dick] Cheney is reading it, I knew they knew the Constitution. And I thought, before he got this job, he really should have read it."

The next day, March 2, Attorney General Jeff Sessions, one of Trump's most steadfast allies, the man who served at the vanguard on immigration and other policies at the heart of the president's agenda, recused himself from oversight of the Russia investigation. During his January 10 confirmation hearing, in response to a question from the Democratic senator Al Franken, Sessions had testified under oath that he "did not have communications with the Russians" during the 2016 campaign. He did not disclose that he had had two conversations during the campaign with Russian ambassador Sergei Kislyak, a fact later revealed in a *Washington Post* story.

The morning of March 2, the president got worked up at the prospect of Sessions bowing to escalating public pressure and recusing, believing the attorney general would look guilty for forgetting an inconsequential meeting, and, most importantly, leave him unprotected and vulnerable. So the president called White House counsel Don McGahn to insist that he stop Sessions.

"Sessions doesn't have to recuse," Trump bellowed, speaking so loudly that people in the West Wing hallway could make out what he was uttering from the Oval Office. "Whatever he said to Franken, so what?"

Trump was incredulous. "Everyone is now saying he has to recuse," he repeated to McGahn. "He doesn't have to!"

McGahn was convinced that some of Trump's reasoning made sense, despite the angry tone he used to explain it. But other reasons were purely political. McGahn's mind raced through the risks, knowing the president's order had the potential not only to be a fool's errand but also to get Trump into trouble for obstructing justice.

McGahn had been loyal to Trump since the early days of the campaign. A veteran campaign lawyer, he was not the typical Trump supporter, yet he was one of the first to recognize the power of Trump's campaign and to join his team. In January 2015, he had watched the real estate developer and reality-television star in action by flying with him to the Iowa Freedom Summit, hosted by Congressman Steve King. McGahn had calculated that due to a seismic shift in the GOP and the rising disaffection of rural white voters in both parties, a traditional Republican candidate like Mitt Romney or Jeb Bush could never win in 2016. The hulking billionaire that McGahn saw onstage in Iowa, home to the nation's first presidential caucuses, made a big impression and connected with the crowd in a way that surprised him. Trump took note that McGahn was in the greenroom, sizing up all the candidates, and figured he was an important player. When Trump later asked McGahn to be the lawyer for his campaign, McGahn said yes. Trump could tell that McGahn, a former member of the Federal Election Commission, knew his field and could see all the angles. Trump knew zip and was unapologetic about it. The candidate gave his lawyer broad autonomy and normally followed his advice.

Once they were in the White House, however, their dynamic changed. Trump believed he was cornered early with a series of rules rigged to box him in and limit his power. It often fell to McGahn to deliver bad news. Cabinet secretaries and other aides pleaded for McGahn to come to the Oval Office to explain to Trump why he couldn't do this and couldn't do that. In one of the counsel's first discussions of executive power with the president, McGahn told Trump he couldn't automatically issue an executive order to impose tariffs on foreign countries' goods—unless he had a grave reason.

"I just want to do it. I'm the president. Can't I do it?" Trump asked him.

"No," McGahn said, pointing out the standard role of Congress in imposing duties and tariffs on imports. "You need a study under the statute. There's a process. They have to do reports, and there has to be public notice."

To Trump, McGahn became Dr. No. The White House counsel labored to keep bad ideas from germinating. McGahn, who carried a pocket Constitution, saw it as his duty to protect Trump from the novices in his administration who knew less about governing than a newly elected congressman coming out of a two-week orientation session. McGahn had also rankled Ivanka Trump by riding herd on the ethical questions of the first daughter joining the West Wing staff.

On March 2, McGahn called Sessions to tell him that Trump was not happy about the idea of his removing himself from the Russia investigation. Sessions responded that his hands were tied and that he intended to abide by the Justice Department's rules of recusal and follow the advice of the career ethics staff who were evaluating the situation. Other White House advisers also pressed Sessions and his deputies against recusing. Still, Trump went public with his feelings. Asked by reporters whether Sessions should recuse, Trump said, "I don't think so." The president said he had "total" confidence in Sessions.

It was too late. Sessions hastily called a news conference and announced that he would not oversee any existing or future investigations that pertain to the Trump campaign. Sessions was following the rules, which plainly stated that no Justice Department official could participate in a criminal investigation if he or she has a personal or political relationship with an individual or organization substantially involved in the investigation. When a reporter asked Sessions about Trump's and White House press secretary Sean Spicer's comments that the attorney general didn't need to recuse, the attorney general smiled awkwardly and shrugged. "They don't know the rules, the ethics rules," he said. "Most people don't."

Trump watched Sessions's news conference from aboard Air Force One, returning from a short afternoon trip to Newport News, Virginia, to visit the USS *Gerald R. Ford*, the navy's newest nuclear-powered warship. He was furious. As the diminutive Alabaman spoke from his lectern at the Justice Department, all the president saw was weakness and disloyalty. He railed about how "weak" and "horrible" the attorney general was. He said he should never have picked him for the job. To Trump, this was the end of Sessions. His attorney general had betrayed him. But this was also the moment Trump started to turn on McGahn, one of his earliest backers, for failing to stop the recusal. He began shutting out the very lawyer who had been working thanklessly to protect him from his own dangerous impulses.

"He should've told me he was going to do this," Trump fumed about Sessions. "If he couldn't handle this, he should've told me and we could've put him down at the border," Trump said, meaning naming him secretary of homeland security.

Trump's Air Force One eruption was the maddest his aides had ever seen him to date. He was so loud that some more junior staffers took a seat in a rear cabin of the plane and put on headphones to drown out the president's yelling. Still, some aides shared their boss's anger.

"This is fucked-up," said Johnny McEntee, the president's body man.

McGahn gave Trump a directive aimed at protecting the president from his own emotions: he could not call Sessions, under any circumstances. Otherwise it could appear as if he were seeking to obstruct justice.

When Air Force One touched down at Joint Base Andrews, the president was still so hot that he was urged to sit on board for a while so he could stew in private. Aides explained to him that the press corps would be waiting under the wing, so he shouldn't stop to talk to them, nor should he stalk down the steps of the plane with a scowl on his face.

Trump managed to deplane without causing a ruckus. But his fury had not subsided. Rather, it was a rage that boiled into the next day. He went thermonuclear. "The rages, they build and they build," one of his advisers said. "He's screaming and he's a big guy and he looks like he could get physical."

Trump is famously short-tempered, a trait that predated his presidency. A large physical presence even when he is sedate, Trump becomes monstrous when something sets him off. "He is scary," said Barbara Res, a former Trump Organization executive who worked for Trump between the 1970s and the 1990s. She recalled Trump losing his cool during a tour of renovations at the Plaza hotel shortly after he purchased the crown jewel overlooking Central Park in 1988. Inspecting the knockoff furniture purchased for guest rooms, Trump tried to slide back the doors to an armoire and one of them got caught on a rail. He shook the door, and still it wouldn't move. So he pulled the door off its hinges and threw it to the floor. Then, inspecting one of the bathrooms, he launched into a tirade at Res over the green Chinese marble. An Italian verde this was not.

"You're no fucking good!" Res recalled Trump yelling at her. "You're making me look bad! This is cheap shit! Who told you to buy this?"

Res had shown Trump three samples of green marble—one for $5, one for $9, and one for $13—and he had picked the cheapest one. "I just stood there and said, 'Donald, you approved it,'" Res recalled. "I thought he might explode. He was that angry. He was that volatile. His face gets red and his lips get white. He gets in these rages. The screaming. The cursing."

The morning of March 3, 2017, Trump was in one of these screaming, volatile rages. In the Oval Office, the president gave Priebus and Bannon an earful about how much he despised Sessions and then summoned McGahn. He wanted to make clear to the White House counsel that he had failed him as well. Trump's words were blistering as he conjured the ghost of Roy Cohn, his former personal lawyer, fixer, and mentor who had previously been a top aide to Senator Joseph R. McCarthy during the Senate's hunt for communist sympathizers in the 1950s. Trump complained that he wished Cohn were still alive because McGahn wasn't properly protecting him.

"I don't have a lawyer!" the president screamed. "Where's my lawyer?"

McGahn felt Trump's fury was aimed at him, although the president appeared to tilt back and forth in his tirade about his "attorney," appearing to be complaining about the abdication of both his White House counsel and his attorney general. Neither was actually *Trump's* attorney, an important constitutional detail lost on the president.

"Roy wouldn't have handled it this way," Trump said, directing his ire at McGahn. "He would have told them all to go to hell."

McGahn, Priebus, and Bannon explained to Trump that Sessions had no choice. But Trump wouldn't listen. To him, everything was personal, and he saw Sessions's recusal as a betrayal. The attorney general is the top federal law enforcement official in the country, serving the American people and leading a quasi-independent institution, the Justice Department. In Trump's mind, however, the attorney general's job was to protect the president, and by that measure Sessions had failed.

"Sessions should be fired," he said.

"I never would have appointed Sessions if I knew that he would have recused himself," the president said at another point.

"Where is my Bobby Kennedy? Where's my Eric Holder? Where's my Roy Cohn?" Trump bellowed to his advisers.

Trump held up Holder as a model attorney general because of what he perceived as his unwavering loyalty to Obama and his political savvy. He believed Holder acted as Obama's protector, much the way Robert F. Kennedy had protected his older brother President John F. Kennedy as attorney general. Trump cited yet another example: J. Edgar Hoover, the politically cunning FBI director who served under eight presidents and was later found to have abused his powers.

Trump's advisers tried to explain that the attorney general is not the president's personal attorney. Independence was expected at the Justice Department, and the attorney general could not be seen as the president's fixer. Bannon told Trump that times had changed. "There's something that happened between those days of having Bobby Kennedy and J. Edgar Hoover bringing over the files," he said. "It's called Watergate. It just doesn't work like that anymore."

Trump believed Sessions should have protected him and his family at all costs. Now oversight of the probe was transferring to Deputy Attorney General Rod Rosenstein, whom Trump hardly knew and therefore did not trust. Trump accused McGahn of not fighting hard enough to defend his oversight of the probe and told him to persuade Sessions to unrecuse himself. That was not legally or ethically possible, and McGahn told him it would look as if the president were interfering with an investigation if anyone at the White House tried to pressure the attorney general. Trump pushed back on McGahn, saying it was a stupid rule.

"You're telling me that Bobby and Jack didn't talk about investigations?" Trump said, throwing up his hands in disgust. "Or Obama didn't tell Eric Holder who to investigate?"

Once the yelling subsided, Trump gathered a couple of his grandchildren to walk across the South Lawn to board Marine One. They were headed to Mar-a-Lago for the weekend. Bannon and Priebus were planning to accompany the president for the trip to Florida, but they stayed at the White House. "Figure this out," Trump told them.

In Trump World, people's fortunes can rise and fall based on the president's changing moods, but the speed with which Sessions went from confidant to persona non grata was breathtaking. Trump and Sessions had known each other for twelve years, first meeting over a shared interest in a New York real estate project. A backbench, ultraconservative senator from the Gulf Coast of Alabama, Sessions led the crusade in Congress against building a new headquarters for the U.S. Mission to the United Nations in New York. He discovered an unexpected ally when he read an article in *The New York Sun*. The headline: "Trump Scoffs at U.N.'s Plan for New H.Q."

Sessions invited Trump to testify before a Senate Homeland Security and Governmental Affairs subcommittee on July 21, 2005, and Sessions was spellbound. He told the other senators on the subcommittee, "Mr. Trump is a breath of fresh air for this Senate," and praised the star witness for his construction know-how. Sessions then invited Trump to his office to have lunch. Sitting at a conference table in the Russell Senate Office Building, the two men—one practiced discipline as a Sunday school teacher at his family's Methodist church and kept the Boy Scout motto, "Be Prepared," engraved on a stone on his office desk, the other was a bombastic braggart from Queens who broadcast his sexual exploits on Howard Stern's radio show and survived life by winging it—bonded over Subway sandwiches.

In Sessions, Trump saw a man who shared his worldview and instincts and could help him establish credibility with conservative base voters. In August 2015, Trump, a newly minted presidential candidate, swooped into Sessions's hometown of Mobile for what was his biggest mega-rally to date. It was something between a Lynyrd Skynyrd concert and the Daytona 500. Just before sunset, the sweaty masses in Ladd-Peebles Stadium heard the roar of a jet engine and snapped their heads toward the sky. Gliding toward them was a gleaming Boeing 757 with "T-R-U-M-P" stretched across its navy blue fuselage, dipping its wing toward the sloped stadium bleachers as if to say hello. The flamboyant candidate soon strode onstage to "Sweet Home Alabama" and ticked through all the polls where he was leading Jeb Bush and the other Republican candidates.

Sessions was blown away. "I've never seen anything like this before," he told one of his political advisers. "Something is happening here." After Trump finished speaking that August in Mobile, he invited Sessions and his wife, Mary, into his motorcade of Cadillac Escalades to ride to the airport, where Trump took the couple onto his plane to show it off—the white leather, the gold trim, the big-screen TV, everything.

In February 2016, Sessions became the first U.S. senator to publicly back Trump, and helped craft the candidate's first major foreign policy speech in April 2016. He also lent some of his top staffers to the campaign, including Stephen Miller. Trump bragged about how smart Sessions was. Whenever he saw the senator, he would point at him and say, "So respected!" or "Totally gets it!" In his mind, there was perhaps no greater attribute than toughness, and Trump would tell aides about Sessions, "That guy is tough."

Trump had signaled that Sessions could have whatever job he wanted. Initially, Kushner, Bannon, and others in Trump's inner circle favored Rudy Giuliani for attorney general. During the campaign, Giuliani had contorted himself every which way to defend Trump, including after the release of the devastating *Access Hollywood* tape in which Trump bragged about sexually assaulting women. They thought the former federal prosecutor and longtime Trump friend was the closest thing to a modern-day Cohn. The trouble is, Giuliani was not interested.

"I don't have the energy," Giuliani told Bannon one Saturday afternoon in November, talking through a possible cabinet role. "You don't understand how tough a job that is."

Bannon replied, "You've gotta do this. We need you. It will only be for a year, but we have to have you."

"Steve, you're not a lawyer," Giuliani said. "You don't understand. It's the worst job. . . . I'm too old. I'm not going to do it."

Instead, Trump installed Sessions at the Justice Department with a mandate to oversee a hard-line anti-immigration agenda and start rolling back civil rights protections. In a statement, Trump hailed Sessions as "a world-class legal mind" who is "highly respected" and "greatly admired." For Sessions, becoming attorney general was a personal triumph. His network of aides and advisers called him "Joseph," referring to the Old Testament son of Jacob and Rachel who was shunned by his brothers and sold into slavery as a boy outcast. But Joseph eventually came under the good graces of an Egyptian pharaoh, rising to become his right hand and oversee the grain supplies of Egypt, ultimately helping civilization survive famine.

At Mar-a-Lago the weekend of March 3, Trump was joined by his daughter Ivanka and Kushner, who are often described by their admirers as calming influences on the tempestuous president. Ensconced at the Palm Beach castle, the kids were helpless to contain the president. Trump had a tendency to try to distract from bad news stories by creating new stories, and starting at 6:35 a.m. on March 4 he pecked out four tweets accusing Obama of orchestrating a politically motivated plot to tap the phones at his Trump Tower campaign headquarters in the run-up to the election. "How low has President Obama gone to tapp my phones during the very sacred election process," Trump wrote. "This is Nixon/Watergate. Bad (or sick) guy!"

Trump made this explosive allegation without citing any evidence, although a Breitbart article posted the day before about the Obama administration's alleged "police state" tactics had been circulating among Trump's senior staff. An Obama spokesman, Kevin Lewis, called Trump's allegations "simply false." But that didn't seem to bother Trump, who went golfing later that morning and vented to friends. "This will be investigated. It will all come out. I will be proven right," Christopher Ruddy said Trump told him. "This is bad; this is really bad. I hope the media focus on this."

Just six weeks in office, Trump believed he was being tormented in ways known and unknown by a group of Obama-aligned critics, federal bureaucrats, intelligence figures, and, most especially, the news media. His angst over the "Deep State," already well established, was fomenting daily and fueled by rumors and conspiracies.

Four

A FATEFUL FIRING

On March 21, 2017, Trump directed Don McGahn to find a way to get James Comey to tell the public the president himself was not under investigation. Trump was upset about the FBI director's confirmation in congressional testimony the day before that the bureau was probing possible coordination between Russia and Trump's campaign, leading to speculation that the president was a suspect. Over the next five days, Trump made similar requests of Director of National Intelligence Dan Coats, CIA director Mike Pompeo, and National Security Agency director Michael Rogers. On March 30, he personally called Comey to ask him to help "lift the cloud." Yet none of these government officials, sworn to serve the public and protect the integrity of investigations, complied with Trump's requests. They observed a professional code of honor Trump knew little about.

Increasingly vengeful, Trump considered delivering a prime-time televised address to the nation debunking what he dubbed the "Russian hoax." When aides resisted, Trump shot back, "This is the only thing they're talking about in politics. Why shouldn't I grab the bully pulpit?" Eventually, Reince Priebus and others persuaded Trump not to give the speech, in part by arguing that a prime-time address would help define his legacy and it would be unwise to make it about the Russia investigation.

On May 3, Trump reached the boiling point when Comey declined in his testimony before the Senate Judiciary Committee to say that the president was not under investigation. One by one, the officials he considered his servants had failed him. The president flew into a rage—"Like DEFCON 1," one of his advisers recalled—that set in motion a quick progression of events culminating in the appointment of a special counsel that would threaten the president for two years to come.

Trump repeatedly insisted to aides, "I don't know any Russians" and "I've never been to Russia." Both statements were outright lies. Trump also groused about Comey. *He's a bad guy! He's a showboater! He's a grandstander! Rank-and-file FBI agents don't respect him! The Democrats all hate him! Our base hates him!* As they watched Comey's testimony together, Steve Bannon told Trump that even if every single FBI agent hated the director, "The moment you fire him, he's the greatest martyr. He's Joan of Arc."

Bannon argued that "the fucking deplorables don't give a fuck" about the Russia investigation, referring to Trump's base voters. "It's the C block on *Anderson Cooper*. People are tired of talking about it," he added. But, he explained to Trump, "you fire him and the FBI is going to bleed you out because they have to. They're the FBI. You're just a guy passing through here. They're the FBI and they're going to be here a hundred years from now."

Trump was indignant. As he saw it, Coats, Pompeo, Rogers, and Comey were tools he could use to improve his situation, even if it meant lying or asserting something they did not know to be true. He issued an edict to four different officials he thought worked at his personal beck and call, yet none complied. "The president knew he didn't collude with any Russians," Trump's longtime friend Thomas Barrack said. "It was infuriating to him to continue to have that whiff of scandal out there." Trump's orders to Comey and the others violated precedent and standard. But the fact that federal intelligence and law enforcement leaders were not working to protect him frightened and infuriated the president.

The next day, May 4, Trump unloaded on Jeff Sessions.

"This is terrible, Jeff," Trump said in a meeting that included Mc-Gahn and the attorney general's chief of staff, Jody Hunt. "It's all because you recused. AG is supposed to be the most important appointment.

Kennedy appointed his brother. Obama appointed Holder. I appointed you and you recused yourself. You left me on an island. I can't do anything." Sessions again explained that he had no choice but to recuse himself, considering the Justice Department's ethics rules, but Trump was still furious.

On Friday, May 5, he flew to Bedminster, New Jersey, to spend the weekend at his private golf club. The rainy and windy weather did little to improve the president's sour mood. He hung around, watched television, drank Diet Cokes, and stewed. He mused about how badly Comey had let him down. Over dinner that night, Trump told Jared Kushner, Stephen Miller, and some family members that he wanted to dismiss Comey. Kushner encouraged the firing and noted that congressional Democrats already viewed Comey with contempt because of his handling of the Hillary Clinton email investigation. Trump had ideas for what to say in his firing letter. Miller took notes as Trump dictated specific language, including that the letter should begin by clearing the president: "While I greatly appreciate you informing me that I am not under investigation concerning what I have often stated is a fabricated story on a Trump-Russia relationship . . ." Over the weekend, Miller drafted a four-page termination letter, and Trump offered several rounds of edits, insisting that the letter establish that Comey had been "under review" and that the president and the American people had lost faith in his judgment.

On Sunday, May 7, when Trump returned to Washington, he was champing at the bit to fire Comey. Around 10:00 a.m. on May 8, the president summoned McGahn to the Oval Office. When McGahn arrived, Trump was at the Resolute Desk surrounded by nearly a dozen aides, including Priebus, Kushner, and Miller. Also present was strategic communications director Hope Hicks, who had received a download on the Comey plan when she caught a ride Sunday on Air Force One after spending the weekend in Connecticut with her parents. Trump greeted McGahn with a smile and waved him in. "You're here. Wonderful," he said. "We're going to fire Comey."

McGahn was surprised. He thought of himself as an independent agent of value to Trump precisely because of his objective eye and was unique among White House aides because he did not fawn over the president, though he could get prickly when he felt pushed. As McGahn told colleagues, he was never entirely sure when the president barked out a plan whether he was giving orders or merely crowdsourcing an idea by saying it aloud. But this time it was clear Trump was determined to fire Comey. The president read aloud from the firing letter Miller had drafted and told his advisers, "Don't talk me out of this. I've made my decision."

McGahn went through two threshold questions with the president. The first: Would it be legal to fire Comey? The answer was yes, absolutely. FBI directors served ten-year terms but could be dismissed at any time. The second: Would it be a good idea? McGahn felt reasonably sure Trump would get roasted by Democrats and even by some Republicans for such a drastic action. But the White House counsel also had grown tired of being Trump's Dr. No and figured it would be impossible to talk the president out of it.

To buy some time, McGahn told the president that the Justice Department had already been discussing Comey's status and suggested that Trump first talk with Sessions, who was to meet with McGahn for a previously scheduled lunch. They could invite the new deputy attorney general, Rod Rosenstein, to join them and see what they both thought.

Over lunch in McGahn's second-floor West Wing office, Sessions told McGahn he supposed firing Comey would be legal. "I assume he can," the attorney general said. McGahn figured Rosenstein might raise concerns and warn of the political dangers of something this rash, but McGahn was a little taken aback when Rosenstein said there were justified reasons to fire Comey, including his handling of the Clinton case, and even sounded gung ho about the idea. McGahn couldn't catch a break.

Rosenstein was just two weeks into the job, and he was oblivious to the nightmare he was walking into at the White House. He didn't realize McGahn expected him to help slow walk the president's decision or caution Trump on the politics of firing Comey; he heard only McGahn insisting they had to stop Trump from sending the "terrible" termination letter he had crafted with Miller, because it mentioned Comey's public handling of the Russia case as one of his fireable offenses. At that moment, Rosenstein had ample reason to recommend removing Comey. He had once considered Comey a personal hero, but after the FBI director twice discussed the Clinton email case in public, his credibility was irrevocably damaged in Rosenstein's mind. Rosenstein also had been briefed about an internal probe that would likely cite Comey's actions as violating department policy.

During the lunch, Rosenstein got his first clue that something was seriously wrong in the White House. Priebus knocked on McGahn's door at least two or three separate times to check in, and each time looked more frantic. Where was the letter? the chief of staff demanded to know. "The president wants to get this done," Priebus said. Amid the fearful rush, there was no orderly planning for who might replace the man they were going to fire.

Some time after 5:00 p.m., Sessions and Rosenstein met with Trump in the Oval Office. This was Rosenstein's first official meeting with the president, and the experience was disquieting. For the first twenty minutes or so, Trump did all the talking, gesticulating and rat-a-tat-tatting his grievances with Comey: the Clinton investigation; the political bias of his deputy, Andrew McCabe, and his wife's campaign in Virginia; and, most of all, Comey's slippery May 3 testimony on Capitol Hill. The president even imitated Comey's sanctimonious manner, explaining that he had watched him testify for hours on TV and said he planned to fire him pronto.

"How do we do it?" Trump asked.

Uttam Dhillon, a deputy White House counsel, suggested they let him resign. Rosenstein chimed in to say that Comey would never resign. Then Trump called for his assistant to bring in his draft termination letter and showed it to Sessions and Rosenstein, asking them what they thought. As Rosenstein tried to read it, Trump kept talking and peppering him with questions. Rosenstein finished reading and said he agreed with some of it but not all. "For one thing, the first sentence is about Russia," he said. Why did Trump have to get into that at all?

"Oh, it's very important to put that in there. I don't want anyone to think it's about Russia," Trump said, prompting confused looks in the room. Trump's point was that Comey had told him he wasn't a subject of the Russia probe; therefore, he couldn't be trying to fire Comey to stop an investigation of himself.

Trump then directed Rosenstein to write a memo to Sessions outlining his case for firing Comey and told Sessions to write a letter with his recommendation. It was around 6:00 p.m. Trump said he wanted both on his desk at 8:00 the next morning.

Rosenstein returned to his office at the Justice Department and huddled with a few staffers to begin writing. They ordered in pizza, with Rosenstein's still unpacked boxes stacked around the room, and the deputy attorney general stayed until about 3:00 a.m. to finish his draft. Although Trump asked Rosenstein to include in the memo "the Russia stuff," meaning Comey's refusal to state publicly that the president was not under investigation, Rosenstein was adamant that it contain only his own views of why Comey should be terminated. He wanted to be able to defend the memo should he ever have to. So he stuck to his own complaint about Comey's violation of department standards and his public discussion of evidence in the Clinton investigation. "The FBI's reputation and credibility have suffered substantial damage, and it has affected the entire Department of Justice," Rosenstein wrote.

After perfecting his prose, Rosenstein delivered the memo to the White House on May 9, several hours after his 8:00 a.m. deadline. He naively expected it would likely go into a West Wing file folder to document the president's decision process. Instead, the Rosenstein memo became Trump's golden ticket. The president liked Rosenstein's critique of Comey and agreed with McGahn to adjust the language of his termination letter, though he still insisted they mention that Comey had told him he wasn't under investigation in the Russia probe. Still, Trump would lean on Rosenstein's memo as a key justification for firing the FBI director.

That afternoon, as Trump prepared to set his plan in motion, Priebus came into the Oval Office with a final piece of advice. He spoke loudly. "I want everyone to hear what I'm going to say," the chief of staff said.

"There's a right way to do this and there's a wrong way to do this. This is the wrong way to do this. The right way is you bring someone in and you sit down and talk. . . . This is not the right way to go about business." But Priebus was unpersuasive. Trump had no interest in slowing down, and certainly not in giving Comey a gentleman's goodbye.

The staffers the president was counting on to spin the firing to the public were still in the dark. At about 4:00 p.m., press secretary Sean Spicer and communications director Mike Dubke were called into the Oval Office. They had no idea why. Dubke hurried in, although it took a while to track down Spicer, who was out on the South Lawn mingling with military families at an ice cream social. Trump handed Dubke a piece of paper and said, "What do you think of this?" It was his letter firing Comey. It took a minute for Dubke to process what was happening, and then he said, "You can't just put this out in a press release. You actually have to deliver this to him, and there's some protocol we have to follow here."

"Fine," Trump said. "Keith, come in here."

Keith Schiller was single-mindedly loyal to Trump. The physically imposing former New York Police Department counter-narcotics officer had been Trump's personal bodyguard and director of security for nearly two decades. He would do just about anything for Trump, from punching protesters he considered a threat to forcibly removing journalists to fetching his Big Macs from McDonald's. At the White House, Schiller was director of Oval Office operations and worked out of a closet-sized office within earshot of the Resolute Desk. Now Trump believed he was honoring his trusted lieutenant with a momentous mission.

"Keith, would you like to fire the head of the FBI?" Trump asked.

"Yes, sir, I would," Schiller said.

"All right, Keith, you're going to take this over," the president said, handing over a big manila envelope that Trump wanted him to use as the delivery package.

Trump was so excited about memorializing this moment in history that he asked the official White House photographer, Shealah Craighead, to come into the Oval to take pictures. Schiller set off to personally deliver the envelope to FBI headquarters, and only then did the White House realize that Comey was traveling on business in Los Angeles. Amid all the hubbub, nobody checked on the FBI director's whereabouts.

Trump then notified congressional leaders but was surprised when Senate Democratic leader Charles Schumer was not supportive. "I thought you'd be on board with this," Trump told him. "You wanted him gone. Why isn't this good?"

Spicer and Dubke scrambled to put together a press rollout plan in a matter of minutes. News of Comey's firing broke at about 5:48 p.m., and bedlam broke out. In the months to come, such firings would feel commonplace. But at this moment Rosenstein was floored. It had never occurred to him that Comey would be executed in so haphazard a way.

Trump, meanwhile, sat in front of the television watching the news coverage and grew angry as the night wore on that his aides weren't on camera defending him. He was getting crushed rather than cheered. The trouble was, his spokespeople were still hurrying to come up with reasons for Comey's firing and to settle on their talking points. Exasperated, Trump called Chris Christie.

"What the hell is going on? I'm getting my ass kicked on this," Trump told his friend.

"You've created a shit storm," Christie told him. "And what about the worst staff work ever? You didn't fucking know the guy was in Los Angeles? You sent Keith Schiller with a letter for a guy who was twenty-nine hundred miles away?"

"I know, I know, fucking incompetence," Trump said. "Drives me crazy."

Christie asked Trump why he fired Comey, and the president told him it was because Rosenstein had written a memo outlining the reasons why.

"I've got your solution," Christie said. "Get Rosenstein out on TV now. If this is Rosenstein's memo, have fucking Rosenstein go out and do it."

"That's brilliant. I'm going to call Rod right now and get him out on TV," the president said, signing off with Christie in a hurry.

Sarah Isgur Flores, the Justice Department's communications chief, received a call from the White House passing along Trump's instructions for Rosenstein. "They need you to hold a press conference and say the Comey firing is your idea," Flores told Rosenstein.

"I can't do that," Rosenstein said. "I can't lie."

Soon thereafter, Spicer, deputy White House press secretary Sarah Sanders, and counselor to the president Kellyanne Conway did a round of television interviews from Pebble Beach, the area along the West Wing driveway from which network correspondents did live shots with the illuminated White House in the background. The Trump aides tried to distance the president from the decision and push the false claim that the idea to fire Comey came from Rosenstein. They insisted this firing wasn't about Russia and that it was a Justice Department recommendation, but they were out of the loop—so much so that both Spicer and Conway stumbled when trying to say the deputy attorney general's name, pronouncing it both *Rosensteen* and *Rozenstine*.

On CNN, Anderson Cooper argued to Conway that it was illogical that Trump, now in his fourth month in office, all of a sudden, after all those "lock her up" chants at his rallies, decided Comey had been unfairly harsh to Clinton in the emails case. "That makes no sense," Cooper said testily.

"It does make sense," Conway insisted.

Watching from home in New Jersey wearing gym shorts and a T-shirt, Christie realized that if Conway was on air struggling to explain the decision, Rosenstein couldn't be persuaded to go on TV. A few minutes later, Christie's phone rang. It was Conway. Whispering because she was now in the president's private dining room, Conway told him that CNN was airing a live special at 11:00 p.m. and the president wanted Christie to go on to defend him. Christie was floored.

"You tell the president I'll go on right after Rosenstein—right after him," he told Conway.

"I think you'd better tell him," she replied, handing the phone to Trump.

"You won't do this for me?" the president asked Christie.

"No, that's incorrect, sir," he replied. "I will do it for you right after

Rod. I want to hear Rod say on national television that he gave you this memo and that because of this memo you fired Comey. As soon as Rod says that, then I know the words of the hymnal and I can sing from the hymnal."

There would be no Rosenstein TV appearance. At the Justice Department, he was in his office that night growing red-faced at having been used for cover. Rosenstein called McGahn to relay a warning: He would resign if the White House persisted with its "fake story" that his memo was the pretext for Trump's firing Comey. "I'm not going to be able to stay here if the whole administration is telling a fake story about me," he told McGahn.

Rosenstein, fifty-two, one of the George W. Bush appointees who had been trained in the Justice Department rather than elevated for his partisan loyalty, had an unblemished reputation as a scrupulous and methodical U.S. attorney in Maryland. The straitlaced Rosenstein resembled a modern-day Jimmy Stewart, reminding his staff to "always stay humble and kind." But now, on his fourteenth day on the job, some would say Rosenstein more closely resembled Tom Hagen, the Corleone crime family's lawyer and consigliere from *The Godfather*, played in the films by Robert Duvall. He worried his career might be reduced to ashes by a destructive president.

Among his many peers at the Justice Department, there was deep concern that Rosenstein had crossed a dangerous line. "There were only two possible interpretations you could take from what he did," one department veteran said. "Either he knowingly helped the president fire the FBI director to try to rid himself of this investigation, or Rod was an unwitting tool who got used by the president. Both of them were terrible."

On May 10, a sense of panic took hold at the FBI headquarters, the hulking Soviet-style J. Edgar Hoover Building on Pennsylvania Avenue, and at the Justice Department headquarters across the street. Many wondered if the Russia probe was now in peril. Deputy FBI director Andrew McCabe, a close ally of Comey's, overnight became the bureau's acting director, but he and his colleagues expected he could be removed. "This was a tumultuous time to say the least. It was one, frankly, crazy thing after another," FBI counsel Jim Baker later recalled in congressional testimony. "The Director being fired because the President doesn't like the fact that we're investigating Russia was pretty crazy to my mind."

The FBI had secretly been considering opening an investigation on Trump for obstructing the Russia probe ever since Comey had returned from a private February 14 meeting with the president in which he referenced the Michael Flynn investigation and said he hoped Comey could "see your way clear to letting this go, to letting Flynn go." Comey had resisted ruling it out in public; he knew one day he might be under investigation. Now some felt Trump's firing of Comey gave the FBI an urgent reason to investigate. "We need to open the case we've been waiting on now while Andy is acting," the FBI counterintelligence agent Peter Strzok wrote in a text message to the FBI lawyer Lisa Page, a view supported by McCabe.

Also on May 10, in the middle of the tumult following Comey's firing, Sessions, Rosenstein, and McCabe ended up in the same room, at a farewell party for Mary McCord, the acting assistant attorney general for the national security division. She was leaving because she feared the Trump administration's recklessness and detested Sessions, someone she considered a xenophobic misogynist with little respect for the law. Unexpectedly, Rosenstein asked if he could join the list of people making remarks about the Justice Department lifer. He spoke of McCord's impeccable reputation for putting her duty to the public above politics. In praising her, he tried to remind people who he was and what he valued at a time when many had palpable doubts.

On Capitol Hill, meanwhile, Democratic and Republican lawmakers alike were expressing serious concerns, with some comparing Trump's firing of Comey to President Nixon's firing of Archibald Cox, the Watergate special prosecutor. "This is nothing less than Nixonian," said Senator Patrick Leahy, a senior Democrat on the Judiciary Committee. "No one should accept President Trump's absurd justification that he is now concerned that FBI director Comey treated Secretary Clinton unfairly."

On May 10, Vice President Pence traveled to the Capitol, and reporters shouted out questions about whether Trump was trying to stop the FBI investigation of Russian interference in the election. "Let me be clear with you, that was not what this is about," Pence said. The vice president knew more than he was sharing, however. He had been in the Oval Office meeting where Trump explained his plan.

That same day, Russian foreign minister Sergey Lavrov happened to be in town. Trump invited Lavrov and Russian ambassador Sergei Kislyak into the Oval Office for a meet and greet. With the Comey story dominating the news, the White House blocked the press pool from observing the session with the Russians. But a photographer with the Russian state-run news agency TASS accompanied the Russian contingent and snapped pictures of the jovial, relaxed U.S. president grinning and shaking hands with the Kremlin envoys, images the Russian Foreign Ministry almost immediately posted on Twitter. Trump boasted to the Russians, "I just fired the head of the FBI. He was crazy, a real nut job. I faced great pressure because of Russia. That's taken off." Then the president told them what he considered the most important fact everyone doing business with him should know: "I'm not under investigation."

On May 11, frustrated that his press team had failed to stem the tide of bad headlines, Trump decided he would be his own spokesman. The president sat down with the NBC anchor Lester Holt and told him that he had been going to fire Comey regardless of Rosenstein's recommendation. He also acknowledged that the Russia investigation influenced his decision. "When I decided to just do it, I said to myself, I said, 'You know, this Russia thing with Trump and Russia is a made-up story, it's an excuse by the Democrats for having lost an election that they should have won,'" Trump told Holt.

On May 11, Rosenstein called together the Justice Department's senior officials overseeing counterintelligence, national security, and criminal cases for a private strategy session. There was rampant speculation in the media that Trump fired Comey in order to torpedo the FBI's Russia investigation, but Rosenstein told them to keep at it and to leave no stone unturned. "In my capacity as acting attorney general of the United States, I'm instructing you that you should follow every available lead, and if there's any wrongdoing, you should uncover it," he said.

Rosenstein asked those assembled if they believed the Justice Department was capable of continuing to run the Russia investigation or if they thought he should consider appointing a special counsel, as McCabe had been urging. Rosenstein seemed inclined to let the Justice Department continue to run the show. Some officials in the room who felt they did need a special counsel later dubbed it Rosenstein's "CYA meeting," or cover your ass, figuring he wanted to later be able to say he asked all his top officials and they agreed.

By Friday, May 12, Rosenstein seemed rocked by the stress of the week. He was scheduled to give short remarks at the Drug Enforcement Administration's green-glass headquarters in Arlington, Virginia, as part of an annual wreath-laying ceremony in honor of personnel who died trying to investigate drug traffickers. He arrived early. He was a jumble of exhaustion and emotion. And his host was one of Comey's best friends, Chuck Rosenberg, the agency's acting director and a standout career prosecutor. Like Rosenstein, Rosenberg had come up through the department and been named a U.S. attorney by President Bush.

Rosenberg ushered the deputy attorney general into a nearby office and closed the door. They spoke privately for a few minutes. Rosenstein had some trepidation at seeing Rosenberg, and tried to explain to him that things were more complicated than they appeared and he was sorry he couldn't say more. The two men walked out, and Rosenstein delivered the remarks he had prepared. He spoke with reverence for the rule of law—that framework of principles that promised impartiality, accountability, transparency, and basic fairness—which Trump was undermining daily.

McCabe had been pushing Rosenstein to appoint a special counsel to safeguard the Russia investigation, but Comey took matters into his own hands. Comey didn't trust Rosenstein to be independent or aggressive enough in overseeing the probe nor to dig into the president's efforts to obstruct it. Trump taunted his fired FBI director with a tweet the morning of May 12: "James Comey better hope that there are no 'tapes' of our conversations before he starts leaking to the press!" Over that Mother's Day weekend, Trump's tweet about "tapes" wormed itself into Comey's subconscious, and he woke up in the middle of the night on Monday, May 15, and realized he had a weapon he could use: his own version of "tapes." Comey decided to leak the contemporaneous memo he had written about Trump saying "letting this go" regarding the Flynn investigation, which showed the president trying to interfere with and obstruct a criminal investigation, asking a friend, the Columbia University law professor Dan Richman, to share details of the memo. On May 16, Michael Schmidt of *The New York Times* published them: "Comey Memo Says Trump Asked Him to End Flynn Investigation."

Rosenstein was dumbfounded. The memo was a critical piece of evidence for investigators, but instead of giving it to the Justice Department, Comey had directed that it be publicized in the press. "Why would Comey do that?" Rosenstein asked McCabe that night. Rosenstein thought to himself, "Why didn't anyone tell me the FBI director was keeping a book on the president?"

Rosenstein realized Comey's memo changed the landscape. He rationalized that he would name a special counsel only if he were confident that that man or woman could do a better job leading the Russia investigation than the FBI's career investigators on the team known as Crossfire Hurricane. It had to be someone who understood national security and cyber warfare, someone with unimpeachable credibility, deft management skills, and absolute discretion. In Rosenstein's estimation, there was only one person who fit the bill. So he called Robert Mueller.

Five

THE G-MAN COMETH

President Trump was deep into his search for a new FBI director on May 16, 2017, when a stone-faced, central-casting G-man was secretly escorted into the White House. Robert Mueller had the kind of law-and-order credentials and don't-mess-with-me look that Trump prized: champion athlete, Princeton grad, Marine Corps platoon leader, federal prosecutor, FBI director through the first twelve years of the war on terrorism, chiseled jaw, neatly cropped silver hair, and permanent glower.

A living legend in the law enforcement community, Mueller, seventy-two, was now finally in a kind of semiretirement in private practice at WilmerHale, one of Washington's most prestigious firms. He made clear to Trump's advisers that he had no interest in returning to the FBI, which he directed for two years longer than the standard ten years at President Obama's request, before retiring in 2013. But Attorney General Jeff Sessions had urged him to meet with the president nevertheless.

The plan was simple: Get Mueller to explain the modern FBI to Trump—its evolution from helping put mob bosses in jail to spotting terror cells before they could strike—as well as to emphasize its historically important political independence. Trump advisers figured the president might be drawn to Mueller's résumé and therefore internalize his points. Maybe then Trump would have a better idea of who should succeed James Comey as FBI director and, importantly, restrain himself from improper interference.

Mueller arrived in the West Wing through a back entrance, so as not to be spotted by the media. He was intimidating. He stepped toward Steve Bannon, who was going over an unrelated task with communications adviser Hope Hicks just outside the Oval Office, and extended his hand to introduce himself. "Hey, Steve, Bob Mueller," he said.

Mueller made a friendly aside about their shared background in the military. "I can't believe a member of the senior naval service allowed his daughter to matriculate at West Point," Mueller told Bannon, who had been an officer in the navy. Bannon was surprised and impressed that Mueller knew where one of his daughters, Maureen, was in college. "Here's the bad news," Bannon said. "She actually was recruited by the Naval Academy."

They both laughed and talked a bit longer, but Bannon couldn't help feeling distracted, even a little spooked. He thought about how much homework Mueller must have done to study up on a Trump aide he wasn't even scheduled to meet. "This guy is so fucking good to do the research," Bannon thought to himself.

The curved door of the Oval Office opened, and Mueller was waved inside to meet Trump. Joining them were Sessions, Rod Rosenstein, and Don McGahn. Mueller tried to explain that he wasn't interested in becoming FBI director again, but Trump seemed to be the only person in the room who didn't catch on to the fact that this wasn't a real job interview.

There was something else Trump didn't know. Rosenstein had privately called Mueller the previous week and asked him to consider taking the job of special counsel if Rosenstein decided to appoint one. Rosenstein had told Mueller that he hadn't yet decided, and Mueller had been courteous but noncommittal, giving Rosenstein neither a yes nor a no.

Normally, aides could count on Trump lighting up in the presence of someone with Mueller's pedigree, but his body language—crossed arms, a mildly bored expression—revealed he wasn't taking a shine to the former FBI director. Trump puffed himself up, eager to impress, but Mueller had a taciturn and nonplussed demeanor, the look of a man trying to be polite but biting his tongue. During their session lasting less than an hour, Mueller made no effort to praise the man sitting behind the Resolute Desk.

The next day, May 17, Trump delivered a commencement address at the U.S. Coast Guard Academy. Families and faculty gathered to celebrate a transformative milestone of young lives, but the president vented to the graduates about his personal pain. "No politician in history—and I say this with great surety—has been treated worse or more unfairly," he said.

Back in Washington that afternoon, Trump had another raft of interviews with FBI director candidates. Vice President Pence, Sessions, Rosenstein, and McGahn, along with a few other aides, were typically present for these sessions. They would brief Trump on each person's background and confer with him between each interview, to see what he had thought of the candidate who had just come through. Rosenstein took a special interest in the process and was proud to have lassoed top-notch contenders. But after the first interview that afternoon, McGahn noticed that someone was missing.

"Where's Rod?" McGahn asked.

"I haven't seen him all day," replied Jody Hunt, chief of staff to Sessions.

They continued with the next interview, but a few minutes into the session an aide peeked her head into the Oval to tell McGahn he had an important call. The White House counsel ducked out and picked up the line.

"It's Rod," the voice on the phone said.

McGahn was relieved. "Hey, we're interviewing FBI directors over here," he told Rosenstein. "Where are you?"

"I gotta tell you something," the deputy attorney general said. "I just appointed a special counsel to oversee the Russia investigation."

McGahn was surprised. He felt as if a flash from a camera had gone off in his face and closed his eyes.

"What?" McGahn said, trying to get some purchase. "You did what?"

Rosenstein repeated himself.

McGahn inhaled and exhaled slowly, thinking of all this would mean.

"Okay, Rod," he said, regaining his composure. "Got it. How much time do I have?"

Rosenstein told McGahn he had a few hours. "This won't be public right away," he said.

McGahn returned to the Oval and the interview in progress. His brain was working so fast on this new development he barely processed anything the candidate or Trump said. He couldn't wait for it to end. In the meantime, an aide poked her head in to say there was someone waiting on the line for Sessions. The attorney general stepped out of the room. Rosenstein delivered the same news he had just given McGahn.

Sessions returned to the Oval, his face white as a piece of paper. He sat down in one of the armchairs forming a semicircle in front of the president's Resolute Desk. He turned sideways to look at McGahn, his gallows expression revealing his fear of what was to come. McGahn cut short the interview, telling Trump and the candidate that their allotted time had come to an end. After the door closed behind the candidate, McGahn said, "I think the attorney general needs to tell you something."

"What is it, Jeff?" Trump said.

"Well, uh, Mr. President," Sessions said, lifting a finger up, then pausing and looking down at the floor. "Well, uh, we have a special counsel." He explained Rosenstein had appointed Mueller.

Trump looked at McGahn, genuinely confused.

"What he's trying to say is Rod just appointed a special counsel and has picked Bob Mueller to investigate the Russia stuff," McGahn told him.

"What did you just say?" Trump asked, aghast.

"Jeff, is this true?"

Sessions nodded, looking down to avoid the president's gaze.

"You're serious?" Trump asked.

"Serious as a heart attack," McGahn replied.

There was a palpable pause in the room, unlike anything any of them had experienced from the voluble Trump, who could fill any air-time. The president slumped in his chair and sighed deeply, like someone making room in his lungs to take in more oxygen for a powerful scream.

"Oh, my God," Trump exclaimed. "This is terrible. This is the end of my presidency. I'm fucked!"

He went on.

"It doesn't matter what the truth is," the president said. "They just fuck you up the whole time. They never find anything. They just put a bunch of people who never talked to you through the ringer."

Then Trump turned his full venom on Sessions.

"It's your fucking fault," he said. "You're weak. This is all your fault."

Sessions said blaming him was not fair. "If you feel that's wrong, then I'll resign," the attorney general said.

"You know what, Jeff?" Trump said. "You're fucking right. You should fucking resign!"

Sessions's eyes welled up. He was holding back tears with everything he had. By this point, McGahn, Pence, and Hunt were watching the president break the attorney general in front of their eyes. The vice president interjected. "Do you mind giving us a minute, gentlemen?" Pence asked, looking at Hunt and McGahn. McGahn told Pence that was a good idea and got up to leave. He and Hunt didn't need to see this.

Once safely outside the Oval Office, Hunt turned to McGahn, his mouth wide open. "Oh, my Gawd . . ." Hunt said in his southern drawl. The two men could hear the presidential tirade coming from the historic room they had just left. Tearing into Sessions, Trump said, "You were supposed to protect me" but "let me down."

A few minutes after his private session with Trump and Pence, Sessions emerged from the Oval Office, and McGahn put his arm on his back. "Don't resign," McGahn told him. "We need you. This will blow over. I'll call you tonight. Don't resign."

As Sessions headed toward the West Wing exit, McGahn charged down the hallway to Reince Priebus's office and stuck his head in the door. "I've got some bad news," McGahn said hurriedly, his face red and in a huff. "Sessions just resigned, and we've got a special counsel."

"No!" Priebus said, looking horrified. "Where's Sessions?"

The chief of staff rushed past McGahn in his doorway and took off in a trot for the Oval, where he saw Pence. "Where's Jeff?" Priebus asked the vice president. Pence confirmed for him that Sessions had resigned and was leaving the building. Priebus then raced out to the parking lot to try to catch the attorney general before he drove off. Priebus climbed into the backseat of Sessions's black vehicle and asked him, "What's going on?"

Humiliated, Sessions said, "He doesn't want me around. I'm done. I'm tired of this."

"You can't resign," Priebus said. "We cannot have the attorney general, a special counsel, and the FBI director fiasco all at the same time."

Priebus brought Sessions back up to his office, where he, along with Pence and others, persuaded the attorney general not to resign immediately but rather to take some time to consider his actions.

Trump was genuinely frightened. In Mueller, Trump found a tenacious and unblemished antagonist. Stern, secretive, and straitlaced, Mueller was a registered Republican and in private conversations would espouse the old GOP principle of individual responsibility over government action. But he was perceived as apolitical and above reproach because of his well-regarded service in both the Obama and the George W. Bush administrations.

Mueller's longtime friend Tom Wilner described the life lessons Mueller learned at St. Paul's School in New Hampshire, which were similar to those ingrained in students at other elite prep schools at the time, including at St. Albans School in Washington, Wilner's alma mater. "You always take the path of the hard right against the easy wrong," he said. "You never compromise your principles. You do what is right no matter what is the cost. What matters is honesty, integrity, loyalty to your family and to your principles. That's Bob. I kid because he's so straight he's a pain in the ass. He will never cross the line in doing something he thinks is improper or looks partisan. Never. Never. He is just so straight."

Mueller had spent two decades prosecuting mob bosses, murderous gangsters, and drug lords in Boston, San Francisco, and Washington before becoming FBI director on September 4, 2001, exactly one week before Osama bin Laden's hijackers orchestrated the worst terrorist attack in U.S. history. He then led a wholesale reorganization of the nation's premier investigative agency to hunt down terrorists around the globe and thwart future plots before they could be executed.

A gruff and often humorless boss, Mueller had high demands for his subordinates at the FBI—and a temper that occasionally flared. He would grill his investigators on every inch of the evidence they had gathered in their cases, often exposing holes in their work. He also had a lifelong habit of getting to work around 6:00 a.m. By the time FBI agents and detectives arrived at 7:30 or 8:00 a.m., they would find yellow sticky notes Mueller had left on their chairs:

"I came by and you weren't here. Where are you?"

"Come find me when you get in, Bob."

Yet Mueller, a square-jawed "Joe Friday," inspired deep loyalty from his colleagues. "I would walk on hot coals for Bob Mueller, that's how much I admire and respect him," said Chuck Rosenberg, his former counsel. "And there have been times in my career working for Bob that it felt like I was."

Frank Figliuzzi, who worked under Mueller as assistant director for counterintelligence, noted that Louis Freeh, who led the bureau for the eight years prior to Mueller, titled his memoir *My FBI*. "That title alone is something that Mueller would never say," Figliuzzi said. "Rather, what he would say is, 'I am a temporary caretaker of the FBI. It's not my FBI. It's the American people's FBI, and I am supposed to run it for a while.'"

Lisa Monaco, Mueller's chief of staff, recalled she would never allow the word "I" to appear in drafts of his speeches. "He literally would cross out 'I'—every time—and replace it with 'we' or 'the FBI and its partners,'" Monaco said. "The theme was, it's never about him. I started getting out my red pen and taking 'I' out so he didn't have to do it. I just knew no 'I' could ever survive first contact with him."

At the White House the afternoon of Mueller's appointment, Trump and his staff scrambled to respond. They had only a short time before the Justice Department made its public announcement. Hicks and other aides went back and forth with the president editing a statement. She would type a draft on her computer and print it out in 16-point font; Trump would make changes with a black Sharpie. She would type up the changes, and so on. As Hicks typed one version, a handful of other advisers stood behind her, including Jared Kushner, who put a positive spin on what was transpiring.

"This is great," Kushner told his colleagues. "We're not going to have to worry." Kushner was referring to the Senate Select Committee on Intelligence's investigation of Russian interference. He assumed that with a special counsel appointed, the Senate probe would be moot.

"You don't understand how any of this works," communications director Mike Dubke told Kushner. "These will all go on simultaneously. There is going to be Mueller; there's going to be investigations in the House, in the Senate. They are coming after you."

Dubke then looked at Hicks. She had proven herself loyal to Trump as his campaign press secretary and traveling companion and was savvy beyond her twenty-eight years, especially when it came to spinning Trump's failings and managing his moods. But Hicks was new to Washington, and Dubke feared she might be naive about some of its ways, especially when it came to investigations. Given her close relationship with the president, she was bound to be called as a witness. Dubke thought she needed to hire a lawyer. Little did he know, she already had one.

———

George Conway, a credentialed and well-respected conservative lawyer, cried tears of joy when Trump was sworn in as president. The
lifelong Republican, who had labored to expose Bill and Hillary Clinton's misconduct in the 1990s, felt a rush of relief when Hillary's march
to the White House was thwarted. And he felt a special swell of pride
for his wife, Kellyanne. She received—and, in George's estimation,
deserved—a lot of credit for guiding Trump to victory. She tried to hone
his populist message to appeal to a broad group of voters, including the
working-class union members peeling away from Democrats and well-
heeled, establishment Republicans more than mildly suspicious of
Trump. She was his spin warrior, sparring with news anchors at all hours
of the day to seemingly wash away Trump's troubles.

At a black-tie gala the night before the inauguration, Trump profusely thanked Conway for more than holding her own with his adversaries. He called "my Kellyanne" up to the stage for a bow. "She gets on
[television] and she does destroy them," Trump said. "Thank you, baby,
thank you."

As Trump scouted for smart loyalists to fill hundreds of government
positions, his lieutenants asked if Kellyanne's husband, a graduate of
Harvard and Yale Law School, would consider running the civil division
of the Justice Department. George Conway had initially hoped to be
named solicitor general but said yes. He was honored. But as chaos en-
gulfed nearly every move the Trump White House made in its first
months, Conway grew worried about his decision, then reluctant. He
realized he was dawdling on filling out the personal financial disclosures
that were required before he could be formally nominated. In late April,
Rachel Brand, a friend from the Federalist Society and then in line for a
top job at the Justice Department, asked Conway why he had not yet
turned his papers in; Conway assured her he was working on it.

Then came May 9. Trump fired Comey. The next day, Conway was
sitting in a doctor's waiting room in New Jersey, reading *The Washington
Post* on his iPad. The story at the top of the website was titled "Inside

Trump's Anger and Impatience" and, citing thirty sources in Trump's orbit, reported that Trump had been brooding about Comey's loyalty and the Russia investigation, contrary to the White House's claim that Trump fired Comey because of Rosenstein's memo about his handling of the Clinton probe. Conway felt his mouth falling open wider with each line of the story.

"Oh no," Conway thought. "No, no, no."

Assuming the story was true, he figured, Trump was patently seeking to obstruct a Justice Department investigation that revolved around him and his campaign. "If that's why he did it, this is going to be a disaster," Conway thought. That night, May 10, Conway ferried one of his daughters to an elementary school auditorium in Englewood, New Jersey, and took a seat in the back to watch her flute recital. As his daughter and her classmates tuned their instruments, Conway could barely concentrate. He tried to figure out how he could delicately back out of the job he had told Sessions he would take in his Justice Department. He alerted his wife by text that he was having serious doubts. Kellyanne was displeased.

Over the coming days, George stewed about what to do, almost to the boiling point. On the afternoon of May 17, as he was walking across Madison Avenue heading back to his office, Conway used a few free minutes to call Brand. A smart lawyer and highly regarded among conservatives, Brand was Trump's nominee to be associate attorney general and was awaiting her confirmation vote in the Senate.

"Hey, Rachel, can we talk off the record for a minute?" Conway began.

She assured him that she would be a sounding board for whatever he needed to talk through.

"I'm really concerned about how this administration is operating," Conway said. "I'm not sure I can go through with it."

Conway was half expecting Brand, a no-drama midwesterner, to buck him up. He figured she would tell him everything he read about the White House was worse than the reality and that it was important he serve his country and his party. Instead, the typically stoic Brand sighed, indicating she, too, had at least some momentary reservations.

"I know how you feel. I heard [the Senate] just held my cloture vote," Brand said. She explained her mixed feelings. "I love DOJ. What an honor. But this is going to be nuts."

It was a sunny afternoon in New York, and Conway left the office a little early to head home to New Jersey. He drove north on the Henry Hudson Parkway, and as he turned the car in to the cloverleaf curve to get onto the George Washington Bridge, he heard CBS News radio break in with a bulletin: Rosenstein had appointed a special counsel to take over the Russia investigation.

Conway thought to himself, "This will never work." How could he serve in the senior ranks of the Justice Department when his wife's boss was going to be at war with that same department? In the time it took to cross the bridge, he had made up his mind. He would not join the Trump administration. Within a few days, George called Kellyanne. George agreed to let his wife help shape his explanation to preserve her relationship with Trump—as long as it was factual.

At the same time, another Justice Department figure was preparing an exit. After being torn to shreds by Trump, Sessions huddled in his office with his advisers to draft a resignation letter. He was angry about how the president had treated him. The next morning, May 18, he hand delivered a signed copy to Trump. "Pursuant to our conversation of yesterday, and at your request, I hereby offer my resignation," the letter read. Trump put it in his pocket and asked Sessions whether he wanted to continue serving. Sessions told him he wanted to stay, and Trump agreed that he would remain as attorney general. They shook hands, but Sessions did not take the letter back.

Leaving the signed resignation letter with Trump was a mistake. When Sessions told Priebus about the letter, the White House chief of staff said, "Jeff, hang on a second. The DOJ has to be independent of the president. Do you understand what you just did? You basically gave the president a shock collar and put it right around your neck. You can't do that. We've got to get the letter back."

All day, Trump was in a defiant mood, beginning with a 6:39 a.m. Twitter post in which he made a baseless allegation against Democrats. "With all of the illegal acts that took place in the Clinton campaign & Obama Administration, there was never a special councel [*sic*] appointed!" the president wrote, adding in a second tweet that the Russia investigation was "the single greatest witch hunt of a politician in American history!"

Trump continued his claim of victimhood in an afternoon news conference where, standing beside Colombian president Juan Manuel Santos, he insisted, "There is no collusion between certainly myself and my campaign, but I can only speak for myself and the Russians. Zero."

Around this time, Trump told Chris Christie, "Can you believe fucking Rosenstein? He appoints Mueller. Why couldn't he just handle it himself? There's nothing here. I didn't do anything."

Christie warned Trump about how a special counsel probe could spiral and create new dangers. "Your problem is that this thing will expand and grow because they're going to find other crimes," he said. "You give a prosecutor and an FBI agent enough time, they'll find a crime. That's what I used to do for a living. They'll find it."

On May 19, Trump departed for his maiden foreign trip, a nine-day, five-city tour that would take him from Saudi Arabia to Israel to the Vatican to NATO Headquarters and to Italy for a global leaders summit. The stakes were high, especially for a temperamental president whose knowledge of foreign affairs was relatively scant. But, consumed as he was by the Mueller development, Trump was entirely unprepared. As the president and his team took off from Joint Base Andrews for the twelve-plus hour flight to Riyadh, *The New York Times* reported for the first time what Trump had told the top Russian diplomats during their May 10 Oval Office meeting: Comey was "a real nut job," and by firing him, he had relieved the "great pressure because of Russia."

Trump lit up. Although the *Times* story bore no direct connection to the special counsel, Trump read it as a signal that he was now at war with his own Justice Department and that mysterious leakers inside the government were trying to help investigators. The president sat in the forward cabin of the plane grousing. Aides strode in and out to try to calm him down. They tried to shift his focus to his meetings in Saudi Arabia and the landmark speech he was planning to deliver before dozens of Arab leaders. There was much preparation left to do, but Trump's furor did not subside. He stayed awake for the red-eye flight across the Atlantic.

"This is a witch hunt!" Trump screamed. "There shouldn't be a special counsel!"

"How did they get this?" Trump said of the *Times*. Then he illogically complained they had gotten some details wrong, when he knew they had not. "This is made-up. There's no sources."

The next day came another blockbuster story that further stoked Trump's rage and paranoia. *The Washington Post* reported on May 20 that the Russia investigation had identified a senior White House adviser, who would later be identified as Kushner, as "a significant person of interest," the first sign that the probe had reached the top echelons of Trump's administration.

On the ground in Riyadh, Trump stayed at the Ritz-Carlton, a massive, lavish palace of a hotel that to mark the occasion lit its facade in the evenings with a huge image of Trump's portrait. In the president's suite, the television was set to CNN International—which, like CNN's domestic channel, was heavy with coverage of Trump. He simmered with anger as he watched with some of his advisers. Despite the distractions, however, Trump managed to make it through his first few days abroad as president without incident. In fact, his speech imploring the Muslim world to confront "Islamic extremism" and eliminate "fanatical violence" was well received. Miraculously, he refrained from tweeting about the Russia investigation, even as he nursed his feelings of persecution with every cable television panel he watched.

On May 22, Trump carried on with the next stop on his trip, meetings in Jerusalem and Bethlehem with Israeli and Palestinian leaders, without his top two advisers, Bannon and Priebus, who had caught a ride to Washington on the government jet of Secretary of Commerce Wilbur Ross and returned to the White House. They had a president to protect from the fast-expanding investigation. They had a war room to build.

PART
TWO

Six

SUITING UP FOR BATTLE

L anding in Tel Aviv on May 22, 2017, Trump strode down a red carpet to the triumphal sound of a military band and vowed to bring peace to the Middle East. He toured Jerusalem's Old City, visiting the Church of the Holy Sepulchre to honor Christians and placing a prayer in the Western Wall, where he put his palm on the ancient stones while wearing a yarmulke in solidarity with Jews. Over dinner with Prime Minister Benjamin Netanyahu, Trump sketched the broad outlines of a peace plan between Israelis and Palestinians and declared newfound resolve to confront Iran. The hastily rehearsed words coming out of his mouth all day were about the unending conflict in the Middle East, but Trump's mind was focused on the mushrooming special counsel investigation into his campaign.

Trump's aides knew he needed to hire a seasoned member of the white-collar defense bar with experience in both law and political combat. The trouble was that most of the pros did not want to represent him. Trump's search for representation became a haphazard and painful obstacle course made more difficult by the competing loyalties, false promises, and backstabbing within his team. Trump was insecure about his worth as a client and feared personal exposure, which both infected his work as president and drove him to want to thwart the investigation. The most powerful man in the world could not get a lawyer.

On May 22, Trump placed a call from the Middle East to Marc Kasowitz, asking him to officially saddle up as his lawyer. Kasowitz had long been the president's dragon slayer, the attorney who for years had represented Trump in his business and personal matters, including a series of bankruptcies and the fight to keep his divorce records sealed. Aggressive and wily, Kasowitz had championed tough cases for Trump and won. He also had represented two of Trump's children, Ivanka and Donald junior, against accusations of fraud. Trump trusted the street fighter and wanted him in his corner right away, although he would still need to recruit lawyers with a specialized set of skills navigating Washington crises, which the New York–based Kasowitz lacked.

Kasowitz agreed, but he soon faced a mutiny from some of his law partners. The white-haired, sixty-four-year-old litigator had built an intensely profitable firm and wooed major Wall Street players and corporations by pledging to outwork stodgier white-shoe firms. He was a rainmaker, but his firm—Kasowitz Benson Torres—had already been singed by its association with Trump during the 2016 campaign. After Kasowitz threatened *The New York Times* for reporting on sexual assault allegations against then-candidate Trump, some of the firm's bigger corporate clients, including those with women as key in-house lawyers, complained. Several of the firm's liberal-leaning partners were personally aghast when Trump won the presidency, but they recognized the possible financial upside to being "of counsel" to the president.

That optimism of those lawyers ended dramatically after May 17, when Mueller was appointed special counsel to investigate election interference and any links or coordination between Trump or his campaign associates and a hostile foreign power. The partners were mindful that their share of hefty yearly profits depended on Kasowitz's prodigious talents as a rainmaker, yet they feared the firm's bottom line could take a hit if Kasowitz took on a highly public role defending Trump in the Mueller probe. The anxiety was compounded by the fact that Kasowitz, a commercial lawyer, lacked the legal chops for a white-collar, major-league Washington scandal. But Kasowitz had something almost no one else did, not even some of the most senior people in the White House: Trump's trust.

Kasowitz imagined assembling a "dream team" to shield the president. He and one of his partners, Mike Bowe, the fifty-year-old son of a fireman with conservative leanings whose hard-charging gut instincts Kasowitz trusted, set out to recruit an experienced scandal lawyer. The first few outreaches to top legal talent ended in rejection. But one offered to help for free: John Dowd. On May 18, Bowe was in his New York office near Times Square when he got an email from Dowd.

"Happy to help DJT quietly behind the curtain. . . . I am not sure he needs counsel but it would not hurt to keep an eye on it and independently advise him. I know Bobby Mueller," wrote Dowd, who attached a *New York Times* article reporting that Trump's advisers were urging him to hire a D.C.-based attorney.

Bowe told Dowd he'd think about it and talk it over with his partner. The early reaction of seasoned pros to Kasowitz's outreach foreshadowed the difficulty to come. Kasowitz called Brendan Sullivan, the crème de la crème of the white-collar criminal defense bar; he offered to help make recommendations but told Kasowitz he couldn't take Trump on as a client. On May 23, news broke that Trump had retained Kasowitz. The next day, Dowd wrote again to Bowe: "Great news. Happy to help pro bono anytime."

Dowd, seventy-six, was a legal legend whose best years had been two decades prior. A former marine, he had served in the JAG Corps and become a captain in the Vietnam era. He joined the Justice Department, where in the 1970s he led the strike force on organized crime, taking on hired hit men and mobsters. Bowe and Dowd had formed a friendship consulting with each other on some cases representing marines whom they felt were getting the shaft from their command. The two lawyers liked each other and had much in common, both macho Irishmen and dogged fighters for their clients.

Bowe figured Dowd could play a supporting role on Trump's legal team. Dowd knew well the inner workings of the Justice Department and also had a lot of contacts in Washington. On May 25, he emailed Bowe yet again to say he was on his way to New York on the Acela for an event that evening at the Intrepid Museum on the Hudson River and offered to meet up. Bowe told him to swing by at 4:00 p.m. and he would introduce him to Kasowitz. The three men met briefly in Kasowitz's office. "Good to meet you, John," Kasowitz said as they parted, saying he thought there might be a place for him on the team. "Mike will let you know."

That Memorial Day weekend, shortly after 7:00 a.m. on Sunday, May 28, the president fired off a tweetstorm ranting about news coverage of his troubles. He was particularly incensed at a May 26 *Washington Post* story, still dominating the headlines, claiming his son-in-law, Jared Kushner, had suggested a back channel to the Russians during the campaign. The story had spawned media commentary about whether Kushner had committed treason, making the president's son-in-law radioactive and feeling as if he were the victim of a lynch mob. Trump decried leaks from inside his own White House as "fabricated lies" and posited that journalists "made up" sources, adding, "#FakeNews is the enemy!" Trump wanted fighters defending him on television and devising legal methods to derail the investigation, but so far only Kasowitz and Bowe were on board.

Trump summoned two trusted hands to pay him a visit: Corey Lewandowski and Dave Bossie, his former campaign manager and deputy campaign manager, respectively. Both men were political brawlers, the kind of operative Trump most admired, and Bossie was well versed in navigating Washington scandals, having worked as a senior Republican House investigator during the Clinton presidency, leading congressional probes into Whitewater and other matters.

Trump wanted to know if Lewandowski and Bossie were interested in joining the administration and running the war room operation. The pair had already met with Reince Priebus and Steve Bannon about just that proposition, and everything seemed set. But Trump changed his mind. He told Lewandowski and Bossie, "I don't want you guys to come here and then when I fire everybody you're part of that."

That same day, Kasowitz and Bowe had left their home base in New York for Bedminster, New Jersey, to meet up with Kushner and Ivanka Trump to travel from the president's private golf club to Washington together. The couple were rattled by the back channel story and wanted their advice. Before arriving in Bedminster, Kasowitz had confided to others about his growing concerns about Kushner's presence inside the White House, telling them Kushner might have to leave due to the complications his Russian contacts created. When he and Bowe arrived, Kushner complained about the scrutiny and claimed the *Post* story was inaccurate. As he would argue repeatedly, Kushner said the Russians asked him for the back channel and he was confident he had done nothing wrong. Kushner and Ivanka Trump also asked Kasowitz and Bowe to help them calm down the president. The couple complained the West Wing was a circus, horribly mismanaged by Priebus and Bannon.

Meanwhile, Priebus and Bannon were hard at work on what they knew the president would consider the most important pillar: a television-ready spokesman to lead the Trump defense. They were working from a deficit because Mike Dubke, who had helped lead the White House's response to such crises as the firing of James Comey, had just resigned as communications director in his third month on the job.

After Memorial Day, Bannon met with Mark Corallo, a seasoned Republican operative whom Trump's advisers had unsuccessfully tried to get to join the communications shop at the start of the administration. Corallo, fifty-one, was an army veteran who had worked at the Justice Department during the George W. Bush administration, giving him a base of knowledge about criminal probes that could prove valuable. He also had "the look" that Trump would want in his front man: wiry and fit, with close-cropped silver hair and tailored suits.

Corallo counted Mueller and Comey as former colleagues. He explained that he had admired Comey at first. Over time, however, Corallo said he came to see Comey as a "sanctimonious phony." Comey had a habit of tut-tutting and frowning at anyone who disagreed with him, Corallo told Bannon. Comey would lecture with a little eye roll, which

Corallo said had one message: "I'm just really disappointed in you. Your moral compass is askew."

"I wouldn't trust him as far as I could throw his six-foot-eight frame," Corallo told Bannon.

"Oh, wow, that's interesting," Bannon said. "So you must know Mueller, too."

Corallo began to gush: "Oh, I love Bob. He walks on water."

"Really?" Bannon said.

"I have very few heroes in life that are not ballplayers, and [former attorney general] John Ashcroft and Bob Mueller are at the top of the list," Corallo replied. "If you have to have a special counsel, there is nobody better than Bob Mueller. If there's nothing there, there will be a report that says there's nothing there. He's your golden ticket."

Bannon and Priebus then wanted to take Corallo to meet Trump. It was in the middle of the afternoon. "I don't have a tie on," Corallo said, surprised. In the George W. Bush administration, the president's schedule had been tightly choreographed, weeks ahead of time, and nobody popped in to see him unless it was urgent—and certainly not on a weekday without a tie. But such formalities did not matter to Trump. Off they went, down the hall and to the president's private dining room, where the television was on and Trump was perusing a stack of papers. He was warm and gracious to Corallo, and they got down to business. Bannon explained to Trump that Corallo knew Mueller well and Trump said, "I'm all ears."

"Here's the deal, Mr. President," Corallo told him. "If you're going to get a special counsel, you couldn't get a better guy. Mr. President, Jim Comey and Bob Mueller, despite what you might think, they're not best friends. There is no conflict. And Bob Mueller is the most honest guy in town. You've got to understand, this guy is a public servant's public servant. He's only interested in facts. He doesn't have a political ax to grind. He's not for you or against you when it comes to the law. He really is as honest a human being as this country's ever produced."

"Oh, I don't know," Trump said. "This whole thing . . ."

His words trailed off.

"I don't blame you," Corallo said. "I understand that it would be uncomfortable. But I do believe at the end of the day, if there's nothing there, you'll get a clean bill of health. And if it comes from Robert Mueller, it's unassailable."

Trump seemed to enjoy the practical, cut-to-the-chase way Corallo spoke, but not to be convinced that Mueller was trustworthy. Trump asked him to return later that day to join a meeting about the Russia investigation, for what would be Corallo's first time in the Oval Office. He felt chills as he took a seat across the Resolute Desk. Trump railed about the Mueller investigation—how unfair it was to him, how persecuted he felt—but Corallo was thinking, "Reagan sat there. FDR sat there. Truman sat there. Ike sat there."

Corallo immediately hit it off with Trump's lawyers, especially Bowe, a practicing Catholic about the same age who also grew up in New York's blue-collar outer boroughs. Corallo agreed on the spot to work for Kasowitz and Bowe as communications strategist for the president's outside legal team. He had one condition: "I will never say anything untoward about Bob Mueller. I will never attack him personally. Ain't gonna happen. And if I'm asked to, I'm out of here, and if anyone on this team attacks him personally, I'm out of here."

Kasowitz and Bowe agreed: they would never malign Mueller's integrity or motivations.

Still without a prominent Washington attorney, Trump was vulnerable. He did what he often did at anxious moments. He grabbed the wheel. Trump thought there might be a way to play to Mueller's patriotism and convince him the investigation needed to end quickly because it was hurting the president and therefore weakening the United States in the view of adversaries around the world.

"Go see Mueller. You gotta go see him," Trump instructed Kasowitz and Bowe several times. "Tell him this is really impairing my ability to function as president. Let's find out what this is. Maybe we can get out in front of it."

This was a classic Trump method for fixing problems. He thought he could talk his way out of anything by cultivating a personal relationship and working out the problem man-to-man. After Trump learned that Corallo knew Mueller from their work together in the Justice Department, he was elated. Trump at once asked Corallo to talk to Mueller on his behalf.

Corallo's eyes widened with trepidation. He thought to himself, "No way." Kasowitz spoke up and told Trump absolutely not.

"That's totally inappropriate and legally unsound," Kasowitz told the president. "Mark is not a lawyer."

Then the president invoked Secretary of Defense Jim Mattis, who stood out in the administration because of his reputation for honor. He thought that because they were both marines, Mattis might engender sympathy in Mueller. Trump told his lawyers to tell Mueller, "General Mattis says this is a problem."

Bannon and Priebus shared their view that it was best to steer clear of Mueller for the immediate future, but Bowe gave them some advice: don't assume you can always corral Trump.

"I don't know if you fish," Bowe told them. "Sometimes you have to let the line run. You run the risk of having the line snap if you pull it in all the time. You can't reel him in constantly. You can't say no to him every time."

As its public face, Trump's legal team also included Jay Sekulow, whom Trump hired in late May. A lawyer with deep ties to Washington's conservative establishment, Sekulow, sixty, was chief counsel to the American Center for Law and Justice, host of a radio talk show, and a longtime commentator on Fox News Channel and the Christian Broadcasting Network. He also was close to Sean Hannity, the Fox host and Trump friend. The president had been impressed at Sekulow's telegenic qualities and how well he thought on his feet. He felt the smooth-talking, savvy Sekulow could lend credibility to his defense in the media as well as help him navigate the political scene.

By now, Dowd had made his way onto the president's team, and he recommended they consider also hiring Ty Cobb, a Hogan Lovells partner and veteran of independent counsel investigations back in the Clinton years. Dowd knew Cobb from their previous careers at Justice and their overlapping work in a massive Wall Street insider-trading case. Cobb was drawn to the challenge of representing Trump, but his firm refused to let him, largely because Trump was too toxic a client. Cobb agreed to retire from his partnership, with his full pension, and went to work in the White House as a special legal adviser rather than as one of Trump's personal attorneys.

Yet Trump still lacked a big-name, credible Washington attorney on his personal legal team, one with the backing of a powerhouse firm. In an all-hands-on-deck push, Trump's advisers reached out to Ted Olson, A. B. Culvahouse Jr., Emmet Flood, Robert Giuffra, Paul Clement, and Dan Levin. All of them followed Sullivan's lead, giving a polite no.

Flood had been considering the team's request that he join them, but as the president's White House adviser. In a call in the first week of June, Flood was surprised to hear the team was considering setting up shop in the Eisenhower Executive Office Building, as Bannon planned, for an on-site war room. Working from the White House grounds would look inappropriate, both for the president and for his private team, but Flood made his warning plainer. "That is absolutely insane," he said.

Bowe thought he found the perfect recruit in Dan Levin, a white-collar pro who had worked as Mueller's chief of staff at the FBI and the Justice Department, and who had turned down Mueller's request to join his special counsel team. Levin had warned Mueller about hiring aggressive prosecutors like Andrew Weissmann because he thought they might seek a scalp and push to "make" a case, even if the facts didn't merit prosecution. Levin wasn't a Trump supporter but felt strongly that even unpopular people deserved lawyers. But Levin's firm didn't want Trump as a client.

For those hunting for a lawyer for the president, the most memorable contender, the one that got away, was Reid Weingarten. The longtime partner at Steptoe & Johnson, Weingarten was a legend because of his uncanny ability at trial to simultaneously woo the jury, eviscerate the government's star witness, and cultivate a fan worship among some of the prosecutors he whupped. One of his billionaire clients, the Las Vegas casino mogul Steve Wynn, told Trump he had to meet Weingarten: "He's the best. I love the guy."

Weingarten was a lifelong independent, a social progressive, and close friends with Eric Holder, President Obama's first attorney general. He told his recruiters that he doubted he could represent Trump. He agreed ultimately to talk with Trump in June, however, explaining to White House counsel Don McGahn that he did not feel he could turn down a president's request to meet.

Weingarten had a folksy charm and, at times, a mouth like a sailor, giving him and the president a small bit of common ground when they met in the Oval Office. As he did with most of the lawyers, Trump went through a well-worn checklist of questions about how this kind of investigation worked, all of which were softballs for Weingarten, who had cut his teeth as a public corruption prosecutor for many years. Trump wanted to know: What was Mueller up to? What would he be looking at?

Trump would later tell confidants he was shocked by Weingarten's answer: By now Mueller would certainly have copies of Trump's tax returns, likely going back at least five or ten years. This was a basic request any prosecutor would make for anyone under investigation for potential conflicts, the lawyer explained. Trump also asked Weingarten two questions he had been asking other attorneys in recent days: Could Trump pardon his family members? Could he pardon himself?

Weingarten declined to describe his meeting with the president. Yet Trump told others that Weingarten warned him he might be technically able to, but this legally dubious method would amount to political suicide. At the end of their meeting, the two men parted amiably, if awkwardly. Trump still wasn't entirely sure he needed a criminal defense lawyer. After all, the president believed he hadn't committed any crimes.

"Thanks, Reid," the president said. "If I smell trouble, when I smell the jail cell, I'll call you."

Then the lawyer was gone. Weingarten met with McGahn for a postbrief after his sit-down with Trump. As McGahn would tell a few close allies, the seasoned lawyer warned him he had just one critical job now: do not let the president remove Mueller. Although Weingarten did not end up working for Trump, the president would repeatedly mention to his aides how much he liked him and recalled details from their conversation.

Ordinarily, for a veteran of the white-collar defense bar, representing a president would be a prestigious career capstone. Not so with Trump, however. These high-profile attorneys understood that many people who have an affiliation with Trump ultimately get discarded and diminished. He saw his attorneys as tools to help bend the law for him and to protect him as he took suspect or outright illegal actions. Then there was the issue of money. No one in Trump's orbit could provide clear answers about who would pay, and Trump had a history of stiffing professionals, be they lawyers or construction contractors. What's more, Trump had a reputation for being a notoriously stubborn client. As one lawyer who said no to Trump's offer explained, "It's like being the captain of the Titanic. 'Turn left. Turn left.' 'No, no, I'm going straight.'"

Trump was incensed that Comey was going to testify before Congress on June 8. He did not understand how a man he fired one month earlier could discredit him on premium television airtime. Trump's lawyers began studying whether the president's conversations with Comey could be shielded by executive privilege. Bowe had done some preparation by calling Flood, who said he was willing to give him some general advice about asserting executive privilege. Flood told him he would never assert it without the Justice Department's Office of Legal Counsel first conducting an analysis of whether it was warranted and issuing a legal opinion. Bowe thought this sounded complicated and time-consuming. Comey was going to testify in a few days. "Sorry, those are the norms," Flood said. "That's just the way it works."

Trump's team decided not to try to block Comey from testifying. Trump watched the hearing on live television from his dining room off the Oval Office, surrounded by Kasowitz, Bowe, Sekulow, and other aides. He got angrier by the second, and even before Comey finished, the president howled that Kasowitz had to hold a news conference—that afternoon—rebutting everything Comey had said. A free-for-all drafting party then began with the president barking out the language Kasowitz should bash Comey with. At one point, Trump suggested that Kasowitz point out that Comey was a liar, but his lawyers said no to ad hominem attacks.

As often was the case when aides rushed to satisfy Trump's demands, Kasowitz ended up damaging his reputation with his televised appearance that day at the National Press Club. Speaking from prepared remarks, he inaccurately described key events in the timeline of Comey's memo about Trump's request that he "let this go" regarding the Flynn investigation. Kasowitz's errors would have been easy to avoid, but he jumped to say what his client wanted.

White House advisers thought Kasowitz looked foolish and ill-prepared. As one seasoned white-collar lawyer who had been asked to help recruit attorneys for Trump put it, "That was terrible. I was watching that thinking, 'How does it advance his client's interests for him to be saying these stupid things?' He wasn't prepared. His answers were not good."

As they settled into a work pattern with the president, the lawyers increasingly saw Kushner and Ivanka Trump as problems. The kids wandered in and out of strategy sessions about the investigation, without so much as a knock on the door, asking what was going on. Ivanka would walk in, say, "Hi, Dad," and the lawyers would stop talking about substance and simply smile at her awkwardly, waiting for her to leave. She and Kushner talked openly about details of the investigation with other staffers, as well as with the president, and privately offered him their own advice.

"The kids are always there," Corallo later explained. "The discomfort is with the kids always being there and talking about the case with other people in the White House, which makes everybody a witness." The dynamic, he added, "makes it impossible for the White House to function in a normal way."

Bannon and Priebus had warned Kasowitz and Bowe back in May about the problems created by having the president's daughter and son-in-law working in the White House in the midst of a special counsel investigation. McGahn shared their concerns. But the kids wanted to be part of the action, and they wanted the lawyers on their side. They worked to charm Dowd, who was immediately taken by Ivanka as she profusely thanked him for joining the legal team and remarked about how valuable he would be to her father.

Others who interacted with Ivanka found her to be a spoiled princess who had absorbed her father's worst narcissistic, superficial, and self-promoting qualities. "As a twelve-year-old, she was put on the phone with CEOs, and her father told her she was the most amazing thing in the world and her opinion was valued," one administration official explained. "She is a product of her environment."

As the lawyers for Trump, his family members, and his business began poring over Trump campaign records in mid-June, they were finding no evidence that linked the president to any coordination or collaboration with Russians. But they did find issues with Kushner. The presidential son-in-law had failed to disclose all of his meetings with foreign officials, and specifically Russians, in his required government forms. He had had more than a hundred in-person meetings or phone calls with representatives of more than twenty countries, many of them between Trump's election and inauguration. A failure to include every foreign contact the first time that a senior White House official applied for a security clearance was serious and might nix someone's chances at a job, but it could be excused if there were mitigating circumstances. A failure to fully correct the mistake by disclosing all additional contacts a second time, as was the case with Kushner, would likely disqualify an official from public service in normal circumstances.

Kushner retained a renowned white-collar defense attorney, Abbe

Lowell, to represent him. Lowell had defended many high-profile clients, including Senators Robert Menendez, on charges of public corruption, and John Edwards, on charges of campaign finance fraud, and had been chief counsel to the House Democrats during impeachment proceedings against President Clinton. Although Lowell was a Democrat, he had just the kind of résumé Trump would have liked leading his own legal defense.

On June 13, Bowe, Dowd, Sekulow, and Corallo gathered at the Washington offices of Kasowitz's firm just two blocks from the White House to discuss the kids. Sekulow broached the subject the team was wrestling over: "Should Jared and Ivanka be in the White House?" Some of the lawyers were wary of staking out a position. They wanted to maintain their standing with the president, and they figured that whatever they advised Trump to do about the kids, he would share with Kushner and Ivanka, and then they would be "roadkill," as one of the advisers put it.

Still, in the confines of Kasowitz's law office, they were frank with one another about the challenges created by the presidential family members. Corallo said he worried that Kushner could make other staffers witnesses in the investigation and that he would not be able to assert privilege to protect conversations he had with them. Corallo also argued that Kushner's security clearance problems alone made it impossible for him to remain a true adviser in the White House. "The politics are really bad," he said. Bowe said the legal team should at least prepare for the possibility that their departure might be necessary. And Sekulow agreed they needed to be ready to discuss the pros and cons with Trump. "Prepare some talking points if it comes to pass that we need to recommend it," Sekulow said. But Dowd defended Kushner and Ivanka, stressing that Trump relied on them and the lawyers shouldn't get involved.

"We're not going to get between family," Dowd said.

Seven

IMPEDING JUSTICE

Monday, June 12, was a day of ritual, which masked the president's agita. Trump convened his first full cabinet meeting, a now infamous session in which U.S. government officials took turns pledging fealty to their master. "On behalf of the entire senior staff around you, Mr. President, we thank you for the opportunity and the blessing that you've given us to serve your agenda and the American people," Reince Priebus crowed. But no one was loyal to anyone in the orbit of Donald Trump.

The groveling of Priebus and others did little to distract Trump from his aspiration to end the special counsel investigation. Priebus and Steve Bannon met that same Monday with Christopher Ruddy, telling him the president had seriously been considering abruptly firing Robert Mueller. That evening, Ruddy said in an appearance on the PBS *NewsHour* that Trump was weighing whether to terminate the special counsel, a revelation that transfixed Washington.

Trump was motivated by his conviction, fueled partially by the analysis of his lawyers, that Mueller had conflicts of interest. Mueller was rapidly building his team, hiring experienced litigators from top firms and hard-charging federal prosecutors. By mid-June, he had hired thirteen lawyers. The team included Aaron Zebley, Mueller's former FBI chief of staff; James Quarles, a former Watergate assistant special prosecutor; Jeannie Rhee, a former prosecutor and partner with Mueller at WilmerHale; Michael Dreeben, a deputy solicitor general known as one of the country's foremost legal thinkers; and Andrew Weissmann, a famed Enron prosecutor and a former chief of the Justice Department's criminal fraud section. Many additional lawyers were itching to be a part of this historic investigation, and Mueller was preparing to hire some of them.

Trump's lawyers closely studied the backgrounds of Mueller's hires and saw a pattern. Though Mueller was registered as a Republican and appointed FBI director by Bush, many of the lawyers joining his team were Democrats, and some had given money to Hillary Clinton's 2016 campaign. Trump's lawyers also thought there was a decent legal argument that Mueller was conflicted out of being special counsel because he had met with Trump the day before his appointment for what the president claimed was a job interview. Mueller could have learned Trump's thinking about the probe and whether Trump implied he required loyalty in his next FBI director. Either way, he could be a witness who had an improper window into the mind of the investigation's key subject.

Marc Kasowitz and Mike Bowe shared this information with Trump during a meeting with his legal team, and he was elated. A one-two punch, he thought. The special counsel's team was politically biased, and Mueller himself could be disqualified from leading the probe. The president became particularly enamored with the idea that Mueller was conflicted because the two men had what he called a "business dispute." Mueller once belonged to Trump National Golf Club in Northern Virginia and sought to recoup some of his membership fees when he moved. Trump's lawyers tried to get their client to realize this was not a strong case of a conflict of interest, but the president could not be persuaded. He wouldn't stop mentioning the business dispute as a fatal flaw in Mueller's appointment.

Testifying June 13 before a Senate Appropriations subcommittee, Deputy Attorney General Rod Rosenstein, who officially oversaw the special counsel probe, tried to assuage fears building in Washington that Trump intended to terminate Mueller. "I'm not going to follow any orders unless I believe those are lawful and appropriate orders," Rosenstein said. He added, "Special Counsel Mueller may be fired only for good cause." Rosenstein's remarks were intended to affirm the Justice Department would uphold the rule of law, irrespective of any impulsive decree by the president. But they did not persuade Trump to drop the issue.

About 7:00 p.m. the next day, June 14, *The Washington Post* reported that Mueller had expanded his Russia probe to include an examination of whether Trump had attempted to obstruct justice. Trump himself was now under investigation, which was precisely what he had spent the spring pressuring his FBI director and intelligence agency heads to publicly deny. The administration was stuck in an unremitting season of investigations and the president was enraged. Around this time, he called Chris Christie.

"Should I fire Mueller?" Trump asked the New Jersey governor.

"Mr. President, if you fire Mueller, you're going to be impeached," Christie replied. "Sure as day follows night, you will be impeached."

"Do you really believe that?" Trump asked.

"I absolutely believe that," Christie said, arguing that even Republicans in Congress could vote to impeach him for terminating the special counsel. "If there's anybody who's encouraging you to fire Mueller and somehow that will end your problems, it will only compound your problems. Don't do it."

Around 10:00 p.m. on June 14, Trump called Don McGahn on his cell phone. He was steaming hot and wanted to find out if the investigation really was trained on him—and, if so, how could this have happened? He told the White House counsel to talk with Rosenstein and push the deputy attorney general. He had to remove Mueller because of what the president believed were conflicts of interest.

"You gotta do this," Trump told McGahn. "You gotta call Rod."

McGahn was more than a little annoyed by Trump's obsession with Mueller's conflicts, which he considered silly and of little merit. He again told the president that the conflicts case was not very strong and that his personal lawyers should be raising the issue, not the White House counsel. But on a night when every cable news channel was fixated on the news that Trump was a subject of a criminal investigation, the president was not thinking rationally and would not take no for an answer.

"I'll see what I can do," McGahn said, giving his boss a noncommittal answer to get him off the phone. McGahn hung up, shaking his head at the president's unreasonable demands.

The next day, June 15, should have been a moment of celebration for both Trump and McGahn. The Supreme Court associate justice Neil Gorsuch's investiture ceremony was at 2:00 p.m. that Thursday. Installing a conservative on the court was the first major achievement of Trump's presidency, a key campaign promise fulfilled, and Gorsuch's smooth nomination had largely been orchestrated by McGahn.

But Trump rose early and began venting his anger at the obstruction probe on Twitter. For weeks, his lawyers and aides had tried to wean Trump off Twitter, fearful that his comments could create greater legal exposure for him. Kasowitz would plead with Trump, "Enough of the tweeting. You've got to stop talking about the case. Enough. Just let us do our jobs." But they eventually resigned themselves to merely managing his missives.

"They made up a phony collusion with the Russians story, found zero proof, so now they go for obstruction of justice on the phony story. Nice," Trump tweeted.

"You are witnessing the single greatest WITCH HUNT in American political history—led by some very bad and conflicted people!" he wrote in a second tweet.

McGahn later told associates that he contemplated skipping the ceremony altogether because the testy talk with Trump over the phone the night before had so deflated him. But he attended, figuring the investiture was history and he would be mad at himself if he didn't witness it. The leaders of all three branches of government came together for the solemn ceremony and congratulated McGahn as the proud father.

That weekend, Trump made his first visit to Camp David, the famed presidential retreat in the Maryland mountains. He seemed to be in good spirits as he boarded Marine One for the twenty-minute helicopter flight there, and McGahn assumed Trump had put his reckless Mueller plan behind him. But on the morning of Saturday, June 17, Trump called McGahn on his cell phone again. It was Father's Day weekend, and Mc-Gahn had slept in and was at home getting ready for a full day of family events planned for his son's birthday.

"Call Rod," Trump told McGahn. "Tell Rod that Mueller has conflicts and can't be the special counsel."

McGahn put a hand to his forehead. This idea wasn't dead after all.

"Mueller has to go," Trump continued. "Call me back when you do it."

This was an inflection point. As McGahn would later tell confidants, it was "Comey II: The Sequel." He did not want to participate in another obstructive episode. He had no intention of actually calling Rosenstein, out of fear Rosenstein would also consider it a directive and that it might trigger him to take some drastic and irreversible step. But McGahn also did not want to fight Trump on his idea. Instead, he just replied methodically, "Yeah, boss," and "Okay." He was worn down, so tired of Trump's bullshit. He just wanted to get off the phone and think through the choice he now faced.

McGahn drove from his home in a gated community near Mount Vernon to the White House and began to collect his things. He felt he had to quit. He figured the next time Trump called to confirm that his orders were being carried out, he would tell him he was resigning. Mc-Gahn told his chief of staff, Annie Donaldson, he was submitting a letter of resignation but didn't tell her the details of why. He was specifically trying to shield her from exposure to this obstruction of justice, so he told her only that Trump demanded he contact the Justice Department to do something McGahn did not want to do.

McGahn later called Priebus. "I'm done," he told the chief of staff. "I've packed up my car. There's nothing in my office. I packed up all my things. I'm done."

"What are you talking about?" Priebus asked. "Why are you done? What happened?"

"I'm tired of the president asking me to do crazy shit," McGahn said, declining to elaborate further.

"You're not resigning," Priebus told him. "You can't resign. You're going to relax for today and we're going to talk tomorrow, but you're not resigning. You can't do that to the staff. You cannot instantly resign from your position at a time when we need you."

McGahn then spoke with Bannon, who tried to talk him out of resigning by underscoring how valuable he was to the president by taking stands like the one he was taking now.

"It's already Saturday night," Bannon told McGahn. "You can't do anything now."

Trump did not call back that night, so the urgency McGahn had felt that afternoon passed as the night wore on. McGahn reluctantly agreed to stay on but told Bannon things had to change.

"We gotta get a real lawyer in here because I can't keep being put in the middle of this shit," McGahn said. "This is all fucked-up."

Trump would later claim that he never asked McGahn to help him "fire" Mueller, which technically was true. He hadn't used the word "fire." But it was clear to McGahn what Trump wanted him to do.

On Friday, June 16, as Trump was preoccupied with trying to remove Mueller, his lawyers had their first meeting with the special counsel. This was the meeting Trump had been pushing them to have since he had officially hired Kasowitz in May. In Mueller's temporary offices near Union Station, Kasowitz, Bowe, and Dowd introduced themselves. Accompanying Mueller were Quarles and Zebley. The Trump team soon broached the elephant in the room: the news reports that Mueller was now investigating the president himself.

"You know, Bob, I don't know if you are investigating the president," Dowd said. "Maybe you're doing a preliminary inquiry. But we have several views about why you can't have a president obstructing justice."

Bowe walked through the law, point by point, that gave the president broad constitutional powers to fire any appointee and take action on investigations. Mueller listened carefully. His stone-faced expression never changed. The lawyers said they had two more concerns, about Comey's credibility as a witness and the conflicts they felt Mueller had in serving as special counsel. They asked if the prosecutors would like their legal arguments spelled out in memo form. Polite but revealing nothing, Mueller said, "We're happy to take any presentation you have."

Dowd said a lengthy investigation could hurt Trump.

"We've got a president who's got to govern. We'll get you whatever you need. In exchange, I want a decision. We'll move it, you move it." Mueller replied, "You know me, John. I don't let any grass grow under my feet."

Mueller had been in the job only a month at this point and made clear to Trump's lawyers that his team had a lot of work to do. The week before, Mueller's deputies had interviewed Andrew Goldstein, who would become a key investigator into whether the president obstructed justice. In the days just before and after their meeting with Trump's lawyers, Mueller's team held strategy sessions about getting a legal agreement with Cypriot authorities to obtain evidence they might be able to seize inside a storage locker belonging to Paul Manafort, Trump's former campaign chairman.

While Trump's legal team presented a united front with Mueller, some were suspicious about a mysterious enemy slinging arrows their way, targeting those who had raised concerns about Jared Kushner. On June 19, Corallo alerted his bosses, Kasowitz and Bowe, that he had been contacted by *The New York Times* that day for comment on a story about tweets he sent in 2016 criticizing Trump's candidacy and disparaging Ivanka Trump and Kushner by suggesting their hiring raised doubts about Trump's commitment to "draining the swamp." Corallo had actually flagged the tweets to Trump senior advisers before his hiring on the legal team and found it odd and unsettling they were being reported as news.

The next day, June 20, a client contacted a lawyer at the Kasowitz firm to alert him that a ProPublica reporter had been asking him about allegations that Kasowitz had been absent from the firm for lengthy periods in the recent past. ProPublica had received a humiliating trove of secrets, which had been known to only a tiny handful of firm insiders, including allegations that Kasowitz struggled with alcohol abuse. Kasowitz assumed someone inside his firm had betrayed him, but he did not know who.

On June 21, Kasowitz and Bowe briefed Trump on several pressing topics, which others would learn included their review of possibly problematic campaign emails they might have to turn over to Congress, and highlights of their first meeting with Mueller on June 16, a subject Trump was eager to hear about. The two lawyers told the president they had conveyed his message, that the probe created a cloud over the president and was unfair. They reported Dowd's request that this not drag on, and Mueller's assurances he would "not let any grass grow under my feet."

Not long after, the president said, "I gotta meet this guy Dowd."

In mid-June, Kasowitz and Bowe still believed they could recruit someone else as lead attorney, with Dowd playing a supporting role. But they didn't have one yet. Bowe agreed to bring Dowd over one afternoon for a late lunch with the president. Bowe liked and respected Dowd but also never expected to put him in charge of representing the president. For his meeting with the president, Dowd entered the president's offices seeming to be in awe. Inside were Trump, Bowe, Corallo, and Jay Sekulow. The men exchanged some pleasantries and took seats in the dining room to enjoy steak, fries, and Diet Coke, one of Trump's frequent lunch menus. The president asked Dowd, "So, do you have a relationship with this guy, Mueller?"

"He's a marine like me," Dowd said. "I can relate to him, Mr. President. I can talk to him."

"What do you think he's doing, John?" Trump asked.

Dowd told the president he felt this could be wrapped up quickly. "I think I can talk to Bob Mueller and get this done in a matter of weeks," he said.

Attendees remembered Dowd's comment differently. Some thought he told the president he could get it resolved in a matter of months. Dowd disputed giving a time frame. Bowe was stunned and looked over at Corallo, then stared at Dowd. He told associates later, "He was working the president."

At first, Trump sounded skeptical.

"Oh, I don't know," Trump said. "Are you sure?"

"Yes, sir," Dowd said.

"That's great; that's just great," the president replied.

Corallo sensed in Dowd that day a "satisfaction that, 'Hey, this is what I've worked for my whole life.' It's like a crowning achievement. 'I'm in the Oval Office and the president is my client now.' That's a big deal. It went to John's head and he decided to take over."

K asowitz and Bowe tried to persuade Trump to stay calm and wait for Mueller to act, but that proved impossible. The self-proclaimed master counterpuncher used every platform he had to decry the investigation and cast himself as a victim of an unfair "witch hunt." The president at first followed his lawyers' advice not to personally attack the special counsel, but pleaded daily with those on his legal team to blast Mueller as conflicted, "dirty," and staffed by Democrats.

Steaming mad over press coverage of the investigation, Trump was taping his weekly video address on an unrelated topic in the Diplomatic Reception Room of the White House one day when he sought help outside his cautious legal team. He gave an unusual directive to Cliff Sims, one of the press aides helping with the taping. "I want you to go write the most scathing thing you've ever written about the Mueller investigation, about this witch hunt, and come back to me by the end of the day and I'll record that video," Trump told Sims.

Sims scurried back to his desk and quickly typed about five hundred words. The rhetoric was bellicose and conspiratorial. "This is a coup," the script read. It went far beyond the language Trump had used to date to describe the Russia investigation. Sims envisioned the president's remarks not only eviscerating Mueller but also rallying his supporters to his defense. His conceit was that Mueller and his prosecutors were coming after not Trump but rather the voters who put him in office by seeking to overturn the election results. "We're in this together against these people who are trying to delegitimize our victory," the script read.

Sims knew his "coup" script was over the top. He showed it to Hope Hicks, the West Wing's wisest interpreter of Trump's instincts and decrees.

"This is insane," Hicks said.

"What do you want me to do with this?" Sims asked.

"Well, the president asked you to do something," she replied. "Go show it to him."

Sims found Trump behind the Resolute Desk and handed him the script.

"I wrote this because you asked for it," Sims said. "But this would be a disaster if you record this video."

Trump read it and agreed.

"You're right," Trump said. "We won't do it this time, but just hold on to it in case we ever want to use it."

For once, Trump exhibited restraint. Fresh in his mind that afternoon was his lawyers' advice not to attack Mueller. Yet at least part of Trump believed Sims's script was right, that this had been an attempted coup.

The Mueller probe was not Trump's only fixation during this period. He also was unnerved by the Russia investigations under way on Capitol Hill. The president felt somewhat protected by the House Permanent Select Committee on Intelligence because it was chaired by a Trump devotee, Republican Congressman Devin Nunes of California, but the Senate Select Committee on Intelligence was another story. That committee's chairman, Senator Richard Burr of North Carolina, was an establishment-minded Republican with no particular affinity for Trump. Burr rightfully saw his committee as nonpartisan and worked closely with the panel's top Democrat, Senator Mark Warner of Virginia. Burr and Warner together had spoken forcefully about Russia's interference in the election, which the intelligence community determined was directed by the Kremlin with the explicit aim of helping Trump prevail.

Trump was deeply insecure about the intelligence community's conclusion about Russian interference. He hated for anyone to think that he did not defeat Hillary Clinton entirely on his own, that his victory was somehow illegitimate. Suddenly the president had an idea: he could somehow convince Burr of his innocence by sending him a pile of printed-out news articles and fact sheets that he believed exculpated him. So during one of his meetings with McGahn in the Oval Office, Trump told the White House counsel he wanted to write a letter to Burr, with the news clippings attached.

McGahn knew it was a dangerous idea. He told Trump that sending this letter would be unwise. If Burr interpreted such a letter signed by the president as demeaning or even hostile, it could jeopardize not only the Russia investigation but also the administration's overall agenda in the Senate, including confirmation of federal judges, a top priority for both Trump and McGahn. What's more, it's not as if Burr didn't have his own easy access to such facts.

"We can't do this," McGahn told the president.

Trump came up with a Plan B: McGahn would sign the letter instead.

"Send the letter," Trump said.

"I can't send the letter, sir," McGahn said. "We have other priorities up there."

At that moment, Chris Christie walked into the Oval for a visit. Trump asked the New Jersey governor whether he would send the letter.

"If Don believes that it will upset your ability to get judges confirmed by the Senate, then the answer is no," Christie told Trump. "That's more important than whatever the fucking letter says."

McGahn was visibly relieved. So often he had been the West Wing's lone voice of resistance. Finally, someone else backed him up in refusing the president's order.

Their defiance irritated Trump.

"You're both jokes," the president told McGahn and Christie. "Okay, leave. Bye."

As they departed the Oval, McGahn said to Christie, "I wish you were around every day."

"Why is that?" Christie asked.

"Because then I wouldn't be the only dick in the building," McGahn deadpanned.

On June 21, *The Wall Street Journal* published a story by Eli Stokols and Michael Bender reporting that the White House was "riven by division between senior aides" and that the expanding Russia investigations had frustrated Trump and exacerbated the administration's struggle to recruit new talent. The piece reflected poorly on Bannon and Priebus. Bannon was furious and lit into Hicks, screaming like a deck seaman at the former fashion model. He confronted her in front of Trump, accusing Hicks of having "leaked" a negative story to the *Journal.* She explained that her interactions had been entirely proper; it was, after all, her job to talk to reporters. Bannon was effectively taking on the president's family. No senior White House staffer, other than Ivanka Trump and Jared Kushner, had a longer or deeper relationship with the president than Hicks, whom he treated like a surrogate daughter.

The next day, June 22, Bannon, Hicks, Priebus, and Sean Spicer met in the chief of staff's office. Hicks knew she had done nothing wrong interacting with the *Journal* and expected Priebus and Spicer to defend her. But they did not.

"You've been running around here for months just working for Ivanka and Jared," Bannon said to Hicks. "Your client is the man in the Oval Office." He added, "You don't actually work for the president. You forgot how you got here."

Sitting at the end of Priebus's long conference table and looking down at his phone, Bannon threatened Hicks: "That's it. I'm going to war. You have no idea who you're messing with. I will end you."

"You're *going* to war?" Hicks replied. "What the fuck have you been doing for the last three months? You've been twiddling on your Black-Berry leaking to everybody."

Hicks was furious. "The fact that my integrity is being questioned in front of the three of you, I can't believe this," she told Bannon, Priebus, and Spicer. "I'm leaving. When you guys are ready to apologize to me, I'll come back, but I'm leaving."

That would be the last time Hicks spoke with Bannon.

In early June, George Conway finally withdrew himself from consideration to lead the civil division as assistant attorney general. The night of June 24, he came face-to-face with the president he decided not to serve. Conway and his wife, Kellyanne, were among the guests attending the wedding of Secretary of the Treasury Steve Mnuchin and the Scottish actress Louise Linton. The opulent event was held at one of Washington's grandest venues, the Mellon Auditorium, a historic neoclassical building named after the former Treasury secretary Andrew Mellon. Vice President Pence officiated, and everyone who was anyone in the administration attended, including President Trump and First Lady Melania Trump.

After taking their vows, Mr. and Mrs. Mnuchin were whisked away for formal pictures while guests were ushered into the cocktail reception. As guests nibbled on hors d'oeuvres before the formal seated dinner, Kellyanne Conway spotted Trump talking to a small cluster of people nearby, and she suggested to her husband that they walk over to say hello.

Trump greeted them with a big smile. But without engaging in any basic pleasantries—no "Hey, good to see you," or "How are the kids?"—Trump brusquely jumped into a stream of complaints and epithets about how badly Jeff Sessions had failed him as an attorney general. He described how "terrible" and "crazy" it was for Sessions to recuse himself from the Russia investigation. Somehow, Trump had convinced himself that George Conway retreated from the Justice Department job because he did not want to work for someone as terribly weak as Sessions.

"Hey, you know, I heard from some people that the lawyers at DOJ felt he had to recuse," George Conway said.

"No, no," Trump said. The president then pointed a finger at George Conway's chest.

"You're a smart guy, not going to work for that weak guy," Trump said, grinning. "Very smart!"

George Conway smiled uncomfortably. After a few more minutes of Sessions bashing by Trump, the Conways said their goodbyes, explaining that others wanted to talk to Trump and they had better make their way to their table for dinner. Ironically, Sessions was supposed to sit at the Conways' table but never showed.

The Conways stopped to get a drink, and as they stood alone together, George Conway chuckled about the president's one-track mind. The president was uncontrollably obsessed with the "weak" Sessions. George laughed harder and was eventually doubled over.

The next morning, though, George Conway replayed in his mind the parody that was Donald J. Trump. In the light of day, he now saw the events of the previous night as deeply disturbing. He had been cackling like a kid about Trump's buffoonish behavior. He was laughing at him, not with him. And the object of his ridicule was the president of the United States.

Eight

A COVER-UP

Trump was impatient to meet Vladimir Putin. So much so that during the transition he interrupted an interview with one of his secretary of state candidates by glancing at Reince Priebus and asking, "When can I meet with Putin? Can I meet with him before the inaugural ceremony?" Trump's advisers told him that would be inappropriate, of course. A U.S. president was expected to meet with NATO allies before ever sitting down with the president of Russia, an adversary whose forces had just illegally interfered with the American election. Then there was the matter of protocol, which dictated that presidents-elect should not meet with foreign counterparts until they took office, out of respect for the sitting president. But Trump was hardly a disciple of diplomatic protocol. He knew what he wanted, and he did not want to take no for an answer. In the same meeting, he piped up again: "When do you think I can meet with Putin?"

Trump had to wait 168 days into his presidency for the big moment. By now, he and Putin had talked on the phone several times, and Trump liked to brag that he shared a special bond with Putin because they were "stablemates" on *60 Minutes*, having been interviewed separately for unrelated segments that happened to air in the same 2015 episode of the venerated CBS News show. But they had never met face-to-face until

July 7, 2017, when Trump and Putin sat down on the sidelines of the Group of Twenty summit for world leaders in Hamburg, Germany.

"It's an honor to be with you," Trump said as he greeted Putin, flashing the tough-boss smirk he had practiced over so many years on *The Apprentice.*

"Your Excellency, Mr. President," Putin said, gamely flattering a man uniquely susceptible to it. "I spoke over the phone with you several times on very important bilateral and international issues, but phone conversation is never enough."

The two men shook hands firmly. What they lacked in warmth, they tried to make up for in machismo. Joined by Secretary of State Rex Tillerson and Russian foreign minister Sergey Lavrov, Trump and Putin conversed for two hours and sixteen minutes. Trump raised the matter of Russia's interference in the 2016 presidential election, but once Putin denied any involvement by his government, they moved on to other topics. Putin convinced Trump that U.S. intelligence officials were trying to damage the U.S.-Russia relationship with phony claims of meddling. The Russians emerged with the distinct impression that Trump would not hold them accountable. "The U.S. president said that he heard clear statements from President Putin about this being untrue and that he accepted these statements," Lavrov said, summarizing the meeting for reporters. Trump saw Hamburg as the start of a new era of diplomacy between the United States and Russia. He directed Tillerson to tell reporters that the tête-à-tête produced "very clear positive chemistry."

Yet Trump, who harbored deep suspicions about the loyalty of national security and intelligence officials and had previously accused them of leaking information about his private discussions with foreign leaders to try to make him look bad, went to extraordinary lengths to conceal details of his conversation with Putin. Trump personally took possession of the notes of the American interpreter and instructed the linguist not to discuss what had transpired with other administration officials.

As a result, high-ranking officials at intelligence agencies and elsewhere in the government had no detailed record of what was discussed between the two presidents, beyond the readout Tillerson provided to the media. The only detail administration officials received from the interpreter was that after Putin denied any Russian involvement in the U.S. election, Trump responded by saying, "I believe you."

As he watched footage of Trump and Putin interacting, John Brennan's blood boiled. As CIA director throughout President Obama's second term, Brennan had a front-row seat not only to Russia's systematic interference in the U.S. elections but to Putin's annexation of Crimea from Ukraine and his murderous authoritarian rule.

"When I saw Mr. Trump lean over and say to Mr. Putin, it's a great honor to meet you, and this is Mr. Putin who assaulted one of the foundational pillars of our democracy, our electoral system, that invaded Ukraine, annexed Crimea, that has suppressed and repressed political opponents in Russia and has caused the deaths of many of them, to say up front, person who supposedly knows the art of the deal, I thought it was a very, very bad negotiating tactic, and I felt as though it was not the honorable thing to say," Brennan told national security professionals gathered a couple weeks later at the Aspen Security Forum.

That day in Hamburg, there was still more Trump wanted to discuss with Putin. The evening of July 7, the two men attended a gala dinner hosted by German chancellor Angela Merkel for the G20 leaders and their spouses. Inside the gleaming modern Elbphilharmonie concert hall on the banks of the Elbe River, the presidents and prime ministers and their spouses ate at a long white-clothed banquet table.

Putin was seated next to Melania Trump, and Donald Trump feared he was missing out on the action. When the dessert course was served, he stood up from his own seat next to Japanese prime minister Shinzo Abe to take a chair next to Putin. Trump and Putin, joined only by an official Kremlin interpreter, chatted for an hour as the other leaders circulated the room looking bemused and befuddled by their animated conversation. They kept talking so long that they were among the last leaders to leave the concert hall, Putin at 11:50 p.m. and Trump at 11:54 p.m., long after their host, Merkel, had departed.

An iron rule of diplomacy is that one of the most important components of the relationship between any two states is the personal rapport between their leaders. Franklin D. Roosevelt had Winston Churchill. Ronald Reagan had Margaret Thatcher. And by this point in his presidency, the list of foreign leaders auditioning to be Trump's closest ally and confidant was long. It was in most countries' interests to be friends with the United States, and foreign governments calculated that Trump could be won over relatively easily, with flattery and deference.

Abe raced to Trump Tower during the transition to ingratiate himself by presenting Trump with a $3,755 gold-colored golf club. The two played twenty-seven holes of golf together in Florida in February. British prime minister Theresa May jetted to Washington on only Trump's seventh full day in office, hoping to reaffirm the "special relationship" between their two countries. They even held hands as they strolled the West Wing Colonnade.

But Trump had his eyes on Putin. His guide in navigating this flowering relationship was Tillerson. Of all the president's advisers, Tillerson knew Putin the best, having negotiated with him as Exxon's leader on Russian exports and later as the energy giant's chief executive. They first met in the 1990s, and they had sat across from each other several times in the years since in Putin's ornate conference room in the Kremlin.

Their relationship was so close that in 2013—the same year Putin snubbed Trump by declining his invitation to attend the Miss Universe pageant in Moscow—Putin personally invited Tillerson to a celebratory event in Sochi to show off Russia's progress in redeveloping the resort city for the upcoming Winter Olympic Games. During that summer trip, Putin brought Tillerson aboard his yacht for a private lunch. Whisked to the dock by Putin's Mercedes, Tillerson stepped aboard the boat and noticed his aides were left on land when Putin's crew tossed the lines overboard and pushed off. Black gunboats flanked the yacht as they took a short jaunt out into deeper waters of the Black Sea. As they dined alfresco, Putin confided to Tillerson that he detested Obama. He argued that Obama had lied to him about claims he wanted to partner with Russia and seemed unable to make a clear decision.

"I've given up on your president," Putin told Tillerson. "I'll wait for your next president and see if I can get along with him."

Tillerson got along with Putin but also had his number. Once he became secretary of state four years later, he tried to use his extensive experience with Putin wisely to tutor Trump. He explained Putin's deep desire to restore Russian greatness and credibility, or at least give it the sheen of a country to be feared, in part by forging a partnership with a world power such as the United States. He stressed that Putin would always look to save face with his citizenry. And he said Putin's hidden default move was picking at his enemies' scabs.

"The only thing Putin understands is truth and power," Tillerson explained to Trump. "He will lean in as far as he can until he fears defeat. The last thing he wants is a defeat with his own people."

Tillerson emphasized the most important trait he thought Trump should know: Putin's moves might seem slick and quick, but he was playing a long game, always thinking several moves ahead, years in the distance. He impressed upon Trump the fact that Putin sought to destabilize Western alliances and remake the post–World War II power structure to weaken America's global influence. Putin, Tillerson told Trump, "wakes up every morning asking, 'Where is America having problems? Let's go there now and make it worse.'" He explained that Putin's government was nimble and sparked brush fires around the world to which the United States was slow to respond.

By helping Bashar al-Assad in Syria, Putin was creating a toehold for Russia in the Middle East. In North Korea, Putin was hoping to befriend Kim Jong Un and keep the United States from consolidating power in the Asia Pacific. And Putin annexed Crimea in eastern Ukraine, dead set on proving that Mother Russia was the rightful ruler of the land and showing resolve on a matter of nationalistic pride.

Before Trump's meeting with Putin in Hamburg, Tillerson visited Moscow in April 2017 to lay the groundwork, sitting with the Russian president in the same Kremlin conference room where they had met when Tillerson worked for Exxon. As he entered Putin's bastion, Tillerson pointed first to his head, "Different hat," he said, then to his chest. "Same man."

"Da," Putin said, smiling and nodding at the gesture.

They discussed contentious issues, not the least of which was the Kremlin's aid to the Assad regime, which was using Russian firepower to slaughter civilians. Tillerson also delivered a message that the United States would resist Russian aggression in Ukraine. Upon his return to Washington, Tillerson counseled Trump that the key to working with Putin was steady discipline.

"With Putin, you have to stay on it every day," Tillerson explained. "He'll wait to see the pressure ease and then seize his opportunity."

Trump listened to Tillerson, but to those watching, he seemed absentminded. He did not ask questions or try to keep the conversation going. He had only one direct comment. He rejected the notion that Putin would try to take advantage of the United States.

"I don't really think that's what Putin is up to," Trump said.

Trump's confidence about how to handle Putin changed dramatically after their face-to-face meeting July 7 in Hamburg. Trump believed he was the expert on Russia now. He owned the relationship. Tillerson's years of negotiating with Putin and studying his moves on the chessboard were suddenly irrelevant.

"I have had a two-hour meeting with Putin," Trump told Tillerson. "That's all I need to know. . . . I've sized it all up. I've got it."

Tillerson's moral code and experience climbing the corporate ladder taught him to respect America's commander in chief. In this moment, he had to deploy every diplomatic skill he had acquired to tell his boss to be careful, reminding him that Putin had a history of taking advantage if he saw an opening. Putin was a master manipulator, a former KGB agent trained to find the soft spots of his foes and to exploit them. But Trump waved him off.

"I know more about this than you do," Trump said.

On July 7, while Trump was focused in Germany on making a friend out of Putin, his lawyers back in the United States were bracing for a public relations catastrophe, the biggest since Robert Mueller was appointed special counsel. Over the previous few weeks, lawyers representing the president, his company, his campaign, and some of his family members had been reviewing tranches of campaign and transition-period emails in preparation for turning over the records to the Senate and House intelligence committees, which were investigating Russian interference.

The lawyers had discovered correspondence suggesting Russians had a special pipeline into the campaign and that some people around Trump knew the Kremlin was trying to help his candidacy. They thought these exchanges were horrifying and certain to show Trump had lied, but did not necessarily pose a legal problem.

"Anybody with half a brain realized it's politically explosive even if legally irrelevant," recalled one of the lawyers reviewing the material. "It's just awful stuff."

The emails revealed that Donald Trump Jr. excitedly and naively set up a meeting at Trump Tower in 2016 with Natalia Veselnitskaya, a Russian lawyer with ties to the Kremlin. In the exchanges, Rob Goldstone, a British talent promoter who was helping broker the meeting, relayed that the Russians were offering "to provide the Trump campaign with some official documents and information that would incriminate Hillary and her dealings with Russia and would be very useful to your father. This is obviously very high level and sensitive information but is part of Russia and its government's support for Mr. Trump."

"If it's what you say I love it," Trump junior wrote in one of the emails to Goldstone.

Jared Kushner attended the meeting on the twenty-fifth floor of Trump Tower on June 9, 2016, at Trump junior's invitation, as did then-campaign chairman Paul Manafort.

The lawyers all knew that as soon as they provided the records to Congress, Democrats would release the most damaging details. After months of Trump's claiming "no collusion," here was the first known meeting between top Trump campaign officials, his own family, and a Russian national. This had the makings of a full-blown crisis.

Trump lawyers Marc Kasowitz and Mike Bowe had alerted the president to the existence of the emails on June 21 but explained they likely would not become known outside their circle of lawyers until the fall, when they had to be produced to congressional committees investigating Russian meddling in the election.

Hope Hicks also was working to help contain the fallout, but the president rejected his communications director's advice. As she later told the special counsel, Hicks met in the White House residence in late June with Trump, Kushner, and Ivanka. Kushner tried to show his father-in-law the emails that Congress would soon have, but the president shut the conversation down and said he did not want to know about it. Then, on June 29, Hicks spoke privately with Trump to convey her concern about the political firestorm the emails would unleash. He told her he did not think they would leak so long as only one lawyer handled them. Later that day, in a second meeting that was attended by Kushner and Ivanka, Hicks told Trump that the emails were "really bad" and the news story would be "massive" when it broke. Hicks suggested Trump junior proactively disclose the existence of the emails and summarize their content in an attempt to soften the blow, but Trump reiterated that he did not want to know the details and insisted he did not believe the emails would leak to the press.

Around the same time, the lawyers for Trump, his campaign, and his family members plotted different ways to get in front of the story. Kushner's lawyer, Abbe Lowell, urged that one of them should leak the story to a friendly news outlet first, just before turning over the material, to shape the story in a way that put all their clients in the best light. Considered one of the very best Washington scandal attorneys, Lowell believed the meeting with the Russian lawyer was embarrassing and showed the Trump team's naïveté, but he did not think it amounted to a conspiracy to collude with Russians. Lowell was elated one day when, combing through the evidence, he found emails showing Kushner arrived late to the meeting and tried to leave early.

As Lowell saw it, Trump junior, Kushner, and Manafort took a meeting with some goofy folks, including Veselnitskaya, that they shouldn't have, but no deals were struck and nothing came of it. Kushner had repeatedly joked that the Democrats' claim that Trump or his advisers might have colluded with Russians was ridiculous because the campaign was so disorganized "we couldn't even collude with ourselves."

Lowell wanted Trump junior to shoulder the responsibility for setting up the meeting and "own" the story. "Everyone knew Abbe wanted Don junior to tell it," said one insider familiar with the plan. "The lawyers knew it. We had all talked about it," another said.

Lowell pushed the other lawyers to get on board with a plan to leak the story to a responsible organization, such as *The New York Times* or *The Washington Post*, around the time they turned over the records. Trump junior's newly hired lawyer, Alan Futerfas, respected Lowell and saw some wisdom in this idea. But Futerfas, hired just a week before, was still learning the facts of the meeting and wasn't comfortable going public until he knew what exactly had happened. Another lawyer who was privy to some of the information, however, was executing a plan of his own.

Reginald "Reg" Brown represented Manafort in the ongoing congressional investigations of Russian interference in the election, and that May he had provided several congressional committees with answers to their questions for his client. In written letters, Brown reported that Manafort didn't recall any one-on-one meetings with Russians during the campaign. However, by June, Brown had been alerted by other lawyers with access to Kushner's campaign emails that Manafort had attended the mystery meeting and had given Congress inaccurate information. Brown didn't want his client to be accused of lying to Congress and also saw an opportunity to show that his client was transparent and open. A veteran of congressional investigations, he didn't want this revelation to come out and let his guy be tagged with trying to conceal something. Brown conferred with Lowell and got his sign-off to notify various committees of Manafort's attending a meeting with a Russian. Brown's notice to the committees—which he conveyed by phone on about June 30, just before Congress left for the July 4 recess—volunteered that Manafort attended the meeting at the invitation of Donald Trump Jr. He made no mention of Kushner's attending.

Neither the Trump Organization nor Trump junior knew how quickly the world was about to come crashing down on their heads. Word of Brown's notification to Congress soon reached *The New York Times*, where on July 7 reporters called White House officials and Trump family lawyers saying the paper planned to write about a mysterious meeting at Trump Tower in 2016 with a Russian lawyer. Trump was four thousand miles away from his lawyers in Washington and New York, and his aides scrambled to buy more time. Hicks proposed a conference call with the *Times* reporters the next morning. But the morning of July 8 came and went with no call from the White House. And by this time, Trump and his entourage had boarded Air Force One in Hamburg to fly home to Washington. The *Times* reporters had put together a list of questions and emailed them to White House aides, who discussed them on the plane. They immediately realized they had a crisis on their hands.

The lawyers had been dreading this looming public relations nightmare but did not expect it to burst wide open this soon and were caught flat-footed. The president's own lawyers, Marc Kasowitz and Mike Bowe, hadn't yet fully briefed Trump on the digital trail. They had been working with a friendly conservative outlet, *Circa*, which also knew a little bit about a meeting with Russians. Bowe and communications strategist Mark Corallo hoped to cast the story in a very different light than Lowell had envisioned. They told the *Circa* reporter that the Russian lawyer had ties to a Democratic opposition research firm and appeared to be trying to set up the Trump campaign to look stupid. But they hadn't been able to settle on a media plan with the other lawyers by that Saturday.

Lowell, Kushner's attorney, was playing tennis when he was dragged off the court by an urgent call. The *Times* was about to publish details of the Trump Tower meeting. This was the very story Lowell had persuaded the broader legal team to carefully shape and communicate on their own terms, but now the dam was about to break and none of them had control.

When the *Times* inquired about the Trump Tower meeting, the person with the most firsthand knowledge of it, Trump junior, could not easily be reached. An avid outdoorsman, the president's namesake son, then thirty-nine, was on a fishing boat on a lake in upstate New York.

He had spotty cell service, and people struggled to reach him, but Hicks got to Trump junior with a series of texts.

Trump junior had already carefully reviewed the emails with his lawyer the previous week, primarily to prepare a press strategy, because the emails would likely have to be released to Congress. Trump junior had explained that although he had been eager to take the meeting with Veselnitskaya and hoped to learn something incriminating about Clinton, he came to consider the meeting a dud. He remembered being mildly annoyed that Veselnitskaya offered no actual evidence linking Clinton to a scandal. Instead, the brunette lawyer spent most of the meeting talking about a proposed deal: the Russian government would lift a ban on U.S. adoptions of Russian children if the U.S. government revoked a law sanctioning prominent Russian billionaires. This was a personal priority of Putin's, and Veselnitskaya had for years lobbied against the Magnitsky Act, which imposed sanctions on a so-called black list of accused human rights abusers. As Trump junior later recalled, it was a "wasted 20 minutes." He and his lawyers had crafted a few versions of statements for him to explain the meeting when the time came, and Trump junior's preference was a detailed account: a page-long description of how he came to hold the meeting and everything that happened.

Kushner, too, had reviewed his emails and texts with his lawyer before the *Times* call. He had remembered the meeting with Veselnitskaya as being fairly odd and unimportant. When Trump junior had gone fishing, Kushner and Ivanka Trump were traveling home from Germany with the president and conferred with Hicks and Kushner's communications aide Josh Raffel to strategize about Kushner's response to the inquiry.

Those in Germany knew the disclosure of the meeting carried political and potentially legal peril and quickly agreed on a strategy. Trump junior would release a statement to the *Times* to contain the fallout. His account would be truthful—including the fact, which they considered helpful, that Veselnitskaya's offer of damaging information on Clinton never materialized—so it could not be repudiated later if the full details emerged or, as the family's lawyers knew would eventually happen, copies of the emails surfaced.

"It's all going to come out eventually," Futerfas told some of those discussing what to do. He advocated for Trump junior's position: don't try to hide that the Russians had offered unflattering information about Clinton.

A statement was drafted in Trump junior's name stating, truthfully, that he was asked by an acquaintance to meet "with an individual who I was told might have information helpful to the campaign."

Once Trump boarded Air Force One, however, the president changed course. Retrofitted for presidential travel, the military's iconic Boeing 747 is segmented by cabins. The president's personal cabin is at the front of the fuselage, near the nose, and separate cabins flow back from there, with passengers assigned to seats in descending order of seniority: top advisers, then other staff, then Secret Service agents, then guests such as friends or members of Congress, and finally, in the rear, a traveling pool of thirteen journalists. For the first few hours of the flight, Trump worked furiously in the front cabin with Hicks to strategize about the brewing story about the Kremlin lawyer. Other aides, including White House press secretary Sean Spicer and his deputy, Sarah Sanders, were seated in the main staff cabin, feeling excluded from the action up front.

By nature a micromanager, Trump sought to minimize what he considered a public relations disaster—for his son, but primarily for himself. As was often the case with Trump, he didn't know all the details, and yet he also knew what he planned to say wasn't entirely true. He was just trying to wrest control of that day's headline and survive.

"You all think that he has some master strategy, but really he's just trying to get past the crisis of that moment," said one top adviser. "He thought to himself, 'Those emails aren't going to see the light of day until the fall,' and we're talking about this story right now. That was an eternity to him."

So Trump took charge to cover up the truth. Hicks sent Trump junior a series of text messages from the plane explaining that the president was proposing a different tack. They would emphasize that the meeting with Veselnitskaya was about Russian adoption policy and say nothing about the campaign. In conferring with Kushner and Hicks, Trump insisted that the statement not touch upon his campaign but rather focus on the obscure policy connections between the ban on Russian adoptions and the U.S. Magnitsky Act. Trump junior conveyed his irritation that his father was crafting a statement that sidestepped the Clinton element, a glaring and problematic omission.

Because the president and his aides were on a plane an ocean away, there was little chance for a thoughtful, strategic conference call with all the parties. Hicks continued to confer with Trump junior over text, while Trump junior discussed options with his lawyers, Futerfas and the Trump Organization's general counsel, Alan Garten. Lowell was conferring with Kushner and Ivanka Trump. Other White House aides were messaging with Garten. The president was adamant, however. In the front cabin of Air Force One, Hicks took Trump's dictation, typing up a draft she kept trying to perfect.

At the last minute, Trump junior urged Hicks to add one final word, to state that they "primarily" discussed adoptions at the meeting.

"I think that's right too but boss man worried it invites a lot of questions," Hicks texted Trump junior.

"If I don't have it in there it appears as though I'm lying later when they inevitably leak something," Trump junior replied.

A little bit after 1:30 p.m., Garten emailed the *Times* with a statement attributed to Trump junior, never conveying that the president himself had drafted it.

"It was a short introductory meeting," the statement read. "I asked Jared and Paul to stop by. We primarily discussed a program about the adoption of Russian children that was active and popular with American families years ago and was since ended by the Russian government, but it was not a campaign issue at that time and there was no follow up. I was asked to attend the meeting by an acquaintance, but was not told the name of the person I would be meeting with beforehand."

Trump junior, Lowell, Futerfas, and Garten were stymied. They all knew what was contained in the full email exchange, and they knew it would eventually come back not just to bite Trump junior but to ensnare Trump himself. However, none of them could overrule the president from afar. By the time Trump's personal lawyers weighed in, it was too late. After Garten issued the statement to the *Times*, he forwarded copies to other lawyers for the president and his advisers. Bowe had been trying to reach Futerfas since Friday; he wanted to get a statement from Trump junior for the *Circa* story. Futerfas had put him off, saying he'd call at 1:00 p.m. He didn't. At nearly 2:00 p.m., Bowe was driving to LaGuardia Airport to pick up his wife and got the email reporting the statement that had been sent to the *Times* at about 1:30 p.m. He pulled over and read the statement with fury. He had crafted a press strategy that would contain a fuller explanation of the meeting, and now Trump junior had issued an entirely different account. He got back on the road and dialed Futerfas on his cell.

"Alan, what the fuck is going on?" Bowe bellowed. "Our client is the fucking president of the United States. Why the fuck didn't you contact me?"

Futerfas tried to keep calm amid the string of expletives. "I didn't have a lot of control on this one, Mike," he said.

"We had a plan!" Bowe yelled back. "You totally screwed up the plan. You didn't call me back. What the fuck?"

Bowe explained in more detail the plan he, Kasowitz, the lawyer Jay Sekulow, and Mark Corallo had set in motion a day earlier with *Circa* to neutralize the embarrassing Trump Tower meeting emails. As Bowe talked, he was racing along the highway in Queens, a section of road he had driven probably a hundred times. Only this time, he was so angry he missed his exit for the airport.

Futerfas was frustrated, too. He didn't like being in this spot any more than Bowe. He had studied the Trump Tower meeting extensively in the previous week and actually now knew more about it than almost anyone. He had debriefed some of the lesser-known people who had attended, including Goldstone, the British publicist who had encouraged Trump junior to take the meeting in the first place.

Futerfas snorted at Bowe's strategy, which he figured no good journalist would believe. "You were planning a story on my client?" Futerfas asked Bowe. "When were you going to tell me this?"

"You never fucking called me back," Bowe said.

Futerfas said he was instructed not to call the president's lawyers. Bowe demanded to know who told him that. Futerfas said he wasn't going to say. Bowe was left to wonder. He picked up his wife, took her to City Island for a waterfront lunch, and tried to calm down. Bowe called Kasowitz to let him know about the shit their client had stepped in without the assistance of counsel. Kasowitz called Trump on his secure phone on Air Force One. Just before 3:00 p.m., the president consulted with his own attorney for the first time. The *Times* already had the misleading statement, and there was little the president's lawyer could do except listen to his client explain his strategy. Trump's version of events was now as good as written in stone. The *Times* published its story later that afternoon. Kasowitz got Trump's approval for a statement he would issue to *Circa*, alleging the meeting appeared to be an effort to entrap the Trump campaign, but that story line would immediately be overshadowed by the *Times* report of Trump family members meeting with Russians who wanted to hurt Hillary Clinton and help Trump.

Lowell read the story online with dismay. The statement issued from Air Force One was highly misleading at best. There was only one silver lining. The story zeroed in on the role of Trump junior, not on the failure once again of Kushner to disclose all of his foreign contacts. Lowell reached Kushner by phone on Air Force One at close to 6:00 p.m. and urged his client to deflect future questions about the meeting to Trump junior's team.

"Let's let this one fall to Don junior," Lowell told Kushner. "It's Don junior's meeting to tell."

At roughly 8:00 p.m., Air Force One touched down at Joint Base Andrews outside Washington. Trump's family members and advisers departed the aircraft exhausted and anxious. They knew the damage was done. The problem they scrambled to contain would only grow bigger. That night, Corallo was at the Masonic temple in Alexandria, Virginia, watching a fireworks show, when he received a call on his cell phone from an angry Hicks.

As Corallo recalled the conversation, Hicks asked him, "What are you guys doing? Who the hell is *Circa*?"

Corallo said he told Hicks the plan to provide information to *Circa* was approved by Trump's attorneys and he assumed they ran it by the president himself.

"I had it handled with *The New York Times*," Corallo said Hicks told him. "Now it's this blowup."

"You had it handled?" Corallo said he responded. "You work for the White House. You work for the president. You're a federal employee. Since when do you handle this stuff?" He added, "You just made yourself a witness in a federal investigation, young lady. Way to go."

Hicks knew she would be a witness regardless, considering her proximity to the president.

The next day, July 9, tensions were still running high. Corallo got a call from the White House. Trump and Hicks were on the other line. Accusations flew back and forth, according to Corallo's account of the conversation.

"Who authorized the statement to go out in my name?" Trump asked.

Corallo explained that the statement provided to *Circa* was not under Trump's name but rather in Corallo's name on behalf of the president's legal team.

"You guys made this a big story," Trump said.

"Mr. President, this was going to be a big story no matter what," Corallo replied. He added, "We really can't have this conversation without the attorneys. This is not a privileged conversation. You really need to have your attorneys on the line. Talk to them."

Hicks then told Corallo, "You guys really screwed this up. We had this all planned out. It was going to go away."

"The meeting was about adoption," Trump said, defending the statement he had dictated for his son.

Corallo felt a lump in his throat. He resented that Hicks was seeming to berate him in front of Trump, and he thought she was displaying a level of foolishness and arrogance that suggested she was not up to the job if she couldn't see the danger of providing a partial account. Hicks, meanwhile, was exasperated from several stressful days urging transparency and truthfulness in managing the crisis despite the president's insistence otherwise. And she believed the statement to *Circa* represented an egregious lapse in judgment. Rather than containing the fire, Hicks believed, Corallo and Kasowitz had poured gasoline on it. Corallo reiterated that it was unwise for them to continue the conversation without lawyers on the line, and everyone hung up.

At the same time, reporters from every news organization were pressing their sources to learn what prompted the June 2016 meeting. For the Trump team, the pressure to provide answers was intense. By midday on July 9, several reporters were hearing from their sources that the original purpose of the meeting was not Russian adoptions but an offer of incriminating information about Clinton. The *Times* had enough sources diming out Trump junior that Garten and Futerfas agreed it was best for their client to lay out the truthful account that they had unsuccessfully argued for the day before. So Trump junior issued a statement to the *Times* explaining that he had met with Veselnitskaya at the request of a mutual acquaintance from the 2013 Miss Universe pageant, which his father had hosted in Moscow.

"After pleasantries were exchanged," Trump junior said, "the woman stated that she had information that individuals connected to Russia were funding the Democratic National Committee and supporting Mrs. Clinton. Her statements were vague, ambiguous and made no sense. No details or supporting information was provided or even offered. It quickly became clear that she had no meaningful information."

Trump junior went on to say that Veselnitskaya redirected the conversation to adoption of Russian children and the Magnitsky Act. "It became clear to me that this was the true agenda all along and that the claims of potentially helpful information were a pretext for the meeting," Trump junior's statement said.

Revoking the 2012 Magnitsky Act, a little-known law, was actually one of Putin's biggest priorities. The U.S. legislation had infuriated Putin because it froze the assets and limited the travel of a circle of powerful Russian businessmen he relied upon as extensions of his own power. In retaliation, Putin had halted American adoptions of Russian children. Whenever Putin raised the issue of Russian adoptions, it was really code for his jihad to revoke the meddlesome U.S. sanctions. But when Veselnitskaya raised the "adoptions" code word with Trump junior at Trump Tower in June 2016, it sailed right over his head.

Inside the West Wing, tempers flared as aides realized the magnitude of the cover-up. The story only got worse. The morning of July 11, the White House learned the *Times* now had a copy of Trump junior's original email exchange with Goldstone proposing the meeting with Veselnitskaya, just as Hicks had warned the president would happen. Trump junior was normally a cool customer, but now his emotions were running high, alternating between fury at the media and misery. He and his father had faced three straight days of withering news coverage because of a meeting he agreed to take and were now about to take another hit for the fourth day in a row. Reporters and lawyers would later joke that the way the president and his aides mishandled the Trump Tower story could be the case study of a graduate seminar on how not to manage crisis communications. After long existing in the shadow of his superstar younger sister whom their father openly favored, Trump junior had enjoyed playing a valued role in the campaign, but revelations about the Trump Tower meeting made him a liability to his dad.

Trump junior and his lawyers, all in New York, agreed to hurriedly get on a conference call with the president, who was in his private chambers in the White House residence, and several other lawyers and aides. It was a quick conversation. The son had to explain to Trump the bombshell about to hit about the embarrassing emails. The president listened intently, interrupting once in a while with a groan. "I'm really sorry about this, Dad," Trump junior said.

Trump made clear he wasn't happy, but did not acknowledge that he had caused much of the problem himself by dictating the misleading statement. "It's a fucking mess," Trump said. "It's interfering with my agenda. This is screwing up what I'm trying to do."

Then the president, his son, and their advisers debated whether to release all the emails or only a portion. Trump junior and his lawyers recommended all of them.

"The rest of them are going to leak anyway," Trump junior said. Trump agreed.

"Fuck it," the president declared. "Publish them all."

After he hung up, at a little after 10:00 a.m., Trump tweeted a defense of his son for the world to see: "Most politicians would have gone to a meeting like the one Don jr attended in order to get info on an opponent. That's politics!"

Trump junior, meanwhile, uploaded images of all sixteen emails among him and Goldstone, Kushner, and Manafort about the June 2016 meeting with Veselnitskaya. At 11:00 a.m., Trump junior published them on Twitter. He had scooped the *Times*.

Trump was furious about the mess that had transpired over the past four days. At a White House meeting with some advisers, according to Corallo, Trump tore into Corallo again, now blaming him for leaking details of the emails to the *Times*, which Corallo denied.

"Are you one of these Never Trumpers?" the president asked his legal communications adviser.

"Mr. President, I voted for you. I supported you," Corallo replied. "That doesn't mean I'm going to agree with everything you do, but I serve at your pleasure. You can dismiss me at any point."

Corallo was crushed. Somehow, he had become the fall guy. He was looking for an out, and he found one a week later. On July 19, Trump ripped into Attorney General Jeff Sessions, questioned the loyalty of Deputy Attorney General Rod Rosenstein, and disparaged Mueller's probe during an interview with Peter Baker, Michael Schmidt, and Maggie Haberman of the *Times*. The interview was a turning point in how Corallo viewed Trump. He considered Sessions, Rosenstein, and Mueller honest public servants who did not deserve to be trashed. Trump had made his job untenable. Corallo called Bowe.

"I'm done," he said.

"Yeah," Bowe replied. "I totally get it."

Corallo resigned from the legal team without so much as a presidential tweet thanking him for his service.

Behind the scenes, a quiet internal Justice Department investigation about the handling of the Clinton email investigation was learning about some soap-opera-style impropriety between a pair of FBI officials, a discovery that would forever tarnish the Mueller probe. Though the two officials' extramarital affair and careless texts long predated Mueller's appointment, their seeming political bias against Trump while launching an investigation of his campaign was used to smear the entire probe. On July 27, Inspector General Michael Horowitz convened a group of senior Justice and FBI officials to alert them to the texts he had uncovered between the senior counterintelligence supervisor Peter Strzok and the FBI lawyer Lisa Page. Their exchanges had made it appear that some in the FBI hoped to stop Trump from becoming president. Strzok was then working on Mueller's team; the FBI immediately yanked him off based on the embarrassing texts.

Trump didn't yet know the full details about the exchanges, but he and his allies in Congress were already bashing Mueller's team as politically tainted Democrats trying to undermine his presidency. Outside the secure conference room at the Justice Department command center where the inspector general had briefed everyone on the texts, Rosenstein pulled Mueller aside in the hallway to apologize. He felt badly that a national hero was getting assailed by the president and lawmakers whose idea of public service was appearing on television and tweeting. He knew the texts, when they came out, would only make Mueller's job harder.

"I'm really sorry I got you into this," Rosenstein said.

Mueller waved it off. "I would've really regretted it if I hadn't agreed to do it," he said.

Nine

SHOCKING
THE CONSCIENCE

Here is no more sacred military space than room 2E924 of the Pentagon. A windowless and secure vault of a conference room where the Joint Chiefs of Staff meet regularly to wrestle with classified matters, its more common name is "the Tank." It got its name from the Joint Chiefs' original meeting location during World War II, in the basement of a federal building on Constitution Avenue in Washington, where attendees had to walk through an austere arched portal with exposed wires that gave the impression of entering a tank. Unlike the command centers conjured in Hollywood thrillers, the Tank at the Pentagon resembles a small corporate boardroom, with midcentury stylings including a gleaming golden oak table and leather swivel armchairs. The room, saturated by history, also is known as the Gold Room for its thick carpeting and ornate drapery.

Uniformed officers think of the Tank a bit like a church. Inside its walls, flag officers observe a reverence and decorum for the wrenching decisions that have been made here. To sit at its table is a great honor. The room is controlled by four-star generals, not the president's civilian appointees, and it is a safe space for them to speak candidly without intrusions from the political dramas of the day. The Tank is reserved for serious discussions of military tactics. Here is where matters of war and peace are determined, where the Joint Chiefs decide to send young men and women to their deaths.

Hanging prominently on one of the walls, along with the American flag and the banners of the military branches, was *The Peacemakers*, a painting that depicted a historic meeting of a president and his three service chiefs: an 1865 Civil War strategy session with President Abraham Lincoln, Lieutenant General Ulysses S. Grant, Major General William Tecumseh Sherman, and Rear Admiral David Dixon Porter. One hundred fifty-two years after Lincoln hatched plans to preserve the Union, President Trump's advisers staged an intervention inside the Tank to preserve the world order. The July 20, 2017, meeting in the Tank has been documented numerous times, most memorably by Bob Woodward in *Fear*, but subsequent reporting reveals a more complete picture of the moment and the chilling effect Trump's comments and hostility had on the nation's military and national security leadership.

Secretary of Defense Jim Mattis, Director of the National Economic Council Gary Cohn, and Secretary of State Rex Tillerson had grown alarmed over the first six months of the Trump administration by gaping holes in the president's knowledge of history and of the alliances forged in the wake of World War II that served as the foundation of America's strength in the world. Trump had unnerved trusted friends by dismissing existing relations with Western democracies as worthless, including by questioning the value of NATO, while cultivating friendlier ones with Russia and other authoritarian regimes. He wanted to tear up trade deals to squeeze more out of partners. And he advocated withdrawing troops not only from active theaters like Afghanistan but also from strategic outposts like South Korea, where U.S. forces were helping keep the peace, complaining that the military presence around the world was a waste of billions of dollars.

Trump organized his unorthodox worldview under the simplistic banner of "America First," but Mattis, Tillerson, and Cohn feared his proposals were rash, barely considered, and a danger to America's super-power standing. They also felt that many of Trump's impulsive ideas—and their continuing difficulty communicating U.S. interests abroad with the president—stemmed from his lack of familiarity with U.S. history, and even with the map of the world. Cohn had confided to his peers he had been surprised at the many gaps in Trump's understanding of world affairs. To have a useful discussion with him, the trio agreed, they had to lay a foundation with Trump and create a basic knowledge, a shared language. So on July 20, Mattis invited Trump to the Tank for what he, Tillerson, and Cohn had carefully organized as a tailored tutorial on the state of the world and America's interests abroad.

The meeting was billed as a briefing on Afghanistan, because Trump was in the midst of developing a long-term strategy to defeat the Islamic State there, but in reality the session was to be a gentle lesson on American power, with the president as a student. The organizers viewed it as a course correction, an intervention to educate Trump and give him some fundamentals for analyzing the world.

The Tank was selected as the venue because Trump was impressed by the room when he first visited it in January 2017, telling advisers that it was cool and classic, a relic from an earlier era. He marveled at the idea that he, Donald Trump, sat in the same room where commanders in chief before him had drawn up war plans. If it hadn't been across the Potomac River in Virginia and such a schlep from the White House, Trump would have liked to have held all his national security meetings there.

On July 20, just before 10:00 a.m. on a scorching summer Thursday, Trump arrived at the Pentagon. He stepped out of his motorcade, walked along a corridor with portraits honoring former chairmen of the Joint Chiefs, and stepped inside the Tank. The uniformed officers greeted their commander in chief. Chairman of the Joint Chiefs General Joseph Dunford sat in the seat of honor midway down the table, because this was his room, and Trump sat at the head of the table facing a projection screen. Mattis and the newly confirmed deputy defense secretary, Patrick Shanahan, sat to the president's left, with Vice President Pence and Tillerson to his right. Down the table sat the leaders of the military branches, along with Cohn and Secretary of the Treasury Steven Mnuchin. Steve Bannon was in the outer ring of chairs with other staff, taking his seat just behind Mattis and directly in Trump's line of sight.

At one end of the room, opposite Trump, an opaque screen hung on the wall for the slide projections to come, with another sliding screen showing maps of different parts of the world. Mattis, Cohn, and Tillerson and their aides decided to use maps, graphics, and charts to tutor the president, figuring they would help keep him from getting bored.

In his regular intelligence briefings, Trump would ravenously ingest glinting nuggets and latch onto names he recognized or hot spots he knew from the news, but he would not read written materials or have the patience for lectures. So his briefers would huddle around the Resolute Desk and show Trump maps and charts and pictures and videos, as well as "killer graphics," as CIA director Mike Pompeo described them. One surefire way to get Trump's attention, they found, was to feature his name somewhere in the text. "That's our task, right? To deliver the material in a way that he can best understand the information we're trying to communicate," Pompeo said.

Mattis opened the July 20 Tank meeting with a slideshow, sprinkled with charts and maps and punctuated by lots of dollar signs. Mattis devised a strategy to use terms the impatient president, schooled in real estate, would appreciate to impress upon him the value of U.S. investments abroad. He sought to explain why U.S. troops were deployed in so many regions and why America's safety hinged on a complex web of trade deals, alliances, and bases across the globe. Normally, trade wouldn't be considered relevant to a national security briefing, but Trump, unlike past presidents, directly connected trade agreements and treaties with foreign countries to the overall power dynamic. To Trump, America's economic power was part of its military might. If another country was imposing tariffs on U.S. goods, he reasoned, it was taking advantage of and disrespecting the United States and therefore should lose the security blanket that U.S. troops provided. An opening line flashed on the screen, setting the tone: "The post-war international rules-based order is the greatest gift of the greatest generation." Mattis then gave a twenty-minute briefing on the power of the NATO alliance to stabilize Europe and keep the United States safe. Bannon thought to himself, "Not good.

Trump is not going to like that one bit." The internationalist language Mattis was using was a trigger for Trump.

"Oh, baby, this is going to be fucking wild," Bannon thought. "If you stood up and threatened to shoot [Trump], he couldn't say 'postwar rules-based international order.' It's just not the way he thinks."

For the next ninety minutes, Mattis, Tillerson, and Cohn took turns trying to emphasize their points, pointing to their charts and diagrams. They showed where U.S. personnel were positioned, at military bases, CIA stations, and embassies, and how U.S. deployments fended off the threats of terror cells, nuclear blasts, and destabilizing enemies in places including Afghanistan, Iran, Iraq, the Korea Peninsula, and Syria. Cohn spoke for about twenty minutes about the value of free trade with America's allies, emphasizing how he saw each trade agreement working together as part of an overall structure to solidify U.S. economic and national security.

Trump appeared peeved by the schoolhouse vibe but also allergic to the dynamic of his advisers talking at him. His ricocheting attention span led him to repeatedly interrupt the lesson. He heard an adviser say a word or phrase and then seized on that to interject with his take. For instance, the word "base" prompted him to launch in to say how "crazy" and "stupid" it was to pay for bases in some countries.

Trump's first complaint was to repeat what he had vented about to his national security adviser months earlier: South Korea should pay for a $10 billion missile defense system that the United States built for it. The system was designed to shoot down any short- and medium-range ballistic missiles from North Korea to protect South Korea and American troops stationed there. But Trump argued that the South Koreans should pay for it, proposing that the administration pull U.S. troops out of the region or bill the South Koreans for their protection.

"We should charge them rent," Trump said of South Korea. "We should make them pay for our soldiers. We should make money off of everything."

Trump said U.S. troops and defense systems in South Korea did not make Americans safer. He said he could eliminate the nuclear threat on the peninsula simply by striking a deal with North Korean dictator Kim Jong Un. "This is all about leader versus leader. Man versus man. Me versus Kim," he said.

Trump proceeded to explain that NATO, too, was worthless. U.S. generals were letting the allied member countries get away with murder, he said, and they owed the United States a lot of money after not living up to their promise of paying their dues.

"They're in arrears," Trump said, reverting to the language of real estate. He lifted both his arms at his sides in frustration. Then he scolded top officials for the untold millions of dollars he believed they had let slip through their fingers by allowing allies to avoid their obligations.

"We are owed money you haven't been collecting!" Trump told them. "You would totally go bankrupt if you had to run your own business."

Mattis wasn't trying to convince the president of anything, only to explain and provide facts. Now things were devolving quickly. The general tried to calmly explain to the president that he was not quite right. The NATO allies didn't owe the United States back rent, he said. The truth was more complicated. NATO had a nonbinding goal that members should pay at least 2 percent of their gross domestic product on their defenses. Only five of the countries currently met that goal, but it wasn't as if they were shorting the United States on the bill.

More broadly, Mattis argued, the NATO alliance was not serving only to protect western Europe. It protected America, too. "This is what keeps us safe," Mattis said. Cohn tried to explain to Trump that he needed to see the value of the trade deals. "These are commitments that help keep us safe," Cohn said.

Bannon interjected. "Stop, stop, stop," he said. "All you guys talk about all these great things, they're all our partners, I want you to name me now one country and one company that's going to have his back."

Trump then disputed every point Cohn had made advocating the benefits of existing trade agreements.

"Gary, I don't want to hear about free trade," Trump said. "We're upside down. They're ripping us off. All the jobs are gone. They're ripping us off."

The president added, "I want reciprocal trade deals where it's balanced. I want these guys to start picking up the load. We can't keep doing this."

Trump then repeated a threat he'd made countless times before. He wanted out of the Iran nuclear deal that President Obama had struck in 2015, which called for Iran to eliminate its uranium stockpile and cut its nuclear weaponry.

"It's the worst deal in history!" Trump declared.

"Well, actually . . . ," Tillerson interjected.

"I don't want to hear it," Trump said, cutting off the secretary of state before he could explain some of the benefits of the agreement. "They're cheating. They're building. We're getting out of it. I keep telling you, I keep giving you time, and you keep delaying me. I want out of it."

Before they could debate the Iran deal, Trump erupted to revive another frequent complaint: the war in Afghanistan, which was now America's longest war. He demanded an explanation for why the United States hadn't won in Afghanistan yet, now sixteen years after the nation began fighting there in the wake of the 9/11 terror attacks. Trump unleashed his disdain, calling Afghanistan a "loser war." That phrase hung in the air and disgusted not only the military leaders at the table but also the men and women in uniform sitting along the back wall behind their principals. They all were sworn to obey their commander in chief's commands, and here he was calling the war they had been fighting a loser war.

"You're all losers," Trump said. "You don't know how to win anymore."

Trump questioned why the United States couldn't get some oil as payment for the troops stationed in the Persian Gulf. "We spent $7 trillion; they're ripping us off," Trump boomed. "Where is the fucking oil?"

Trump seemed to be speaking up for the voters who elected him, and several attendees thought they heard Bannon in Trump's words. Bannon had been trying to persuade Trump to withdraw forces by telling him, "The American people are saying we can't spend a trillion dollars a year on this. We just can't. It's going to bankrupt us. And not just that, the deplorables don't want their kids in the South China Sea at the 38th parallel or in Syria, in Afghanistan, in perpetuity."

Trump mused about removing General John Nicholson, the U.S. commander in charge of troops in Afghanistan. "I don't think he knows how to win," the president said, impugning Nicholson, who was not present at the meeting.

Dunford tried to come to Nicholson's defense, but the mild-mannered general struggled to convey his points to the irascible president.

"Mr. President, that's just not . . . ," Dunford started. "We've been under different orders."

Dunford sought to explain that he hadn't been charged with annihilating the enemy in Afghanistan but was instead following a strategy started by the Obama administration to gradually reduce the military presence in the country in hopes of training locals to maintain a stable government so that eventually the United States could pull out. Trump shot back in more plain language.

"I want to win," he said. "We don't win any wars anymore. . . . We spend $7 trillion, everybody else got the oil and we're not winning anymore."

Trump by now was in one of his rages. He was so angry that he wasn't taking many breaths. All morning, he had been coarse and cavalier, but the next several things he bellowed went beyond that description. They stunned nearly everyone in the room, and some vowed that they would never repeat them.

"I wouldn't go to war with you people," Trump told the assembled brass.

Addressing the room, the commander in chief barked, "You're a bunch of dopes and babies."

For a president known for verbiage he euphemistically called "locker room talk," this was the gravest insult he could have delivered to these people, in this sacred space. The flag officers in the room were shocked. Some staff began looking down at their papers, rearranging folders, almost wishing themselves out of the room. A few considered walking out.

They tried not to reveal their revulsion on their faces, but questions raced through their minds. "How does the commander in chief say that?" one thought. "What would our worst adversaries think if they knew he said this?"

This was a president who had been labeled a "draft dodger" for avoiding service in the Vietnam War under questionable circumstances. Trump was a young man born of privilege and in seemingly perfect health: six feet two inches with a muscular build and a flawless medical record. He played several sports, including football. Then, in 1968 at age twenty-two, he obtained a diagnosis of bone spurs in his heels that exempted him from military service just as the United States was drafting men his age to fulfill massive troop deployments to Vietnam.

Tillerson in particular was stunned by Trump's diatribe and began visibly seething. For too many minutes, others in the room noticed, he had been staring straight, dumbfounded, at Mattis, who was speechless, his head bowed down toward the table. Tillerson thought to himself, "Gosh darn it, Jim, say something. Why aren't you saying something?" But, as he would later tell close aides, Tillerson realized in that moment that Mattis was genetically a marine, unable to talk back to his commander in chief, no matter what nonsense came out of his mouth.

The more perplexing silence was from Pence, a leader who should have been able to stand up to Trump. Instead, one attendee thought, "He's sitting there frozen like a statue. Why doesn't he stop the president?" Another recalled the vice president was "a wax museum guy." From the start of the meeting, Pence looked as if he wanted to escape and put an end to the president's torrent. Surely, he disagreed with Trump's characterization of military leaders as "dopes and babies," considering his son, Michael, was a marine first lieutenant then training for his naval aviator wings. But some surmised Pence feared getting crosswise with Trump. "A total deer in the headlights," recalled a third attendee.

Others at the table noticed Trump's stream of venom had taken an emotional toll. So many people in that room had gone to war and risked their lives for their country, and now they were being dressed down by a president who had not. They felt sick to their stomachs. Tillerson told others he thought he saw a woman in the room silently crying. He was furious and decided he couldn't stand it another minute. His voice broke into Trump's tirade, this one about trying to make money off U.S. troops.

"No, that's just wrong," the secretary of state said. "Mr. President, you're totally wrong. None of that is true."

Tillerson's father and great-uncle had both been combat veterans, and he was deeply proud of their service.

"The men and women who put on a uniform don't do it to become soldiers of fortune," Tillerson said. "That's not why they put on a uniform and go out and die. . . . They do it to protect our freedom."

There was silence in the Tank. Several military officers in the room were grateful to the secretary of state for defending them when no one else would. The meeting soon ended and Trump walked out, saying goodbye to a group of servicemen lining the corridor as he made his way to his motorcade waiting outside. Mattis, Tillerson, and Cohn were deflated. Standing in the hall with a small cluster of people he trusted, Tillerson finally let down his guard.

"He's a fucking moron," the secretary of state said of the president.

The plan by Mattis, Tillerson, and Cohn to train the president to appreciate the internationalist view had clearly backfired.

"We were starting to get out on the wrong path, and we really needed to have a course correction and needed to educate, to teach, to help him understand the reason and basis for a lot of these things," said one senior official involved in the planning. "We needed to change how he thinks about this, to course correct. Everybody was on board, 100 percent agreed with that sentiment. [But] they were dismayed and in shock when not only did it not have the intended effect, but he dug in his heels and pushed it even further on the spectrum, further solidifying his views."

A few days later, Pence's national security adviser, Andrea Thompson, a retired army colonel who had served in Afghanistan and Iraq, reached out to thank Tillerson for speaking up on behalf of the military and the public servants who had been in the Tank. By September, she would leave the White House and join Tillerson at Foggy Bottom as undersecretary of state for arms control and international security affairs.

The Tank meeting had so thoroughly shocked the conscience of military leaders that they tried to keep it a secret. At the Aspen Security Forum two days later, longtime NBC News correspondent Andrea Mitchell asked Dunford how Trump had interacted during the Tank meeting. The Joint Chiefs chairman misleadingly described the meeting, skipping over the fireworks.

"He asked a lot of hard questions, and the one thing he does is question some fundamental assumptions that we make as military leaders—and he will come in and question those," Dunford told Mitchell on July 22. "It's a pretty energetic and an interactive dialogue."

One victim of the Tank meeting was Trump's relationship with Tillerson, which forever after was strained. The secretary of state came to see it as the beginning of the end. It would only worsen when news that Tillerson had called Trump a "moron" was reported in October by NBC News.

The following weekend, Attorney General Jeff Sessions was back in the president's crosshairs. He was under scrutiny anew for his two 2016 conversations with Russian ambassador Sergei Kislyak. On July 21, *The Washington Post* reported that U.S. intelligence agencies had intercepted Kislyak's accounts of the conversations to his superiors in Moscow, telling them that he and Sessions had discussed matters related to the Trump campaign. This was important because Sessions had denied discussing the campaign with Kislyak.

Again, the news coverage triggered a spasm of fury from Trump, who in conversations with advisers had called the attorney general "fucking worthless," a "fucking idiot," a "fucking jerk off," a "fucking moron," and a "fuck head." Trump had been openly imitating Sessions's Alabama drawl and mocking him for being portrayed by a woman, Kate McKinnon, on *Saturday Night Live.*

On July 22, Trump traveled to Newport News, Virginia, to attend the commissioning ceremony for the USS *Gerald R. Ford*, the navy's newest battleship. Aboard Marine One, as they choppered onto the ship, Trump gave Reince Priebus an order. "We gotta get rid of Jeff," Trump told his chief of staff. "You have to get his resignation, and don't give me any of this slow-me-down Reince bullshit, either. You've got to get it."

Trump told Priebus to write down his reason for forcing the attorney general's resignation: "The American people cannot withstand any more of this," referring to negative publicity. Treasury secretary Steven Mnuchin and White House senior policy adviser Stephen Miller, the former Sessions protégé, both were on board the helicopter and said nothing to try to talk the president out of the rash action. At one point, Trump asked Mnuchin what he thought of removing Sessions, and Mnuchin told the president he agreed. Priebus was alone in trying to stop the president.

On board the battleship, Priebus hovered backstage calling White House counsel Don McGahn to figure out what he should do. He knew it would be disastrous to follow Trump's orders. Regardless, Jody Hunt, the attorney general's chief of staff, had already told Priebus that Sessions would not quit and would have to be fired. So Priebus and McGahn decided to slow walk Trump. After the ceremony, Trump followed up with Priebus about the resignation letter. "Did you get it?" the president asked. Priebus persuaded Trump to hold off. The next day was Sunday, and he said the president would not want the ouster to dominate the Sunday political talk shows. "Let's deal with this tomorrow," Priebus told him. Trump relented. Over the next few days, Trump's complaints to other advisers about Priebus being too "weak" would reach a fever pitch. "If we heard it once, we heard it 20 times [that] week, this erosion of confidence," recalled a senior White House official. "The word was 'weak'—'weak,' 'weak,' 'weak.' Can't get it done."

On Monday, July 24, with no action taken against Sessions, Trump took to Twitter to vent. In a 7:49 a.m. missive, the president admonished "our beleaguered A.G." For Sessions and his aides, the tweet was devastating. Over the next twenty-four hours, the media were on Sessions's death watch. The next afternoon, shortly after 3:00, Trump strode out to the Rose Garden for a news conference. The Justice Department's senior leadership gathered in the attorney general's office to watch on television. Sessions and his deputies thought he would use the occasion to announce his firing. The president called on Margaret Talev of Bloomberg News, who stood up to ask her question: "Your, kind of, catch-phrase or motto before the White House was, 'You're fired.' So I'm wondering if you would talk to us a little bit about whether you've lost confidence in Jeff Sessions, whether you want him to resign on his own, whether you're prepared to fire him if he doesn't, and why you're sort of letting him twist in the wind rather than just making the call for him."

Watching on television, Sessions was calm. He leaned back in his desk chair as if he were watching a football game. Hunt had his hand over his mouth. Rachel Brand, the department's No. 3 who was considered a possible successor, focused intently. Noel Francisco, the solicitor general, held his hand to his head. And the attorney general's spokeswoman, Sarah Isgur Flores, and legislative affairs chief, Stephen Boyd, both leaned forward in anticipation of what the president would say.

"Well, I don't think I am doing that, but I am disappointed in the attorney general," Trump said. "He should not have recused himself almost immediately after he took office. And if he was going to recuse himself, he should have told me prior to taking office, and I would have, quite simply, picked somebody else. So I think that's a bad thing not for the president, but for the presidency. I think it's unfair to the presidency. And that's the way I feel."

Sessions had survived to live another day. But in the days that followed, he and his aides made plans for a "Saturday Night Massacre," a reference to the series of Justice Department resignations triggered by President Nixon's 1973 order that his attorney general fire the Watergate independent special prosecutor. They prepared for several scenarios: if Trump fired Sessions, if Trump fired Rosenstein, and if Trump ordered the firing of Mueller. Senior officials considered whether they would resign, too, and some had even drafted resignation letters. For instance,

Hunt later told the special counsel that Sessions prepared a resignation letter during this period and for the rest of the year carried it in his pocket every time he visited the White House. At times, aides joked that the planning for a Saturday Night Massacre resembled 1950s nuclear drills: *Get under your desk! Duck! Cover!*

Rosenstein warned the White House that the Justice Department building would effectively clear out within an hour of any such move by Trump. His objective was to instill fear of a mass exodus that could be politically crippling for the president. Secretly, however, Rosenstein and the team developed a different plan. Whether to stay or quit was dependent on each person's conscience, of course, but it was important to Rosenstein that enough senior people remain in their jobs to protect the Justice Department and the integrity of the special counsel investigation. He and his team warned Brand to constantly be ready to assume control at a moment's notice. If Trump named her acting attorney general, the plan was for Brand to hold a news conference within forty-five minutes to reassure public confidence in the probe.

Rosenstein told Brand around this time that there was a good chance he would get fired, and if she took over the Russia investigation, the most important thing to do would be to buy herself time and to not act immediately on any White House orders. He said she should consult right away with the three officials under him who were up to speed on the probe. "It's under control," he told Brand. "It's not a witch hunt. It's not a fishing expedition. We're monitoring it closely. We're meeting with Mueller's team every other week. If I get fired, my advice to you is, whatever they tell you, tell them, 'I need time to sort this all out.'"

On July 24, Sessions and Priebus were not the only advisers to draw Trump's attention. Jared Kushner publicly defended his 2016 meeting with the Russian lawyer at Trump Tower, saying, "I did not collude with Russia," and insisting that all of his actions during the campaign were "proper." Because Kushner's appearance in the West Wing driveway was his first on-camera press statement, it was covered as major news, and the president tuned in. "Jared looks like a little boy," Trump told other advisers.

Ever since the Trump Tower meeting story broke on July 8, Trump had been feeling sorry for his daughter Ivanka and Kushner. He thought they were being unfairly maligned in the news media, and he feared they could suffer from Mueller's glare. He was convinced they were being targeted not for their own misdeeds or failures of judgment but because they were members of his family.

"You guys should have never come here," Trump told Ivanka and Kushner around this time, in the presence of other White House advisers. "You see what kind of a mess this is? You're getting killed. Why would you come here? There's a better life back in New York. I don't understand why you want to stay here."

July 24 turned out to be an eventful Monday for Trump. He flew to Mount Hope, West Virginia, to address the annual Boy Scout Jamboree. Some forty thousand boys, ranging in age from twelve to eighteen, assembled under the hot summer sun to hear inspiring words from their president. Onstage in West Virginia, Trump described Washington as a "cesspool"; attacked President Obama; trashed Hillary Clinton; threatened to fire Secretary of Health and Human Services Tom Price; lambasted the "fake news" media; mocked pollsters; and told a meandering tale about a famous home builder who frequented the Manhattan cocktail party circuit and engaged in "interesting" activities aboard his yacht, which he left to the boys' imaginations. "Should I tell you?" Trump asked, teasing the crowd. "Oh, you're Boy Scouts, but you know life. You know life."

As Trump rambled off script, speaking for thirty-five minutes in total, his aides cringed. Standing at attention behind him were two former Boy Scouts in his cabinet, Secretary of the Interior Ryan Zinke and Secretary of Energy Rick Perry, but two others, Tillerson and Sessions, were not included on the trip. Zinke wore a scouting uniform, which White House aides mocked as a "Smokey the Bear" costume and said made the former Navy SEAL look absurd. At one point in his remarks, Trump reflected on Boy Scout values, saying, "As the Scouts law says, a Scout is trustworthy, loyal—we could use some more loyalty, I will tell you that."

The boys then chanted ten other attributes in Boy Scout law: "Helpful, friendly, courteous, kind, obedient, cheerful, thrifty, brave, clean, and reverent." But the president did not easily embody a single one. The head of the Boy Scouts of America later apologized to scouting families who were offended by the president's comments.

Four days later, July 28, Trump provoked similar outrage from his critics when he addressed a gathering of law enforcement officers at Suffolk County Community College in New York. The president used stark language in describing the violent transnational gang MS-13 to effectively approve of police brutality in combating illegal immigration. He said when police throw "these thugs" into the backs of paddy wagons, "Please don't be too nice. . . .

"When you guys put somebody in the car and you're protecting their head, you know, the way you put their hand over, like, don't hit their head, and they just killed somebody—don't hit their head," Trump said. He mimed an officer shielding a suspect's head from hitting the police vehicle. "I said, 'You can take the hand away, okay?'"

A number of police officers attending Trump's event chuckled and applauded. The scene led the Suffolk County Police Department to distance itself by tweeting, "We do not and will not tolerate roughing up of prisoners."

In Washington, Chuck Rosenberg, the acting administrator of the Drug Enforcement Administration, watched the speech with horror. The career prosecutor, already disgusted by Trump's treatment of his friend Jim Comey, felt he had to say something to make clear that law enforcement agents would reject the president's coarse proposal. Rosenberg sent an all-staff memo to DEA personnel mentioning Trump's remarks and assuring them he trusted they would continue to respect defendants' rights and conduct themselves with integrity.

"The President, in remarks delivered yesterday in New York, condoned police misconduct regarding the treatment of individuals placed under arrest by law enforcement," Rosenberg's memo said. "So why do I write? I write to offer a strong reaffirmation of the operating principles to which we, as law enforcement professionals, adhere. I write because we have an obligation to speak out when something is wrong."

"You know you can't do that," Rosenstein, who oversaw the DEA administrator at the Justice Department, told Rosenberg after reading his email. Rosenberg was a career employee, not an appointee, so Trump could not summarily fire him. Still, his position was untenable. Rosenberg would stay at the DEA a while longer and announce his resignation on September 26, 2017.

On the flight home on July 28 from Long Island after his rough-'em-up speech to cops, Trump roughed up one of his own in humiliating fashion. When Air Force One touched down at Joint Base Andrews early that Friday evening, while most of his staffers deplaned the president stayed in his cabin and pecked out a tweet: "I am pleased to inform you that I have just named General/Secretary John F Kelly as White House Chief of Staff."

Priebus, who had been on board, was fired. Just like that. Priebus walked across the tarmac in the drenching rain and tucked into a black government SUV, which ferried him off alone, separate from the presidential motorcade, with no fanfare. Minutes later, when Trump stepped off the plane, he shouted at reporters from beneath a giant umbrella, "Reince is a good man."

Trump had had his eyes on Kelly for a while. After firing Comey in May, the president had asked Kelly to be FBI director. Kelly had declined, saying he preferred to stay as homeland security secretary, but he had observed to Trump that he had been poorly served by his staff because they had let him fire the FBI director without a Plan B. That conversation stuck with Trump, and the last week of July he asked Kelly to step in as chief of staff. Kelly asked to take the weekend to consider the offer, but the president was too impatient. He tweeted Kelly's appointment before he had agreed to take the job.

Priebus had been in an impossible position. Despite tireless efforts, he never could manage to assert control over basic White House functions, such as communications and policy development, in large part because of the president's impulses. Trump never fully empowered Priebus, either, allowing Bannon, Kushner, and Ivanka to operate as independent forces outside the chief of staff's authority. Priebus complained to friends that he often felt demeaned by the president's treatment of him. Trump had undermined Priebus by calling him "Reince-y." When they flew to Priebus's hometown of Kenosha, Wisconsin, for an April manufacturing event, the chief of staff peered out the window of Air Force One and spotted his home down below. The president mocked him for it. These episodes illustrated what some of Trump's subordinates considered his cruelty as a manager. He was willing—eager, really—to belittle the people working for him.

Ten

UNHINGED

The morning of Monday, July 31, John Kelly was sworn in as chief of staff in a small, private ceremony in the Oval Office. Kelly had just run homeland security, a bureaucratic behemoth overseeing a number of competitive agencies, each with its own individual culture. A former combat veteran whose valor on the battlefield had been chronicled in books, Kelly won at first the respect of Trump's staff, including even Ivanka Trump and Jared Kushner. "This is the eleventh time I've taken this oath to defend the Constitution and I want everybody here to know I'm here to defend the Constitution and to defend the rule of law," Kelly told the other officials in attendance. When he later addressed the larger staff, in the soaring lobby of the Eisenhower Executive Office Building, he pointed out that the oath "doesn't say anything in there about being loyal to the president. It doesn't say anything in there about the GOP being more important than your integrity."

Kelly's first chore was deciding what to do with communications director Anthony Scaramucci, fifty-three. The flashy Manhattan financier, who called himself the Mooch, was friends with the president and had been recruited as communications director by Ivanka and Kushner in part to help oust Reince Priebus. Scaramucci unloaded on Priebus and Steve Bannon in an expletive-filled interview with *The New Yorker*'s Ryan Lizza that was conducted on July 26 and published the next day.

Minutes before Kelly's July 31 swearing-in ceremony, Scaramucci approached the defense secretary in the West Wing lobby. "Hey, General Mattis," he said. "I know you're close to Kelly. Can you get me a meeting with him? He won't see me."

Startled, Mattis replied, "Maybe you ought to talk to his scheduler."

"Oh, no," Scaramucci said. "They're blowing me off. General, you don't understand."

Mattis tap-danced away from the request. Later that day, Kelly fired Scaramucci. He lasted just eleven days on the job.

July 31 also was Ty Cobb's first day in the White House as special counsel for the Russia investigation. Cobb was not personally representing Trump, but was brought in to oversee the White House's involvement in the probe, in part because Don McGahn had recused himself and most of the lawyers in his shop from the investigation because some of them were now witnesses.

On his first day, Cobb came to learn that such distinctions were rather blurry in Trump's world. Cobb was filling out administrative paperwork and preparing to move into his new office when two senior officials raised the same request. McGahn and Bannon both asked for Cobb's help removing Kushner and Ivanka from the White House staff. Each of them tried to convince Cobb that this was the most important way to protect the president.

McGahn, who was already on bad terms with the president because of his refusal to comply with some of his demands, including to ask Rosenstein about having Robert Mueller removed as special counsel, told Cobb he needed to persuade Trump about the problems his daughter and son-in-law created. Bannon was more forceful, stressing the many obstacles they presented. "You need to shoot them in the fucking head," Bannon jokingly told Cobb.

Cobb was wary of making any snap decisions this early. But Cobb's view was also partly shaped by a careful reading of the palace intrigue.

Priebus had just been fired, and Bannon might be the next to go, while McGahn had an especially prickly relationship with the president and the kids. Cobb reasoned that he could not get his job done without the support of Kushner and Ivanka, and he came to like and trust them.

Cobb had his own instant tensions with McGahn, who had lobbied Trump to appoint other lawyers for Cobb's job. Cobb's first big task was reviewing documents and submitting them to Mueller's team. But he did not initially have a staff, and McGahn initially would not lend him lawyers to help. Cobb learned on his first day that McGahn had been trying to deny Cobb the premium West Wing office Trump had promised him. By September, however, Cobb would have as a deputy Steven Groves, an able lawyer and skilled strategist who had been U.S. ambassador Nikki Haley's chief of staff at the United Nations.

On August 1, his second day at work, Cobb called James Quarles, Mueller's deputy who was in charge of the special counsel's interactions with the White House, to try to introduce himself. Cobb got a phone call back from Quarles and Michael Dreeben, a soft-spoken and well-known appellate lawyer on the Mueller team. Dreeben explained that Mueller's team was a bit frustrated. They had made a series of requests of the White House and thus far had not received a satisfactory reply. In particular, they wanted White House permission to review a key document, one of the draft statements Trump wrote in May in Bedminster as he prepared to fire Comey. Mueller's team felt they were getting stonewalled. They had a general idea about the contents but had been waiting for the White House to decide if they wanted to hold the document back due to executive privilege concerns.

Dreeben laid out for Cobb one way the White House could cooperate. He cited a 2008 opinion under Attorney General Michael Mukasey that found the White House could share sensitive internal documents with another executive branch office, such as the Justice Department, for the purposes of an investigation. As Dreeben explained, the White House wouldn't have to deal with the question of whether these records should be shielded by executive privilege because under the Mukasey memo the executive branch would agree not to divulge any of the records without White House permission. Cobb consulted with a career attorney in the Justice Department's Office of Legal Counsel who confirmed Dreeben's interpretation: the White House would not waive executive privilege or risk anything by sharing internal notes or the recollections of staff with the special counsel.

A veteran of previous independent counsel fights, Cobb felt cooperation was the right path for several reasons. Trump had been emphatic with Cobb that he had done nothing wrong and that he wanted to get the investigation over with as quickly as possible. As Cobb saw it, that could be achieved by cooperating fully with the investigators, turning over every document they needed, helping to provide staff witnesses for interviews, and reaching a resolution without subpoenas and court fights. Cobb laid out this cooperative approach to John Dowd and fellow attorney Jay Sekulow, who then explained its virtues to Trump. The Mukasey memo meant no potentially sensitive or embarrassing material would automatically become public without White House agreement, and sharing broadly with Mueller would speed up the investigation. Trump immediately embraced what lawyers on the team dubbed an "open kimono" strategy.

On August 1, Cobb authorized the Justice Department to give Mueller's team the draft of Trump's letter to fire Comey. Trump lawyers had reviewed four drafts of the termination letter, including the final version that Keith Schiller—"the Manila Killa," as one adviser called him—carried in a manila envelope to FBI headquarters. They felt that the letter exonerated Trump of obstructing justice because they believed it showed he was firing Comey for declining to state publicly that the president was not under investigation, not because of corrupt intent to end the Russia probe.

Over the next several days, Cobb further consulted the Office of Legal Counsel, reviewed the law, and became even more convinced. He was familiar with a ruling in an independent counsel investigation of Mike Espy, an agriculture secretary under President Clinton, which set a very high bar that investigators had to meet in order to question a president and force his or her testimony. Investigators had to show they couldn't get the information any other way. Under the Espy precedent, the more the White House cooperated by providing detailed records and responsive witnesses, the more difficult it would be for Mueller to subpoena the president himself.

"You can build a record of cooperation every day that you're cooperating, and every time you're making a production and every time people are testifying voluntarily, that builds a big mountain," Cobb told Trump and his advisers. Cobb argued that this mountain of cooperation could therefore shield the president from having to answer investigators' questions, which Trump's personal lawyers wanted to avoid in part out of fear that he might perjure himself, given his tendency to embellish or fabricate.

Dowd, who had been meeting with Mueller's team, told Cobb he thought he could see light at the end of the tunnel and a speedy end to the probe, at least as it related to concluding the Trump campaign had engaged in no collusion. Dowd believed that Mueller had assured him he would make a rather quick decision on this and would alert Dowd in the near term. Dowd was cheered by Mueller's insistence that he would move speedily. Cobb liked the sound of that because he felt he could use Mueller's promise of a swift investigation to apply pressure in public by telling reporters that the White House could turn over all its records and witnesses by Thanksgiving or the end of the year, and so the probe could be completed then as well. Dowd shared a rosy outlook with the president.

"This could be over by the end of January," Dowd told Trump.

Cobb, sixty-seven, noticed right away that he and Trump had different styles. Cobb liked to think before he spoke, while Trump liked to talk off the cuff, as part of his process of testing ideas and gathering information. Cobb watched Trump throw up in the air theories and proposals to get reactions, but recognized the president as nobody's fool. Cobb was intrigued by Trump's habit of keeping a running score on his senior aides' popularity and "performance ratings."

Others noticed that the president was obsessed with knocking down as inferior what his predecessors had built. "His whole DNA is, whatever anybody else has done is stupid, I'm smarter, and therefore that's why he goes around breaking glass all the time," one senior Republican senator recalled. "He's torn a lot of things up. He likes to break things. But what has he put together yet?"

In August, the West Wing underwent a renovation for two weeks, so Trump had a change of scenery. The staff was displaced, just as Kelly was settling into his new post, and Trump decamped to his golf club in Bedminster, New Jersey. Trump was hypersensitive to any suggestion that he was on vacation, even though he effectively was, and he ordered aides to plan public events each day: a briefing on health care or a roundtable session on opioids, for instance. But they occupied only an hour or so of his time, and he spent the rest of each day playing a round of golf, chatting with friends in the clubhouse, and hanging out in his private cottage.

Trump was accompanied by a small coterie of aides, including Kelly, communications director Hope Hicks, and staff secretary Rob Porter. But he spent hours each day alone in the cottage watching cable news and reading newspapers. Aides carted up from Washington boxes that contained back issues of *The New York Times* and *The Washington Post* that the president had not had a chance to fully peruse in the White House. The extensive news coverage about Mueller's investigation—"pure hate," as Bannon would refer to it—put Trump in a foul mood.

"Can you believe how obsessed they are with this?" Trump fumed to aides. "It's so overblown. That's all they want to talk about. This is so ridiculous. We didn't do anything."

Trump was not only bothered by the Russia investigation. He was confounded over what to do about North Korea. Ever since Obama had told him, back in November 2016, that North Korea would be the greatest challenge he would confront as president, Trump had been vexed by the security threat posed by Kim Jong Un. A series of missile tests in the spring and summer of 2017 rattled him, and as he vacationed at Bedminster, he was getting regular updates from National Security

Adviser H. R. McMaster and other officials about the rogue regime. On August 8, Trump issued a fresh warning to Kim after North Korea vowed to develop a nuclear arsenal capable of reaching the U.S. mainland.

"They will be met with fire and fury and, frankly, power, the likes of which this world has never seen before," Trump said, folding his arms and staring straight into the cameras.

The bellicose threat was interpreted as yet another unscripted presidential eruption, but one with the consequence of escalating the war of words between the two countries and their unpredictable leaders. Trump's advisers rushed to reassure suddenly jittery world leaders that Trump's statement was part of an agreed policy of pressure on Pyongyang. But Trump's intimates recognized that there was no grand strategy at play and that the president was unsettled.

During his stay in Bedminster, Trump invited Chris Christie and his wife, Mary Pat, over for dinner one night. The three of them ate in private on the patio. Melania was away (and in fact had visited the White House only occasionally in the winter and spring, living instead in New York so that their son, Barron, could finish the school year there). Trump was usually punctual to dinner, but he got to the table about fifteen minutes late and seemed preoccupied, even rattled. Trump had known the Christies for nearly two decades, and he and Mary Pat always hugged and kissed when they saw each other. But this time, the president extended his hand for a more formal shake.

Once Trump sat down, he didn't say much. The Christies were used to dinners in which they listened to Trump gab for two hours straight, but this time the president was mostly silent. Trump eventually explained the reason for his delay: he had just been on calls with Japanese prime minister Shinzo Abe and South Korean president Moon Jae-in, discussing the nuclear brinkmanship with North Korea.

"It's really complicated," Trump told the Christies, adding that he needed the New Jersey governor to give him regular advice on what to do. It was immediately clear to his guests that the North Korea quandary simply overwhelmed Trump.

———

The Mueller investigation kept needling Trump at every turn. On August 9, while he was still in Bedminster, the president watched the jarring news reports that FBI agents had raided the home of Paul Manafort, his former campaign chairman. Using a search warrant, agents had entered Manafort's Alexandria, Virginia, home in the early-morning hours of July 26 and seized a trove of documents and other materials related to the Russia probe. This was Mueller's first shock-and-awe move, and it signaled a newly aggressive phase of the investigation.

Trump was unnerved. "Pretty tough stuff," he told reporters of the FBI's tactics. Privately, Trump told his advisers he was at once worried about Manafort's well-being and upset that the media portrayed them as close. "The press is acting like we're best friends," Trump lamented to Kelly, Porter, and Hicks.

That weekend, a group of white supremacists and neo-Nazis held a "Unite the Right" rally in Charlottesville, Virginia. People marched in a nighttime parade on August 11 holding tiki torches and chanting, "Jews will not replace us," and on August 12 their daytime celebration of white nationalism turned deadly when one of the white supremacists deliberately drove his car into a crowd of peaceful counterprotesters, killing one woman and injuring twenty-eight others.

Trump said there were "very fine people on both sides" and initially refused to condemn white supremacy, a stunning ambiguity that drew bipartisan opprobrium. This abdication of moral leadership was one of the lowest points of his presidency and inspired one of his top advisers, National Economic Council director Gary Cohn, to do an on-the-record interview with the *Financial Times* condemning his handling of Charlottesville.

The white supremacist rally occurred during the time that cities around the country, from Annapolis to New Orleans to Louisville, were removing monuments to the Confederacy. Trump opposed what was happening. "Sad to see the history and culture of our great country being ripped apart with the removal of our beautiful statues and monuments," he tweeted on August 17. Trump had told his aides many times that summer, "This is a shame. They're destroying our heritage. This is ridiculous."

On August 18, after almost a week of racial unrest over Trump's handling of Charlottesville, and with Kelly trying to break up the West Wing's warring factions, Trump dismissed Bannon, putting out to pasture the adviser who had most zealously channeled his pugilistic and nationalist impulses. Locked in a tortuous ideological and personal feud with Kushner, McMaster, and other senior aides he derided as "globalists," Bannon came to embody the White House's dysfunction and self-destructive tendencies.

Bannon considered himself a historical figure, likening his work for Trump to leading a revolution, and he cast his departure as the end of an era. "The Trump presidency that we fought for, and won, is over," he said in an exit interview with *The Weekly Standard*, adding that he felt liberated and vowing to achieve even greater influence from outside the government. "I feel jacked up. Now I'm free. I've got my hands back on my weapons. Someone said, 'It's Bannon the Barbarian.'"

The discarding of Bannon underscored the fact that the president wanted all the glory for himself. He had deeply resented the *Saturday Night Live* portrayal of Bannon as the Grim Reaper making presidential decisions behind the Resolute Desk while Trump played with an expandable toy from behind a kiddie desk. With Bannon out, Kelly centralized power inside the White House and inspired new confidence that he could get the president to act more like a president.

On August 23, Trump flew to Phoenix for a rally, his first since Charlottesville. His supporters had waited for hours in 107-degree heat to get through security, and a quartet of introductory speakers, including Alveda King, a niece of Martin Luther King Jr., and the evangelist Franklin Graham, delivered carefully scripted speeches denouncing racism and praising Trump as a unifier. Then the president took the stage and ranted and rambled for seventy-five minutes, sixteen of which he spent attacking the "damned dishonest" media for their coverage of his Charlottesville equivocations. At one point, Trump called Kelly onto the stage. "Where's John?" the president asked. "Where is he? Where's General Kelly? Get him out here. He's great. He's doing a great job."

Kelly did not go onstage, which irritated Trump, who later vented to other aides that his chief of staff did not follow his command. Trump had begun chafing against Kelly's restrictions, which his deputy, Kirstjen Nielsen, brusquely enforced. She ordered shut the doors of the Oval Office to block staffers from wandering in without appointments; screened the president's phone calls, making it harder for outside friends to get patched in; and mandated prescreening any papers, including the printouts of news stories about himself that Trump liked to read, before they reached the president's desk.

Just about everything Kelly did ran counter to Trump's spontaneity, setting the two men on a collision course. Trump was embarrassed by the media narrative that Kelly was "managing" the president with his rigid structures. Kelly instructed White House operators to patch him into many of Trump's calls so that he could hear what people told the president and vice versa. And Kelly tried to restrict who had direct access. When some of his friends complained that their calls were not connected, Trump sometimes yelled at his personal assistant, Madeleine Westerhout. "People say they've not been able to reach me for two weeks," the president fumed. Westerhout blocked the calls under Kelly's orders. Worse, though, Trump thought Kelly was acting morally superior. Trump started derisively dubbing him "the church lady" behind his back.

The danger for Kelly was that insiders, too, were starting to turn against him over his strict new procedures. It was Trump, of course, who birthed this nest of vipers, allowing his staff to snipe at foes and sometimes rewarding them for it. Some Trump loyalists had come to consider the West Wing's chaos a ladder for personal ambition, back channeling to the president and influencing the government in ways beyond the scope of their positions. But once their wings were clipped, they sought to undermine Kelly, in ways the new chief of staff did not necessarily see.

"When you take Fallujah, you know the incoming is coming directly in front of you because you can see it," one Trump adviser explained. "When you're in Washington, it's coming from everywhere. . . . You don't know if I'm killing you from inside the tent or outside the tent."

At the outset, Kelly decided not to give Ivanka and Kushner special treatment, a move that would later lead the kids to conspire against him and imperil his ability to manage effectively. Corey Lewandowski, Trump's former campaign manager, who remained close to the president and was among those outsiders Kelly tried to isolate, sought to warn the new chief of staff. Early in Kelly's tenure, Lewandowski explained what he saw as a survival mechanism in Trump World: "Embrace the family, because when you're home having Thanksgiving dinner with your family, they're with the president, and if you don't embrace them, you're going to lose."

But Kelly did not embrace the family. He made clear he expected Ivanka and Kushner to act as regular staffers and abide by his rules, including that they first seek his approval before discussing any policy or political matters with the president. Privately, Kelly told Mattis and other administration officials that he thought Ivanka and Kushner were "idiots" and needed to leave the White House because "we've just got to run this country." Naturally, the kids came to resent Kelly, believing he and his enforcers, chief among them Nielsen, were trying to erode their influence and access, which in the Priebus era had largely been unfettered.

"They're trying to fuck me," Kushner told confidants.

Kelly was nearly killing himself in the job. He woke up most mornings at 4:00, and his Secret Service detail waited outside his home in Manassas, Virginia, to drive him to work. On the roughly forty-five-minute drive—there was no traffic at that predawn hour—Kelly read *The Washington Post*, *The New York Times*, *The Wall Street Journal*, *Politico*, the Fox News and Breitbart websites, and *Axios*. He learned early in the job that the president's addiction to press accounts of himself was so strong that Kelly's daily tasks and discussions inevitably would be determind by the news cycle.

Once he got to the White House, CIA officials went over the latest intelligence with him for the President's Daily Brief. Until Trump came down from the residence, usually between 11:00 a.m. and noon—a remarkably late start time for a commander in chief—Kelly did normal staff work. But the moment the president arrived in the Oval Office, all normalcy flew out the window, and Kelly stayed glued to his side. Once Trump went back to the residence, around 5:00 or 6:00 in the evening, Kelly snuck in a couple more hours of work. On many days he slept only four or five hours.

Famously blunt, Kelly routinely commiserated with other staffers about the difficulties of working for Trump. "He can't make up his mind," the chief of staff once told aides. "He says one thing and does another thing. Look what I have to deal with."

Still, Kelly was considered a stabilizing force on Capitol Hill, where veteran lawmakers had been watching Trump's presidency aghast. They saw Kelly, Mattis, and Secretary of State Rex Tillerson as essential guardrails for an erratic president. Bob Corker, the Senate Foreign Relations Committee chairman, gave voice to this sentiment on October 4, when he told reporters, "I think Secretary Tillerson, Secretary Mattis and Chief of Staff Kelly are those people that help separate our country from chaos, and I support them very much."

Corker's willingness to say what he believed about Trump made him a rare breed among Republican lawmakers, and his "separate our country from chaos" quote immediately made the rounds on cable television, drawing notice from the nation's viewer in chief. Concerned about the president's agitation, Kelly called Corker that afternoon.

"Bob, what in the hell happened today?" he asked.

Corker explained that he simply responded truthfully to a question he was asked by a reporter. "If you want me to quit complimenting you, I will," Corker said. Kelly laughed. Trump got more spun up the more the Corker quote was replayed on television, and on October 8 the president attacked Corker on Twitter. Trump stated falsely that Corker had "begged" him for his endorsement and that after the president said "NO," the senator decided not to run for reelection. In fact, Trump had told Corker several times he would endorse him and earlier that week had called, asking the senator to reconsider his decision and seek another term. Corker responded about an hour later with a tweet of his own: "It's a shame the White House has become an adult day care center. Someone obviously missed their shift this morning."

As Kelly and others were trying to help steer Trump away from dangerous impulses, Mueller and his team were trying to excavate every detail of the Russian cyberattack on the 2016 election. These investigators were combing through tens of thousands of Democratic emails the Russian government had stolen, on orders from Vladimir Putin, to damage Hillary Clinton's bid for the White House. This required old-fashioned detective work, like tracing the footprints of a burglar but through the dark digital trails traveled by shadowy spies and hackers. The team compared which of the Democratic National Committee emails were held—in identical form—in the computer troves of WikiLeaks.

The team, led by the former federal prosecutor Jeannie Rhee and her tireless partner Rush Atkinson, informally called the search "Hack-n-Dump," though they would later settle on the catchier name "Matchy Matchy." This was serious work, however. They charted "the hack" to establish the computer theft, pulled off by the GRU's secret political dirty tricks division, Unit 26165. The elite team of computer scientists, based in offices in central Moscow, was formed in the cold war as a critical signals decrypting office for the Soviet military and had recently been described on a Russian website as "able to decipher any code within three minutes and re-encrypt it without breaking away from writing a doctoral dissertation on quantum physics." The unit's officers had created "buffer" servers between their own operation and the Democratic servers to store what they stole and based them in Arizona, an apparent effort to throw people off their trail.

Tracking "the dump" was in some ways far more important to establishing proof of criminal interference in the election. Another GRU division, Unit 74455, pushed out the material after creating two phony personas:

the website DCLeaks, which hosted the hacked goodies, and the social media figure Guccifer 2.0, who pretended to be an individual hacker and tried to communicate with journalists and other key influencers. Tracing the hackers' theft was like chasing a house burglar.

"It's like, the house was robbed, some jewelry was taken," said one person familiar with the work. "The bracelet that was taken is now in this pawnshop on the corner. We found the same bracelet. We've got a match!"

On October 30, Trump woke before dawn, clicked on the television, and burrowed in to await the bombshell he expected that morning. It was a Monday, the day before Halloween, and all weekend there was rampant media speculation that Mueller was preparing his first indictments. After being given a heads-up from the Justice Department about the imminent indictments from Mueller, Trump watched live footage of Manafort and his deputy Rick Gates, both onetime confidants of the president, turning themselves in to the FBI. They were being charged with tax fraud, hiding millions of dollars in income, and deceiving the federal government about their secret lobbying work for pro-Russian leaders in Ukraine. Trump was pleased and relieved that the charges against Manafort and Gates were focused primarily on activities that began before his campaign. At 10:28 a.m., he tweeted, "There is NO COLLUSION!"

Within minutes, the media discovered a link between the Trump campaign and Russia. Prosecutors unsealed court documents showing that three weeks earlier Trump's campaign adviser George Papadopoulos pleaded guilty to making false statements to the FBI about having received advance warning from a Russian intelligence operative that Russia had obtained damaging information about Hillary Clinton. Trump grew angry, and in the corridors of the White House that day the mood was one of weariness and fear of the unknown. Staffers were in freak-out mode. The president had detested Gates but genuinely felt bad for

Manafort, believing prosecutors were charging him with long-ago crimes as a means of ensnaring Trump.

"It's a shame," Trump told McGahn not long after the charges were brought. "It had nothing to do with the campaign. It was all this stuff before he met me."

Most of all, Trump was furious that the charges created so much bad publicity for himself, a sort of guilt by association. The president urged his lawyers to point out publicly that the charges had no connection to him or his campaign.

"Why don't the papers report that?" Trump groused. "This was when he worked for President Reagan!" He added, "I barely knew him. I need you to tell the press that."

Trump's advisers had seen him fall into this pit before. He couldn't sit still and ride out the storm. He always wanted to be on offense. Cobb had to explain to him that the White House should never say anything about Manafort.

"Nothing Manafort's charged with involves the White House and it's very defensive," Cobb said. "It suggests some anxiety about Manafort."

Trump often raised his voice at other aides but not to Cobb. He seemed to respect Cobb's calm, matter-of-fact tone. He slumped in his chair and complied with his lawyer's advice. Cobb reminded Trump and his political advisers that Manafort's lawyers had already addressed the media from the federal courthouse steps and made clear Manafort had no unflattering information about Trump to share with prosecutors.

"You should just let that be the record rather than muddying the record," Cobb told him.

That was welcome news to Trump. But unbeknownst to the president, Mueller was working to secure another cooperating witness. The special counsel's team would next move in to talk to Trump's former national security adviser.

Eleven

WINGING IT

Secretary of State Rex Tillerson worked to advance the U.S. relationship with India throughout the first year of the Trump administration. The South Asian republic, the world's most populous democracy and one of its fastest-growing economies, was a natural ally to the United States. Tillerson felt strongly that America needed to fortify its alliances and block rivals, chief among them China, from taking advantage of any gaps or friction between the United States and its strategic partners. To that end, he believed that if the United States strengthened its transpacific alliance with India, Japan, and Australia, with open trade and shipping routes, it could keep China at bay.

In October 2017, Tillerson telegraphed the administration's hopes for the region and India in a speech at the Center for Strategic and International Studies and then jetted to New Delhi to discuss the alliance in person with Prime Minister Narendra Modi. Tillerson was immediately impressed by Modi. The prime minister was a serious person, an experienced deal maker who was motivated by the prospects of a strategic partnership with the United States. Modi was candid with Tillerson about his challenges. He was operating in a tough neighborhood. On one border was Pakistan, India's greatest threat, and on another was China, which had been trying to partner with Pakistan. To the north was Afghanistan, which was ravaged by war, highly unstable, and vulnerable to

Russia and other countries. As he considered allies for India, Modi had options. He was inclined to deal with the United States, but if things ever went sour, Russia was knocking on his door.

The second week of November, President Trump took his first trip to Asia, a five-country, ten-day journey that concluded in the Philippines, where he attended a global summit of leaders. On November 13, Trump sat down with Modi in Manila on the sidelines of the summit. Tillerson had high hopes for the meeting—even though, back at the White House, Trump was known to have affected an Indian accent to imitate Modi, a sign of disrespect for the prime minister.

As with most of his foreign leader meetings, Trump had been briefed but didn't appear to have retained the material and instead tried to wing it. He took a hard right turn into a nitpicky complaint about trade imbalances. Modi tried to refocus on the threats India faced from Afghanistan, China, and Pakistan. His mention of Afghanistan led Trump off into a lengthy tangent about how stupid it had been for the United States to maintain its military presence in Afghanistan for so many years. When Modi mentioned his concern about China's ambitions and aggression in the region, Trump revealed a stunning ignorance about geography.

"It's not like you've got China on your border," Trump said, seeming to dismiss the threat to India.

Modi's eyes bulged out in surprise. Aides noticed him giving a sidelong glance at Tillerson, who accompanied Trump as part of the U.S. delegation. The Indian prime minister considered Tillerson among the best-versed Americans on the region's security challenges, and together they had been plotting a new partnership. Tillerson's eyes flashed open wide at Trump's comment, but he quickly put his hand to his brow, appearing to the Indian delegation to attempt not to offend the president as well as to signal to Modi that he knew this statement was nuts.

Trump did not appear to notice their silent exchange. He just kept rolling, droning on about unrelated topics. Modi tried to keep the conversation on an elevated plane, hoping to follow the path Tillerson had laid out for them in the previous weeks to work together to protect India and fend off China's Belt and Road Initiative. But each time Modi tried to get Trump to engage on the substance of U.S.-India relations, the American president veered off on another non sequitur about trade deficits and the endless war in Afghanistan. Those who witnessed the meeting that day in Manila were disheartened. Modi's expression gradually shifted, from shock and concern to resignation.

"I think he left that meeting and said, 'This is not a serious man. I cannot count on this man as a partner,'" one Trump aide recalled. After that meeting, "the Indians took a step back" in their diplomatic relations with the United States.

The meeting with Modi was a major setback not only for U.S.-India relations but also for the administration's hopes of checkmating China in the region. The meeting came at a time when Tillerson's influence with Trump was growing simply because the president had tired of others in his orbit. In preparation for the Asia trip, John Kelly asked Tillerson if he could add another duty to his already-full portfolio: Could he give Trump his national security briefings on the road?

This request was odd. Briefing the president was normally the responsibility of the national security adviser. Tillerson asked Kelly why.

"He doesn't want to see McMaster," Kelly responded.

The signs of Trump's fraying patience for H. R. McMaster had been painfully obvious throughout the fall. McMaster's loyal staff hated to admit it, but they knew this relationship was no longer working.

A military intellectual and policy maestro, McMaster was widely respected in Washington's foreign policy establishment and on Capitol Hill, but he did not easily fit into Trump's orbit. This much was evident right away. In his first town-hall meeting of the National Security Council staff after being appointed in February 2017, McMaster emphasized that as a nonpartisan army officer he did not vote. He wanted the professional staff to know that he valued their input, but his admonition about voting unwittingly sent a message to Trump, who demanded political loyalty from everyone in his administration.

McMaster lived by paperwork and process. He believed his duty was to give the president information so that he could make the best decisions, and then to help carry out the commander in chief's will. But his briefings to Trump were academic and detail-oriented, and the two men's stylistic differences inspired epic clashes.

McMaster had difficulty holding the president's attention. Trump, meanwhile, would get annoyed with what he considered McMaster's lecturing style. The president felt his national security adviser was always determined to try to "teach me something." Indeed, Trump constantly shifted and grumbled when staff were trying to bring him up to speed on a topic, immediately threatened by the notion that his knowledge wasn't sufficient if he needed experts. As the president repeatedly told Kelly when he proposed a subject briefing: "I don't want to talk to anyone. I know more than they do. I know better than anybody else."

McMaster came across as a tank commander in his bearing and didn't seem able to change gears to the far more politically cautious mode of White House hedging and dodging. He had a barking kind of voice, which had reliably conveyed strength and directness in his previous world. But it proved to be a pitch Trump disliked instantly, as if it were a piercing dog whistle.

Some mornings, Trump would come down to the Oval Office and see the President's Daily Brief on his schedule, followed by a meeting with the national security adviser, and complain. "I'm not fucking doing that," he told aides. "I'm not talking with McMaster for an hour. Are you kidding me?" Instead, the president would step into his private dining room, turn on the television, and summon National Economic Council director Gary Cohn, Treasury secretary Steven Mnuchin, or commerce secretary Wilbur Ross to come over and keep him company.

In March, McMaster was in the Oval Office briefing Trump on the visit of the German chancellor, Angela Merkel, a favorite foil for the president. Trump got so impatient that he stood up and walked into an adjoining bathroom, left the door ajar, and instructed McMaster to raise his voice and keep talking. It was unclear if the strange scene was a reflection of Trump's feelings about McMaster or Merkel or both.

McMaster felt it was his duty to speak truth to his commander, to notify the president of critically important issues, and even to highlight bad news and the cons of a particular strategy Trump was considering.

That's how McMaster had always spoken to his wartime commanders when he was reporting from the battlefield: "Things have gone to hell, sir. Here's how bad it is." But Trump's intelligence briefers downplayed or withheld new developments regarding Russia's election interference or cyber intrusions, so as not to agitate the commander in chief. When they left a key piece of information out of the verbal President's Daily Brief, McMaster would later raise it directly with Trump, only to become a punching bag for the president when he inevitably blew up. The routine frustrated McMaster.

Part of McMaster's process entailed providing Trump with written briefing documents on each big decision, with detailed descriptions of the risks and possible rewards. He had tried to be concise from the get-go, boiling the material down to three pages, but McMaster and his team almost immediately realized the president wasn't reading any of the briefing books, or even the concise three-page version. Staff secretary Rob Porter would synthesize the memos in a one-page cover letter, written in prose the president might find easier to digest. As one of Trump's confidants said, "I call the president the two-minute man. The president has patience for a half page." But McMaster understandably resented the fact that Trump was reading Porter's version of CliffsNotes. Porter and Reince Priebus suggested an alternative approach: McMaster could deliver verbal briefings to Trump. Nothing in writing.

"Everyone agreed we needed to stop giving the president paper to read," one former National Security Council staffer recalled. "H.R. was uncomfortable with this. McMaster kept saying, 'How are we not going to give the president any papers?'"

McMaster and his deputies were mindful of history and fearful of failing to document a risk or of missing an important alarm. President George W. Bush had faced withering criticism when it was discovered that in the summer of 2001 he had been briefed on intelligence suggesting Osama bin Laden planned to orchestrate terror attacks using airplanes. Bush had actually received briefing books on this, but the intelligence did not prompt any corrective action. Eliminating briefing books for the president seemed to tempt disaster. McMaster came up with yet another plan that the staff put into full effect in September: note cards with bulleted factoids.

Other top officials in the White House saw McMaster and some of his top deputies as overly suspicious. They fretted about the national security adviser's standing with the president and fought at times with others in the building, including Keith Kellogg, another army lieutenant general who served as the chief of staff on the NSC but was loyal to Trump above all.

By the time of the November trip to Asia, Trump was openly mocking McMaster. When McMaster arrived in his office for a briefing, Trump would puff up his chest, sit up straight in his chair, and fake shout like a boot camp drill sergeant. In his play, he pretended to be McMaster. "I'm your national security adviser, General McMaster, sir!" Trump would say, trying to amuse the others in the room. "I'm here to give you your briefing, sir!"

Then Trump would ridicule McMaster further by describing the topic of the day and deploying a series of large, complex phrases to indicate how boring McMaster's briefing was going to be. The National Security Council staff were deeply disturbed by Trump's treatment of their boss. "The president doesn't fire people," said one of McMaster's aides. "He just tortures them until they're willing to quit." The cruelty also was uncomfortable for Secretary of Defense Jim Mattis, Kelly, and other advisers to watch. Kelly was weary of McMaster's inability to take the hint that Trump was done listening. One day in the fall, Trump was meeting with a group of his advisers in the Oval Office, and Kelly decided the president was growing more obstinate on an issue and it was time for the gathering to break up.

"Thank you very much," Kelly said. "Everyone can leave now."

McMaster moved closer to the Resolute Desk and said, "Mr. President, I'd like to keep talking to you. I have a few more things."

Kelly did not take kindly to McMaster disobeying his order. The chief of staff stood nose to nose with the national security adviser and decreed, "I said the meeting was over."

Here was a four-star marine general and a three-star army general nearly coming to blows in front of the president of the United States. Trump loved it, later telling another adviser that he was impressed by Kelly's willingness to confront McMaster and the sheer machismo he exuded. "This guy is an animal," the president remarked, complimenting Kelly. That the president's narrow bandwidth might have been the root cause of the disagreement didn't seem to cross his mind.

On the Asia trip, both Tillerson and McMaster hopped into the president's vehicle in succession to give Trump his morning update before the motorcade took off for its appointed meetings. But as McMaster spoke, Trump frowned, turned his back, and interrupted him midsentence to ask Tillerson a question. It was a not-very-gentle cue for Tillerson to take over the role of updating the president on the key facts he needed to know. Tillerson engaged in a little small talk, then returned to tee up the debates Trump would tackle in his meetings that day.

"As H.R. was saying, Mr. President," Tillerson began, a sign of respect and deference to the national security adviser at an otherwise painful moment. Tillerson didn't always agree with McMaster on style or process, but he told aides the man was selfless and dedicated to the mission.

McMaster had occasional disagreements with Trump, such as over the long-term strategy in Afghanistan and the Iran nuclear agreement. Unlike several other senior advisers, though, he genuinely tried to help implement the president's wishes. Rather than impose his own agenda, McMaster generally sought to curate the opinions of the relevant administration officials and present a range of options to Trump.

"Sometimes you have very forceful differences of opinion among the president's senior advisers," Senator Tom Cotton, a McMaster ally, said at the time. "H.R. is indispensable in helping the president hear all those viewpoints and have the information he needs, and framed in time for the president to make a decision."

U.S. ambassador to the United Nations Nikki Haley added, "When we're in those meetings, he's all about getting options on the table for the president."

Another episode startled Trump's advisers on the Asia trip. As the president and his entourage embarked on the journey, they stopped in Hawaii on November 3 to break up the long flight and allow Air Force One to refuel. White House aides arranged for the president and first lady to make a somber pilgrimage so many of their predecessors had made: to visit Pearl Harbor and honor the twenty-three hundred American sailors, soldiers, and marines who lost their lives there.

The first couple was set to take a private tour of the USS *Arizona* Memorial, which sits just off the coast of Honolulu and straddles the hull of the battleship that sank into the Pacific during the Japanese surprise bombing attack in 1941. As a passenger boat ferried the Trumps to the stark white memorial, the president pulled Kelly aside for a quiet consult.

"Hey, John, what's this all about? What's this a tour of?" Trump asked his chief of staff.

Kelly was momentarily stunned. Trump had heard the phrase "Pearl Harbor" and appeared to understand that he was visiting the scene of a historic battle, but he did not seem to know much else. Kelly explained to him that the stealth Japanese attack here had devastated the U.S. Pacific Fleet and prompted the country's entrance into World War II, eventually leading the United States to drop atom bombs on Japan. If Trump had learned about "a date which will live in infamy" in school, it hadn't really pierced his consciousness or stuck with him.

"He was at times dangerously uninformed," said one senior former adviser.

Trump's lack of basic historical knowledge surprised some foreign leaders as well. When he met with President Emmanuel Macron of France at the United Nations back in September 2017, Trump complimented him on the spectacular Bastille Day military parade they had attended together that summer in Paris. Trump said he did not realize until seeing the parade that France had had such a rich history of military conquest. He told Macron something along the lines of "You know,

I really didn't know, but the French have won a lot of battles. I didn't know."

A senior European official observed, "He's totally ignorant of everything. But he doesn't care. He's not interested."

Tillerson developed a polite and self-effacing way to manage the gaps in Trump's knowledge. If he saw the president was completely lost in the conversation with a foreign leader, other advisers noticed, the secretary of state would step in to ask a question. As Tillerson lodged his question, he would reframe the topic by explaining some of the basics at issue, giving Trump a little time to think.

Over time, the president developed a tell that he would use to get out of a sticky conversation in which a world leader mentioned a topic that was totally foreign or unrecognizable to him. He would turn to McMaster, Tillerson, or another adviser and say, "What do you think of it?"

"There was always the concern when no one was there that he would be maneuvered into a condition or an agreement that he didn't realize he had committed to," one former senior adviser said. "They tell him to do something and he does it."

Oftentimes after meetings with Trump, Kelly and Secretary of Defense Jim Mattis would huddle together—sometimes with McMaster in the national security adviser's office, sometimes without him—to compare notes on the presidential performance they had just witnessed. In words and sometimes simply facial expressions, they communicated a shared concern: "This guy doesn't know what he's doing."

In the spring of 2017, as aides gathered in the Oval Office one day to brief Trump on upcoming meetings with foreign leaders, they made a passing reference to some foreign government officials who were under scrutiny for corruption, for taking bribes. Trump perked up at the mention of bribes and got rather agitated. He told Tillerson he wanted him to help him get rid of the Foreign Corrupt Practices Act.

"It's just so unfair that American companies aren't allowed to pay bribes to get business overseas," Trump told the group. "We're going to change that."

Looking at Tillerson, Trump said, "I need you to get rid of that law," as if the secretary of state had the power to magically repeal an act of Congress.

The business developer turned president was angry about the FCPA ostensibly because it restricted his industry buddies or his own company's executives from paying off foreign governments in faraway lands. Other aides in the room turned to Tillerson to gauge his reaction. Surprised at Trump's request, Tillerson first paused, then found his words.

"Mr. President," he said. "I'm not the guy to do that."

Tillerson explained the way laws work. He said the Justice Department should be consulted about a series of statutes that now made it a crime for American businesspeople to give bribes to foreign officials or business leaders to get contracts or deals struck in other countries. Then, in a somber kind of *Schoolhouse Rock!* episode that had become a regular feature of the Oval Office education of this president, Tillerson said that Congress would have to be involved in the repeal of the law.

Trump didn't miss a beat. He was unmoved by Tillerson's explanations and turned to Stephen Miller, the White House's senior policy adviser who had long before proved that he could be relied upon to dutifully execute almost all of the president's wishes.

"Stephen, I want you to draft an executive order and repeal that law," Trump decreed, evidently still unaware or unconvinced that he alone did not have the power to repeal the FCPA.

Later, after the meeting broke up, Tillerson caught up with Miller in the hallway. Miller, who had championed many of the president's most unpopular plans, told Tillerson he had some skepticism that the EO idea would work, a rare moment of agreement between the two men.

There was a sign of trouble in the Russia investigation after Trump returned from Asia. The lawyers for various witnesses and subjects in special counsel Robert Mueller's probe had been sharing information and strategies as part of a joint defense agreement. On November 22, the Wednesday before Thanksgiving, former national security adviser Michael Flynn's lawyer Robert Kelner alerted Trump's attorneys that Flynn was withdrawing from the joint defense agreement and could no longer communicate confidentially with the president or the White House. Though Kelner did not explicitly say so on the call, John Dowd, Trump's lead personal attorney, took Flynn's withdrawal from the agreement as an indication that he had begun to cooperate with Mueller's office or was actively seeking to do so. In either case, Flynn's lawyers could have a duty to shut off communications with other defense teams.

The night of November 22, Dowd left a voice mail for Kelner saying he would not be surprised if Flynn had "gone on to make a deal" with the special counsel's office but that if he had "information that implicates the president, then we've got a national security issue." Dowd asked for a "heads-up" for the sake of "protecting all our interests," then reminded him of Trump's warm regard for Flynn.

"Remember what we've always said about the president and his feelings toward Flynn and, that still remains," Dowd said in closing. He sounded conciliatory, friendly even.

It was a tricky situation. Flynn's lawyers were hoping they could eventually secure a presidential pardon for Flynn if he was charged or pleaded guilty to charges. The next day, Kelner returned Dowd's message and reiterated over the phone that he couldn't discuss anything with Dowd or any other attorneys for the president. Dowd's mood shifted dramatically. He grew incensed, warning Kelner that he took this as a sign of Flynn's hostility toward the president and that he planned to let President Trump know that. Kelner and his co-counsel Steve Anthony saw it for what it was: Dowd was indirectly threatening the wrath of Trump if they didn't change their plans to have Flynn cooperate. They also knew, as did Dowd, that Flynn didn't want to anger the president.

The Flynn news came at a stressful time for Trump's attorneys. Since the summer, Dowd and White House lawyer Ty Cobb had persuaded Trump to buy into their strategy to cooperate fully with the investigation by assuring the president that if he did so, Mueller would have to wrap up the probe more quickly. Dowd first told Trump that Mueller's investigation into possible collusion with the Russians could be over within weeks or months, but that didn't pan out. Cobb had been telling reporters the White House portion of the probe could be complete by Thanksgiving, but that deadline slipped away, and he suggested instead the end of the year. Dowd felt growing pressure to satisfy his impatient client, but he had no control over delivering what Trump wanted: a public exoneration from Mueller.

By now, the White House, the Trump Organization, and the Trump campaign had turned over the reams of documents and internal emails that Mueller had requested, and all the members of the White House staff Mueller had requested had either sat for interviews or scheduled them with the special counsel's office, with Don McGahn being the last on Mueller's list. They wondered now, what if Mueller wants to interview the president? That would be a natural request. Cobb said they couldn't reject the idea of an interview publicly. Dowd was wary but thought an interview might give "the old man" what he wanted.

Jay Sekulow, another Trump attorney, was cautious. One day after Thanksgiving, he called Mike Bowe, who also represented the president, to talk it over.

"What do you think about an interview with the president?" Sekulow asked Bowe, who was working in his garage.

After a brief pause, Bowe told him what he really thought: "It's legal malpractice."

Having any client testify was risky, but the risks increased manyfold with a client like Trump who tended to exaggerate and had his own brand of reality. Trump's lawyers had prepped CEOs for depositions for hundreds of hours and always carefully reminded them of the rules. If you couldn't remember key parts or every detail, simply say, "I can't recall." If you didn't know for certain, say, "I don't know." But such executives were bred to have answers and tended to be impossibly stubborn. It was as if they were genetically unable to say, "I'm not sure." Trump was an extreme version of this. His lawyers took note that Mueller's team had proved they would charge people for inconsistent accounts.

The lawyers continued to game out the possibilities when the reason for the Flynn team's silence was revealed. The former national security adviser pleaded guilty on December 1 to lying to the FBI about his contacts with Russian ambassador Sergei Kislyak, the first White House aide to face charges in the probe. The guilty plea revealed that Flynn was cooperating with Mueller's team in their ongoing work and had shared with them his discussions with unnamed senior officials in Trump's transition. Though it was unclear what else he might have told the special counsel about the Trump campaign or administration, his cooperation indicated that Mueller's probe was heating up rather than cooling down and would likely continue for many more months.

Trump was anxious and increasingly furious as he watched CNN coverage of Flynn's guilty plea that day. He called Steve Bannon, who was traveling in Scotland. "How can Flynn be charged?" the president said. "Flynn didn't do anything. Flynn's innocent."

Trump said the whole scene made him angry. He said he was worried Flynn hadn't done anything wrong.

"They targeted him because he worked for me," Trump lamented.

Bannon seized this opportunity to share his view of Trump's lawyers and their strategy. Bannon had long been skeptical that Mueller would ever clear the president of wrongdoing so quickly and believed Dowd and Cobb were effectively wearing rose-colored glasses and misleading their client.

"You gotta get rid of Cobb and Dowd," Bannon told Trump. "They're walking you into a trap that's going to blow up. You gotta get real lawyers. You gotta get a law firm. You gotta hire Jones Day. They're the only law firm that will work with us. You need a ton of associates. You've got to exert executive privilege and not send any more documents and not produce any more witnesses."

Bannon tried to play to Trump's pugilistic and litigious impulses.

"You've gotta fight this," he told the president. "You can stretch it out for a number of years."

Trump replied that Dowd and Cobb had assured him that cooperating was the best strategy.

"They tell me I'm going to get a letter of exoneration," Trump told Bannon. It was going to be over any day now. Trump was sure of it.

Bannon shook his head at the notion that Mueller was about to give Trump a clean bill of health.

On the morning of December 2, Trump was upset that none of his lawyers were speaking up for him in the media and pushing back against speculation that the reason Flynn lied to the FBI might have been to avoid implicating the president. At 12:14 p.m., about twenty-four hours after Flynn's plea agreement was entered in federal court, Trump took to Twitter to defend himself, as he often did, and in so doing offered a striking new view on Flynn's criminal acts.

"I had to fire General Flynn because he lied to the Vice President and the FBI," Trump tweeted. "He has pled guilty to those lies. It is a shame because his actions during the transition were lawful. There was nothing to hide!"

The tweet surprised and frustrated Cobb. This was explicitly what he thought he and Dowd had persuaded Trump not to do. Plus, the substance of the message created a whole new firestorm, indicating that Trump had long known Flynn had lied about his contacts with Kislyak, something the president had never before acknowledged. It covered the cable news stations all Saturday morning, and reporters were barraging the White House press shop for comment on this new development.

Cobb confronted Dowd about the tweet.

"Where did that come from?" Cobb asked his colleague. "This is contrary to everything we agreed to."

"The old man asked me to," Dowd said, referring to the president. Dowd later challenged this account, claiming that Cobb had advance notice of the tweet language.

Dowd then issued a statement asserting that he had drafted the language for Trump's tweet.

Meanwhile, Dowd and Sekulow were preparing for a meeting they had scheduled with Mueller in the third week of December. They were hopeful it would lead toward some closure, at least in terms of concluding the president and his campaign had not colluded. The president had been telling friends that the probe would be largely complete within weeks, and when that was reported in *The Washington Post*, his lawyers felt even greater pressure to somehow bring the investigation to an end.

On December 6, Bowe flew to Washington to see Dowd. They met at Shelly's Back Room, a cigar bar two blocks from the White House. Bowe was worried enough by what he was hearing to make a special trip. He wanted to make sure Dowd didn't agree to a presidential interview as a means of making good on his promise to Trump, in part because there was no guarantee that putting the president in front of Mueller would necessarily end the probe.

"I'm sure this will be over soon," Dowd told Bowe. "I'm confident we can get a letter." Bowe feared Dowd would agree to an interview to try to end the probe; Dowd later said he had no intention of considering an interview.

"It would just be malpractice, John," Bowe replied, waving the red flag that he knew lawyers would pay attention to. "And there's no need. In order to try to get it done quickly, we shouldn't make a bad mistake."

The lawyers were in a bind, with no clean bill of health on the horizon. Meanwhile, Trump continued to deny the conclusive evidence gathered by his own intelligence agencies that Russia waged an assault on American democracy by interfering in the 2016 election in support of his candidacy. Even as he proclaimed total innocence of conspiring with the Russians, Trump still couldn't bring himself to state definitively that the Russians interfered in the election.

"What the president has to say is, 'We know the Russians did it, they know they did it, I know they did it, and we will not rest until we learn everything there is to know about how and do everything possible to prevent it from happening again,'" Michael Hayden, who served as CIA director under President George W. Bush, told Greg Miller of *The Washington Post*. Trump "has never said anything close to that and will never say anything close to that."

As the year came to a close, Trump and his administration did little to hold Russia to account for its illegal actions or to deter future Kremlin attacks and safeguard U.S. elections. The only punishment for Russia came from Congress, which voted in August to impose additional penalties against Moscow despite fierce resistance from Trump. As Trump pursued an alliance with President Vladimir Putin, he never convened a cabinet-level meeting on Russian election interference in 2017.

In December, Trump had gathered his generals and top diplomats for a meeting as part of the administration's ongoing strategy talks about troop deployments in Afghanistan in the Situation Room, a secure meeting room on the ground floor of the West Wing. Trump didn't like the Situation Room, because he didn't think it had enough gravitas. It just wasn't impressive.

But there Trump was, struggling to come up with a new Afghanistan policy and frustrated that so many U.S. forces were deployed in so many places around the world. The conversation began to tilt in the same direction as it had when Trump met with top military and national security officials in the Pentagon's Tank back in July.

"All these countries need to start paying us for the troops we are sending to their countries. We need to be making a profit," Trump said. "We could turn a profit on this."

General Joseph Dunford, the chairman of the Joint Chiefs of Staff, tried to explain to the president once again, gently, that troops deployed in these regions provided stability there, which helped make America safer. Another officer chimed in that charging other countries for U.S. soldiers would be against the law.

"But it just wasn't working," one former Trump aide recalled. "Nothing worked."

After the Tank meeting in July, Tillerson had told his aides that he would never silently tolerate such demeaning talk from Trump about making money off the deployments of U.S. soldiers. Tillerson's father, at the age of seventeen, had committed to enlist in the navy on his next birthday, wanting so much to serve his country in World War II. His great-uncle was a career officer in the navy as well. Both men had been on his mind, Tillerson told aides, when Trump unleashed his tirade in the Tank and again when he repeated those points in the Situation Room in December.

"We need to get our money back," Trump told the room.

That was it. Tillerson stood up. But when he did so, he turned his back to the president and faced the flag officers and the rest of the aides in the room. He didn't want a repeat of the scene in the Tank.

"I've never put on a uniform, but I know this," Tillerson said. "Every person who has put on a uniform, the people in this room, they don't do it to make a buck. They did it for their country, to protect us. I want everyone to be clear about how much we as a country value their service."

Tillerson's rebuke made Trump angry. He got a little red in the face. But the president decided not to engage Tillerson at that moment. He would wait to take him on another day.

Later that evening, after 8:00, Tillerson was working in his office at the State Department's Foggy Bottom headquarters, preparing for the next day. The phone rang. It was Dunford. The Joint Chiefs chairman's voice was unsteady with emotion. Dunford had much earlier joked with Tillerson that in past administrations the secretaries of state and Defense Department leaders wouldn't be caught dead walking on the same side of the street, for their rivalry was that fierce. But now, as both men served Trump, they were brothers joined against what they saw as disrespect for service members. Dunford thanked Tillerson for standing up for them in the Situation Room.

"You took the body blows for us," Dunford said. "Punch after punch. Thank you. I will never forget it."

The fateful meeting between Dowd and Sekulow and Mueller finally came in late December. As Dowd asked what else was needed to wrap up this investigation that was hampering the presidency, Mueller gave them the answer for which they had been warily bracing.

"Well, we're going to need to interview the president," Mueller said.

Then the special counsel clarified why. Mueller confirmed that he needed a presidential interview to finish a report he was writing about his investigation of Trump. The special counsel regulations described a report as the method by which Mueller could communicate his findings to the attorney general, but the lawyers had never heard Mueller mention it before.

Dowd and Sekulow didn't say no to the interview. They asked more questions.

"You've got to tell us what you want to interview him on," Dowd said.

At first, Mueller's deputies insisted they weren't going to provide questions, but later they agreed that James Quarles, one of Mueller's deputies, would relay some basic topics they would ask about. Dowd and Sekulow did not have a problem with the special counsel asking Trump about his connections with Russians or participation in any interference conspiracy during the campaign. They believed he had none. But they were wary of other interview topics, such as questions that would probe what Trump had said to former FBI director James Comey about Flynn. Trump said flatly he didn't remember saying he had hoped Comey could "let this go" in discussing the investigation of Flynn, as Comey wrote in his contemporaneous notes, but a prosecutor could conclude that Comey had been honest and Trump had not. Those kinds of questions were Perjury Trap 101 for prosecutors.

The meeting ended without an agreement about an interview. Dowd and Sekulow then briefed Trump on what Mueller and his team had said. The president was excited. He was raring to get in a room with Mueller.

"Will they agree it's over?" Trump asked his lawyers. "Do I get my letter now?"

"Well, they want an interview," Dowd said.

Dowd explained how they might negotiate the terms of an interview.

"Great," Trump answered. "Let's do it."

Trump had an unyielding faith in his own abilities to persuade Mueller. "The president thought, 'I can do this. I can get this done,'" one of his advisers recalled.

What Trump's lawyers viewed as a legal matter with some political fallout, the president saw as a political event, with a legal component. He felt he was being bludgeoned in the media over all things Russia, perse-cuted in historic, even biblical proportions. Trump was adamant that the cloud be lifted by any means necessary, even if it meant taking control of the crisis himself.

"Any other president would have said, 'Do your thing and come to us when you are done,'" this adviser said. "That was not President Trump. President Trump wanted it done now. . . . You couldn't give him comfort by saying, 'We're going to deal with this the way we normally handle cases.' He would say, 'That's a fucked-up strategy. This isn't normal.'"

PART
THREE

Twelve

SPYGATE

January 11, 2018, began as a typical weekday morning in the White House. President Trump woke up and flicked on the television. This was a part of the day he loved. Alone in his bedroom, no aides to pester him, Trump manned the remote and surfed among channels on his two large screens. His television system was programmed to record all of the cable news shows so that he could fast-forward and rewind to when anchors and their guests discussed him—which, of course, was most of the time. "Television is often the guiding force of his day, both weapon and scalpel, megaphone and news feed," Ashley Parker and Robert Costa wrote in *The Washington Post*. He loved watching MSNBC's *Morning Joe* and CNN to see how the enemies were describing him, but *Fox & Friends*, with its sycophantic hosts, was where the president picked up some of his preferred ideas.

Deep into the first hour of *Fox & Friends*, on January 11, at 6:46 a.m., Andrew Napolitano came on the air. Napolitano was one of Trump's favorite Fox analysts, so much so that some of Trump's advisers had talked seriously about the former New Jersey judge as a possible Supreme Court nominee. The Republican-controlled House of Representatives was expected to vote that day to reauthorize a key part of the Foreign Intelligence Surveillance Act, a move the White House had endorsed. Known as the Section 702 program after its numerical reference in the statute, the measure was essential to U.S. intelligence agencies because it authorized government surveillance on foreigners abroad as a way of catching terrorists before they struck.

"I'm scratching my head," Napolitano said. "I don't understand why Donald Trump is in favor of this."

Napolitano said he did not trust the surveillance program and warned, erroneously, that it had likely been used to spy on the Trump campaign and give birth to the Russia investigation. Then, forty-seven minutes later, at 7:33 a.m., a gap in time explained perhaps because Trump had been watching *Fox & Friends* on a delay, the president announced his opposition to the bill that his own White House had been championing in language that eerily echoed Napolitano's commentary.

"House votes on controversial FISA ACT today," Trump wrote on Twitter, quoting verbatim the headline that had been used on Fox during Napolitano's appearance. "This is the act that may have been used, with the help of the discredited and phony Dossier, to so badly surveil and abuse the Trump Campaign by previous administration and others?" Trump's tweet was only thirty-nine words long, but it instantly sparked mayhem at the White House and on Capitol Hill. Key officials tore up their schedules for the morning to try to fix the mess created by the president.

Trump was confused. He conflated, as Napolitano had, Section 702 with the broader FISA law, which governs a vast assortment of surveillance practices. Trump and his allies were angered by FISA warrants, signed and approved three times by three judges, that had been issued to surveil the former Trump campaign aide Carter Page. But Section 702 was a separate and valuable classified program that could primarily target foreigners overseas, when they were suspected of plotting to kill Americans or of helping to support terror cells. The program allowed intelligence agencies to eavesdrop on these foreign citizens, though it could also pick up incidental communications with Americans who were in touch with those targets. Section 702 had been a backbone of the FBI's post-9/11 efforts to both spot these plots in the making and provide critical pieces of intelligence in the President's Daily Brief.

John Kelly intervened to reiterate the program's importance to the president. He asked House Speaker Paul Ryan to give Trump a thirty-minute primer on the difference between surveilling Americans with a judge-approved warrant and spying on foreigners. Kelly and Marc Short, the White House legislative affairs director, then huddled with lawmakers on Capitol Hill who were in a state of disbelief over the president's out-of-left-field tweet, trying to calm them down and round up votes.

Tom Bossert, the White House's homeland security and cybersecurity adviser, was traveling that morning but received an emergency call from the White House asking him to draft a cleanup tweet that the president could send immediately to reverse his position on renewing Section 702. Meanwhile, lawmakers were speaking out against Trump's position with opprobrium for his clear lack of knowledge.

"This is irresponsible, untrue, and frankly it endangers our national security," the Democratic senator Mark Warner tweeted. "FISA is something the President should have known about long before he turned on Fox this morning."

The White House's task to shore up votes for renewing Section 702 was further compounded by the opposition to it from two Republican lawmakers who were close to the president. Senator Rand Paul, a libertarian-minded Republican, called Trump the morning of January 11 to raise concerns that surveilling foreign targets could capture information on U.S. citizens. Paul said he would filibuster the bill if it reached the Senate because of his privacy concerns. Congressman Mark Meadows, who led the conservative House Freedom Caucus and was one of Trump's most faithful defenders, also called the president that morning to reiterate his opposition to the program because of concerns about civil liberties.

When a CNN reporter caught up with Kelly in the halls of Congress to ask if Trump's behavior made legislating more difficult, the chief of staff said, "It's not more difficult. It's a juggling act." Meanwhile, Kelly hurried to clean up the mess, arranging for FBI director Christopher Wray and Director of National Intelligence Dan Coats to explain to Trump how the Section 702 program worked and its value in keeping Americans safe. Throughout the tutorial, Trump never acknowledged making a mistake, never expressed any regret about wasting his staff's time and imperiling his administration's own legislative agenda.

"He's incapable of saying sorry," said one senior government official.

Trump finally tweeted a correction at 9:14 a.m., using language recommended by Bossert, as a reply to his original tweet, as if he were merely continuing the same thought.

"With that being said," Trump's message read, "I have personally directed the fix to the unmasking process since taking office and today's vote is about foreign surveillance of foreign bad guys on foreign land. We need it! Get smart!"

The tweet was as much an explanation of the policy for Trump himself as for anybody else. House Republicans were meeting at that very moment, alarmed by Trump's initial tweet, and their anxiety did not subside until Trump's second tweet registered. Later that day, the House voted overwhelmingly to reauthorize the foreign surveillance program, 256 to 164, and the Senate immediately took up debate on the measure. Crisis averted. Yet the president's misstep continued to reverberate.

At her afternoon briefing on January 11, White House press secretary Sarah Sanders struggled to explain Trump's tweets, insisting there was no discrepancy, and said any confusion over the president's position on the policy was with the media. "The president fully supports the 702 and was happy to see that it passed the House today," she said. "We don't see any contradiction or confusion in that."

When the NBC News correspondent Hallie Jackson asked about Trump's contradictions, Sanders snapped. "I think that the premise of your question is completely ridiculous and shows the lack of knowledge that you have on this process."

Privately, however, Trump's top advisers were exasperated by a crisis they believed would likely recur, considering how much value this president placed in cable news musings and how little value he placed in the expertise of his own government. Some of Trump's aides felt pity for him, too. He was so obsessed with the belief that the "Deep State" was trying to undermine his presidency by spying on his campaign adviser that the simple acronym "FISA" was like a red flag waved at a bull.

Also on January 11, Trump met in the Oval Office about immigration policy with a group of lawmakers, including the Democratic senator Dick Durbin, the Republican senators Lindsey Graham and Tom Cotton, and the Republican congressman Bob Goodlatte. As the group discussed a possible bipartisan immigration deal that would protect migrants from Haiti, El Salvador, and African countries, Trump grew frustrated.

"Why are we having all these people from shithole countries come here?" the president asked. He specifically denigrated Haiti, an impoverished Caribbean nation made up mostly of descendants of African slaves, and said the United States should instead allow migrants from Norway, a Nordic country that is one of the world's whitest and wealthiest, and other countries.

Trump's comment in the closed-door meeting, which was first reported by *The Washington Post*'s Josh Dawsey, triggered a days-long backlash. White House officials knew Trump had used the vulgarity and did not try to deny the story. The next morning, on January 12, Durbin told reporters that he had personally heard Trump say "things that were hate-filled, vile and racist."

But Trump later denied what his aides would not, tweeting that his language had been "tough, but this was not the language used."

The night of January 19, sitting in an oversized chair in the White House residence, Trump plotted aloud on the phone with Kelly late into the evening. His voice had a self-assured confidence. Trump believed he had finally found the silver bullet to snuff out the Mueller investigation.

"This can end the investigation into us," Trump told Kelly. "This is our opportunity to fire Rod. . . . And then it's over."

The president sounded pleased, pumped even. "Rod" was Rod Rosenstein, the deputy attorney general and the man empowered to restrain Mueller. Trump's excitement stemmed from a secret Republican memo that Meadows and other conservative allies in the House had been whispering to him about. They said if they could get permission from the Justice Department to release the memo to the public, the document would undermine Rosenstein by showing his early role in approving questionable surveillance and prove that the Mueller investigation was tainted.

Devin Nunes, who chaired the House Permanent Select Committee on Intelligence, had authored the four-page memo with a key staffer, Kashyap Patel, based on classified documents from the FBI investigation of Trump's campaign. Hailed as a hero by pro-Trump conservatives and dismissed as a reckless conspiracy theorist by some in the FBI, Nunes claimed in the memo that the bureau had abused its top secret surveillance powers and misled a federal judge in order to launch the Trump investigation in the first place. The memo alleged that the FBI used information from the former British spy Christopher Steele to obtain a warrant to conduct surveillance on Carter Page, a former Trump campaign adviser. Nunes insisted the FBI failed to alert the court to Steele's anti-Trump agenda. For weeks now, Nunes had been sparring with top Justice Department officials over releasing the memo. He and Rosenstein had had a cordial, at times even friendly relationship, but the congressman's obsession with alleged malfeasance in the Russia investigation drove a wedge between them.

On January 10, Nunes and Patel had met in a secured room at the Capitol with Rosenstein, Wray, Justice Department legislative affairs chief Stephen Boyd, FBI legislative affairs chief Gregory Brower, and others to go over their declassification requests. The meeting got off to a hostile start when Patel, who in 2017 had already established himself as a Justice Department antagonist by threatening to hold Rosenstein and Wray in contempt, insisted that Brower leave the room because he said Nunes's committee was investigating him for obstructing their congressional investigation.

Rosenstein thought this was more childish bullying from the Nunes crowd. "We are trying to accommodate your requests," he told Patel. "Director Wray and I cannot personally review all the documents. We need congressional liaisons to accomplish that. Threatening them over bogus allegations is not helpful if you want them to cooperate with you."

Later in the meeting, Rosenstein brought up Patel's past shenanigans and told Nunes, "If you really did prosecute me for contempt, I would call you and your staffers as defense witnesses to prove that I am operating in good faith, so I request that you preserve relevant text messages and emails."

On January 19, Nunes called Rosenstein and Wray with an update. He told them he would soon be releasing a memo criticizing the FBI's FISA process. Rosenstein took the call as he was being driven to a memorial service for his former colleague in the U.S. Attorney's Office in Maryland Deborah Johnston. Rosenstein was upset with Nunes. "You told Director Wray and me that you were not working on a report attacking the FBI," he told the congressman. "I repeatedly asked you to give us any evidence of wrongdoing so that we could investigate."

"It is a memo, not a report," Nunes replied. He said he believed there had been "systematic FISA abuse" and a "conspiracy."

"Who are the suspects and what are the crimes?" Rosenstein asked.

Nunes did not say.

On the phone the night of January 19, Trump told Kelly that public chatter about the Nunes memo and its revelations of a corrupt investigation were "gaining traction." He predicted that when the memo's contents became public, he would have ample justification to fire Rosenstein for not reining in such a flawed investigation. Finally, Trump said, the memo would reveal efforts by the intelligence and national security establishment he dubbed the "Deep State" to delegitimize his election victory.

"It's great, right?" Trump asked Kelly.

"Yes, sir," the chief of staff replied.

Trump's burst of optimism about ending the Mueller investigation came amid secret preparations by his legal team and the White House for an interview with the special counsel. Since New Year's Day, Trump's lawyers had been working with Kelly to set up a tentative interview at Camp David, the private presidential retreat in Maryland where guests could go undetected by the media. They were so far along in the process that they had made arrangements for helicopters to fly in Trump and his lawyers, and for Mueller and his team to enter the compound secretly. They had even set a date: January 27.

Trump's personal lawyers, John Dowd and Jay Sekulow, recognized the dangers of letting their client sit down with prosecutors and how a man who had such difficulty sticking to the facts could carelessly walk into a perjury accusation. Sekulow had been the most wary of the idea, and didn't think Mueller was justified in asking. But Trump was adamant about doing the interview because he believed he could convince Mueller of his innocence and be cleared of wrongdoing. Trump's lawyers concluded that disappointing the boss could be far more ominous. Dowd was wary of a presidential sit-down, but the lawyers moved ahead with preparations.

Trump's lawyers tried to hedge the risks for the president by pressing Mueller and James Quarles for more specificity about the nature of the questions they would ask Trump. Quarles complied with more details. But in several discussions with Mueller's team, Dowd felt Mueller was backing away from what Dowd considered earlier commitments and adding new conditions for the interview. Within days, Dowd decided to pull the plug. He called Quarles to tell him the interview was off. Sekulow and Cobb were surprised when they learned of the decision a few days later; Dowd had not run the idea by his fellow lawyers first. Explaining his reluctance to proceed with the interview, Dowd told Trump that it would have been a suicide mission and he could not have sent him into that maw.

"I'll just go talk to them," Trump replied. "Why can't I just talk to them?"

Dowd told the president, "We can't do this."

"Why can't I do this?" Trump shot back.

In various conversations, Dowd tried to lay out the risks of just one misstep in one answer to one question—to show Trump how easy it would be for him to say something that wasn't true, even if he didn't mean to lie.

Contrary to previous accounts, Dowd did not hold a murder board session or mock interview with the president. It was just Dowd face-to-face with the president, trying out a few questions to attempt to convince him that an interview with Mueller would be not some boardroom handshake deal but rather a torture session and final exam that he was bound to fail.

Dowd got through only one or two questions before it became obvious the president was winging it. It was palpably clear that he was not versed on the facts of the case and had not given much if any thought to how he might answer Mueller's questions. He said versions of "I did this" and "I did that"—framing himself as the guy in charge, the one at the wheel. Dowd pointed out that several of his claims were inaccurate and conflicted with the accounts of events provided by multiple witnesses.

Trump disputed the facts. He got frustrated when Dowd pointed out his errors and imperfections. Dowd tried to explain to Trump something he had sought to ingrain in his client many times before: there was a momentous difference between saying "No" and saying "I don't recall." Trump often bragged of having "the world's greatest memory," but Dowd reminded him that in a legal setting it was perfectly fine—even preferable—to say, "I don't recall."

Trump's friends and advisers had long observed that he had an amazing ability to disconnect from facts and remember experiences the way it suited him at the moment, a dangerous habit when being interviewed by federal prosecutors in a criminal investigation.

"The problem with him: he tells you what he thinks he knows or what he thinks he remembers," said one adviser. "He might actually believe it. And he may not think he is lying. When you confront him and say, but no, 'Remember this fact?' He'll say, 'That's right.' He'll work closer to the truth. It's not an inattention to the detail. It's his feeling that the details and pieces are irrelevant. He's a big-picture, broad-point guy. He says, 'Hey, I know this big point is true. Who cares about the other stuff?'"

Lying has been part of Trump's act all his life. "People ask me if the president lies. Are you nuts? He's a fucking total liar," Anthony

Scaramucci said. "He lies all the time. Trump called me one night after I was on *Bill Maher* and he said, 'How come you always fucking figure me out?' I said, 'I've seen you around for twenty years. I know your act. I know when you're saying shit you don't really mean, and I know when you're saying bullshit.' He laughed."

Scaramucci recalled that he then asked Trump, "Are you an act?" Trump replied, "I'm a total act and I don't understand why people don't get it."

In his back-and-forth with Dowd over the interview in mid-January, Trump continued to fume about the shift in plans. He was confused and angry that he couldn't proceed and get the interview over with. Dowd later called a colleague to complain about the tongue-lashing he had received from Trump. "I don't need this shit. I'm seventy-six years old," Dowd told the colleague. "I don't need to be treated like this." Dowd later contested this account and claimed Trump always treated him courteously.

Trump begrudgingly resigned himself to the notion that his lawyers were making the right call in deciding to cancel the interview. However, he then tried to convince the public of the opposite, announcing that the interview was very much still on the table even after Dowd had privately canceled it.

On the afternoon of January 24, Trump was meeting with some of his advisers when he abruptly stood up and said, "Wait here. I'll be right back." Down the hall in the chief of staff's office, Kelly had been meeting with a group of about twenty reporters for a briefing on the administration's immigration policy. Trump was loath to have a group of reporters' tape recorders running for someone other than himself, so he surprised the journalists—and their host, Kelly—by swinging open the door and walking in.

"Hello, everybody," the president said cheerfully. "How're we all doing?"

Trump was in a jovial mood and began an impromptu question-and-answer session. He bragged about how well the economy was doing and talked up his efforts to secure the border and set new standards about "chain migration." Less than ten minutes into the freewheeling session, a reporter asked Trump one of the questions dominating press coverage that month: Was the president still willing to sit down for an interview with Mueller?

"I'm looking forward to it, actually," Trump said. "Here's the story, just so you understand. There's been no collusion whatsoever. There's no obstruction whatsoever, and I'm looking forward to it."

Kelly pursed his lips. He knew Trump had just stretched the truth, suggesting an interview was just over the horizon. "I guess they are talking about two or three weeks," Trump said about when the interview would likely take place. "I have to say, subject to my lawyers and all of that, but I would love to do it."

That caveat—"subject to my lawyers and all of that"—was a major one for Trump. To the reporters and the public, Trump sounded as if he were planning an interview. To his lawyers, his careful word choice telegraphed that he was finally on board with their plan to resist the interview.

Trump also told the reporters that he felt it was "disturbing" that the FBI investigation of his campaign was so biased, with two FBI officials, Peter Strzok and Lisa Page, discussing their fear of a Trump presidency. Trump insisted that he had defeated Hillary Clinton entirely on his own merit.

"The fact is you people won't say this, but I'll say it," Trump added. "I was a much better candidate than her. You always say she was a *bad* candidate. You never say I was a good candidate. I was one of the *greatest* candidates. Nobody else would have beaten the Clinton machine, as crooked as it was. But I was a *great* candidate. Someday you're going to say that! Goodbye, everybody."

And then he was gone.

The president's sudden visit with reporters led to another classic White House cleanup. By the time press aides learned that Trump had said he was looking forward to his interview with Mueller, it was leading the cable news channels. Cobb issued a statement explaining that Trump had spoken hurriedly off the cuff and intended to say only that he was willing to meet with Mueller, not that he would be meeting with Mueller.

"He's ready to meet with them, but he'll be guided by the advice of his personal counsel," Cobb said.

Later that afternoon, Trump headed up to the residence to get ready for a big trip. The president was scheduled to fly out that evening to Switzerland to attend the World Economic Forum in Davos, where he was slated to meet with a number of foreign counterparts. With Trump up in his room, Kelly returned to his long list of chores. He called Goodlatte to talk with the Republican congressman about a budget resolution. Standard preparation for the legislative week ahead. Then Kelly let down his guard a bit. In a woe-is-me tone, he shared with Goodlatte that Trump's pop-in to the press and claim of doing an interview with Mueller came out of nowhere and were not part of any plan or strategy.

"I don't envy you," Goodlatte told Kelly.

That evening, January 24, waiting in the White House before departing for Davos, Trump fumed at the television screen. He was engaging in one of his guilty pleasures: hate-watching CNN. He called Kelly, this time incensed. He cursed the Justice Department.

White House aides sometimes informally measured the power of Trump's moods on an informal scale of one to ten. When Trump rated a one or two, advisers worried that he was so bored he had stopped listening entirely. At a nine or ten, he sounded over the phone to his advisers as if he might be jumping up and down, and some fretted whether they should ask a Secret Service agent to check on him.

This night, Kelly was experiencing Trump at a nine.

By now Kelly had gone home for the day. He was skipping the Davos trip to stay in Washington and work with lawmakers on an immigration plan. Trump shared with Kelly that he found the guest on CNN's 7:00 p.m. newscast riveting and the topic infuriating. The Republican congressman Trey Gowdy was criticizing the latest "Deep State" insurgency against the president: The Justice Department's senior leaders and the FBI director were saying that House Republicans could not make their secret memo public because it could reveal sensitive secrets about an ongoing probe. Gowdy told the CNN host Erin Burnett that the Justice Department appeared to be trying to hide something. Trump was supposed to walk out to the South Lawn to board Marine One, but first he conferred with Kelly about Gowdy's comments.

What followed was Trump once again plotting to snuff out a federal investigation, an episode that apparently went undetected by Mueller, for it garnered no mention in the special counsel's final report.

Trump howled to Kelly, with the chief of staff able to hear Gowdy talking on the television in the background.

"These fucking Justice people are blocking the release, and they are supposed to be my people!" Trump roared. "I don't understand why the Trump Justice Department won't release a pro-Trump memo that helps me! It's the worst thing anyone has ever seen."

Trump grew more enraged as he kept talking.

"This is *my* Justice Department. They are supposed to be *my* people," Trump told Kelly. "This is the 'Deep State.' . . . Mueller's all over it."

Gowdy described on television the advice he would give the president. He suggested Trump intervene to declassify the memo, then share these secrets of the origins of the FBI probe with the American people.

"My counsel to him is . . . release it in an appropriate forum and let the public decide," Gowdy told Burnett.

Trump ordered Kelly to call Jeff Sessions or Rosenstein to make sure the Justice Department stopped blocking the memo's release. He promised his chief of staff that this was not the end of the story. He would show them who was in power.

"If they won't release it," Trump said, "I will."

Trump soon boarded Marine One en route to Joint Base Andrews and took off for Davos. But even in the snowcapped Swiss Alps, where he had journeyed ostensibly to promote America's economic interests, the president remained obsessed with thwarting the investigator who infuriated and vexed him every day: Mueller.

I n late January, when Trump returned to Washington, he resolved to
ensure the secret Nunes memo would be released. The House Permanent Select Committee on Intelligence, which Nunes chaired, voted on
January 29 to declassify the memo, giving the president five days to review the document and raise any objections.

The White House immediately heard serious reservations from
throughout the intelligence community. Wray, Coats, and Rosenstein
all argued with Kelly against the memo's release, saying it could set a
dangerous precedent by exposing classified information and revealing
sources and methods of U.S. intelligence gathering. Furthermore, they
said, the document was an inaccurate depiction of the bureau's investigative methods.

The worries of intelligence and law enforcement officials mattered
little to Trump, however. He was determined to grasp onto anything,
even a partisan memo, to bolster his claim that the Russia investigation
was a "witch hunt."

"He believed it really was going to be the panacea he hoped for," one
adviser recalled.

White House aides were adamant that the president appear to follow
a fair and deliberative process in reviewing the declassification decision,
but Trump was caught on tape revealing his mind-set the night of January 30, when he delivered his State of the Union address to a joint session
of Congress. When a Republican lawmaker asked him to "release the
memo," Trump said, "Don't worry, 100 percent," and waved his hand
affirmatively.

By week's end, Trump got his wish and declassified the Nunes memo.
"It's a disgrace what's happening in our country," he told reporters in the
Oval Office on February 2. "A lot of people should be ashamed of them-
selves, and much worse than that."

The decision brought recriminations from congressional Democrats,
who warned that any firings at the Justice Department would trigger a
constitutional crisis. But the memo did not have Trump's intended effect.

Its central claim was that the warrant application to spy on Page relied on the Democrat-funded Steele dossier and that the Justice Department and senior FBI officials concealed this partisan bias from the judges reviewing the warrant application. Nunes's memo argued there was an anti-Trump conspiracy in hiding this pro-Clinton detail from the judges, and that Rosenstein lacked objectivity because he, too, had approved one of those dubious warrants.

Republicans ultimately had to concede, with the release of the memo's black-and-white text, that the government had in fact revealed the role of Trump's political opponents in funding the research. Rosenstein stayed on the job, and the Mueller investigation continued apace. At the FBI, Wray's response to the memo's release was remarkable. He issued a video and written statement to employees in which he took indirect aim at the president's tactics and urged agents to stay focused on their missions for the country.

"The American people read the papers, and they hear lots of talk on cable TV and social media. But they see and experience the actual work you do—keeping communities safe and our nation secure, often dealing with sensitive matters and making decisions under difficult circumstances," Wray said. "And that work will always matter more. Talk is cheap; the work you do is what will endure."

Thirteen

BREAKDOWN

R ob Porter, the White House staff secretary, had a title that belied his power and influence. He controlled the flow of paper to the president; managed the policy process, including mediating the often unruly internal debates over trade; and spent many hours a day at Trump's side, internalizing his preferences and shaping the direction of his presidency. He was Chief of Staff John Kelly's reliable partner.

In a White House staff notable for its renegades and misfits, Porter, forty, cut a singular figure. He was high achieving, smooth, and charismatic. He earned undergraduate and law degrees from Harvard, studied at Oxford as a Rhodes scholar, and then climbed the ranks on Capitol Hill to become, by only his midthirties, chief of staff to senior Republican Senator Orrin Hatch. Friends and former colleagues of Porter's told *The New York Times'* Katie Rogers, "He was articulate enough to be secretary of state. Intelligent enough to be a Supreme Court justice. Driven enough to be president."

But on February 6, 2018, the British tabloid the *Daily Mail* reported accusations of domestic abuse against him by both of his ex-wives. Porter denied abusing the women and claimed a "coordinated smear campaign." Kelly and other senior officials had adopted a bunker mentality in a White House constantly under siege. At first, they were defensive of Porter and viewed scrutiny from journalists as "gotcha" questions.

Kelly's initial statement on the matter, which he largely dictated to White House press secretary Sarah Sanders as she typed it on her computer, called Porter "a man of true integrity and honor, and I can't say enough good things about him." But on February 7, *The Intercept* posted photographs of one of the women, Colbie Holderness, with a black eye. Kelly then issued a second statement saying he was "shocked" by the allegations and that "there is no place for domestic violence in our society." Porter announced that day he would resign.

When Porter began as staff secretary in January 2017, he had been granted an interim clearance so that he could handle classified materials, often passing them directly to the president for his review or signature. But troubling allegations emerged in his background investigation. FBI agents interviewed his ex-wives as part of their standard investigation for his security clearance, and in July 2017 the bureau flagged the White House that they found derogatory information.

The specifics of who did what and when throughout the Porter saga remain murky and vary based on each person's account, but there was consensus among many staffers about one thing: Kelly misrepresented his own actions. At a February 9 senior staff meeting, after he had issued two divergent public statements about Porter, Kelly said that he had taken action to remove Porter within forty minutes of learning that abuse allegations were credible. But many staffers said Kelly's claim of swift action was dishonest, and it contradicted the public record.

"We were like, 'What are you saying?'" one White House adviser recalled. "He was blatantly lying. No you did not."

Sanders and her deputies, who were tasked with accounting for the administration's actions to a restive news media, were exasperated. Sanders was a willing warrior for Trump, at times sacrificing her own credibility in service to a president who obfuscated and lied for sport, but one day during the Porter scandal she lost it. She had had enough with the incomplete and misleading information she had been provided by her colleagues.

Standing in a hallway outside Deputy Chief of Staff Joe Hagin's West Wing office, Sanders lit into Don McGahn, a shouting match so loud that more than a dozen staffers heard it. She told him she would not continue to speak publicly on behalf of the administration unless she was provided more information about Porter's situation. Sanders quickly received the clarity she sought. The dispute was resolved and Sanders briefed reporters, but tensions between the press office and McGahn and Kelly persisted. "You couldn't get a straight answer from John Kelly," one aide recalled. "Either he was dishonest or an old man who can't remember things."

As Kelly refashioned his explanations for how he handled the Porter matter, he was consulting regularly with Trump. They both liked Porter a great deal and were disappointed to see him leave the White House. "We absolutely wish him well," Trump told reporters on February 9. The president continued, saying that Porter, "as you probably know, says he's innocent, and I think you have to remember that."

On the night of February 9 and the morning of February 10, Trump and Kelly spoke at length about the scandal. Trump complained that lots of women make things up about men for their own benefit. "He's a good guy," Kelly told Trump of Porter. Maybe, Trump said, Holderness purposefully ran into a refrigerator to give herself bruises and try to get money out of Porter? The president urged his chief of staff to have the White House trumpet this injustice and explain why it was so unfair to accuse or judge a man without all the facts. The parallels between Porter and the president were obvious. More than a dozen women have accused Trump of sexual assault and harassment, and he denied each claim— although he was infamously recorded in 2005 bragging to *Access Hollywood* host Billy Bush about grabbing women by their genitals against their will.

In addition, the Porter case coincided with the burgeoning Stormy Daniels scandal, which had been flaring since January when *The Wall Street Journal* first reported hush-money payments to the porn star. Daniels, whose real name is Stephanie Clifford, had been paid $130,000 in the final weeks of the 2016 campaign by Michael Cohen, Trump's longtime personal attorney and fixer, in exchange for her silence about a sexual encounter she claimed to have had with Trump in 2006, during his first year of marriage to Melania.

The morning of February 10, Trump decided he wanted to speak out again about Porter. At 10:30 a.m., he tweeted his view to the world: "Peoples lives are being shattered and destroyed by a mere allegation. . . . There is no recovery for someone falsely accused—life and career are gone. Is there no such thing any longer as Due Process?"

The Porter scandal put a harsh spotlight on the process for obtaining security clearances. Dozens of White House officials worked under interim clearances of varying levels, having access to some of the nation's most sensitive material while their FBI background investigations were pending. But only one of these officials mattered to the press corps—and ultimately to Trump—and that was Jared Kushner. The presidential son-in-law held a broad range of responsibilities that necessitated access to classified information, and he enjoyed regular access to the "holiest of holies" in the CIA trove of intelligence. Typically, senior officials did not stay on interim clearances for more than three months; Kushner by now had had his for thirteen months.

Amid the media scrutiny of the Porter case, Trump had directed McGahn to find out the status of the FBI investigation into Kushner's background. On February 9, McGahn received a call on a secure phone line from Rod Rosenstein. The deputy attorney general delivered some bad news. He didn't go into details but said there were continuing problems with Kushner's obtaining a high-level security clearance, and to expect further delay. Rosenstein said additional investigation was required.

As Mark Corallo had foreshadowed in May 2017, there was no way someone who failed multiple times to disclose all of his or her foreign contacts would receive the highest-level security clearance through a normal process. And Kushner, who had an unusually complex history of financial transactions and business dealings with foreigners, was no exception.

Bill Daley, a former White House chief of staff and commerce secretary under Presidents Obama and Clinton, respectively, said the right course was for Kushner to follow the same rules as every other senior government official, regardless of his lineage. "A family member with no experience at anything other than real estate, no real profile other than a family-run business with a shady past, given incredibly complicated tasks was a joke," Daley said. "People elect a president knowing so much about them, good or bad, but no one knows Jared Kushner in the game he is playing. The fact that he made so many blunders, starting with the back-channel talks with Russians, should have told one how in over his head he was."

Kelly had been concerned with Kushner's high level of access without a permanent clearance and was under pressure in the wake of the Porter scandal to overhaul the process for all White House clearances. On February 16, the chief of staff announced that he would be enforcing rigorous new rules that would prevent some officials with interim clearances from accessing top secret information. An aide briefed on Kelly's thinking told *The Washington Post* that the chief of staff knew his policy put a "bull's eye" on Kushner but that the rules were designed for national security and could not be ignored.

"The events of the last ten days have focused immense attention on a clearance process that has been in place for multiple administrations," Kelly wrote in a memo outlining the new policy. "We should—and in the future, must—do better."

The credibility that made Kelly such an asset in Trump's White House, which he had earned on the battlefield, was now tainted by his work in the Porter saga. Kelly's friends said the portrait of him in service to Trump bore little resemblance to the leader they had come to know. "This is a man who, across the Corps for 40 years, was considered to be the exemplar of moral principle and integrity," John R. Allen, a retired four-star Marine Corps general, said amid the Porter scandal. "He was a selfless servant in every possible way—a lot of personal courage, moral courage to do the right thing. His values were very powerfully formed, and it's just difficult for me to find in my memory of my service with him a flaw."

The problems for Kelly had been building. He came under sharp criticism in October 2017 for leveraging his standing as a Gold Star father who lost a son at war to help contain a political crisis over Trump's botched calls to the families of fallen soldiers and for falsely attacking the Democratic congresswoman Frederica Wilson. After the Florida Democrat criticized Trump's call to one soldier's widow, Kelly called the congresswoman an "empty barrel" and alleged that she wrongly claimed responsibility for a new FBI field office in Miami. When the *Sun Sentinel* released video showing she had made no such claim, Kelly said he would "absolutely not" apologize.

Then, in January, Kelly got crosswise with Trump when he said in a Fox News Channel interview that Trump's views on immigration had evolved because he wasn't "fully informed" when he first proposed a border wall during the campaign. "Campaign to governing are two different things, and this president has been very, very flexible in terms of what is within the realm of the possible," Kelly told Fox's Bret Baier. He added, "There's been an evolutionary process that this president has gone through."

Cable television's viewer in chief was not pleased. "Based on what you said, I'm totally misinformed and don't know what I'm talking about!" Trump thundered to Kelly after the interview aired. "You said I don't know what the fuck I'm talking about!"

"That's not what I said," Kelly told the president, explaining that Trump's position on the wall had indeed evolved since he initially took office and envisioned a forty-foot concrete barrier stretching across every mile of the border, from the Gulf of Mexico to the Pacific Ocean.

"No," Trump shot back. "That *is* what you said."

Both easily combustible, Trump and Kelly were used to recurring and escalating clashes. Some of them would conclude with Kelly's threatening to quit. "I'm out of here," the chief of staff would say, though he was merely venting his anger.

Trump was upset that the Porter story had dominated the news for several days straight and that week he began quietly calling friends to complain about Kelly and crowdsource possible replacements. After this moment, Kelly stopped lurking around the Oval Office as often or listening in on as many of the president's calls. Trump stopped consulting him on some key personnel decisions. And Kelly lost the trust and support of some on the staff.

"When you lose that power, when you lose the ability to really direct the White House staff as you need to in order to support the president, you've essentially lost the ability to do the job. You can stick around. I guess you can let the president decide when he is or isn't going to use you. But what happens is you become a virtual White House intern, being told where to go and what to do," Leon Panetta, a Democratic former White House chief of staff, defense secretary, and CIA director, said later in the spring.

"I think it won't take long before John says, 'What the hell am I doing here?'" Panetta added. "If you're true to yourself, you know that it's reached a point where you have to make the decision about who you are and what history's going to say about it."

On Friday, February 16, Rosenstein announced a sweeping indictment of thirteen Russian nationals and three Russian companies with an extensive criminal scheme to interfere with the 2016 U.S. presidential election. The thirty-seven-page indictment laid bare in exhaustive detail an ambitious Russian campaign of internet trolls and propaganda to trick Americans into supporting Trump. Rosenstein accused the Russian suspects of conducting what he termed "information warfare against the United States." While this indictment did not charge anyone from Trump's campaign, it dealt a fatal blow to one of the president's favorite talking points, that Russian interference was a hoax created by Democrats as an excuse for losing an election they should have won.

That weekend in Florida, Trump lashed out about the Russia probe in a defiant and profane tweetstorm that was exceptional even by his own standards, beginning after 11:00 p.m. Saturday, February 17, and ending around noon Sunday, February 18. He accused Democrats of enabling a foreign adversary to interfere in the election. He attacked the FBI for missing signals of the school shooting in nearby Parkland, Florida. He undermined his own national security adviser, H. R. McMaster. And he lit into some of his favorite targets: the media, Congressman Adam Schiff, and Hillary Clinton.

Trump faulted the Mueller investigation and other Russia probes for sowing discord in America. He wrote in one of his Twitter messages, "If it was the GOAL of Russia to create discord, disruption and chaos within the U.S. then, with all of the Committee Hearings, Investigations and Party hatred, they have succeeded beyond their wildest dreams. They are laughing their asses off in Moscow. Get smart America!"

Trump spent much of his weekend watching cable news and venting to friends that the Russia investigation was dominating the news cycle. He had dinner Saturday night with the talk-show host Geraldo Rivera before retreating to his private quarters and firing off the first in his series of controversial tweets. Trump was especially irritated with McMaster, who was in Germany addressing the annual Munich Security Conference. He said in his speech there that evidence of Russian interference in the U.S. election was "incontrovertible."

Trump, who firmly believed any acknowledgment of Russia's crimes took away from the validity of his own election victory, upbraided the national security adviser on Twitter: "General McMaster forgot to say that the results of the 2016 election were not impacted or changed by the Russians and that the only Collusion was between Russia and Crooked H, the DNC and the Dems. Remember the Dirty Dossier, Uranium, Speeches, Emails and the Podesta Company!"

The pressures remained when Trump returned to the White House. On February 21, he invited Corey Lewandowski, his former campaign manager, whom he regarded almost as a son, to the Oval Office. Kelly and Lewandowski had an especially acrimonious relationship. Earlier that month, for instance, Lewandowski had criticized Kelly on television for his handling of the Porter scandal. Much like Trump, Lewandowski was crude, combative, and cocky. During the campaign, he was charged with misdemeanor battery for grabbing the arm of a reporter. Kelly thought Lewandowski was nothing but trouble, a Trump sycophant and palace infighter who revved up the president's riskier instincts and profited off their relationship with a lucrative consulting business. Just a couple months earlier, Kelly and Lewandowski had clashed in front of the president and other advisers during a meeting about political strategy. Lewandowski delivered a fatalistic outlook on the 2018 midterm elections: "You're going to get fucking crushed. You guys don't have your shit together." He proceeded to fault Kelly, as well as White House political director Bill Stepien, for deficiencies in the political operation and congressional outreach. He argued that the staff was not being strategic enough in using the powers of incumbency to build a foundation for the midterms, now less than one year away.

In the February 21 meeting, Trump and Lewandowski had spent about fifteen or twenty minutes alone, catching up and talking politics, when the president called for Kelly to join them. The conversation was acrimonious and interrupted by an urgent phone call for Trump. Kelly and Lewandowski stepped out of the Oval Office to leave Trump to take the call. As they stood just outside the Oval, Kelly and Lewandowski argued. Kelly told other people to "throw him out of my fucking house."

That's when the shouting match began, with Lewandowski standing close to Kelly's face. They were so loud their voices could be heard in the front lobby of the West Wing, where an aide rushed to shut a door to try to muffle the noise.

"This isn't your house," Lewandowski yelled back at Kelly. "This is the people's house. Fuck you. I don't work for you."

The two men argued so loudly their faces turned red. Kelly grabbed Lewandowski by his collar and tried to push him against a wall. The chief of staff was a Secret Service protectee, so agents rushed in to ensure he would be safe.

"If you put your hands on me, you'll spend the rest of your career in Siberia," Lewandowski told one of the agents. "I don't work here. I'm a friend of the president. Do not touch me."

The two men quickly cooled down and agreed to a truce. But before going their separate ways, Lewandowski told Kelly, "The day you are walking off the campus is the day I will walk back on because I'm not leaving, ever."

On February 27, Kelly spelled out the administration's new security clearance policy in more detail. All those operating on an interim top secret clearance or the more specialized TS/SCI clearance for a year or more would have their access downgraded to secret. That was a far lower level of access, one that literally millions of government employees had in their jobs and would normally hamper a senior White House adviser's ability to do his or her work. Kelly's policy effectively downgraded Kushner's clearance, a severe limitation on the Trump family member's access to intelligence and other classified information.

Kushner was the classic profile of a person who would be rejected for a national security clearance, and Kelly's move to downgrade his clearance level provided comfort to the CIA. Agency officials had been wary of allowing Kushner to see highly sensitive information about sources and methods, based on his pattern of talking to foreign leaders in the Middle East—including Mohammed bin Salman, Saudi Arabia's crown prince—without State Department diplomats or other government experts guiding him.

The intelligence agencies were on guard in part because, as the *Post* reported on February 27, they had intercepted private conversations of leaders in China, Israel, Mexico, and the United Arab Emirates talking about the ease with which they could manipulate Kushner. Some of these foreign leaders described Kushner as naive and easily pushed; others said his financial debts and search for refinancing for an underwater Manhattan skyscraper were one route that made him vulnerable to pressure.

Immediately after Kelly's order, national security staff at the White House got new standing orders for how to deal with Kushner. They could no longer provide particularly sensitive intelligence products to him and tailored his reports to ensure he had necessary information on subjects on which he worked. Kushner and Ivanka Trump wanted Kelly to restore his clearance, telling him this was a problem. When they couldn't move him, Ivanka lobbied her father, complaining at least twice to the president that Kelly was taking away her access as well. She said that she and Kushner would be marginalized and unable to do their jobs without higher-level clearances and pleaded with him to fix it. When Kelly soon learned what Ivanka was telling Trump, he became incensed—because it wasn't true. Ivanka had joined the White House staff in April 2017, meaning she had had an interim security clearance for less than one year and therefore was not affected by the new policy.

"Ivanka lied to her father's face, saying her security clearance had been downgraded as well," a White House adviser recalled. "She told her father that Kelly had taken her clearance. It was a complete lie."

Publicly, Trump had sought to distance himself from the security clearances dilemma. When reporters asked him about Kushner's access earlier in February, the president said, "I will let General Kelly make that decision, and he's going to do what's right for the country. And I have no doubt that he will make the right decision."

Privately, however, Trump intervened and applied pressure on Kelly. He asked his chief of staff, wasn't there a way to get the kids permanent top secret clearances? Trump never gave a direct order, but left a strong suggestion that Kelly should prioritize this problem and fix it for him.

"I wish we could make this go away. This is a problem," Trump told Kelly, stressing that this was making him and his family look bad.

Kushner and Ivanka disputed to associates that they had sought to apply improper pressure, and Kushner later denied publicly that he had ever talked about his clearance status with the president. "I have not discussed it with him," Kushner told *Axios*.

But others in the administration felt unrelenting pressure from Kushner and Ivanka. The president's daughter tried to prod McGahn to intervene, something she later denied to associates, but when the White House counsel didn't deliver what she wanted, Ivanka whispered to her father and to other White House aides that McGahn was a "leaker" and not to be trusted. "Leaker" was about the worst red-flag name you could give someone in the presence of the bull named Donald Trump.

There was no love lost between McGahn and Ivanka. The lawyer was already highly wary of the first daughter, and they had had a number of run-ins the year prior. But the security clearances issue ultimately ruined Kelly's relationship with the kids. He was furious that Ivanka was using her standing as first daughter to cajole her father to intervene on an issue of national security importance. Kelly would never trust her or Kushner again.

A pair of departures threatened to wreak more havoc on the White House. On February 28, Hope Hicks, the communications director who had become the president's de facto therapist and could be counted upon to manage his moods and talk him out of hazardous ideas, announced that she would soon depart. The timing of her exit seemed significant; a day earlier, she had spent more than eight hours testifying before the House Intelligence Committee as part of its Russia investigation and admitted to telling white lies on behalf of the president. But her departure had been in the works for several weeks and had nothing to do with the various probes. After more than three tumultuous years at Trump's beck and call, Hicks was burned out and eager for a fresh start outside Trump's orbit. Months later, she would settle far away in Los Angeles as an executive at New Fox, the Murdoch family media empire.

A week later, Gary Cohn resigned as National Economic Council director amid a fierce internal clash over trade policies. A former president of Goldman Sachs, Cohn had served as a free-market counterweight to Trump's protectionist impulses and as an interlocutor with the business community. When the president decided to proceed with tariffs on steel and aluminum imports, which threatened to touch off a global trade war, Cohn called it quits.

The departures of Cohn, Hicks, and Porter represented an inflection point in the presidency. Some of Trump's stabilizers, the advisers who urged caution and found consensus, were gone. The result was an air of anxiety and volatility in the White House. The president confided to friends that he was uncertain about whom around him he could trust. And he seethed about perceived betrayals, such as a photo obtained by

Axios that made the rounds on cable television showing Rosenstein, At-torney General Jeff Sessions, and Solicitor General Noel Francisco hav-ing dinner together on February 28. The scene was interpreted as an act of solidarity by the Justice Department's top two officials after Trump had again attacked Sessions on Twitter.

Observers registered a new level of alarm. "This is an unprecedented position of chaos," Barry McCaffrey, a retired four-star army general, said at the time. "I think the president is starting to wobble in the emo-tional stability and this is not going to end well."

Kelly did not cloak his disdain for some parts of his White House job when he visited his former workplace on March 1. At an event celebrat-ing the fifteenth anniversary of the Department of Homeland Security, Kelly told department employees that he missed working with them "ev-ery day" and lamented his abbreviated, six-month tenure as homeland security secretary.

"The last thing I wanted to do was walk away from one of the greatest honors of my life, being secretary of homeland security," Kelly said. "But I did something wrong and God punished me, I guess."

Fourteen

ONE-MAN FIRING SQUAD

By March 2018, Robert Mueller's intentions were still completely unknown to those in the president's orbit. Trump aired his state of mind hourly, while Mueller was an enigma. He did no media interviews and made no public appearances. His team of prosecutors and investigators were just as tight-lipped, and the office's spokesman neither confirmed nor denied media reports about the state of the investigation.

Meanwhile, the White House had sent Mueller reams of emails and other documents, Ty Cobb and John Dowd having convinced Trump that full cooperation would be their best strategy. The president's aides and advisers were told they had an obligation to be witnesses and answer questions from the special counsel. By the end of February, Mueller's office had interviewed just about everyone in the White House who might have relevant information to share, including Don McGahn, Hope Hicks, and Avi Berkowitz, the twenty-nine-year-old assistant to Jared Kushner, although sit-downs continued well into the spring.

For some Trump aides, the interview experience was terrifying. Their lawyers instructed them not to talk to colleagues—and certainly not to the president—about the investigation, so they did not quite know what to expect. They were covertly whisked away to a conference room in a windowless government building and seated facing half a dozen or more special counsel prosecutors and FBI agents. Others, including an FBI body language expert, sometimes lurked around the edges of the room, observing.

The questioners were thorough and incredibly well prepared, asking the same questions several different ways to elicit revelatory answers. As one witness recalled, "They don't ask any question they don't know the answer for." The inquiries often lasted for many hours and sometimes for multiple days. The witnesses were afraid both of oversharing, for fear of eventually facing the president's wrath, and of slipping into a lie, for fear of becoming the next Michael Flynn.

Mueller's deputies led most of the questioning, but Mueller would come in and out of the room, looming silently over the sessions with his rigid bearing. A second witness described Mueller's stare as downright frightening: "He comes in and puts those dead eyes on you like a fucking shark. . . . Shark eyes. Dead eyes. Big, old, dead eyes."

Steve Bannon felt ready for his first of several sessions with the Mueller team. He had spent the previous month doing murder boards—practice sessions in which the lawyers interrogated Bannon so he could rehearse answers—with his lawyer, William Burck, and a team of associates. Bannon had studied the events prosecutors were most likely to probe and had reviewed copies of his correspondence. But when he showed up the morning of the interview, he had a bout of stage fright. He peeked into the conference room and saw about twenty-five people—prosecutors, FBI agents, and other investigators. He thought Mueller was about to flip the tables on him and for a moment feared he might not make it out a free man. He pulled Burck aside.

"What the fuck is going on here?" Bannon asked his lawyer. "There's murderers' row in there."

Burck also represented Reince Priebus and McGahn, and Bannon asked him whether such a large showing from Mueller's team was standard.

"How many did Reince have?" Bannon said.

"Reince had about five," Burck said. Then he offered an explanation to his concerned client: "Everybody wants to tell their grandkids they were here when Darth Vader was deposed."

The two men laughed and Bannon calmed down. When they entered the room, Mueller walked up to greet the star witness. He again brought up Bannon's daughter Maureen, just as he had when they first met outside the Oval Office in May 2017.

"I really think Maureen is going to be really happy with the decision she made being back up at West Point," Mueller told Bannon. Maureen had only recently opted to return to the academy, and Bannon couldn't fathom how Mueller knew. Mueller said he had heard the news from a friend.

Later, Bannon told Burck, "He did that just to say, 'You're one of us. Besides all your bullshit, you're actually a naval officer and your daughter is a West Point grad. Remember that.'"

Mueller had set his sights on a much more important witness: the president himself. On March 5, Trump's lawyers met with the special counsel for the first time since Dowd had summarily canceled the tentative interview with Trump scheduled for January 27.

Sitting with Mueller and Quarles, and accompanied by his co-counsel Jay Sekulow, Dowd once again laid out his legal theory for why the president did not need to answer the special counsel's questions. Dowd said Trump had broad executive power to lawfully take the precise actions Mueller's team was scrutinizing. He again cited the ruling in the Mike Espy case, which established that prosecutors needed to show they couldn't get critical and necessary information in any other way before demanding an interview with the president.

The interview wasn't going to happen, Dowd declared. "You've got no right," he said.

For a moment, no one said anything. Silence. Then Mueller piped up. "Well, John, we could subpoena him," Mueller said.

This was a subtle threat and in one sense the most basic statement any prosecutor could make to a defense lawyer. But it was the first time Mueller had used the *S*-word this directly with Trump's lawyers, and it made Dowd rear back. He told Mueller that subpoenaing the president to appear before a grand jury would be highly aggressive, thrusting them into a pitched battle in federal courts that could take many months to be resolved. Surely this would go to the Supremes. And while Dowd was confident Trump's side would prevail, he thought privately that a subpoena battle would be awful. It would keep the cloud over Trump's presidency indefinitely, the exact opposite of what his client wanted.

Dowd hit the conference table with his hand. "Good, go ahead. I can't wait to get you before a federal judge and have you explain why you need this information when you have no evidence [of a crime] and you have all the answers."

He snapped at Mueller: "This isn't some game. You are screwing with the work of the president of the United States."

Mueller sat poker-faced, listening, then reiterated the team needed an interview with the president to "square our corners." His deputies amplified that the president's answers were essential to the investigation. Courts had not previously ruled on the legality of issuing a presidential subpoena for testimony. Although independent counsel Kenneth Starr subpoenaed President Clinton for grand jury testimony in 1998, it was never tested in court, because Starr withdrew it once the president agreed voluntarily to sit for an interview. Paul Rosenzweig, who worked on Starr's investigation as a senior counsel, explained to *The Washington Post* that judges are generally inclined to accommodate presidents so that they can focus on their sworn duties, such as managing world affairs, but also are loath to protect them from investigations because "no man is above the law, and if it's a lawful investigation, then he must respond."

The March 5 meeting ended without an agreement. Trump's lawyers proceeded to debate among themselves how to deal with Mueller's continuing request for an interview. The president, meanwhile, continued to stew about the canceled January interview, believing he could have cleared his own name.

On March 6, amid these discussions of a presidential interview, Rex Tillerson departed on a sensitive diplomatic mission to Africa to mend fences and ease tensions caused by Trump's decidedly undiplomatic rhetoric. Like just about everyone else in Trump World, Tillerson had a target on his back. He had internal enemies. In the fall of 2017, he weathered reports that Trump was cooking up a plan to oust him as the nation's top diplomat. Rumors of his demise were so pervasive that they took on a name of their own—Rexit—even though few people knew how forcefully Tillerson had confronted Trump.

Yet through it all, Trump tolerated Tillerson and kept him at his side. In fact, back in January, following fresh reports about the president's calling some African and Caribbean nations "shithole countries," a diplomatic embarrassment for the United States, Trump sought Tillerson's assurance that he would stay on as secretary of state.

"We're good, right, Rex?" Trump asked as the two finished up a meeting in the Oval Office.

"What do you mean, sir?" Tillerson replied.

"You're staying on, right?" Trump said. "You're going to stay with this?"

"Yes, sir," Tillerson said. "As long as you feel I'm of use to you, I will continue to serve."

The president slapped the secretary of state on the back. "Good, good," Trump said. "You're staying on."

Tillerson's five-country visit to Africa in March was the first trip he had made to the continent as secretary. It was a listening tour more than anything else, an attempt to repair relations that had been strained by Trump's "shithole" remark. His first few days abroad went smoothly, but starting on March 9, Tillerson and some of his staff were suffering from a wrenching food-bourne illness. The doctor who traveled with him concluded they had eaten or drunk something bad and would be sick for a day or two but recover fine. Unbeknownst to Tillerson, trouble was brewing back home.

On Friday, March 9, at about 7:00 p.m. in Washington, White House chief of staff John Kelly told his aides he needed to call Tillerson immediately from a secure phone. It was about 2:00 a.m. on Saturday in Kenya, where the secretary was staying, but Kelly insisted they wake Tillerson up. It was that important.

"The president is really upset," Kelly told Tillerson, urging him to return home. "You should wind up your trip."

Kelly tried to convey the urgency of the situation to Tillerson, whom he trusted as an ally in steering Trump away from calamity. Earlier that day, Kelly spotted U.N. ambassador Nikki Haley, a Tillerson rival, and National Security Adviser H. R. McMaster, who had sometimes tussled with the secretary, leaving the Oval Office. Once Kelly got inside the room, the president was raving about Tillerson and what a terrible secretary of state he was. The chief of staff couldn't be sure, but he assumed that whatever Haley and McMaster had told the president set him off.

First, Tillerson had to think through the logistics. He had a packed schedule for the next three days and was already canceling upcoming events because his staff felt so ill.

"John, I have a lot of events lined up," Tillerson answered. "I can do that, but . . ." His voice trailed off.

Kelly told him he would check into things and call him back. He did.

"It's all patched up," Kelly said. "Don't worry about it. No need to rush back."

Still, Tillerson knew something was up. Later that morning, he made arrangements to cut his trip short by a day, leaving on Monday, March 12, instead of Tuesday.

Kelly called again the next night with another harsh wake-up call. It was Saturday evening in Washington, but roughly 2:00 a.m. Sunday in Africa.

"You really need to get back," Kelly told Tillerson. "The president is going to fire you."

Kelly explained that now Trump wanted to oust Tillerson by tweet, and the chief of staff was trying to stop him. Kelly was treading water, trying to buy time. Tillerson didn't seem that upset about the prospect of losing his job. However, he did stress over the terrible optics. How could the president fire his secretary of state while he was on an overseas mission? It would signal a breakdown in American government.

"John, that is really not good," Tillerson said. "That's going to look terrible. For the country."

Tillerson told Kelly he could get back to Washington by about 4:00 a.m. Tuesday; then he'd go to his Kalorama home to get a few hours' sleep before coming into the office.

On Monday evening, rumors that Tillerson was likely out began to spread through the Washington press corps, but State Department officials flatly dismissed the chatter as false. Tillerson didn't immediately share with the reporters traveling with him to Africa what Kelly had told him, but he also didn't lie as he explained why he was cutting the trip short.

"I felt like, look, I just need to get back," Tillerson told reporters aboard his flight home from Nigeria. "I just felt like I need to get back."

On what Tillerson knew might be his last gaggle with reporters, the secretary decided to break with the president on Russia.

The British government had just accused Russia of orchestrating the poisoning of a former Russian spy and his daughter in Salisbury, England. White House press secretary Sarah Sanders declined to lay blame on Moscow, but Tillerson was clear in his assessment: "Much work remains to respond to the troubling behavior and actions on the part of the Russian government."

Tillerson's plane touched down at Joint Base Andrews right on time, around 4:00 a.m. Tuesday, and his driver spirited the secretary home so that he could get some shut-eye. Then, after Tillerson arose to get dressed and ready for his day, Trump's tweet landed with a thud. It was 8:44 a.m.

"Mike Pompeo, Director of the CIA, will become our new Secretary of State," Trump wrote. "He will do a fantastic job! Thank you to Rex Tillerson for his service! Gina Haspel will become the new Director of the CIA, and the first woman so chosen. Congratulations to all!"

Alerted to the tweet by a phone call from his chief of staff, Margaret Peterlin, Tillerson felt it was important to say something quickly to calm folks down at the State Department. He told Peterlin what he wanted to convey and asked her to have Steve Goldstein, the undersecretary of state for public diplomacy and public affairs, issue a statement on his behalf.

Goldstein had gotten up around 3:00 a.m., just in case he was needed when the secretary arrived at Andrews, but had no idea about the drama over the weekend. At about 8:45 a.m., he was conducting a Skype session with some employees in U.S. embassies of African nations when two aides showed up and gestured with a cutting motion across their throats. You have to go, one finally told Goldstein. He abruptly ended the session. For a moment, he thought that something might have happened to his spouse.

"The secretary has been fired on Twitter," one staffer told him.

"What?" Goldstein said.

They showed him the tweet. Goldstein gulped.

"Let's take the back elevator to my office," he said.

Goldstein glanced down at his phone. He had dozens of phone messages and texts, most of them from reporters.

When he got to his office, TV screens were blaring the news that Trump had booted Tillerson and that Kelly had told him he was out. Goldstein reached Peterlin on her cell phone. She had just gotten off the phone with Tillerson and gave Goldstein the statement he could issue. It conveyed the truth but left out some of the unpleasant details.

"The Secretary did not speak to the President this morning and is unaware of the reason, but he is grateful for the opportunity to serve, and still believes strongly that public service is a noble calling and not to be regretted," Goldstein said in the statement.

Within minutes, Twitter and cable news lit up, emphasizing the differences between the White House's version of events and the State Department's, and citing Goldstein's statement. Watching the coverage on television, Trump seethed. One of Goldstein's aides rushed into his office to say that Steve Doocy was on the phone. Goldstein didn't immediately recognize the name, puzzled over it a minute, and thought it sounded familiar.

"Steve Doocy? From Fox News?" Goldstein said. "I don't know him. I'm not talking to anybody I don't know."

Then the aide came back and said, no, it's *Sean Doocey*.

Goldstein asked him to please find out who that was. The answer: Doocey worked at the White House, in the presidential personnel office. Goldstein called him back.

"The president has relieved you of your duties," Doocey told him.

Goldstein let that sink in.

Into the silence, Doocey's voice came back.

"Do you want something in writing to this effect?" Doocey asked.

Goldstein remained calm and said, "Yes, please."

Once Tillerson got into the office and learned of Goldstein's firing, he was upset.

"This is not right," Tillerson told his public affairs chief. "You just issued my statement."

Tillerson said he would call Kelly to say his staffer shouldn't be faulted for issuing his statement, but Goldstein told him there was no need to try to reverse the decision. He said he was mostly sad about the country losing a stand-up public servant like Tillerson. He didn't care about his own job.

Not long after, Trump called Tillerson from Air Force One as he was flying to California for a fund-raiser. He spoke as if they were friends catching up on their respective days.

"Hi, Rex," the president said. "I hope you saw all the good things I said about you on TV."

Tillerson had not had time to turn on a television, much less to sit and watch one. He had no idea what Trump was talking about, but the president had complimented Tillerson to reporters earlier. "I actually got along well with Rex," Trump told them, "but really it was a different mind-set, a different thinking."

"You should be very happy," Trump told Tillerson. "You never really wanted to do this job. Now you can retire and go back to your ranch and relax."

Tillerson found this summary surreal. He responded without emotion.

"Yes, Mr. President," he said.

"This will be great," Trump said.

"Yes, Mr. President," Tillerson replied, robotically.

"Okay, so I'm back Friday," Trump said. "Come by the Oval and we'll take a picture and I'll sign it."

"Yes," Tillerson said. "Sure, Mr. President."

They hung up.

Trump acted as if he and Tillerson would be buddies, never actually mentioning the firing or offering a rationale for it. At the same time, some of Trump's top aides were privately trashing Tillerson to reporters. They argued that Tillerson had been a poor manager at the State Department, isolating himself from thousands of career diplomats and getting bogged down in a bureaucratic restructuring plan. They said Trump had soured on Tillerson in part because of how much negative press he received and because the president thought he was too arrogant. And they said Tillerson lacked necessary gravitas abroad because foreign leaders did not believe he spoke for the president. They didn't mention the real reason for that: Trump had repeatedly contradicted Tillerson publicly.

Kelly felt defeated. He had struggled to protect Tillerson's job and feared the result of Trump's grinding through another of his guardrails. Aboard Air Force One en route to California, Kelly uttered an ominous view to a handful of other aides: "The forces of darkness have won today."

Tillerson decided he wanted to speak for himself, making an on-camera statement from the State Department at 2:00 p.m. He called Kelly to tell him the general outline of the statement he planned to deliver and to make sure it was okay. He didn't want to create another ricochet of reaction from the White House, as occurred with Goldstein's statement. Kelly gave a green light to the general outline.

In his remarks, Tillerson did not thank or compliment Trump.

Instead, he said he was honored to serve his country, praised Secretary of Defense Jim Mattis, thanked career diplomats for serving with "honesty and integrity," and expressed gratitude to the American people for "acts of kindness."

The omission angered Trump, who was quick to see personal slights in the words of his subordinates.

A few days later, the White House delivered yet another demeaning insult to Tillerson, this time a blunder by Kelly, his friend. The chief of staff convened an off-the-record session with a couple dozen reporters and shared his account of Tillerson's firing. Kelly said that when he reached Tillerson in Nairobi to let him know he may soon be fired, the secretary of state was suffering from traveler's diarrhea.

"He had Montezuma's revenge, or whatever you call it over there," Kelly said. "He was talking to me from the toilet."

The journalists and White House aides in the room grimaced. Kelly later regretted that his off-the-record remark was reported in the media, another humiliation for Tillerson. It hadn't even been true. Tillerson and his staff had all caught a bug that caused violent vomiting and dehydration. He had a mild case compared with some of his senior staff and had canceled some of his appearances to let them rest. When Kelly called Tillerson with the bad news, his very ill chief of staff and another aide had dutifully come to the secretary's room to wake him from a deep sleep. He took the call in his bedroom suite.

Tillerson would stay on the job until March 31, to help ensure an orderly transition, but he never went to the White House to take his picture with the president. Nearly a year would pass before he and Kelly spoke again.

As Trump disposed of his secretary of state, he was also browbeating Dowd to take to television and Twitter to bludgeon Mueller—precisely the sorts of attacks that the president's initial legal team steered away from—and spotlight what the president saw as the partisan motivations of the special counsel and other investigators. Trump believed

Congressman Devin Nunes's theory that the probe was tainted from the start, and on Friday, March 16, he seized an opportunity to exact revenge.

For his role in steering the initial investigation into Russia's election interference and possible conspiracy between the Kremlin and the Trump campaign, Andrew McCabe was a frequent target of Trump's ire. McCabe had already stepped down as the FBI's deputy director under pressure after the Justice Department's inspector general found he had authorized the disclosure of sensitive information to the media about the Hillary Clinton email case, but technically he remained an FBI employee.

As a twenty-year veteran of the bureau, McCabe was set to retire as soon as he turned fifty on March 18 and would be eligible for his full retirement benefits. But Trump, with the help of Attorney General Jeff Sessions, sought to punish a foe. Just before ten o'clock on the evening of March 16, Sessions fired McCabe effective immediately, saying that he was acting on the recommendations of the inspector general and the FBI office that handles discipline. The swift termination threatened to cost McCabe a portion of his retirement benefits.

Though technically the firing was executed by Sessions, the loudest celebrations came from the White House residence, where the president pecked out his reaction on Twitter at 12:08 a.m.: "Andrew McCabe FIRED, a great day for the hard working men and women of the FBI— A great day for Democracy. Sanctimonious James Comey was his boss and made McCabe look like a choirboy. He knew all about the lies and corruption going on at the highest levels of the FBI!"

On March 17, St. Patrick's Day, Trump began a weekend of public and private brooding over the Russia investigation. He tweeted that the Mueller probe was a "WITCH HUNT" that "should never have been started" and claimed it was "based on fraudulent activities and a Fake Dossier." Trump spent the weekend in Washington and complained to friends and advisers that his lawyers were doing a lousy job protecting him. He said the situation was particularly painful because he believed Rod Rosenstein, who oversaw the probe, was up to no good and shielding a corrupt investigation from scrutiny by Nunes and other Trump allies in Congress. Dowd succumbed to Trump's wishes to publicly assail Mueller when he emailed reporters a statement calling on Rosenstein to immediately end the probe.

"I pray that Acting Attorney General Rosenstein will follow the brilliant and courageous example of the FBI Office of Professional Responsibility and Attorney General Jeff Sessions and bring an end to alleged Russia Collusion investigation manufactured by McCabe's boss James Comey based upon a fraudulent and corrupt Dossier," Dowd said in the statement.

Dowd got twisted in knots trying to explain his statement. He first told *The Daily Beast* that he was speaking on behalf of the president. A few hours later, he backtracked, telling *The Washington Post* that he was speaking for himself and not on Trump's behalf.

Regardless, Senate minority leader Charles Schumer warned of "severe consequences" if Trump and his legal team took action to interfere with or end the Russia investigation. Robert Bauer, a former Obama White House counsel, said facetiously, "That is certainly an unconventional way of mounting a legal defense." Dowd increasingly felt sapped by Trump's heaping blame on him for the probe not wrapping up quickly. But on that point, the president was in the right. It was Dowd who had given him an all-too-rosy forecast.

Dowd confided that weekend in another Trump adviser: "He's beating the shit out of me. He's abusive."

Trump, meanwhile, was working to undermine Dowd. Just as Trump had found the counsel of his national security professionals tiresome, he grew frustrated with the people on his legal team. He wanted to shake things up. Without initially confiding in Dowd or his White House counsel, Trump started working to add muscle to his legal defense. He asked to interview Emmet Flood, an expert in impeachment and presidential power, who had been wary of representing Trump if he wasn't going to be the final decision maker.

The final straw for Dowd came on March 19, when Trump announced he was hiring Joseph diGenova, a fiery former prosecutor and longtime critic of the Clintons, who had been alleging, in frequent appearances on Fox News, that Trump was being framed by FBI and Justice Department officials. DiGenova had the advantage of being a vocal, persuasive critic of the Mueller probe in the media. Trump wanted a television warrior as his lawyer, and he admired how diGenova savaged Mueller. He figured diGenova was primed to go on television night after night as his Mueller attack dog, just as the midterm election season was ramping up, with Republican control of the House on the line. But Dowd told colleagues that he saw the new hire as a grievous insult. He congratulated diGenova and publicly supported the appointment. Privately, however, he told a White House adviser that it was too much for him to bear. "DiGenova hasn't tried a case in forty years," Dowd said. "I'm not going to try a case with him."

The morning of March 22, Dowd quit. He alerted the lawyers on the joint defense that he was resigning. Sekulow and Cobb knew Dowd was unhappy and that things were souring between Dowd and Trump; the two had been cursing at each other a lot. And they knew that Trump had been talking about adding more lawyers to his team, a potential demotion for Dowd. Still, they were caught off guard by Dowd's rash decision.

Dowd issued a short, simple statement announcing his exit: "I love the President and wish him well." But he left the legal team in a bind, and without a clear replacement. And he was the only Trump lawyer with a security clearance, meaning no one was left on the president's personal legal team who could review classified information pertaining to the case.

Fifteen

CONGRATULATING PUTIN

In March, President Trump told other aides that he was considering firing his national security adviser, H. R. McMaster, and John Kelly, not a fan of McMaster's style, leaped to line up replacements. Before long, news of the president's intentions leaked to the media. The White House denied that McMaster was on the chopping block, but Trump again told aides McMaster was going to be fired, and the cycle repeated.

During this period, the mood inside the White House verged on manic. The president was emboldened, buoyed by what he viewed as triumphant decisions to impose tariffs on steel and aluminum, and the plans he was putting together for a historic summit in June with North Korean dictator Kim Jong Un.

Tillerson was not the only recent casualty to be humiliated. On March 12, White House aides had witnessed the sudden firing of Johnny McEntee, the president's personal assistant, booted out by Kelly and escorted from the White House grounds after his security clearance was revoked amid an investigation into his personal finances and links to online gambling. "Everybody fears the perp walk," one senior White House official remarked. "If it could happen to Johnny, the president's body guy, it could happen to anybody."

On Sunday, March 18, this was the soft ground on which McMaster was standing when Vladimir Putin was reelected president of Russia. It was a frigid night in Moscow as Putin strode onto a stage erected just outside the Kremlin walls to accept his victory. The Russian government said Putin won in a landslide, with more than 75 percent of the votes, with high turnout thanks to an extensive propaganda campaign. All day, Russian state TV broadcast images of long lines of Russians waiting eagerly to cast ballots for Putin—at polling places from the beaches to the mountains to remote settlements in the Arctic. A Russian on the International Space Station was reported to have cast a ballot while in orbit.

"Success awaits us!" Putin told supporters. "Together, we will get to work on a great, massive scale, in the name of Russia."

The boisterous crowd responded with chants of "Russia! Russia!"

Unsaid was the fact that the Russian election was anything but fair. The most popular opposition leader challenging Putin, Alexei Navalny, had been barred from the ballot. Another opponent, Communist Party candidate Pavel Grudinin, had been relentlessly attacked by the state media, which Putin and his cronies controlled, and finished a distant second with 12 percent of the vote. It was, as the BBC dubbed it, the election Putin "could not lose."

Back in Washington, Trump monitored the election results and swelled with pride for Putin. He was impressed by the size of his victory. A mandate. Trump told McMaster that he wanted to call Putin to congratulate him. McMaster was used to hearing Trump toss impulsive ideas into the air to gauge his reaction. But he knew Trump was adamant about this one. He was calling Putin.

The next day, in their regular Monday meeting, McMaster tried gently to steer Trump away from the idea of congratulating Putin. He explained that the Kremlin would use the American president's words to claim the world's leading democracy had blessed their rigged election. McMaster suggested Trump condemn the Salisbury nerve agent attack. He also suggested Trump bring up the conflict in Syria to try to protect civilians from Bashar al-Assad's attacks on rebel strongholds. Trump listened but mostly remained adamant about making the call, so McMaster reached out to Russia's foreign minister, Sergey Lavrov, and set a time for a call between the two presidents on Tuesday, March 20.

Later that Monday, March 19, in a prep session ahead of the Putin call, Trump again told his advisers that he wanted to give Putin an atta-boy on his election victory. McMaster had resigned himself to the high likelihood that Trump would do whatever he wanted on the call. This is how it went with Trump. "The call was Trump's idea, and his whole point was to congratulate Putin," said one White House adviser. "H.R. couldn't stop him."

McMaster made one last attempt to give his considered advice. He had his National Security Council staff prepare a three-inch-thick over-night briefing book for Trump, which the staff secretary delivered to the president's residence late Monday evening. Notably, the briefing book included four five-by-seven-inch "cue" cards, the kinds used by students cramming for a test. The stock-grade cards, with the White House seal at the top, contained easy talking points Trump could use in the conver-sation. To ensure the president would not miss what it said, the first card had all capital letters and bold lettering: "DO NOT CONGRATU-LATE ON ELECTION WIN."

It was the first time anyone on the White House career staff working on national security could remember a president being handed marching orders from the NSC in all capital letters.

On Tuesday morning, McMaster called Trump at his residence for a quick check-in before the call. McMaster did not reiterate the "DO NOT CONGRATULATE" instructions from the cards. He didn't think he had to. After all, the key points were in all capital letters. How could Trump miss them? Shortly thereafter, the White House Situation Room placed the call, connecting the Kremlin to Trump's residence. Trump opened his conversation with Putin as if greeting an old friend, congratulating him on his amazing election victory.

Trump ignored the first cue card in its entirety. Then he ignored the others. He did not say a word about what Britain had concluded was the Putin-ordered poisoning of a former KGB agent in England, declin-ing to confront the Russian strongman in defense of America's oldest ally. Trump and Putin spoke for roughly forty minutes, with Trump following his gut and riffing with Putin about how the two of them might generate economic deals between their two countries.

Putin had developed a knack for manipulating Trump, making him believe that the two of them could get big things accomplished if they ignored their staffs and worked one-on-one. National security aides feared Putin knew how to feed the unusual combination of Trump's ego and insecurity and to cultivate conspiracies in his mind. He told Trump his ideas were brilliant but warned him that he could not trust anyone in his administration in Washington to execute them.

"It's not us," Putin had told Trump. "It's the subordinates fighting against our friendship."

As he did reflexively when talking to foreign leaders, Trump invited Putin to come to Washington for a state visit. This was one of many Trump tics that befuddled McMaster. Typically invitations were extended strategically and only after considerable internal deliberation about the possible diplomatic and policy gains. But Trump invited everyone, creating headaches for his team. Some major migraines ensued when Trump invited the leaders of tiny nations, such as Prime Minister Dr. Keith Rowley of Trinidad and Tobago, and people deeply controversial in their own home countries, such as Brazil's then-president Michel Temer, to drop by the White House whenever they were in town.

Trump had been scheduled to speak with Temer in March 2017, and at the time the Brazilian president was embroiled in a major corruption scandal. Before Trump and Temer's call, White House aides foresaw what might happen and preventively urged Trump not to invite the Brazilian leader to Washington. Trump did it anyway. White House aides spent the next few weeks politely dodging calls from the Brazilian ambassador, who was trying to make good on Trump's invitation and set up the visit. In the case of Trinidad and Tobago, Trump's invite to Rowley forced the NSC staff to create polite ways to withdraw the offer, explaining that Trump was so busy he could not find time in his schedule to see him.

The morning of March 20, after hanging up with Putin, Trump made his way to the Oval Office. He was excited. He told McMaster he wanted to put out a statement right away. The president liked to dictate what he considered the historic successes of his conversations with foreign leaders for public distribution by the White House. Staffers tried to suggest edits, but it usually fell to McMaster to talk Trump out of ideas that would reveal too much or piss off Western allies. On this day, Trump was adamant about what he wanted the statement to say.

"I want Putin to come here," Trump told McMaster.

"Yes, Mr. President," McMaster said. "We'll start working on it ASAP."

"Let's announce the invitation and put out a statement about it," Trump said.

McMaster didn't think Trump should publicly announce his invitation, much less have Putin visit Washington at all, but figured the situation could be managed. He explained to Trump that state visits or face-to-face meetings of this magnitude should be kept secret until closer to the event and after the two countries negotiated a concrete agenda. Trump seemed to relent, shrugging his shoulders.

McMaster instructed Fiona Hill, the Russia specialist on the NSC, to contact the Russian ambassador and start talks about a possible meeting. But he stressed that she should take her time. If she set up a meeting with the ambassador, they could say they were working on the visit the next time Trump asked. As McMaster was drafting and editing with his staff the White House's statement on the Trump-Putin call, the Kremlin released its own readout of the call. The Russians almost always got their statements out before the Americans, which allowed them to shape the global media narrative on their terms. The Kremlin statement made clear what Trump had said.

"Donald Trump congratulated Vladimir Putin on his victory in the presidential election," the statement began. It went on to say, "Special attention was paid to making progress on the question of holding a possible meeting at the highest level. In all, the conversation carried a constructive, businesslike character, and was oriented toward overcoming the problems that have piled up in U.S.-Russian relations."

British diplomats, talking to their own sources, were incensed. They were hearing that Trump never raised the issue of the poisoning of the former Russian and British double agent Sergei Skripal and his daughter, who had defected to the U.K. They called their American contacts at the State Department and in the White House demanding an explanation. For her part, British prime minister Theresa May chose intentionally not to wish Putin well, still waiting for him to acknowledge the poisoning. Her spokesperson told reporters May wanted to have independent observers assess the Russian election before she commented on it.

The Russians had not exaggerated or misstated the substance of the call, as they often did, and Trump was hardly shy about confirming the truth. Sarah Sanders told White House reporters in the early afternoon that the Kremlin readout was accurate.

Later that day, *The Washington Post* first reported that Trump ignored his "DO NOT CONGRATULATE" instructions. The scoop posted at 7:16 p.m., and it blanketed cable news the rest of the night. Washington's national security professionals and Russia hawks were outraged.

Late that Tuesday night, Fox's Sean Hannity spoke with Trump by phone, part of their ritual of conferring each night after Hannity's broadcast. Trump told aides that Hannity had a lead about the Judases in his midst: McMaster's deputies.

A nor'easter rolled over the mid-Atlantic early Wednesday morning, March 21, dumping six inches of snow on the Washington region, the heaviest snowfall of the season. Metro shut down a large portion of its bus and subway service, and federal agencies in Washington closed, except for essential services. McMaster and other national security staffers reported for duty, and they received a frigid reception at the Oval Office. Trump was furious and demanded that McMaster find whoever shared the detail about the cue cards with *Post* reporters. McMaster told Trump he, too, was furious at the leak and told him he had already begun the hunt. The president made clear he wanted an answer soon. Hours, not days.

Trump and McMaster were not the only officials infuriated by the unauthorized leak. Kelly shared some of Trump's frustration about the unrelentingly negative press coverage of the administration and was irate that confidential briefing materials had become public. He, too, directed a search for the sources. Kelly and the White House lawyers put the search in the hands of a trusted McMaster deputy who had never accessed or reviewed the classified notes, according to the White House's digital system, which tracks who opened or reviewed sensitive documents. That deputy, ironically, was one of the people Hannity had accused of being a leaker.

On Capitol Hill, Republican lawmakers shared in the outrage. "A president's staff shouldn't leak," said Senator Ben Sasse, a Republican who sometimes criticized Trump. "In cases of principle, you may need to resign. So resign. Do the right and honorable thing if you believe your conscience is compelled to do so and resign your position."

Later that afternoon, Trump called McMaster back to his office.

"Did you figure out who did it?" the president asked.

"No, sir," McMaster said. He laid out his strategy for the investigation. They had determined that roughly a hundred people would have had access to the notes, not counting more far-flung diplomatic staff, so it would take some time. He said they had one idea for catching the leaker, but White House lawyers worried it wouldn't be foolproof and might risk identifying the wrong person.

"Well, I know who did it," Trump announced, surprising McMaster and a handful of other aides in the room. "It was your guys."

There is a dispute about whether Trump said their names aloud then or later. But in other conversations with senior White House staff, Trump would explain that Hannity had fingered Fernando Cutz and Ylli Bajraktari as the leakers.

"Get rid of them!" Trump bellowed. "This is fucking outrageous!"

McMaster, who steadfastly refused to fire people based on unfounded suspicions, tried to calm Trump down by saying neither man could be the leaker. "They would never do that, Mr. President," McMaster said. "Never."

The next day, March 22, the snowstorm continued to complicate commutes. Federal agencies were delayed in opening by two hours. McMaster was at his home at Fort McNair, on a peninsula on the edge of

Washington where the Potomac and Anacostia Rivers meet. He had meetings that afternoon with his national security counterparts in the Quad, the strategic alliance between the United States, Australia, Japan, and India. He was hosting a dinner that night for them at his home.

At the White House, McMaster's skeletal staff, those who had come to work that day, were concerned when they learned who was walking up the snowy main driveway to the West Wing just before 4:00 p.m. It was John Bolton. "He wasn't being very discreet," said one McMaster aide, noting that Bolton walked past television camera crews on his way in.

Bolton, a wily old hand from the George W. Bush administration who was known in those years for his hard-line neoconservative views and bureaucratic brawling, was being buzzed about as a contender to replace McMaster as national security adviser. Trump admired him in part for delivering what McMaster never did: fiery performances on Fox News defending the president.

McMaster's aides were suspicious Bolton had come to pay Trump a visit. They asked Ivanka Trump and Hope Hicks, his communications director who was in her final days on the job, to find out what was happening. The NSC staffers wanted to try to stop Trump from firing McMaster without any warning. Ivanka and Hicks talked to the president and persuaded him not to tweet-fire McMaster, as he had Tillerson a week earlier. They argued that the military officer deserved more respect—at a minimum, the courtesy of a phone call. Amid this hubbub, Cutz felt he had to do something. For the first time in his years of working in the White House, he strode directly into the chief of staff's office without making an appointment. He didn't seem to realize this clock couldn't be turned back.

"I need to see the chief right away," Cutz told Kelly's assistant.

Once inside, Cutz explained he couldn't stomach seeing McMaster, a rock-ribbed professional and a role model, go down so that he, a relatively low-level staffer, could remain.

"I beg of you, don't let McMaster do this," Cutz told Kelly. "I'm resigning."

But Kelly shook his head emphatically.

"No, no," Kelly said. "You're great. Just keep doing what you're doing. What are you talking about?"

Cutz blinked. He couldn't believe what he was hearing. Trump was insisting that McMaster fire the leakers. Hannity had fingered McMaster's deputies as the guilty parties. The president's alt-right fans on the internet were openly accusing Cutz by name, even though an early internal investigation ruled out both him and Bajraktari because neither ever had access to the document. And still, here was Kelly, standing in front of Cutz and insisting that both he and the president wanted him to stay.

At the same time or shortly after, Trump called McMaster, summoning him to the phone and away from his meetings with foreign leaders. Trump was terse. He said something to the effect of "I think it's time for you to leave."

"Yes, Mr. President. I understand," McMaster said. "How quickly do you want me to go?"

"Friday," Trump replied, meaning the next day.

McMaster suggested a more structured handoff, perhaps over a two-week period, so that he could share briefing materials with his successor. Trump said that would be fine. But he wanted to announce the change immediately. McMaster quickly called his core team of NSC advisers to gather for a conference call. He wanted them to hear the news from him before Trump tweeted it. When they all hung up, McMaster's two top deputies, the ones accused of the leak, sent Kelly an email informing him they were tendering their resignations, effective when McMaster left his office.

It took only a few minutes for Trump to announce his own news. The tweet posted at 6:26 p.m.: "I am pleased to announce that, effective 4/9/18, @AmbJohnBolton will be my new National Security Advisor. I am very thankful for the service of General H.R. McMaster who has done an outstanding job & will always remain my friend. There will be an official contact handover on 4/9."

McMaster did not go quietly, however. During the two-week handoff period, he delivered a stinging rebuke of Trump's Russia policy. On April 3, in a dinner speech at the Atlantic Council, McMaster denounced

Russia's aggression around the world and said the United States was falling short in confronting it.

"Russia has used old and new forms of aggression to undermine our open societies and the foundations of international peace and stability," McMaster said. "For too long some nations have looked the other way in the face of these threats. Russia brazenly and implausibly denies its actions. And we have failed to impose sufficient costs."

Earlier that same day, Trump said during a news conference with the leaders of the Baltic States that he was hopeful of forging an alliance with Putin. "Ideally we want to be able to get along with Russia," the president said.

McMaster made clear he saw little virtue in getting along with Russia. "Would you rather be part of a small club of autocrats that might rotate their meetings between Moscow, Tehran, Damascus, Havana, Caracas, and Pyongyang, or would you rather be a club of free peoples who respect sovereignty, individual rights, and the rule of law?" he told the Atlantic Council. "I think our club is better."

The audience burst into applause. The Atlantic Council's president, Frederick Kempe, congratulated McMaster "for that ringing voice of clarity." This was the last time McMaster spoke publicly as a member of the Trump administration.

The tumult on Trump's legal team mirrored the chaos in his White House—a virtual Tilt-A-Whirl, with the president pressing the buttons like a carnival-ride operator. Joe diGenova, the lawyer Trump had announced he was hiring based on his Fox News appearances, lasted less than one week. On March 23, Trump met with diGenova and his wife, Victoria Toensing. The couple, both seasoned lawyers with solid track records, came as a package, but Trump told aides he was less impressed with them than he had expected. He explicitly ruled out Toensing speaking for him on television, complaining that she showed up in the Oval Office wearing a flowing bohemian-style wrap and fingerless gloves. DiGenova, meanwhile, wore an ill-fitting suit. Trump envisioned "killers" as his lawyers, and diGenova and Toensing simply did not have "the look."

Trump found a face-saving way to back out of hiring diGenova and Toensing without directly offending them. The couple had responsibly flagged for the president a potential conflict of interest that he would need to be aware of if they represented him. They also represented Mark Corallo, the former spokesman for Trump's legal team who was a potential witness in the probe into the president's possible obstruction of justice. For diGenova and Toensing to continue, Trump would have to be aware of the Corallo conflict and agree it did not concern him. Jay Sekulow announced March 25 that diGenova and Toensing would no longer be joining the legal team.

Sekulow had been expecting to eventually downsize his own role in the Trump legal battle, and though an avid fan of the president, he never planned to lead his legal defense team. But after a week of turmoil, Sekulow, a rock music fan, adopted a Zen attitude and a gallows humor to try to roll with the punches. "Welcome to the Hotel California," Sekulow said in a joking reference to the Eagles hit when a colleague asked him what the turnover meant for him. "You can check out anytime you want. But you can never leave."

Sixteen

A CHILLING RAID

On April 5, 2018, when Michael Cohen visited Miami Beach, a delegation representing a Qatari sovereign investment fund greeted him at the Four Seasons as a dignitary. They bowed at Cohen's feet. The dazzling treatment of Cohen impressed one of his clients, the Tennessee billionaire Franklin Haney, who had hired the long-time Trump lawyer and fixer as a consultant to help him win the Qatari government's financial backing for a nuclear project that could make Haney even richer.

"He was treated like *royalty* with the Qataris because he was the president's lawyer," Haney told his hometown paper, the *Daily Memphian*. "They treated him like we had went to dinner with a prince and all that sort of stuff."

Haney was among more than half a dozen wealthy business executives who paid Cohen generous consulting fees, wagering that his influence with Trump would translate into profits for them and their companies. Cohen spent the night aboard Haney's $35 million yacht moored at a Miami Beach harbor before flying back to Manhattan the next day.

Also on April 5, Trump traveled to West Virginia and was asked by reporters aboard Air Force One about payments to Stormy Daniels, the adult-film star who claimed Cohen gave her $130,000 to keep quiet about a sexual encounter with Trump.

"Did you know about the $130,000 payment to Stormy Daniels?" asked Catherine Lucey of the Associated Press.

"No," Trump said.

"Then why did Michael Cohen make [the payment], if there was no truth to her allegations?" Lucey asked.

"You'll have to ask Michael Cohen," Trump replied. "Michael's my attorney, and you'll have to ask Michael."

Jenna Johnson of *The Washington Post* tried another question: "Do you know where he got the money to make that payment?"

"No," Trump said. "I don't know."

On April 9, four days later, federal law enforcement officers used search warrants to get some ironclad answers to that question. It was a crisp spring Monday morning in Manhattan, just thirty-two degrees outside, the sun rising in a clear sky, when a team of FBI agents showed up at the Loews Regency hotel on Park Avenue. At about 7:30 a.m., they knocked on the door of the room where Cohen and his wife, Laura, had been staying. This was their temporary home while repairmen were fixing damage from a water leak at their Manhattan apartment.

The federal agents in blue windbreakers were polite but firm. They told Cohen they would need to search the premises and asked him to hand over his phones, as well as any laptops or other electronic devices in his possession. Simultaneously, agents showed up at his apartment as well as his office, cordoning off the areas to collect computers, servers, and boxes of files, including tax returns and other financial records. They had to break into the front door of Cohen's office; nobody was there at that hour to let them in. The morning raid was extraordinary. Cohen was not merely Trump's attorney. He was his virtual vault—the keeper of his secrets and executor of his wishes, from business deals to personal affairs. "This search warrant is like dropping a bomb on Trump's front porch," remarked Joyce White Vance, a former U.S. attorney.

The three criminal statutes listed near the top of the warrant they presented were a confusing blur to Cohen. But within hours Trump's trusted fixer would understand that they conveyed a double-barrel threat. The sections of the U.S. criminal codes typed on the legal document showed that FBI agents, overseen by the famously aggressive prosecutors of the Southern District of New York, had significant evidence to suspect that Cohen had engaged in three kinds of federal crimes: bank fraud, mail fraud, and campaign finance violations.

The investigation put Cohen in significant legal peril because prosecutors would dig into whether he had lied to banks to get millions of dollars in loans for his taxi business. The probe was also well on its way to exposing the conspiracy to pay off Trump's mistress at a crucial stage of the 2016 campaign to help him win the White House. This was something much bigger.

Cohen's lawyer Steve Ryan was up early that Monday morning and already at the offices of his Washington law firm. Ryan had been working closely with Cohen to represent him in his handling of testimony to congressional committees regarding his Russian contacts as part of the various election interference probes.

His firm's headquarters were mostly white and sun filled and had sweeping views of the U.S. Capitol and Union Station just blocks away. But at that moment, Ryan was in the basement gym for his regular 8:00 a.m. session with his trainer. He had told his staff he would appreciate their not interrupting this small bit of personal time he had carved out of his deadline-crushed work schedule. So he was surprised when his assistant walked into the gym a few minutes after he had begun his workout.

"You have to come upstairs," she said.

"Why?" Ryan asked. "What is it?"

"They're doing a search warrant on Michael," she said. "It's on live TV. He called you."

Ryan blinked. He rushed to the locker room to quickly get cleaned up and headed upstairs to his corner office. Once he got to his desk, he couldn't reach Cohen. The FBI had seized his phone.

Meanwhile, Trump's lawyers Michael Bowe and Jay Sekulow and some of their associates were meeting at Sekulow's D.C. offices. They were preparing for a meeting that very afternoon with Robert Mueller and his lieutenants, the first one since John Dowd had summarily quit as the president's lead counsel. Sekulow's cell phone rang, and he turned his head away from the conference table to take the call. In his year representing Trump, darting from one drama to the next, Sekulow had proven himself a pretty calm cookie. So his stunned reaction to the caller got everyone's attention.

"What?" Sekulow said in a loud voice.

Everyone went silent and turned their heads toward the lawyer. When he hung up, Sekulow appeared shell-shocked.

"That was Ryan," Sekulow announced. "The FBI is raiding Michael's office."

Ryan told Sekulow what he knew at that hour, which was only the basics about the raid of the three locations, including that agents had to bust open the door of Cohen's law office in Rockefeller Center because no one was there. Later, Trump would get the details slightly wrong when he said agents "broke into" Cohen's office, when they had a proper court-approved warrant to search the premises.

Over the next hour, Ryan would learn worrisome new details about the purpose of the multipronged raid. He called the U.S. Attorney's Office in Manhattan asking to speak to the prosecutor in charge of the Cohen matter and got the gist of the warrant. Ryan immediately realized the magnitude: investigators had opened a new front in their investigation of the president.

The warrant specified that Cohen turn over all of his communications with Trump going back several years, as well as records related to payments Cohen negotiated with two women who had claimed extramarital affairs with Trump—Daniels and Karen McDougal, a former *Playboy* Playmate. Because Cohen had counted himself as Trump's personal lawyer for most of that time, their communications would normally be sacred and protected by attorney-client privilege. But that protection was useless if prosecutors could show the communications were part of a criminal scheme, which was likely the case for Cohen's hush-money payments to porn stars and models on Trump's behalf.

To Ryan, this moment felt like a replay of a previous standoff he had had with the special counsel's office. In November 2017, some lawyers on

Mueller's team told Ryan they wanted Cohen to allow them to review all communications Cohen had had with Trump and other officials from the Trump Organization over the previous ten years. Ryan refused, calling it a ridiculously unfair fishing expedition into every aspect of Cohen's life. He claimed Mueller's team did not have the justification to pry so deeply.

"We'll subpoena you then," Jeannie Rhee, one of Mueller's prosecutors, threatened Ryan.

Ryan, indignant, told her to go ahead and try.

"You're going to lose," Ryan told her. "I grew up in this courthouse. I'll go out on the sidewalk and say this is what the special counsel wants: a dragnet surrounding every guy he's ever known and everything he's ever done in his whole life."

Rhee never sought the subpoena. Ryan figured the Mueller team realized their odds were bad. But now, five months later, prosecutors in the Southern District of New York had obviously found something rotten in Cohen's handling of his taxi business and something about payments he made to women. Ryan saw those bad facts as effectively a crowbar to get what Rhee had wanted in the first place: all of Cohen's communications with Trump.

The morning of April 9, once Ryan reached an assistant U.S. attorney in New York on the phone, he identified himself as Cohen's lawyer but spared the typical pleasantries.

"I want my documents back," Ryan told the prosecutor. "You have privileged documents, and I don't want you to read them. I'm going to fight what you're doing."

Trump was at the White House when he learned of the raid, in calls from Sekulow and also Ty Cobb and John Kelly, who had received a heads-up from the Justice Department. When confronted with new developments in the Russia investigation, Trump typically ranted and raved, seeming as if he had steam coming out of his ears. The president asked Cobb about a dozen questions. He wanted to know if anything like this had ever happened before in history. Had any president ever had his own lawyer become a target of an investigation? He wanted to know the exhaustive background on this type of event. Wasn't this unheard of and likely illegal? What was required before prosecutors could legally seize a lawyer's records? When could you obtain records from a public official's lawyer? Were there any restrictions? Cobb explained that when he was a prosecutor he had sought lawyers' records dozens of times, and usually when he could argue those records contained evidence implicating the lawyers in a criminal scheme.

Trump was more than mad. But he had more questions. Who specifically would approve such a search warrant? How high did the prosecutors need to go in the Justice Department? Cobb replied that he felt certain Rod Rosenstein would have had to sign off on a raid of this nature. Trump vented to advisers about Rosenstein and complained that nobody at the Justice Department was working to adequately rein in these prosecutors and control the scope of their inquiry.

Trump also asked Cobb what he should do now to shield these records from the prying eyes of prosecutors. That wasn't really Cobb's job, as a special adviser to the president on the Russia probe. This battery of questions, combined with Trump's visible discomfort, created awkwardness for Cobb. The president needed to be talking to his personal lawyer, someone to vent to who was inviolable. Cobb worked for the White House and did not represent Trump personally; therefore, his interactions with the president were not protected by attorney-client privilege.

With Dowd out of the picture, that "Trump whisperer" was Sekulow. Cobb called him. "You really need to get over here because this isn't a White House event," he told Sekulow. "This is a personal thing."

The morning of the Cohen raid, Sekulow called Mueller's office and asked what in the world was going on. Did Mueller's team have any role in this raid? Sekulow was told that this was a matter the Southern District was handling independently. Neither Trump nor his lawyers believed Mueller's team. They were convinced the Cohen investigation was a backdoor way by the special counsel to get to the president.

The Trump attorneys did not know whose word they could trust.

They were wary of everyone, worried that Cohen might have engaged in sloppy, secretive plots that could come back to bite the president. The president's lawyers canceled a meeting scheduled for that day with Mueller. Trump's and Cohen's lawyers believed the Cohen investigation was orchestrated as a means of pressuring Cohen to cooperate with the special counsel's investigation and to push him to reveal his private conversations with Trump during the campaign.

One indication was that the two lead prosecutors on the Cohen case—Thomas McKay and Nicolas Roos—were from the New York office's public corruption unit and focused on public officials engaged in conspiracy or fraud against the government. Another indication that the Manhattan prosecutors were investigating the president was the search warrant specifying communications between Cohen and Trump. The prosecutors would later argue to a federal judge that many of the records should not be protected by attorney-client privilege because very little of what Cohen did for Trump was practice law.

"It's all agony, because it's amateur hour," one Trump adviser said at the time. "It's this death by a thousand cuts and they're going to die. Mueller has got everybody rolling on everybody. The president himself was not involved in collusion. But all of this stuff underneath us is going to bring us down."

The afternoon of April 9, Trump chose an ill-fitting moment to reveal his sudden vulnerability: a special all-hands meeting with his Pentagon leaders to discuss how to respond to the Syrian government's latest slaughter of innocent civilians by dousing them with chemical weapons.

Syrian leader Bashar al-Assad had gassed his own people, and the top military brass had come to the White House to meet with Trump to review his options. National Security Council officials had worked with Defense Department officials to prepare specific targets should Trump authorize a mission to take out, or at least temporarily weaken, Syria's ability to fly chemical weapon sorties. But there was only one subject on Trump's mind as the meeting began, and it wasn't dead Syrian children.

"So I just heard that they broke into the office of one of my personal attorneys, a good man, and it's a disgraceful situation. It's a total witch hunt," Trump said sternly as he sat hunched forward slightly over the conference table, his arms crossed at the wrists.

"It's, frankly, a real disgrace," Trump added. "It's an attack on our country in a true sense. It's an attack on what we all stand for. So when I saw this and when I heard it—I heard it like you did—I said, 'This is really now a whole new level of unfairness.'"

The military leaders looked on stone-faced.

The Cohen raid occurred on a day of transition in the leadership of the Justice Department. April 9 was Ed O'Callaghan's first full day at work as the principal associate deputy attorney general. The PADAG, an under-the-radar position yet one of the department's most powerful posts, helps the deputy attorney general run the department and shapes all major investigations and policy decisions. With Rod Rosenstein in charge of the Mueller investigation, O'Callaghan took responsibility for day-to-day interactions with the special counsel and his team.

O'Callaghan would immediately establish himself as Mueller's internal protector and brought a sophisticated understanding of politics and the media to the job that would help Rosenstein navigate the more treacherous turns in the investigation. Officials at the Justice Department took pride in their traditional independence from the White House. Yet the Mueller investigation had become such a public spectacle, with pressure coming from the White House, Capitol Hill, and throughout the media, that Rosenstein valued O'Callaghan's expertise in navigating choppy political waters and his sound legal judgment.

O'Callaghan was the third person to serve as PADAG under Rosenstein, and while his predecessors, Robert Hur and James Crowell, were loyal lieutenants and sound prosecutors, they lacked his political background. By contrast, O'Callaghan had worked on John McCain's 2008 presidential campaign, helping investigate and defend the vice presidential nominee Sarah Palin's background in Alaska, as well as try to manage the ensuing media circus. He also had worked as a prosecutor in the Justice Department's national security division and at the U.S. Attorney's Office in the Southern District of New York, where he first got to know Mueller, Aaron Zebley, and some other members of the special counsel's team.

As he settled into the PADAG's spacious office the morning of April 9, with sweeping views of the Washington Monument and the White House, O'Callaghan turned on a small television screen on his desk and saw that cable news stations were broadcasting images of the front of his building. He knew Trump would be furious about the raid and seizure of his lawyer's private materials. But the president's rage would be Rosenstein's problem to manage. O'Callaghan's job was to counsel Rosenstein, game out contingencies, and ensure all investigative measures were defensible and carried out according to Justice Department principles. Most of all, Callaghan's responsibility was to protect the Mueller probe, keep it running on course and immune from political— or presidential—influences.

On April 19, less than two weeks after the Cohen raid, Sekulow breathed a sigh of relief and announced what he considered a triumph. Trump had hired three new lawyers: Rudy Giuliani, a former New York City mayor who had been a legendary U.S. attorney, and Jane and Martin Raskin, two seasoned criminal defenders.

Giuliani needed no introduction. He had been "America's mayor," leading New York in the aftermath of the September 11 terrorist attacks and, in the 1980s, one of the country's great prosecutors. Now seventy-three years old, Giuliani was widely seen as a faded titan and a committed partisan, after his ad hominem attacks on Hillary Clinton during the 2016 campaign.

Giuliani, who would immediately become a cable-TV fixture as Trump's legal warrior, overshadowed the Raskins. The Raskins were not household names in the defense bar and in the coming months would garner nary a mention in the round-the-clock news coverage of the investigation. But they were content to work in the shadows. They were professionals with the street cred that comes from having worked on both sides of a criminal investigation, and their lawyering proved essential to the president's case.

Cobb, who would end up resigning from the White House on May 1, recommended the Raskins to Trump because he had known Jane from her time prosecuting mobsters as part of an organized crime task force in Boston. The president met with the Raskins at Mar-a-Lago over the previous weekend and had decided to hire them after just one conversation. Both Raskins had worked as Justice Department prosecutors and then built a reputation for good-quality defense work, notching enough wins to open up a small private practice in South Florida. The Raskins were Republicans and had played a supporting role in George W. Bush's legal efforts in the 2000 Florida recount, but were not overtly political, certainly by comparison with Giuliani and Sekulow.

The Raskins brought an added benefit to the Trump operation. Jane had previously worked side by side with Mueller at the U.S. Attorney's Office in Boston and with Quarles at a law firm. And Marty knew the father of Andrew Goldstein, another Mueller deputy who had been focused on interviews of White House officials and was among those gunning to sit down with the president.

The Raskins hoped to follow two core principles. First, they did not want to change how they operated just because their client was the president. They believed they had good facts and sound law on their side to help Trump, and they would stick to that. Second, they had an old-school style and had not interacted much with reporters. They did not want to try their case in the press or rush into TV studios to defend Trump. In fact, not doing so was part of their deal with the president. This would be exclusively Giuliani and Sekulow's territory.

When the trio of new lawyers came onto the scene to join Sekulow, they were shocked to discover they could not find comprehensive case files. The Raskins felt they were operating a bit in the dark. But two facts gave them comfort: there was not a shred of evidence linking Trump personally to any communications or coordination with any Russians, and there were major hurdles preventing Mueller from forcing the president to answer questions under oath.

One of the first tasks for Giuliani and the Raskins was to get up to speed with Mueller and his deputies. Since Trump's lawyers canceled their April 9 meeting, there had been a chill between the two sides. A new date was set: April 24. Mueller arranged for the president's attorneys to get the "secret entrance" treatment. An FBI agent on the case showed up at Sekulow's office in a Capitol Hill town house in a black SUV to pick up Giuliani, the Raskins, Sekulow, and two of their associates to drive them to the special counsel's offices in Southwest Washington, entering through a garage loading dock. As the lawyers entered a hallway, they were asked to deposit their cell phones into lockboxes on the wall and were then escorted upstairs and into a secure windowless conference room with a long table. Trump's representatives stood for a few minutes, waiting for their hosts.

In came Mueller, followed by Quarles, Goldstein, Zebley, and Michael Dreeben. Mueller and Giuliani, who worked together in the aftermath of 9/11, shook hands and exchanged respectful hellos. But Jane Raskin, Mueller, and Quarles greeted each other like the old friends they were, with Mueller kissing her on the cheek as one might do at a friend's wedding. "It's nice to see you, Jane," Mueller said.

As they stood chatting for a bit and asking about each other's families, the other attendees exchanged introductions. The special counsel's team took their seats on one side of the table, with Mueller in the middle. The president's team took this as their cue. They filed into chairs on the opposite side, with Giuliani in the middle, facing Mueller.

Both sides went into the meeting feeling put upon. Giuliani and the Raskins had a lot of facts to master in short order. Sekulow was still smarting from the Cohen raid, a search obviously generated by the early work of the special counsel. Mueller's team, meanwhile, felt they had been left standing at the altar in mid-January, when Dowd unceremoniously canceled a tentative Trump interview at Camp David, and their request had been put on hold for the past three months.

Trump's team had agreed earlier to use this meeting with Mueller to clear the air and introduce themselves as the new lawyers on the case. Then they would ask about Mueller's continuing demand for a presidential interview.

Giuliani took the lead, as they had determined ahead of time, and opened with pleasantries.

"Thanks for meeting with us. We're new and we wanted to say hello," Giuliani said, looking mostly at Mueller. "We're looking forward to working with you. We want to get a sense of where we are."

Mueller, as ever, was matter-of-fact. He said he and his deputies were looking forward to working with the refashioned Trump team.

The real meeting got started when Giuliani asked the key question: Why did the special counsel feel entitled to an interview with the president? As his predecessors had, Giuliani cited the Mike Espy decision in which an appellate court found that prosecutors had to prove they could not obtain key information any other way in order to seek an interview with a president.

"We have a lot of work to do to get up to speed," Giuliani said. "It would help if you would explain to us, under the framework of Espy, what you think you need from the president and are unable to get from the others and the documents?"

"We need to know what the president's state of mind was," Mueller replied. "We need to know the nature of his intent when he was undertaking these various actions we're looking into."

Mueller showed no emotion. He was the first to respond to Giuliani's questions, but he did so with short and direct answers, devoid of color or nuance. Sitting across from Mueller, every Trump lawyer was mildly agitated. Each had something to say and jumped in, one after the other, to push back forcefully.

Giuliani replied, saying something to the effect of "You have other ways of determining his intent." He explained that Mueller and his investigators already had a mountain of evidence, more than prosecutors would in nearly any other case. They had heard Trump's public explanations and interviewed scores of aides who had spoken to him contemporaneously about why he had taken key actions, including firing James Comey.

Jane Raskin said this approach to learning a subject's intent didn't square with the practice of prosecutors in other cases. They routinely charged people with obstructing justice without personally interviewing the suspects.

"Why do you need him to come in and talk about intent?" she asked. "Why?"

"We do," Mueller said. "He's the only one who can tell us."

The special counsel team explained that Trump could have had corrupt, mistaken, or innocent motivations in taking certain steps that impacted the investigation.

"We need to ask him," one of Mueller's deputies said.

Trump's new lawyers picked up some important intelligence in the meeting. Although they never said the word "obstruction," Mueller's deputies made clear their questions for Trump were focused on obstruction of justice. They mentioned nothing about coordinating or communicating with Russians.

At some point, the Trump team raised the question of what prosecutors could learn about Trump's intent from his interview with Lester Holt shortly after the Comey firing. Sekulow had been hot and bothered about the media's take on the Holt sit-down, and he feared that Mueller's team was also misreading what Trump said and meant. Journalists had focused on Trump explaining he had fired Comey because of "this Russia thing," but Sekulow argued they did not consider the full context. In the rest of the interview, Trump made clear he fired Comey out of frustration that the FBI director would not tell the world what he had privately told the president, which was that he was not under investigation. Trump also explained that his advisers warned him that firing Comey would likely lengthen the investigation, but he did it anyway, feeling it was the right thing to do.

"Listen to the rest of the interview," Sekulow said.

Trump's lawyers also floated alternatives to a face-to-face interview. Would they take an attorney's description of Trump's account instead of a sit-down? The special counsel's answer was no. Marty Raskin pressed Mueller and his deputies to consider written questions rather than a sit-down. He stressed that had been done with past presidents. Nope, Mueller said. That's not happening. Dead on arrival.

"We need an in-person interview," Mueller said.

The argument grew circular, from the Trump lawyers' perspective. *Ipse dixit.* Mueller needed the interview because he said so. And the Trump team, as Giuliani later recalled, was determined not to allow the chance. "The fear we always had of his testifying was not that he would lie, not even that he would make good-faith mistakes, but that he would say, 'I never said that to Cohen,' Cohen would say he did. Perjury," Giuliani later explained. "'I never said that to Comey'; Comey said he did. Perjury."

There was some discussion at the end about the parameters of a hypothetical in-person interview, if it were agreed to. Where would it happen? Would lawyers be present and permitted to confer with the president? Would it be videotaped? At the time, Trump's lawyers felt it was entirely possible Mueller would subpoena the president. He wasn't threatening it in this meeting, but it had hovered over such discussions ever since Mueller first uttered the *S*-word in his March 5 meeting with Dowd.

The Trump team also raised a pressing question, one that Dowd had never got answered. Did Mueller believe the special counsel was bound by Justice Department opinions that prohibited federal prosecutors from trying to charge a sitting president? In his March meeting, Mueller had told Dowd he did not consider Trump a target of his investigation, which was a good sign but not a conclusive answer.

What came next was awkward. People in the room remember the exact words of Mueller's response slightly differently. Some believe he replied, "I don't know." Others recall him shrugging and saying something to indicate he wasn't sure. Trump's lawyers remember having the same reaction to whatever it was that Mueller said: surprise.

Could the special counsel not have thought about two seminal opinions from the Justice Department's Office of Legal Counsel that prohibited indicting a sitting president, one from 1973 amid Watergate and the other from 2000 following President Clinton's impeachment? Or was Mueller simply playing coy?

Someone on Mueller's team then changed the topic, which Trump lawyers considered the subordinate's effort to create graceful cover for the boss. Then, toward the end of the meeting, in what the Trump team considered an odd non sequitur, Zebley circled back to the Office of Legal Counsel question. He also appeared to be trying to help Mueller in some way.

"I know the OLC opinion you're talking about," Zebley said. The Trump team felt Zebley was avoiding giving an answer; the Mueller team felt he made clear the OLC opinion was Justice Department policy, signaling the special counsel would have to follow it.

After the meeting, Trump's lawyers believed Mueller's team kept applying pressure about getting an interview, without directly answering their questions about charging a sitting president. Quarles called the Raskins and Sekulow in a follow-up conference call to say that the special counsel's office would feel bound by Justice Department rules. The Raskins' ears perked up. Quarles was so technical in his phrasing but still did not explicitly answer the question. They wondered whether he and Mueller were trying to preserve some flexibility.

Then Quarles pressed them for a decision on a Trump interview.

"When can you give us an answer?" he asked. "A week? Two weeks?"

Trump's lawyers wanted to slow walk a decision. Privately, they were leaning heavily against an interview but had not ruled it out entirely.

"We will do our best. We just got here," one of them said. "As you know, there is a lot to learn."

It would take several phone calls and letters before Trump lawyers felt the special counsel gave an explicit answer about whether they believed they could indict a sitting president. The answer was no.

The April 24 meeting would prove to be one of the only times Trump's new legal team would engage directly with Mueller. The special counsel typically deferred to Quarles or Zebley to interact with the opposing side—so much so that the president's lawyers wondered how much work Mueller was actually doing.

"I always had a feeling they were hiding him," Giuliani would later remark. "He had only one case. It was a case against the president of the United States, a very sensitive case. The inmates were running the insane asylum."

Giuliani would recall John Dowd telling him, "Well, he's not really on top of the case. He's kind of like delegating it."

Trump's team was not the only group to note Mueller's distance. Justice Department officials who had to interact with the special counsel's office from time to time talked about Mueller as the wizard in the classic film *The Wizard of Oz*. They would knock on the door. Zebley or another subordinate would crack it open and hear the question or learn about the problem. Then the door would shut, Mueller's team would discuss it internally, and the door would reopen with Zebley or someone else delivering the wizard's edict.

Mueller did not allow outsiders into his sanctum or to be a part of his team's deliberations, even if there were other stakeholders. To the Justice Department officials on the other side of the door, this was patronizing. Zebley and Quarles in particular were protective of their boss. When talking to Justice Department officials, they referred to him as "Mr. Mueller." For instance, they would say, "You don't need to talk to Mr. Mueller."

In May, the problem of Kushner's lack of permanent security clearance resurfaced in the White House. Sometimes Trump would badger Kelly to "just fix it," with Kushner or Ivanka standing by. Other times Trump would ask Kelly why it was taking so long and if he could do something.

"Look, help 'em out here," Trump once told Kelly. "They want the clearance. They're embarrassed. Why can't [they] have it?"

The chief of staff, accustomed to the military's fastidious care with granting clearances, would explain the importance of following an un-tainted process. But soon after his talks with the president, Kushner or Ivanka would visit Kelly in his office to follow up, with questions about lifting the obstacles. One day, Trump gave what Kelly considered an or-der: "I want you to give it to them." Kelly refused, saying it was improper and politically stupid. He was mindful of the career people who consid-ered the granting of clearances a religion and who would have reason to rat out an abuse.

"No, I won't," Kelly said. "It's not ethical. This will come back and bite us."

Still, Kelly gave Trump some advice about how he could get what he wanted. As president, he was the final authority on access to classified material. He could legally decide on his own to grant Kushner a perma-nent clearance. The conversation went back and forth as Trump tried to get Kelly to do it instead, and the chief of staff held firm. In the end, Trump did what he promised the media he would not do: he bypassed the typical process to grant Kushner permission to see the country's most carefully guarded secrets. Kelly wrote a memo to his file, in shades of Comey's own moves to document his interactions with Trump. The chief of staff then alerted the White House security office, which granted Kushner the privilege he had been denied for months.

The dispute arose anew when the details of Kelly's memo came out nine months later, as well as the fact that McGahn had also documented the president's decision in his own memo. Ivanka and Kushner would insist to associates that Kushner's clearance was obtained through a standard process managed by career professionals. As corroborating evidence, they pointed to Carl Kline, former director of the White House's Personnel Security Office, who testified to Congress in 2019 that he had granted clearances on his own authority and not under orders from anybody in the White House. However, one of Kline's subordi-nates, Tricia Newbold, told Congress that Kline frequently dismissed risks in security applications and overruled security specialists to grant the clearances.

Ivanka would later tell ABC News, "There were anonymous leaks about there being issues, but the president had no involvement pertaining to my clearance or my husband's clearance, zero." And Kushner would later claim to associates that Kelly had assured him he got his clearance through the normal process. But very little had been normal about it.

At the Justice Department, Rosenstein and FBI director Chris Wray were at wit's end with the cadre of House Republicans who had been secretly promising Trump they had evidence of a huge cover-up in the Russia probe. Without first consulting the FBI, House Permanent Select Committee on Intelligence Chairman Devin Nunes had sent a letter to the White House that included highly sensitive intelligence that was not properly marked. Both the intelligence chiefs and the FBI officials were concerned that he had made an inappropriate disclosure. If this was how Nunes was going to handle things, Rosenstein and Wray figured they wouldn't turn over any more information.

Nunes and some of his House GOP colleagues believed the FBI and DOJ had horribly abused their power. Though Nunes had chosen not to read the actual documents himself—he had Congressman Trey Gowdy read them instead—he believed that the two agencies had misled the secret federal court to get approval to spy on Trump's campaign adviser Carter Page. Investigators had omitted the political motivations of a person providing some of the information, Christopher Steele.

Rosenstein, meanwhile, was growing exasperated by the aggression and gamesmanship of Nunes, who he believed was clearly overstepping his oversight authority. On May 4, Rosenstein marked Law Day in the Washington suburb of Rockville, Maryland, by delivering a speech about the separation of powers and the "incredibly complex" interplay among the three branches of government. "Congressional oversight is important," he said. "Congress must be able to hold hearings, conduct inquiries, and require reports so that it knows the laws are being faithfully executed and the money it appropriates is being properly spent. But oversight is not intended to eliminate the line between executive branch authority and legislative branch authority."

What Rosenstein did not say is that congressional oversight into his own actions was endangering his family. On May 8, a whirlwind day of travel that took the deputy attorney general from Washington to Philadelphia back to Washington and on to New York, he received notification from the U.S. Marshals Service about a death threat against his wife, Lisa. The marshals deemed it sufficiently credible to require protection for Rosenstein's family. Suddenly Lisa and their daughters were being driven around in an SUV with a 24-7 security detail.

Around noon on May 10, Stephen Boyd, Rosenstein's deputy for congressional relations, arranged a meeting for the principals to clear the air in the Justice Department's sixth-floor Sensitive Compartmented Information Facility. Attending were Sue Gordon, the deputy director of national intelligence, along with Rosenstein, Wray, O'Callaghan, Boyd, Nunes, Gowdy, and FBI deputy director David Bowdich. Rosenstein and Wray explained their fear about turning over any information that might be compromised and said their reluctance had nothing to do with hiding any funny business.

"The FBI, DOJ are all run by Republican political appointees who were not here during the Clinton investigation. Nobody here has a motive to conceal anything. We are not your enemy," Rosenstein said. "We have a duty to protect classified information."

At first, Nunes denied writing any letter to the White House with sensitive intelligence. Then one of Rosenstein's deputies showed him the letter with his signature. Nunes said nothing. The Justice Department team members found that puzzling. They wondered if Nunes's staff had written it and not told him. For a short portion of the meeting, the conversation turned testy. In three decades of public service, Rosenstein had rarely raised his voice in a meeting, and he had almost never yelled. This was one of the exceptions. Things had gotten personal. Nunes and his Republican colleagues had been rattling their sabers on social media and in Fox News appearances accusing Rosenstein's Justice Department of trying to hold back evidence proving the department's corrupt investigative tactics.

"You've got to stop this," Rosenstein told Nunes. "This is ridiculous. You're ginning up all these ludicrous conspiracy theories. You're accusing me of being part of some vast left-wing conspiracy. I'm a lifelong Republican. My wife is a Republican. She's getting death threats from these nuts."

Rosenstein also knew Nunes was raising money among conservative voters by claiming donations could help expose the secrets Rosenstein was trying to keep hidden from the public. Rosenstein's mother, who lived in Florida, about as far away as one could get from Nunes's central California congressional district, had received some of the congressman's fund-raising letters.

"You're making money off this," an angry Rosenstein bellowed, leaning over the conference table and looking at Nunes and Gowdy. "We're suffering the consequences of your fund-raising. My wife is getting death threats based on what you're doing."

The entire special counsel office, located next to train tracks and the newly opened Museum of the Bible, was a SCIF. Everyone—including investigators, agents, staffers, and visitors—surrendered their phones each day upon entry to avoid any minuscule chance of improper breach or mishandling of classified information. Mueller's team had become experts in the vast and unsettling power of criminals to steal and spy on private email communications, and not surprisingly they often eschewed the typical workplace habit of casually chatting by email with colleagues a few desks away. Instead, when they had updates to share, they often yelled down the hallway.

One day in late May 2018, Rush Atkinson, one of the youngest members of the team and considered a phenom for his diligence and stamina, hollered to Rhee, "You gotta come over here, Jeannie!" Atkinson had been reviewing the attempted intrusions by the Russian GRU's Unit

26165 and had found an amazing coincidence—one he knew couldn't be a coincidence. It showed exactly what the Russian hackers had been up to on July 27, 2016, within just five hours of Trump's making his infamous "Russia, if you're listening" comment at a news conference in Florida, saying he hoped they could find Hillary Clinton's missing thirty thousand emails. In that bizarre moment, Trump had actively encouraged a foreign government to illegally hack his political opponent. Just days earlier, WikiLeaks had published nearly twenty thousand documents that appeared to have been stolen from Democratic National Committee servers, and U.S. intelligence agencies concluded Russia was the thief, in a hit ordered by Putin himself.

At the time the press was reporting Trump's "Russia, if you're listening" comment, it was dinnertime in Moscow. Most Russian government offices were closed. But, as Atkinson discovered more than a year later, some Russian military intelligence operators in Unit 26165 were busy late that July night sending outbound pushes to Clinton's private domain and sending malicious links targeting fifteen email accounts on her server. This was a stunning find, one that U.S. intelligence agencies had not tracked earlier. The digital pushes did not show that Trump or anyone in his campaign had committed a crime, but they established that Russians were doing his bidding in real time, literally working the graveyard shift at his request from half a world away.

PART
FOUR

Seventeen

HAND GRENADE
DIPLOMACY

On June 9, 2018, President Trump was at his second day of meetings at the Group of Seven summit, hosted in Quebec by Canadian prime minister Justin Trudeau. This was an annual gathering of leaders from seven of the world's industrial powers: Canada, France, Germany, Italy, Japan, the United Kingdom, and the United States. It had been an unusually acrimonious summit. European allies, including German chancellor Angela Merkel, French president Emmanuel Macron, and British prime minister Theresa May, were pressing Trump to sign a joint statement committing to "a rules-based international order." The president had resisted, believing his counterparts were ganging up on him, before eventually relenting. Then Trump put his hand in his suit pocket, took two Starburst candies out, threw them on the table in front of Merkel, and said, "Here, Angela. Don't say I never give you anything," according to Ian Bremmer, president of the Eurasia Group.

Traditionally, the G7 has been a forum for the United States and its allies to express common democratic principles and fortify economic partnerships and aspirations. In the recent past, the annual summits had amounted to carefully scripted shows of unity against authoritarian adversaries, including Russia, which had been a member (it was then the Group of Eight) until it was kicked out in 2014 following the annexation of Crimea. But over two days in Quebec, Trump effectively blew up the

G7. He abruptly withdrew the U.S. endorsement of a joint declaration of unity, which his own representatives had already agreed to, and up-braided Trudeau on Twitter as "very dishonest & weak" because the prime minister objected to Trump's tariffs on steel and aluminum imports from Canada and other nations. Then he stormed out of Quebec.

Just before departing Canada, Trump threatened a trade war with any country, including allies. "We're like the piggy bank that everybody is robbing, and that ends," he said. Trump's complaint in Quebec drove to the core of his campaign pitch to the "forgotten men and women" of America: that he would forcefully put U.S. interests first, by renegotiat-ing trade deals to restrict foreign imports and increase U.S. exports. But according to many economists, blocking foreign imports would have been counterproductive and actually harmful to the U.S. economy.

Trump headed directly to Singapore, the island nation in the Pacific, where history awaited him. He was set to meet Kim Jong Un for the first-ever face-to-face talks between an American president and a North Korean leader. On the way, one of Trump's top advisers revealed that the tantrum the president threw in Quebec might have been about more than just trade disagreements. "POTUS is not gonna let a Canadian prime minister push him around," Larry Kudlow, director of the Na-tional Economic Council, said June 10 on CNN. "He is not going to permit any show of weakness on the trip to negotiate with North Korea, nor should he."

"So this was about North Korea?" anchor Jake Tapper asked.

"Of course it was in large part," Kudlow responded.

The president envisioned the historic disarmament summit as the ul-timate Donald J. Trump production. He thought meeting with Kim might even earn him the Nobel Peace Prize. Trump had long ago started imagining the pageantry. Earlier in the year, when he and Kim were first cooking up plans to meet, the White House Communications Agency had manufactured red, white, and blue challenge coins embossed with Trump's silver visage facing off against Kim. Just before leaving for

Singapore on June 9, Trump announced that he would be able to determine whether a denuclearization deal was attainable "within the first minute" of meeting Kim. How? "My touch, my feel—that's what I do," he boasted to reporters.

One longtime Trump adviser summed up the president's mind-set about the North Korea talks: "He looks at it like he looks at everything, which is, this is another guy who is the mouse that roared, who's tied his tail to China, to whom Donald Trump could be the messiah. Why? Because in Donald J. Trump's mind, he thinks that he, the president, has the ability to figure out a way to give [Kim] what he wants and to get what he wants. It's just another deal to him."

The president, this adviser added, had thought to himself, "Am I intellectually as smart as Jimmy Carter? No, but I don't need to be. Do I have the vast reservoir of political cachet that the Bushes have? No, but I don't need that. What do I have? I can go one-on-one playing tennis. I don't need to play chess. I don't need long-range, strategic diplomacy."

On June 10, when Trump arrived in Singapore, approximately thirty-six hours ahead of his meeting with Kim, it was so humid that visitors' shirts stuck to their backs the minute they stepped outdoors. About five hours earlier, Kim had landed aboard a Boeing 747 borrowed from the Chinese government. Trump was restless. He never liked life outside the bubble of his daily life—his bed, his televisions, his steaks and burgers. The antsy president told his aides to move up the start of the summit, scheduled for June 12, to June 11. He wanted to see Kim right away. "We're here now," Trump told them. "Why can't we just do it?"

After weeks of careful diplomatic negotiations by the U.S. and North Korean governments to choreograph the summit, Trump caused a flurry of commotion. His aides, including Secretary of State Mike Pompeo, John Kelly, and Bolton, pleaded against changing the schedule. They told him he needed the extra day to prepare for his talks with Kim. Plus, on June 11, Trump was slated to meet with the prime minister of Singapore, a perfunctory visit that if canceled would insult the host government. Then press secretary Sarah Sanders made the argument that proved persuasive: if he moved the summit up to June 11, a Monday, then it would air live on Sunday night in the United States, because Singapore is twelve hours ahead of Washington. "Sir, you're doing a historic meeting and you don't want it on prime time?" Sanders asked Trump. Of course, he did.

When Trump first met Kim at the lush Capella hotel on the resort island of Sentosa, he shook the dictator's hand for thirteen seconds, patted him on the back, and led him down a rich red carpet. Kim was a pariah, arguably the world's greatest abuser of human rights, and committed to nuclear armament. But Trump threw Kim a party, showering him with respect and declaring himself honored to be in his presence. The summit was carefully staged to put both leaders on equal footing, which normalized the authoritarian Kim. The spectacle was so jarring that even Kim acknowledged the oddity. He was overheard telling Trump, through an interpreter, "Many people will think of this as a form of fantasy . . . a science fiction movie."

Trump's nearly nine-hour day with Kim epitomized the president's reality-show diplomacy. The summit was short on substance but heavy on superlatives. Trump called Kim "very talented," "very smart," and a "very good negotiator." He said the North Korean people were "very gifted" and their country's future "very, very bright." And he claimed personal credit for staving off a North Korean nuclear attack on Seoul, the South Korean capital, which is just thirty-five miles from the border and home to about ten million people. "This is really an honor for me to be doing this, because I think, you know, potentially, you could have lost, you know, 30, 40, 50 million people," Trump said.

Trump began his grand-finale news conference in Singapore by playing a film he had commissioned, first a version in Korean and then one in English. It was startlingly reminiscent of Pyongyang's propaganda videos. The movie portrayed North Korea as some kind of paradise, with gleaming high-rises, time-lapsed sunrises, high-speed trains, majestic horses running through water, and children merrily skipping through a city square. It included a montage of images of Kim and Trump waving their hands and flashing thumbs up, as if running mates in a campaign.

Journalists were flabbergasted. Trump explained that he had it made to show Kim what his country's future would look like if it abandoned its nuclear weapons and normalized relations with the West. The shores of North Korea could be an exclusive resort destination! Trump said he played the video personally for Kim on an iPad—and, yes, the North Korean dictator liked it.

"They have great beaches," Trump told reporters. "You see that whenever they're exploding their cannons into the ocean, right? I said: 'Boy, look at that place. Wouldn't that make a great condo?' And I explained it. I said, 'Instead of doing that, you could have the best hotels in the world right there.' Think of it from a real estate perspective."

The summit put a pause on bellicose rhetoric and threats of war but produced nothing concrete—certainly not a commitment from Kim to give up his nuclear arsenal. In the days following his Singapore trip, Trump spoke with apparent envy of Kim's rule. He admired how the North Korean people "sit up at attention" when their dictator spoke and marveled at how tough Kim's guards appeared. After watching clips from North Korean state television, Trump noted the female news anchor's sycophancy and joked that she was even more lavish in her praise of the dear leader than Fox News hosts were of Trump.

Eliot A. Cohen, a neoconservative who served as a top State Department official in the George W. Bush administration and was a critic of Trump's candidacy, said in the aftermath that the Singapore summit was "just the latest manifestation" of Trump's authoritarianism. He "has classic traits of the authoritarian leader. The one that's always struck me most is this visceral instinct of people's weaknesses and a corresponding desire to be seen as strong and respected and admired," Cohen said. He added, "We've been very fortunate that the institutions have contained him."

Trump's courtship and flattery of Kim also laid bare Bolton's limits and his capacity to influence the administration. For years, Bolton had advocated a hard-line position with North Korea. During the George W. Bush administration, he called Kim's father, Kim Jong Il, a "tyrannical dictator," to which the North Korean leader responded by calling Bolton "rude human scum." In February 2018, just before joining the Trump administration, Bolton had opined that the threat from Pyongyang was imminent and that the United States should launch a preemptive military strike as opposed to negotiating.

Bolton was regarded not only for his ideology but also for his masterful, if sharp-elbowed, manipulation of the federal bureaucracy and disciplined focus. The chaos of the Trump White House gave him the opportunity to seize control of the foreign policy process. Whereas H. R. McMaster ran the National Security Council by hewing to precedent, which included producing reports and leading regular meetings of principals or deputies to surface and vet policy recommendations from subject-matter experts throughout the government, Bolton consolidated power within his personal office of loyalists and ideologues. He stopped holding all but the most essential NSC meetings and made clear to career staffers that he had no use for them. When NSC staff visited his office suite to confer with Bolton's assistant about a scheduling matter or upcoming meeting, Bolton would sometimes emerge from his office with a frown that seemed to ask, "Why are you here?"

Bolton saw his job as being Trump's whisperer, carving out one-on-one time with the president to shape his policy views personally, as opposed to serving as an impartial broker who synthesized ideas and information from the vast array of federal departments and agencies. Bolton's doctrinaire views alarmed some Western allies, but Trump liked having him around. In bilateral meetings with foreign leaders, Trump developed a habit of teasing Bolton for his warmongering instincts. The president would often say a variation of this: "I've got hawks and I've got doves. Bolton will just bomb you. He'll turn your country into a parking lot. That's just how he is."

Gérard Araud, the French ambassador, recalled a senior White House official explaining to him that Trump "can't stand people who try to moderate him, but he loves people who are stronger or harsher than he is. He loves to be the moderator in the building. So compared to Bolton, he knows that Bolton wants to bomb anything. To Bolton, any problem can be solved by bombing, so he gets to be the voice of reason."

Bolton kept to an unusually strict daily regimen. He woke up well before dawn and was in the office by about 5:30 or 6:00 in the morning, giving him five or more solid hours to work before Trump showed up in the Oval Office. Bolton typically left the White House around 4:00 in the afternoon and went to sleep early, telling aides not to bother him after 8:30 at night. He bordered on anal retentive, once scolding an aide who handed him a ream of documents for not placing the paper clips in precisely the right place. Some longtime national security officials saw Bolton as a self-aggrandizing and untrustworthy recluse, calling him "Lone Wolf" because he would spend hours each day burrowed in his office on the first floor of the West Wing, reading with the door shut. Colleagues knew not to disturb him.

Articulating the difference between McMaster's and Bolton's style, one government official said that with Bolton "there's an underlying bias. He's selling when he's talking. . . . One man is being more objective; one man's tone smells of deeper motivation." Acting as the arbiter of what Trump needed to know was made infinitely easier for Bolton by the president's impatience for national security or intelligence briefings and disinclination to study complicated issues.

In the third week of June 2018, Secretary of Homeland Security Kirstjen Nielsen was aboard a government jet returning from giving a speech when she received a call from Sanders. The White House press secretary wanted Nielsen's help selling the administration's "zero-tolerance" immigration policy to reporters. "Can you come over and give the briefing on this?" Sanders asked. Sanders's reasons were obvious. She and her colleagues were getting slammed with questions from journalists about why migrant children were being separated from their parents while crossing the border over the last several days.

The situation was fast becoming a humanitarian crisis. John Kelly had opposed the policy when immigration officials first proposed it in March 2017 and he was the homeland security secretary. "No way. Not on my watch," he told his team. Kelly had held them off for many months, including after he was named White House chief of staff. Once Nielsen took over at the Department of Homeland Security in December 2017, Immigration and Customs Enforcement acting director Thomas Homan and Customs and Border Protection commissioner Kevin McAleenan had pitched her hard on the idea of family separations. Nielsen wasn't sure the policy would actually deter crossings or that the government had the capacity to separate families safely, but Trump loved the policy, as did some of his advisers, including Stephen Miller. They believed it might finally slow illegal migration.

Another agency with a piece of the nation's immigration policy was the Department of Justice, where Attorney General Jeff Sessions was often looking for ways to repair his relationship with Trump. On April 6, Sessions had announced the zero-tolerance policy for prosecuting every immigrant who crossed the border illegally. It had been the existing law, but this was a hard-line interpretation, and it would require the government to separate adults from their children while they faced charges. The attorney general's announcement had caught other leaders in the government by surprise. He had not briefed the other agencies that would be responsible for implementing the policy, including the Departments of Homeland Security and Health and Human Services. Even Kelly had been caught off guard.

By mid-June, the family separations had become a heart-wrenching global news story. At the White House, Sanders and her team were stuck having to answer for "zero tolerance," and they didn't know well the ins and outs of immigration enforcement. The communications team didn't want to put Sessions in charge of defending the policy. The man who had christened it with his no-warning announcement was someone Trump considered a weak performer on television. "Everyone thought Sessions was incapable of selling this in any way," one senior administration official recalled. "He was completely scatterbrained."

So the White House turned to Nielsen, forty-six, a disciplined lawyer with a calm demeanor, as the best choice to explain and defend why children were being temporarily held while their parents were prosecuted for crossing the border illegally. Nielsen agreed she would do it but it would have to be the following day, once she got back to Washington. Those closest to her urged her not to hold the briefing, including her deputy, Chad Wolf, and her chief of staff, Miles Taylor. Kelly was the firmest. If Nielsen did this, he warned, she'd become the face of the policy, which she had already cautioned would be tough to implement and which Sessions had enacted anyway.

On June 18, Nielsen stepped to the lectern at the White House Press Briefing Room. The policy had been rolled out with little planning. Immigrants didn't realize that if they came into standard entry points along the U.S. border, they could file for asylum and wouldn't be prosecuted. Most didn't know that they would be prosecuted for crossing the border illegally—by crossing deserts or riverbanks—and then have their children temporarily taken away from them. And in the United States, the public didn't realize that to prosecute undocumented adults, the government was legally required to separate the children from their parents. By this point, the Department of Homeland Security had separated an estimated twenty-three hundred children from their parents since the zero-tolerance policy began in April. The policy wasn't designed to separate kids in Nielsen's mind, but it didn't matter. Family separations were the result of deciding to prosecute the parents.

Nielsen didn't know how bad the situation really was, and as she stood before the cameras, she didn't realize ProPublica, an investigative news organization, had just moments earlier posted an audio clip of migrant children, ages four to ten, crying and pleading to see their mothers and fathers while being corralled inside a Customs and Border Protection facility. Their misery had been recorded a week earlier by a Good Samaritan who preferred to remain anonymous but felt wrenched by their cries just hours after the children were separated from their parents. As Nielsen answered questions from reporters, Olivia Nuzzi of *New York* magazine played the recording aloud in the briefing room. In addition to the sounds of sniffling and cries of "Mami" and "Papi," a six-year-old Salvadoran girl could be heard pleading to have someone call her aunt and repeating over and over the number she has memorized.

A Customs and Border Protection agent could be heard joking in a deep voice, "Well, we've got an orchestra here."

A reporter shouted out to Nielsen, "How is this not child abuse?"

Nielsen felt blindsided, but she was also wary of assuming that the sounds of crying children automatically meant there had been some government failure and fearful of attacking her own department's employees without the full set of facts. Some claims of abuses by border agents had been exaggerated in the past. Her response was that of a careful lawyer, though she sounded callous. "Be more specific, please," she said.

The tapes brought visceral proof of the warning from the American Academy of Pediatrics that such separations can cause children "irreparable harm." When asked for her reaction to the tapes, Nielsen said coolly, "They reflect the focus of those who post such pictures and narratives." In her head, Nielsen was furious. All the warnings she had given her own agency heads about the difficulty of carefully separating children from parents were proving true. After giving the White House briefing, she became the public face of a government placing kids in cages.

"She should have never gone to the fucking podium," one senior government official said. "I wish she had explained everything. We needed another six months to do it properly. We should have spent months telling migrants, 'If you are with a kid, please, please come to a point of entry, and you won't be separated.'"

The problems at the border only worsened. Agents were overwhelmed. Children were being held longer than expected in makeshift shelters that resembled giant chicken coops. Information wasn't flowing quickly back to Washington, because Immigration and Customs Enforcement leaders, who had been gung ho to deter illegal border crossings by punitively breaking up families, were not reporting significant hiccups quickly enough to Nielsen. As a result, the secretary looked as if she were out of touch.

In the two days following her briefing, Nielsen and White House officials intensely debated whether to reverse course and halt the zero-tolerance enforcement. They all feared pissing off Trump, but other advisers had been quietly lobbying the president—including Ivanka Trump, who told her father that no deterrence policy was worth making the administration appear so cruel.

The president broke first. On the morning of June 20, he called Nielsen at home to say they had to fix what had become a public relations disaster. His conflicting instructions left her scratching her head. "Yeah, yeah, we got to fix this. Just stop it," Trump told Nielsen, referring to family separations. "But I want zero tolerance to continue."

Nielsen called Taylor to explain her predicament. The president's two directions were in clear conflict. "I don't know what the fuck we are supposed to do," she said.

An executive order was the only way to sort it out. Nielsen and her team, Miller, and lawyers from the White House counsel's office debated the wording of the order the president would need to sign to stop Sessions's policy. They considered pausing zero-tolerance prosecutions for anyone who entered the country illegally with a child, but then feared that would encourage child traffickers. They agreed on an order that would pause zero tolerance for families illegally crossing the border.

"So we're going to have strong, very strong borders, but we're going to keep the families together," Trump said while signing the order. "I didn't like the sight or the feeling of families being separated."

Nielsen stood behind the president smiling, thinking she now knew her instructions and the law of the land was clear. But at this exact moment, the White House distributed information showing the president had signed a different order from the one Nielsen thought they had agreed to. It said the United States would stop family separations but continue zero tolerance. She learned the truth only when she returned to her office. Nielsen would later figure out how to interpret and execute the order with administration lawyers. "It's absurdity on top of absurdity with this administration," the senior official recalled.

On July 11, Trump arrived in Brussels for the biannual NATO sum- mit and complained immediately about an alliance he believed was taking advantage of the United States. The visit would become a transatlantic brawl. Sitting for what was billed as a perfunctory break- fast with NATO secretary-general Jens Stoltenberg, Trump accused many countries of being "delinquent" because they were not allocating enough money toward their own defense budgets. Trump then attacked Germany—whose longtime leader, Merkel, was respected as a consensus builder within NATO—as "totally controlled by Russia" because of an oil and gas deal between the two countries. This was a blatant attack on Merkel, who grew up in East Germany when it was actually con- trolled by the Soviet Union and who had worked since the end of the cold war to promote democratic values in unified Germany. As Trump made his case, members of the U.S. delegation were visibly stricken. This set the tone for an acrimonious NATO summit—a repeat of Quebec.

The next day, July 12, the situation went from uncomfortable to dan- gerous. The NATO summit was concluding as planned. European lead- ers were pleased that Trump had been reasonably well behaved, despite the visceral disdain he had long harbored for them because he believed they looked down on him. But late in the morning Trump arrived at NATO headquarters and was visibly fuming. He was frustrated that news reports of his first day in Brussels did not describe him as angry enough. In Trump's mind, the stories failed to convey to people back home the depth of his agitation with allies for failing to up the ante on defense spending.

Several U.S. officials could tell the president was in a foul mood, just by watching him enter the main atrium of the NATO headquarters from the windowed offices on a balcony above. He was about forty-five min- utes late. Though his Secret Service detail entered the building with him, Trump looked very much like a man alone. The president was frowning, his head was down, and he made no effort to look up to greet anyone or say hello. He was walking toward the main NATO meeting hall with purpose.

Trump arrived at the meeting of the North Atlantic Council, where members were already deep into a conference with the presidents of Ukraine and Georgia, and took it over without so much as a courtesy greeting. Holding the meeting hostage, Trump scolded and shamed countries one by one for their defense spending totals. He was on a tear. He harassed individual leaders. He had statistics at the ready, indicating his assault was preplanned. He warned that if NATO member nations did not meet their defense spending targets of 2 percent of their gross domestic product by January, the United States might leave the alliance. Trump had trouble putting his precise threat into words. First he warned there would be "grave consequences" if the allies didn't draw up formal commitments to increase their defense spending amounts. Then he said the United States would "go our own way."

Stunned by Trump's tirade, Stoltenberg tried to calm the room, but the president snapped. "No, we are not playing this game," Trump said. "Other presidents have done this, but I'm not going to." The entire Western alliance scrambled for an hour to keep itself together in the face of the possibility that the United States could withdraw from NATO, which it helped found in 1949 to counter the Soviet Union.

Just ten minutes later, Secretary of Defense Jim Mattis's aides began getting urgent texts on their phones. They were desperately needed in the U.S. holding room. As Dana White, Mattis's press secretary, rushed downstairs, she saw Hogan Gidley, a deputy White House press secretary, and shared what she considered a terrifying development. "I'm getting messages that we're pulling out of NATO," she said. Gidley, who had a self-effacing, aw-shucks manner, counseled in his southern drawl that nobody rush to judgment. He'd been here before. Some of Trump's ideas sound ominous, he explained, but may not end the world. "Eh, you know the president likes to float things," Gidley said. "But it's just a floater."

Katie Wheelbarger, a former aide to Vice President Cheney who was acting assistant secretary of defense for international affairs and who didn't rattle easily, had a panicky look on her face after witnessing the president harangue his fellow NATO partners. "It feels like we just pulled out of NATO," Wheelbarger said. Stoltenberg himself called an emergency session for allies only so they could discuss Trump's demands on expenditures and construct a response on their burden-sharing agreements.

Mattis, a steadfast NATO supporter, had had to miss the emergency session to attend a prearranged meeting with a battlefield commander who had flown from the Middle East to Brussels strictly to brief him. The fact that the defense secretary wasn't attached to Trump's shoulder at this particular moment made Pentagon officials nervous. Who then could prevent Trump from doing something catastrophic?

Kelly soon located and retrieved Mattis for a huddle about what they should do. The defense secretary suggested he, Kelly, Bolton, and Pompeo meet privately with Trump in a secure holding room. Aides said they heard Trump wanted to hold an immediate press conference, but Mattis wanted to talk to the boss first. After Mattis and the others spoke with Trump, the president emerged first from their private conference. Miller, a fellow NATO skeptic, was busy drafting some talking points for the impromptu news conference. Mattis and Kelly hung back, continuing their private discussion. The Pentagon reporters who traveled with Mattis, and had already been screened by security officials, were waiting on the secretary's plane to depart Brussels with him; now they were furious upon finding out they would be missing a major Trump news conference that Mattis was attending.

Before heading to the airport to depart Brussels, Trump addressed throngs of journalists from around the world at a lectern at NATO headquarters. The American president made claims that some of his international counterparts contested. For instance, Macron and other foreign leaders disputed Trump's announcement that countries had agreed to eventually increase their spending "quite a bit higher" than 2 percent of their gross domestic product. However, the U.S. officials traveling with Trump breathed a major sigh of relief when Trump stated, "I believe in NATO." He called the alliance "a fine-tuned machine" and praised its "great unity, great spirit, great *esprit de corps.*"

At his news conference, Trump revealed he had been disappointed with the media's lack of coverage of him scolding the Europeans to pay more. "I was surprised that you didn't pick it up; it took until today," he said, as if his morning threat were a stunt orchestrated to generate headlines. Xavier Bettel, the prime minister of Luxembourg, had reminded reporters that Trump had wireless internet on Air Force One and could reverse his support for NATO in a single tweet once he left Brussels. When a reporter asked Trump if he might attack NATO on Twitter after departing, just as he had maligned Trudeau following the G7 in Quebec, the president replied, "No, that's other people that do that. I don't. I'm very consistent. I'm a very stable genius."

Four days later, Trump warmly embraced Russia, NATO's greatest direct threat. The Trump-Putin summit in Helsinki was long in the making. Trump was under intense pressure to confront Putin over his broad subterfuge operation in the 2016 election, as well as to counter Russia's intervention in Syria and Ukraine.

Trump knew before he clasped Putin's hand that U.S. investigators had built an airtight case proving the Russian government had interfered in the election. When Trump had announced at the end of June his scheduled Helsinki summit for mid-July, Mueller's prosecutors had been getting their ducks in a row to indict a dozen GRU military officers for the email hacks. They faced a diplomatic quandary. They had to give Trump a heads-up and offer to let him decide whether he wanted the indictment to occur before or after he met with Putin. Trump's choice surprised the prosecutors. He wanted the announcement of the indictment to take place prior to the Helsinki summit.

Before leaving Washington, Trump sat down with Deputy Attorney General Rod Rosenstein to preview the Justice Department's charges against twelve Russian intelligence officers for hacking Democratic emails. The indictment, which Rosenstein publicly announced on July 13, was a major development in Robert Mueller's investigation. "When we confront foreign interference in American elections, it is important for us to avoid thinking politically as Republicans or Democrats and instead to think patriotically as Americans," Rosenstein said, announcing the indictment. "The blame for election interference belongs to the criminals who committed election interference. We need to work together to hold the perpetrators accountable."

Trump, however, was not interested in holding the Russians accountable. He was focused on forging a better friendship with Putin during their tête-à-tête in Helsinki. "He's not my enemy, and hopefully, someday, maybe he'll be a friend. It could happen," Trump said. When a *Washington Post* reporter asked him if he intended to confront Putin on election interference, Trump mocked the very suggestion—"your favorite question about meddling"—and said he expected Putin to deny it yet again. Earlier, when the CBS anchor Jeff Glor asked Trump during a one-on-one interview whether he would ask Putin to extradite the twelve indicted Russian agents, Trump replied that he "hadn't thought" of doing so.

On July 16, Trump and Putin spent two hours meeting alone, joined only by their interpreters, inside Finland's neoclassical Presidential Palace along Helsinki's glistening waterfront. Unlike in most foreign leader meetings, there was no note taker to compile an official record of what was said or what promises were made. What came next was historically unprecedented. As he held forth with Putin for a forty-six-minute joint news conference, Trump refused to endorse the conclusion of U.S. intelligence agencies that the Russian government had tried to sabotage the U.S. election to help him win. In fact, he said he took the word of Putin over the collective assessment of his own intelligence agencies. Trump demurred when Jonathan Lemire of the Associated Press asked, "Would you now, with the whole world watching, tell President Putin—would you denounce what happened in 2016? And would you warn him to never do it again?"

"All I can do is ask the question," Trump replied. Referring to his director of national intelligence, the president continued, "My people came to me, Dan Coats came to me and some others and said they think it's Russia. I have President Putin. He just said it's not Russia. I will say this: I don't see any reason why it would be."

Trump then raised a series of questions about Hillary Clinton's emails before adding, "I have great confidence in my intelligence people, but I will tell you that President Putin was extremely strong and powerful in his denial today."

Inside Mueller's office, the prosecutors investigating Russian election interference watched the televised coverage with a mixture of concern and grim resignation. Intelligence operators had determined Putin had ordered the interference. The prosecutors also knew Trump had repeatedly been provided evidence of it.

Trump's performance in Helsinki sparked horror among the national security establishment in Washington. He thought he had come across as strong, but an hour into his flight home Trump's mood darkened as he watched cable news on a satellite feed and was shown printouts of statements from fellow Republicans condemning his comments. Even for some of the president's Republican allies, Helsinki was an out-of-body experience. Coats effectively rebuked his boss, saying that the intelligence assessment of Russia's "ongoing, pervasive efforts to undermine our democracy" was clear and had been presented to Trump in an unvarnished fashion.

Senator John McCain did not mince words in his statement: "Today's press conference in Helsinki was one of the most disgraceful performances by an American president in memory. The damage inflicted by President Trump's naiveté, egotism, false equivalence, and sympathy for autocrats is difficult to calculate. But it is clear that the summit in Helsinki was a tragic mistake." The Arizona Republican senator added, "No prior president has ever abased himself more abjectly before a tyrant."

Suddenly the word "treason" became part of the public debate about Trump. The former CIA director John Brennan called Trump's comments "nothing short of treasonous." A dam had broken.

After consulting with Sanders and other aides in his private cabin aboard Air Force One, Trump issued a tweet trying to seal the leak in the dam: "I have GREAT confidence in MY intelligence people." But the uproar continued. Even such reliable boosters as the former House Speaker Newt Gingrich—whose wife, Callista, served as Trump's ambassador to the Vatican—and Brian Kilmeade, a *Fox & Friends* host, said Trump made an error and should correct his statement. Back at the White House, Trump confided in friends that he did not understand what the big fuss was about. He thought the summit had been an undeniable success. But for the president's aides, a haphazard scramble was under way to blunt the global fallout from Helsinki. This would be a week of corrections and clarifications.

At about 8:30 in the morning on July 17, Trump called counselor Kellyanne Conway, who was at her West Wing desk, and told her to meet him in the private dining room off the Oval Office. The president was upset. He had been watching brutal cable television analysis about his "I don't see any reason why it would be" comment.

"That isn't what I said," Trump told Conway.

"It *is* what you said," Conway told him.

"I didn't say that," the president insisted. "Why would I say that?"

"That's a great question," Conway said. "Why *did* you say that?"

Trump had written down what he meant to say in Helsinki: "I don't see any reason why it *wouldn't* be Russia." He handed Conway the piece of paper. "I meant to say this," he told her. "Here, go out and tell everybody that this is what I meant to say."

"No," Conway said. "I think you should do that. . . ."

"You need to clear that up right away," she added. "That's not just a difference of three letters. That's a difference of intent."

Vice President Pence, newly installed communications chief Bill Shine, Kelly, Bolton, Miller, and Sanders soon came into the room to huddle around and help Trump draft a statement to deliver that afternoon clarifying his Helsinki remarks and addressing the concerns of his intelligence chiefs. Speaking from the Cabinet Room, a day after facing Putin, Trump claimed that when he said "I don't see any reason why it *would* be" Russia, he meant to say, "I don't see any reason why it *wouldn't* be Russia." This, the president explained, was "sort of a double negative."

But on July 18, at a cabinet meeting, Cecilia Vega of ABC News asked Trump whether he believed the Russians were still targeting the United States. The president responded with just one word, "No," once again contradicting his own intelligence chiefs and his own correction. Sanders later told reporters Trump was not answering Vega's question. "He was saying, 'No,' he's not taking questions." But it was too late.

The next day, July 19, Trump gave Bolton an order: schedule a second summit with Putin and invite the Russian president to visit him in Washington. Bolton sprang into action to make an overture to the Kremlin, and by afternoon the White House announced that planning was under way for a fall visit. The Putin trip would not end up happening. At this very moment, Coats, the director of national intelligence, was speaking at the Aspen Security Forum. The intelligence chief acknowledged that he wished Trump had made a different statement in Helsinki and that he ought not to have met with Putin alone. Coats also spoke forcefully about the continuing and "undeniable" threat of Russia's interference in America's elections.

When Andrea Mitchell of NBC News asked Coats what he tells intelligence personnel risking their lives in the field when the president disavows their work, as he did in Helsinki, Coats said he tells them, "We are professionals. We are here to provide professional service to our government. We need to keep our heads down. We need to go forward with the wonderful technological capabilities that we have to produce intelligence. There's a lot of swirl, political swirl, going around. Just do your jobs."

Coats's candor was remarkable, considering some colleagues in national security circles gave him the nickname "Marcel Marceau," after the French mime, because he was typically so tight-lipped and rarely opined freely. Before opening the floor for audience questions, Mitchell made an announcement: "We have some breaking news. The White House has announced on Twitter that Vladimir Putin is coming to the White House in the fall."

"Say that again?" Coats said, leaning forward in his chair.

"Vladimir Putin coming to—" Mitchell replied.

"I hear you," Coats said, cupping his hand to his ear playfully. They both laughed uncomfortably. It was obvious that this was the first Coats had heard of the Putin invitation. He took a deep breath.

"Okaaaaay," Coats said, chuckling. With a wry smile, he added, "That's going to be special."

Eighteen

THE RESISTANCE
WITHIN

On the sidelines of the NATO meetings on July 11, 2018, Trump believed he had struck a bargain with Recep Tayyip Erdogan. News cameras captured Trump and the Turkish president bumping fists and smiling. What the public did not know at the time was Trump thought he had a deal for a straightforward prisoner trade. The United States would win the freedom and return of Andrew Brunson, an evangelical American pastor imprisoned in Turkey for the previous two years on what U.S. officials considered bogus terrorism charges. Brunson was a cause célèbre for Trump's conservative base. Trump would then leverage his close relationship with Israeli prime minister Benjamin Netanyahu to negotiate the release of a Turkish prisoner jailed in Israel on exaggerated claims of terrorist activity. In Trump's mind, he had brokered the deal during a man-to-man meeting with Erdogan. Erdogan had mentioned the Turkish prisoner Ebru Özkan, a twenty-seven-year-old woman accused of acting as a smuggler for Hamas. Trump was intrigued. He, too, had a prisoner in Turkey he wanted released.

On July 27 the deal fell apart. Erdogan had tried to flatter Trump by telling him that surely he could get Özkan released. The American president said he could and then mentioned Brunson. But U.S. officials would later learn that Erdogan never thought this was a tit for tat. "Trump left the meeting believing he had personally negotiated it. He had not," said one person familiar with the talks. On top of that, something went wrong in the conversation. "Somehow, Trump left Erdogan with the impression he could get more for his dollar."

The exchange was complicated for many reasons. First and foremost, delicate negotiations about Brunson's release had been going on for weeks between lower-level deputies in both the U.S. and the Turkish governments. Turkish officials originally said Erdogan would be willing to give up Brunson in exchange for the United States' deporting or extraditing Fethullah Gulen, a reviled political opponent of Erdogan's who had been living in exile in Pennsylvania. U.S. officials shot down that idea. No way. That would be a decision for the Justice Department, and attorneys there had already made clear that an extradition of that nature would break U.S. legal norms. It was obvious to anyone following the situation that Erdogan's unstated goal almost certainly was to have Gulen killed as soon as he left the United States and landed in another country. So the Americans came up with a three-step approach that the Turks liked. The first step, agreed to in June and conveyed by Secretary of State Mike Pompeo, was that the Justice Department and the FBI would more closely investigate whether Gulenist groups in the United States were engaged in illegal activities, such as tax violations. The second step would be helping secure the release of Özkan from Israel. The third step had the feel of a prisoner exchange: After Turkey released Brunson back to the United States, the U.S. government would extradite a Turkish banker and Erdogan ally who was being detained in the United States in a federal case. The banker, who had incriminating information about Erdogan's role in a bribery and money-laundering scheme to avoid U.S. sanctions against Iran, would then be allowed to serve the rest of his short sentence in his home country. Trump had little familiarity with the details of those talks. There was no official transcript of his discussion with Erdogan, no direct proof of his apparent "deal" for U.S.

intelligence or diplomatic officials to hold the Turkish government to account.

On July 14, while Trump spent the weekend at his golf resort in Scotland, he decided in the middle of playing a round to call Netanyahu. His aides brought a secure phone out to the front nine. Trump leaned into the Israeli prime minister and asked him to release Özkan. Netanyahu confessed that he knew nothing about the woman. Her name did not register with him. But he agreed to look into it and to help speed her release, barring some other issue.

The next day, July 15, Özkan was released. She flew from Israel to Istanbul, where she was met by reporters and professed gratitude for Erdogan, who she said "was kind enough to be very interested in my case." Over the next several days, Trump asked his aides for updates on Brunson. The first sign was not encouraging. On July 18, a Turkish court rejected appeals to release Brunson and set another court date for October. At the White House, where the president had just returned from his European trip, officials were taken aback. Trump tweeted that the Turkish court's decision was a "total disgrace."

On July 25, the court convened again and ordered that Brunson be released. Top advisers to Trump, as well as outside Christian advocates who had long been pushing for the pastor's release, prepared that Wednesday night to celebrate Brunson's homecoming. But what happened next surprised Americans familiar with the negotiations: Brunson was released from prison but on the morning of July 26 was taken by national police to his Turkish home and placed under house arrest. Through back channels, the United States learned Brunson would be detained in Turkey. Pompeo wrote on Twitter that the court's decision was "welcome" but "it is not enough. We have seen no credible evidence against Mr. Brunson, and call on Turkish authorities to resolve his case immediately in a transparent and fair manner."

On July 26, Trump called Erdogan and was livid. The call was short, with Trump doing most of the talking and not getting the answers he wanted. Trump then took to Twitter to announce his displeasure. The

United States "will impose large sanctions" on Turkey, he wrote. "This innocent man of faith should be released immediately." Hours later, a senior Turkish official issued a statement calling reports of Trump's making a deal with Erdogan at NATO for a prisoner exchange between the United States and Turkey "completely baseless." According to the Turks, whatever deal Trump believed he had miraculously sealed with Erdogan was one of his own imagination. Trump took this as a personal affront. He had long admired Erdogan, attracted to him because of his ruthless rule in Turkey and the ease with which he dispatched political rivals. Ever preoccupied with optics, Trump told advisers he admired the deep and commanding sound of Erdogan's voice.

"It's un-fucking-believable," one of Trump's senior advisers recalled. "I can't describe it. When he's on that speakerphone, it is like you're hearing Hitler at a Nuremberg rally. You've heard Hitler's voice and it's just different. There's something about it that's powerful and chilling. You feel like you're maybe hearing Satan talking or whatever. When Erdogan talks, it's so powerful it's disturbing. It's just like this booming voice, and said in a cadence."

On August 16, during a cabinet meeting, Trump brought up the "terrible" Turks. "Turkey, they have not proven to be a good friend," he said. "They have a great Christian pastor there. He's a very innocent man." That is when Trump publicly acknowledged for the first time his role in the Israeli prisoner trade. "We got somebody out for him," he said, referring to Erdogan. "He needed help getting somebody out of someplace; they came out."

"They want to hold our wonderful pastor," Trump added. "Not fair. Not right."

Brunson would stay in Turkey for another two months, until he was finally released when a judge lifted the travel ban on the pastor, giving him a window to quickly grab his belongings, race to the airport, and flee the country. Facing unrelenting economic pressure and the added threat of U.S. sanctions, Erdogan gave up the fight with Trump.

On October 13, Brunson's first stop upon returning to the United

States was the White House, where he rested his hand on Trump's shoulder, knelt in prayer, and thanked the president. Trump claimed a diplomatic coup for his administration. It took longer and was messier than the president anticipated, but the pastor was nevertheless free.

On August 15, Trump seized an opportunity to retaliate against the national security professionals who had publicly condemned his handling of Russia's election interference or questioned his fitness to be president. Chief among them was John Brennan, the former CIA director who had delivered an intelligence briefing to Trump about the Russian operation back in January 2017 and had since become an outspoken critic of the president, both on social media and in his role as an NBC News analyst.

Sarah Sanders made a striking announcement at her August 15 press briefing: Brennan's security clearance was being revoked. Reading a statement she attributed to Trump, Sanders said Brennan posed a risk to national security by "his erratic conduct and behavior." She accused the former CIA director of making "a series of unfounded and outrageous allegations—wild outbursts on the Internet and television—about this administration." Ironically, these were the same charges many if not most national security professionals would level against Trump. Brennan, sixty-two, had devoted twenty-five years of his career to the CIA. He worked as a Near East and South Asia analyst, a CIA station chief in Riyadh, Saudi Arabia, and a director of the National Counterterrorism Center. He served under President Clinton, President George W. Bush, and then in the Obama administration, where he was homeland security adviser and later CIA director. Trump was also considering revoking the security clearances of other national security officials, each of whom the president considered a personal enemy: former director of national intelligence James Clapper; former FBI director James Comey; former deputy FBI director Andrew McCabe; former acting attorney general Sally Yates; former CIA director Michael Hayden; and former national security adviser Susan Rice; as well as two recently departed FBI officials,

Peter Strzok and Lisa Page, and one current Justice Department official, Bruce Ohr.

To many professionals in the national security community, this extraordinary action crossed a red line. Among those shocked was William McRaven, who had earned the title "Bull Frog" among special operators for being one of the longest serving in that elite corps. The former navy admiral had been a commander of the U.S. Joint Special Operations Command and led the 2011 raid on a Pakistani compound that killed Osama bin Laden, the al-Qaeda terrorist mastermind of 9/11.

McRaven had considered Brennan a trusted friend and critical partner in that unique mission. Earlier in 2018, McRaven and Brennan had been together in Austin at the University of Texas, where McRaven was finishing his work as university chancellor. They headlined a panel discussing the importance of leadership and praising each other's steady support in the years-long search for bin Laden's hideout and the tense assault on his compound.

McRaven was enjoying his semiretirement, visiting a friend in the Colorado mountains, when he heard the news that Trump was revoking Brennan's security clearance. The next day, August 16, he had plans to go fly-fishing in a beautiful river valley but felt an urge—a duty, even—to speak out in Brennan's defense. McRaven had spotty cell reception and no wireless connection, so sending an email was not an option. He asked his host if he could use the landline at his home. First he gathered his thoughts and scribbled a few phrases on a piece of paper. Then he called the cell phone of a reporter he knew and trusted.

As a child growing up in San Antonio, McRaven had been in the same fifth-grade class as Karen Tumulty, who had become a distinguished political correspondent at *The Washington Post* and had recently moved to the opinions section as a columnist. McRaven figured he would give her an on-the-record quote she could share with whichever *Post* colleague was writing about the Brennan controversy. Tumulty was heading to a doctor's appointment when the admiral dialed. She didn't recognize the Colorado number and let the call go to voice mail. Not sure when he'd be able to call her back later, McRaven decided to speak aloud into the voice-mail message, saying what he would tell Trump directly if he had the chance.

"Here is what I've come up with," he said. "Do whatever you want to with it, Karen."

Then he dictated his comment, verbatim:

Former CIA Director John Brennan, whose security clearance you revoked on Wednesday, is one of the finest public servants I have ever known. Few Americans have done more to protect this country than John. He is a man of unparalleled integrity, whose honesty and character have never been in question, except by those who don't know him.

Therefore, I would consider it an honor if you would revoke my security clearance as well, so I can add my name to the list of men and women who have spoken up against your presidency.

Like most Americans, I had hoped that when you became president, you would rise to the occasion and become the leader this great nation needs.

A good leader tries to embody the best qualities of his or her organization. A good leader sets the example for others to follow. A good leader always puts the welfare of others before himself or herself.

Your leadership, however, has shown little of these qualities. Through your actions, you have embarrassed us in the eyes of our children, humiliated us on the world stage and, worst of all, divided us as a nation.

If you think for a moment that your McCarthy-era tactics will suppress the voices of criticism, you are sadly mistaken. The criticism will continue until you become the leader we prayed you would be.

Waiting in the reception area to see her doctor, Tumulty played the mystery caller's voice mail. She was stunned by what she heard. She called McRaven back but only talked briefly to him because he was finally heading out to fish. She told him she felt sure the *Post* would publish some of his reaction, and McRaven said he'd be out of pocket for a while but trusted her to handle it. They hung up.

As Tumulty sat in the waiting room transcribing McRaven's voicemail recording, she felt certain it deserved more than a few quotes in a news story. A national military hero had called the president a national embarrassment and a poor role model for America's children. He even compared Trump to Joseph McCarthy. She consulted with her editors, and they agreed they should publish McRaven's impromptu speech word for word as an opinion piece.

McRaven's essay went viral. It drew notice deep in the bowels of the country's national security apparatus, where public servants working many rungs below McRaven had been silently disgusted watching Trump disrespect them and their brethren. They took private comfort reading McRaven's words. As one of those low-level cogs described it, finally somebody revered, a boldfaced name, was declaring, in essence, "No more."

Before Trump, this government aide had always felt the presidency had a kind of magic. No matter which party the president came from, he bore the weight of history on his shoulders, with the seriousness it deserved. But not anymore. "He's ruined that magic," this aide said of Trump. "The disdain he shows for our country's foundation and its principles. The disregard he has for right and wrong. Your fist clenches. Your teeth grate. The hair goes up on the back of your neck. I have to remind myself I said an oath to a document in the National Archives. I swore to the Constitution. I didn't swear an oath to this jackass."

As this aide saw it, there has been a silent understanding within the national security community that diplomatic, military, and intelligence officers were doing the right thing, quietly risking their lives to protect the American way of life. This aide saw Trump's move against Brennan as one of the first steps of undercutting America's democratic system of government and the belief system upon which it was founded. According to the aide, it was the president declaring, "It's not okay to disagree with me. I can remove you from this work and your career."

"If he wanted to, how far could he push this?" this aide asked. "Look back. Did people in the 1930s in Germany know when the government started to turn on them? Most Americans are more worried about who is going to win on *America's Got Talent* and what the traffic is going to be like on I-95. They aren't watching this closely.

"I like to believe [Trump] is too self-engrossed, too incompetent and disorganized to get us to 1930," this aide added. "But he has moved the bar. And another president that comes after him can move it a little farther. The time is coming. Our nation will be tested. Every nation is. Rome fell, remember. He is opening up vulnerabilities for this to happen. That is my fear."

On August 21, in a courtroom in lower Manhattan, Michael Cohen was set to appear that afternoon as part of a plea agreement with federal prosecutors related to the hush-money payments he made to women claiming to have had affairs with Trump. More than 250 miles south, in a federal courthouse in Alexandria, Virginia, a jury was deliberating on charges against Paul Manafort, the former Trump campaign chairman.

Just after four o'clock in the afternoon, Cohen pleaded guilty to eight felony counts and agreed to cooperate with prosecutors in New York. He testified that he had made these criminal payments "in coordination and at the direction of" Trump.

At nearly the same time, the jury in Alexandria reached a verdict in the Manafort case. Manafort was also found guilty of, coincidentally, eight counts: five counts of tax fraud, two counts of bank fraud, and one count of failure to disclose a foreign bank account. The judge declared a mistrial on the remaining ten charges.

The news broke as the president traveled to West Virginia for a rally, where he used his bully pulpit to repeatedly denounce the Mueller investigation as a "witch hunt." The president cried out, his voice rising, "Where is the collusion? Where is the collusion?"

Unbeknownst to his throngs of supporters or the journalists covering the day's events, Trump had used this day to try to win the Nobel Peace Prize. He worked the phones, seeking a recommendation for the prize. His main target was Japanese prime minister Shinzo Abe, who had proven to be the most obsequious of his major-nation counterparts, but he called other Asian heads of state, too. As Trump lobbied foreign counterparts, his pitch went along the lines of "It's time. Obama got it without doing anything. I brought peace to North Korea. I need to win the Nobel." Winning a Nobel had been a fixation of Trump's, in large part because Obama was awarded one in 2009, less than one year into his presidency.

Trump's hunger for recognition extended to other prizes, too. Oftentimes when he heard about somebody receiving a lifetime achievement award from a think tank, for instance, Trump would complain to aides and argue that he deserved it more. At one point in late 2017, he even suggested that he might award himself the Presidential Medal of Freedom, which President Harry S. Truman established as the nation's highest civilian award. As Trump reviewed the biographies of potential candidates for the Presidential Medal of Freedom, he remarked to aides, "Well, I've probably done even more. Maybe I should be the one getting this."

On August 27, Trump wanted to turn a personal phone call with Mexican president Enrique Peña Nieto celebrating a new U.S.-Mexico trade deal into a live news conference. This was just another whim from the president, who called himself a game-day player. Aides had to rush to satisfy him. With the press pool whisked into the Oval Office and gathered around the Resolute Desk, Trump pushed the button on his phone to greet Peña Nieto.

"Enrique?" Trump said.

There was no response. Silence. The line was dead. Trump was impatient. "You can hook him up," he called out to aides. "You tell me when. This is a big deal. A lot of people are waiting."

Trump tried again.

"Hellooo?" he said. "Do you want to put that on this phone please? Hellooo?"

Finally, an aide picked up the handheld receiver and patched Peña Nieto through to Trump. The two presidents carried on with a conversation. It turned out Peña Nieto had been properly connected on the other line. The problem was that Trump wasn't used to picking up the handset to ensure that the other side could hear him.

John Kelly and Sanders had green-lighted Trump's idea to conduct his call with Peña Nieto live, with television cameras running, with only twenty minutes' notice. White House communications officials did not have time to do a pretest to make sure the phone lines would connect properly. "Buy two minutes to get it right," one top aide said later. "Mexico is not going to hang up the fucking phone. Nobody—nobody—is going to hang up on the president of the United States."

Trump and his aides had debated whether to tell the Mexicans that Peña Nieto's voice would be played on speakerphone live on TV. Ultimately, they concluded that they had to. The White House would later tell reporters that they coordinated the call in advance with the Mexican government. That was taking major license with the word "coordinated." The White House gave the Mexican president's office only about 120 seconds' notice of what Trump was planning to do. That lack of advance preparation was clear in Peña Nieto's halting language. To celebrate the deal, Peña Nieto offered a tequila toast.

Trump loathed John McCain. Even as the Arizona senator was dying of brain cancer at his Sedona ranch, Trump attacked him at his rallies over his decisive 2017 vote against the GOP's proposed health-care overhaul. After McCain passed away on August 25, 2018, at the age of eighty-one, Trump stubbornly rejected his aides' suggestion to issue a statement about his death. The White House briefly flew the American flag at full staff, even though Washington protocol dictated that it remain at half-staff until the senator was laid to rest.

On September 1, McCain's memorial service at Washington National Cathedral served not only as a memorial for an American hero but also as a stinging rebuke of Trump and Trumpism. The cathedral rang with paeans to bipartisanship, compromise, and civility in a melancholy last hurrah for all that now seemed lost. One by one, mourners celebrated elements of McCain's epic life—basic decency and morality; common values that transcended ideology, class, or race; service to nation over self—that Trump most starkly lacked.

Meghan McCain, the late senator's thirty-three-year-old daughter, delivered the rawest repudiation: "We gather here to mourn the passing of American greatness. The real thing, not cheap rhetoric from men who will never come near the sacrifice he gave so willingly, nor the opportunistic appropriation of those who lived lives of comfort and privilege while he suffered and served."

Gathered in the pews was a collection of global elites: the previous three presidents and every major-party nominee for the past two decades; military generals; intelligence chiefs; senators and representatives; foreign ambassadors and other world leaders. The lone man out was Trump, who spent the day golfing at his Virginia course because the McCain family made clear he would not be welcome at the service. His isolation was underscored by the chumminess inside the cathedral, where Hillary Clinton sat shoulder to shoulder with Dick Cheney and at one point George W. Bush snuck candies to Michelle Obama.

Ivanka Trump and Jared Kushner attended at the invitation of Senator Lindsey Graham, a close friend of McCain's, and rubbed elbows with the very people who so disdained the president. Kelly and Jim Mattis had special roles in the proceedings. The White House chief of staff and defense secretary escorted McCain's widow, Cindy, into the cathedral and were seated prominently in camera view. And as he watched clips of them on television, Trump grew furious, telling other advisers that he felt Kelly and Mattis had betrayed him by sidling up to the McCain family.

On September 5, Trump become irate when *The New York Times* published an extraordinary editorial. The title was "I Am Part of the Resistance Inside the Trump Administration," and the author was anonymous, identified by the *Times* only as a "senior official." The column was without precedent, and it was published a day after the first revelations surfaced from Bob Woodward's *Fear*, also a scalding portrait of the president. The anonymous editorial writer described Trump as "impetuous" and accused him of acting "in a manner that is detrimental to the health of our republic." The official also alleged that there had been "early whispers" among members of Trump's cabinet about invoking the Twenty-fifth Amendment to remove him from office but that they decided to instead work within the government to contain him. It amounted to a portrait painted from within of what Senator Bob Corker had called the "adult day care center."

Administration aides were so alarmed by the column—and by the president's resulting fury—that some texted each other the phrase "The sleeper cells have awoken." One recently departed White House official likened it to the opening sequence in *When a Stranger Calls*, a 1979 psychological thriller: "It's like the horror movies when everyone realizes the call is coming from inside the house."

Trump considered figuring out the identity of Anonymous one of the government's most pressing priorities. Beginning just after dawn on September 6, press statements forcefully denying that they were the author rolled in one by one from more than two dozen cabinet members and other top administration officials. They read as public declarations of absolute loyalty to Trump. On September 7, Trump directed the Justice Department to investigate the author of the "resistance" op-ed. He spoke freely to reporters that day about his fresh paranoia regarding whom in his midst he could trust. "What I do now is I look around the room," he said. "I say, 'Hey, if I don't know somebody . . .'"

White House staff began going through records to see who had outstanding copies of foreign leader calls with the president, as well as other sensitive documents. A White House official made a request to Mattis's assistant: Why hadn't the defense secretary's office returned some of the copies of readouts of the president's calls with foreign leaders? The White House needed them returned ASAP. This was a normal housecleaning request, but some officials at the Pentagon felt the timing conveyed an undeniable message: we're watching you.

In early September 2018, Trump's lawyers finally reached a conclusion with Mueller over his request for a presidential interview. Trump's lawyers had argued to prosecutors all summer why they didn't believe it was necessary to provide the president's responses to their questions and tried to appear open to a possible compromise for him to provide limited answers. The discussion took the form of a volley of emails and memos between Trump's lawyer Jane Raskin and her old law firm friend James Quarles.

Some of the correspondence was rudimentary. The Trump lawyers wanted to know what criminal statutes Mueller's team was investigating as possible crimes and why this would require answers from the president. Raskin's shorthand version was something to the effect of "You have told us our client is the subject of the investigation and you won't even tell us what you are looking at." It took roughly three weeks to get an answer to that question. Quarles responded that the statutes governed the criminal acts of hacking, under the Computer Fraud and Abuse Act, as well as the very general crimes of wire fraud and mail fraud. Trump's lawyers shrugged. That's it? That's useless, they said to each other. They were certain the president hadn't engaged in any of those crimes.

Mueller's team would be silent for long stretches, especially later in the summer. At one point, Quarles told the Trump lawyers that it was important to ask about the president's view of events surrounding his pursuit of the Trump Tower Moscow project, as well as his role in describing Donald Trump Jr.'s 2016 meeting with a Russian lawyer who was expected to provide damaging information on Clinton. Raskin and her colleagues had a shared reaction: "What conceivably is criminal about that? Why do you want to ask about that?" The president's team also argued that prosecutors were not entitled to question Trump on decisions he made as president because anything prosecutors needed to know from Trump's time in office could be obtained from the thousands of documents and dozens of witnesses the White House had helped provide.

In early August, Raskin summed up the team's views on this and made what the team considered their closing argument: the Mueller team had failed to make a compelling case for an interview. The line went dead. The Trump team got no response throughout the remainder of the month. The silence was mildly nerve-racking. Trump's lawyers suspected these lulls were caused by a third party: the Department of Justice, specifically Rod Rosenstein, who was supervising Mueller's work. It felt to Trump's counselors that the special counsel's office was checking with the boss about how strenuously it could threaten the president or what it could claim before it did so. Trump's lawyers figured Rosenstein had been recommending an incremental approach.

"It was like when Princess Diana said there are three people in this marriage," one Trump adviser recalled, a reference to the late Princess of Wales's infamous quip about her husband, Prince Charles, and his relationship with Camilla Parker Bowles. "The Mueller folks felt they were fighting a battle on two sides—against us and against DOJ. My sense is, DOJ was telling them to do certain things."

Raskin and her husband, Martin, went on a long-scheduled vacation over Labor Day weekend to Flathead Lake, a breathtaking part of Montana just south of Glacier National Park. On the first full day of their trip, a family celebration, Jane Raskin was on the main drag in quiet Missoula when she got a call on her cell phone from Quarles. He was providing her with a heads-up that he was sending a new letter to the Trump team.

The Raskins braced for bad news. But as they read the letter together the first week of September, they quickly realized everything had broken Trump's way. Mueller had effectively capitulated. The special counsel would accept written answers from the president, for now, on a limited set of questions. Trump's lawyers were ecstatic. The nuclear missile they had always feared Mueller was just a few keystrokes away from launching—a subpoena—would never come.

"Everything was about the grand jury subpoena," a member of Trump's legal team said. "Until it became obvious there wasn't going to be one. We had won."

Nineteen

SCARE-A-THON

L abor Day marked the unofficial kickoff for the campaign sprint to the November midterm elections. The Democrats were trying to reclaim majorities in the House and perhaps even the Senate. Trump was not on the ballot, but the elections were a referendum on his presidency. For Trump, the very survival of his presidency was at stake. He and his advisers feared that if Democrats seized control of the House, they could bring impeachment charges against the president.

The night of September 6, Trump took the stage at the MetraPark arena in Billings, Montana, which was home to a marquee Senate race, and declared, "There is no place like a Trump rally." Trump defended himself against "all these losers that say horrible things," including against those questioning his mental fitness. "I stand up here giving speeches for an hour and a half, many times without notes, and they say, 'He's lost it.' And yet we have twenty-five thousand people showing up to speeches," the president said. He then extolled his political conquests—"I beat seventeen great Republicans!" "I beat the Bush dynasty!" "I beat Crooked Hillary!"—and lamented that media commentators still ask, "Is he competent?"

Then Trump told his cheering supporters the real reason the Democrats had to be thwarted in November: "They like to use the impeach word. 'Impeach Trump.' . . . But I say, 'How do you impeach somebody that's doing a great job that hasn't done anything wrong? Our economy is good. How do you do it? How do you do it? How do you do it?'" By the time he finished speaking, the president had made thirty-eight false statements, according to *The Washington Post*'s Fact Checker.

Throughout the fall campaign season, Trump spoke regularly by phone, sometimes twice a day, with a handful of Republican loyalists in Congress, including Mark Meadows, the North Carolina representative who led the Freedom Caucus. Among all the Republicans in Washington, Meadows was one of those whose advice the president truly valued and sought out most consistently. Meadows provided Trump with regular updates on the so-called investigation of the investigators—the Republican quest to find wrongdoing in the FBI's handling of its initial investigation, Crossfire Hurricane.

Trump's displeasure with Jeff Sessions had simmered for more than a year now. In his fall conversations with Meadows, Trump periodically expressed interest in firing the attorney general. Meadows urged patience, as did other voices in Trump's ear. You can fire Sessions, he told the president, but just wait until after the midterms, when Trump would have the backing he needed from most if not all congressional Republicans. Meadows and his colleagues on Capitol Hill agreed that the president had every right to have an attorney general he trusted, but firing Sessions before the election risked sparking a political backlash that could hurt the GOP's prospects. If Trump acted like an authoritarian, there was a danger that voters might take it out on Republican candidates, Meadows warned. Trump complained about feeling boxed in, but he agreed to give Meadows his word.

On September 21, Sessions was in his home state of Alabama touring Auburn University to spotlight scientific research to combat the opioid epidemic. As Auburn's president, Steven Leath, showed him around campus, Sarah Isgur Flores's phone was melting down. The Justice Department communications chief was trying furiously to stop the *New York Times* reporters Adam Goldman and Michael Schmidt from publishing what seemed like an explosive scoop: Rod Rosenstein, in his first disorienting weeks as deputy attorney general and in the immediate aftermath of James Comey's firing, had suggested to other Justice Department and FBI officials that he secretly record Trump and had discussed recruiting cabinet members to remove him from office for being unfit by invoking the Twenty-fifth Amendment. If true, it would have been a huge departure from any normal investigative protocol. The supervisor of a high-profile investigation—especially a special counsel probe—would not normally jump into the investigative work or assume a secret undercover role. The *Times* reporters were confident in their reporting. Isgur Flores argued it was preposterous and also feared the report would unfairly spur Trump to fire Rosenstein.

"You're going to cause a constitutional crisis," Isgur Flores yelled into the phone at one of the *Times* reporters. "Go fuck yourself!"

Sessions and Leath were listening to Isgur Flores's end of the conversation. "She's spirited," Sessions told Leath in his thick drawl.

Later that day, a Friday, the *Times* published the story. It landed like a bomb. Rosenstein disputed the account, calling it "inaccurate and factually incorrect." He added, "Based on my personal dealings with the president, there is no basis to invoke the 25th Amendment." But the damage was done. Rosenstein assumed he would be fired. A scramble was under way to protect the Russia investigation and ensure stability at the Justice Department. Those practice drills Sessions, Rosenstein, and their deputies had gone over so many times in their heads were suddenly real.

Sessions continued his trip in Alabama, but Isgur Flores rushed to catch a commercial flight back to Washington to help Rosenstein navigate the storm. Ed O'Callaghan, who had been traveling overseas, cut his vacation short and returned home right away. On Saturday, the president called Kelly with instructions: fire Rosenstein this weekend. Kelly argued against basing a decision on a *New York Times* article alone. The chief of staff had doubts about the story and at least wanted to hear from Rosenstein. "We gotta let him come in and talk to him," Kelly told the president. Trump, Kelly, Rosenstein, and Don McGahn traded calls over the weekend. The president vented his anger. McGahn mostly focused on how this could interfere with the Supreme Court nomination of Judge Brett Kavanaugh. Rosenstein was trying to convince Kelly he should keep his job.

Kelly had found himself in this difficult place more than once with a high-level government appointee. As the president would fume and rail about an appointee and threaten at varying decibels that he was going to give him or her the boot, Kelly would see the writing on the wall and try to ease the public servant out gently. "Go," Kelly would tell someone who had gotten on Trump's bad side. "It's not going to get any better."

Kelly tried this with Rosenstein. But the deputy attorney general didn't want to leave and argued over the weekend that the *Times* reporting was misleading and, in his estimation, bore the fingerprints of former deputy FBI director Andrew McCabe.

Aides at the Justice Department and at the White House nevertheless prepared for the deputy attorney general's ouster. Matthew Whitaker, Sessions's chief of staff who was close to the White House and had been an outspoken critic of the Russia investigation before joining the administration, told Isgur Flores, "Rod will be gone. I'll be DAG. The president told me this." When Rosenstein caught wind of the Whitaker plan, he worried it might appear to outsiders like an effort by the president to interfere with the Mueller probe.

On Monday morning, September 24, Rosenstein showed up at his Justice Department office knowing it might be his last day there. Isgur Flores popped into Noel Francisco's office and said, "Today might be the day. Hope you're ready to go." Francisco, the solicitor general, was slated to take over control of the Mueller investigation should Rosenstein exit.

Rosenstein was still upset about the *Times* story and angry about the rumors that he was being pushed out immediately and replaced by Whitaker. But he also had a strange calm after the harried weekend: he now assumed he'd lose his job and was solely focused on making sure he had a dignified exit. He didn't want to be tweet-shamed out of his office. Rosenstein had adopted a gallows humor over the months of attacks from Trump's GOP allies, who often predicted his demise and were proven wrong. In Rosenstein's tight circle, there was a running joke in the office about his nine lives: "Die another day."

Isgur Flores got inquiries from reporters that morning about Rosenstein's resignation. She assumed the tips were coming from the White House, and she took the queries as a sign that Rosenstein's hours were numbered. Then *Axios* reported that Rosenstein had "verbally resigned" to Kelly. Isgur Flores tracked down Rosenstein, who was in his office taking goodbye photos with his staff. "Sir, we're out of time," she told him.

"Wait, let's take a picture first," Rosenstein told his trusted spokeswoman.

"Sir, I need to talk to you immediately," Isgur Flores said. "It's happening."

Rosenstein then went to the White House in late morning, where he expected to be fired. Isgur Flores put the finishing touches on a Justice Department statement announcing Rosenstein's departure, Whitaker's appointment as deputy attorney general, and Francisco's role overseeing the Mueller investigation.

Inside the West Wing, Rosenstein met with Kelly and made clear he was no longer resisting. He said he would resign; he just didn't want an ignominious, abrupt ending. "If you want me to resign, I'll be happy to talk to the president and we can negotiate a reasonable amount of time," Rosenstein said. "I don't intend to resign immediately." Kelly didn't demand anything, but listened instead.

Rosenstein then went to meet with McGahn, who was about to head over to the Hill for the Kavanaugh hearings. In the early afternoon, just after Rosenstein left a National Security Council meeting, he talked by phone with Trump, who was in New York for the annual United Nations General Assembly. The call was cordial, even friendly, with Rosenstein saying that the *Times* story was wrong.

"I don't want to fire you," Trump told Rosenstein. "Where did you get that idea?"

Trump suggested Rosenstein visit him later that week at his golf club in Bedminster, New Jersey. "I don't think that's a good idea," he told the president. "I'll talk to you when you come back to town."

They decided to meet that Thursday. Despite the pleasantries of the call, Rosenstein still thought, "I'll be fired soon, just not today." Rosenstein became the latest senior government official left hanging in one of Trump's parlor games. "I think it pleases him to sort of paw at a wounded mouse in front of him because it asserts his sense of control and authority, and he enjoys that to no end," Trump's biographer Tim O'Brien told *The Washington Post*'s Ashley Parker.

Both behind the scenes and in public, some of Trump's most important advisers were telling him not to fire Rosenstein. The Friday night after the *Times*' "wire" story broke, Sean Hannity said to his loyal viewers, including Viewer No. 1: "I have a message for the president tonight. Under zero circumstances should the president fire anybody." Hannity, who spoke with Trump nearly every day, warned on air that the president's enemies were "hoping and praying" that Trump fired Rosenstein to lure him into a scandal. "The president needs to know it is all a setup," Hannity said.

Some of Trump's attorneys were also throwing up cautions. Firing Rosenstein would only make it appear he was interfering with the probe once again. Before Trump's planned meeting with Rosenstein on Thursday, the threat of his ouster seemingly vanished, without so much as an acknowledgment from Trump that he had been demanding it.

Trump and Rosenstein spoke several more times on the phone that week. They met in person the following week, aboard Air Force One on October 8 for a day trip to Florida, and had a perfectly cordial conversation about a range of other topics. They were, in the acronym used by one Trump adviser who interacted with them on the flight, "BFFs." Best friends forever.

In mid-September, Trump confronted a political crisis over Kavanaugh's embattled Supreme Court nomination. The #MeToo reckoning had arrived at the doorstep of the White House. Christine Blasey Ford alleged, first in a private letter to Democrats on the Senate Judiciary Committee and then in an on-the-record interview published September 16 in

The Washington Post, that Kavanaugh had sexually assaulted her in 1982, when the two of them had been high school students in suburban Maryland. Ford told the *Post* reporter Emma Brown that Kavanaugh corralled her into a bedroom during a house party, pinned her to a bed, groped her, pressed his body against hers, and, when she tried to scream, put his hand over her mouth to silence her. Kavanaugh denied the allegation.

Ford was not the only woman to accuse Kavanaugh of assault, but she was the most prominent and most credible. Hers was a horrifying and serious allegation against a sitting federal judge, former senior official in the George W. Bush White House, and darling of the conservative establishment. Kavanaugh was under consideration to succeed retiring justice Anthony Kennedy, a longtime swing vote on the bench, and his confirmation would push the high court's center of gravity to the right.

Politically, the Kavanaugh crisis was a grave threat to Republicans on the ballot in November. Polling showed Trump and his party already underwater with women voters. The gender gap was growing wider during Trump's presidency: the percentage of women who said they leaned toward the Republican Party was 32 percent in September, down from 35 percent in 2016, according to *Washington Post*–ABC News polling. But Trump had long been blind to the political liability of gender issues.

Trump's instinct throughout was to defend his Supreme Court pick and muscle Kavanaugh's nomination through the Senate. He calculated that the mere act of fighting to protect a conservative jurist would endear him to his political base and galvanize conservatives in the midterm elections, especially evangelicals. For Trump, however, the Kavanaugh allegations were not just about politics. They were personal. The president himself had been accused of sexual assault by more than a dozen women and infamously bragged on tape of grabbing women by the genitals. The president was hypersensitive to the modern reality that a powerful man's career could be ruined by a single accusation, as had occurred to a litany of business and media figures, some of whom were Trump's friends or acquaintances.

On September 26, Trump inserted himself into the anguished national debate over Kavanaugh allegations and sexual assault more broadly by calling the #MeToo movement "very dangerous." In a defiant and free-wheeling news conference on the sidelines of the U.N. General Assembly, Trump revealed his myopic obsession with his own jeopardy. Asked whether the allegations brought against himself influenced his thinking about Kavanaugh's accusers, the president replied, "Absolutely."

"I've had a lot of false charges made against me, really false charges," Trump said. "I know friends that have had false charges. People want fame. They want money. They want whatever. So when I see it, I view it differently than somebody sitting home watching television, where they say, 'Oh, Judge Kavanaugh this or that.' It's happened to me many times."

The next day, Ford and Kavanaugh both appeared before the Senate Judiciary Committee for one of the most extraordinary days of public testimony in modern political history. The day unfolded like a play in two acts. First Ford declared herself "100 percent" certain that Kavanaugh was the prep school boy who assaulted her. She was credible. Kavanaugh was in trouble. Trump, watching her on television on the flight home from New York, thought Ford came across as Mother Teresa reborn. He was worried. Then, shortly after three o'clock in the afternoon, Kavanaugh appeared. He practically shouted his opening statement denying Ford's allegations. His face was red with righteous indignation. He decried "a calculated and orchestrated political hit." He was positively Trumpian, a performance artist spinning his own reality in direct contradiction to Ford's testimony, and Trump was riveted. He loved it. "This is why I nominated him," the president crowed privately.

On October 2, with senators preparing to vote on Kavanaugh's nomination, Trump took matters into his own hands. At a rally that Tuesday evening in Southaven, Mississippi, he delivered a thirty-six-second, off-script, ruthless jeremiad ripping into Ford's credibility with the pacing and delivery of a stand-up comedian. From the presidential lectern, Trump reenacted Ford's Senate hearing and mocked her memory lapses:

"How did you get home?"

"I don't remember."

"How did you get there?"

"I don't remember."

"Where is the place?"

"I don't remember."

"How many years ago was it?"

"I don't know. I don't know. I don't know. I don't know."

"What neighborhood was it in?"

"I don't know."

"Where's the house?"

"I don't know."

"Upstairs? Downstairs? Where was it?"

"I don't know. But I had one beer. That's the only thing I remember."

Trump's advisers had implored him not to attack Ford, but he did it anyway, relying on his primal instincts for political combat. The Mississippi crowd of thousands was in stitches, hooting and hollering at the president's impersonation of an alleged sexual assault victim.

Predictably, Democrats reacted with horror—as did some Republicans at first—but as Trump's mockery of Ford was replayed many times on television, the national discussion shifted to include doubts about the truthfulness of Ford's allegations. It became a familiar "he said, she said" debate. The president had also helped turbocharge momentum among conservative activists and made Republican senators more emboldened to muscle his nomination through. By week's end, on October 6, the Senate voted to confirm Kavanaugh, 50 to 48. His swearing-in two days later was a crowning achievement for Trump's presidency.

Kavanaugh's ascension to the Supreme Court also was McGahn's swan song. The White House counsel had prioritized judicial appointments during the first two years of the administration, installing two conservatives to the high court and scores more to federal district and circuit courts. This left an enduring legacy. As soon as the Kavanaugh fight was over, McGahn was set to depart the administration and not entirely on his own terms. Since late 2017, his relationship with Trump had been strained, but in the late summer and the fall of 2018 it deteriorated to the point where the two were barely on speaking terms. On August 18, *The New York Times* reported that McGahn had sat for thirty hours of interviews with the special counsel team and that his testimony was central to Mueller's understanding of how Trump acted in key moments under review for obstruction of justice. This was a flash point. The *Times* story did not mention that several other White House advisers also had spent lengthy periods as Mueller witnesses, including Reince Priebus and Steve Bannon. It should not have been news to the president that so many of his aides had been interviewed by the special counsel. But in Trump's mind it was evidence of McGahn's disloyalty.

On August 29, Trump decided to take a public stand and tweeted that McGahn would be leaving his position once Kavanaugh was confirmed. The tweet was preemptive. If McGahn wanted to reconsider his tentative plan to depart, he couldn't do it now. This was Trump's way of saying he was the one who decided which staff left and when. The president telegraphed to everyone that he was the boss.

McGahn's final day was October 17. Trump picked as his replacement Pat Cipollone, a well-respected commercial litigator and a conservative Trump fan. Since early summer, Cipollone had been informally advising Trump and his outside legal team about the Mueller probe. He also had a close working relationship with Emmet Flood, and Jared Kushner and Ivanka supported his hiring.

In the weeks before the November 6 midterm elections, Trump barnstormed the nation, singularly focused on illegal immigration. He fixated on a slow-moving migrant caravan consisting mostly of families fleeing violence traveling on foot from Central America, through Mexico, and toward the United States to seek asylum. Trump warned voters that the "caravans" were in fact a dangerous "invasion" of migrants threatening the safety and prosperity of U.S. citizens. Privately, Trump demanded that his aides take "tough action" at the border to demonstrate "strength." No one came under more pressure from the unrelenting president than Kirstjen Nielsen, the secretary of homeland security and a close ally of John Kelly's.

Trump's relationship with Nielsen had been tempestuous from the start as he made her a battering ram for illegal immigration. He routinely complained to other advisers that Nielsen was not doing enough to secure the border; her defenders said she was doing all she could within the confines of the law. In some instances, the volatile president was verbally and emotionally abusive toward Nielsen. "Kirstjen, you're just not tough enough," Trump would tell her.

Trump complained that Nielsen did not "look the part" of homeland security secretary. He made fun of her stature and believed that at about five feet four inches she was not physically intimidating. "She's so short," Trump would tell others about Nielsen. She and Kelly would try to make light of it. Kelly would rib her and say, "But you've got those little fists of fury!"

A number of federal agencies bore responsibility for managing the influx of migrants. The Justice Department housed asylum judges and administered the legal process. The State Department negotiated with Latin American countries and issued visas. The Department of Health and Human Services oversaw the care of migrant children. The Army Corps of Engineers managed construction of the border wall. But in Trump's mind, everything related to immigration and the border fell under the Department of Homeland Security, and he held Nielsen accountable for it all.

At a cabinet meeting on May 9, 2018, Trump had berated Nielsen in front of roughly two dozen administration colleagues over the rising number of illegal border crossings. In an explosive, extended tirade, a red-faced Trump excoriated Nielsen for not bringing him enough "solutions." Then Trump instructed Nielsen to "shut down" the southern border. Attorney General Jeff Sessions, whose relationship with the president was the most strained of all the cabinet members, seized an opportunity to get on the boss's good side for once. Seated across the table from the president, Sessions interjected, "I just think we're not being tough enough. I think we need to shut down the border."

Trump concurred and, turning to Nielsen at the far end of the table, asked, "Why haven't you shut down the border?" It was more of an admonition than a question. Nielsen knew this would be illegal, not to mention economically disastrous because it could choke off trade routes.

"I'm not sure what we are saying here," Nielsen said. "As the attorney general knows, people have a legal right to cross the border and try to claim asylum. That's just the law."

Trump looked back at Sessions.

"No," Sessions said, "we should just shut the border down."

Trump then lit into Nielsen. Why couldn't she use the power of her department to keep immigrants from flooding into the United States? What was so hard about this? Trump was so worked up that some attendees thought he looked manic. Kelly silently shook his head at Nielsen to signal to her to stop engaging with the president. Kushner made eye contact with Nielsen and moved his finger across his neck to signal to her to cut it off. It was clear to others in the meeting that Nielsen hadn't properly read the room or the president. By the time Trump eventually tired of yelling at Nielsen, nobody had stuck up for her—not even Kelly. He had decided that speaking up would only further provoke the president. After the cabinet meeting had concluded, Mick Mulvaney, the director of the Office of Management and Budget, said to Trump, "You know, the attorney general was wrong about the law. The attorney general is saying this, but that is not the case." But it was too little too late.

Trump's abuse continued episodically through the summer and fall. He harassed Nielsen with angry phone calls, waking her as early as five o'clock in the morning and routinely calling her at 6:30 or 7:00 a.m. as she was heading to work. He also pestered her late at night. Once, after the president had heard a rumor from a Republican lawmaker that a mid-level homeland security official had been "disloyal" to the president during a classified briefing, Trump became obsessed with getting the man fired. He had called Nielsen late at night demanding she remove the official from his job. "That doesn't sound like something he would do, but I'll look into it, sir," she had told him. He had called Nielsen back early the next morning. "Is it done?" the president had asked. Nielsen explained that she couldn't check as her employees had been asleep overnight.

Trump regularly called Nielsen after watching Lou Dobbs's nightly show on Fox Business. Dobbs delivered regular diatribes about illegal immigration, proposing unrealistic solutions and castigating Nielsen as a squish. To Trump, the Dobbs monologues were gospel and created in the White House a near-daily drumbeat. The president would routinely call Nielsen to say a version of "Did you see Lou Dobbs? You're totally fucking embarrassing me. This is my issue!" One of his go-to complaints was, "They're killing me," a reference to Fox coverage of immigration policy. "You've got to fix it," he would demand of Nielsen. Sometimes, Trump would refer to one of Dobbs's proposals and say, "Kirstjen, just do it. Just do it."

"But we can't do it," Nielsen would explain, usually because whatever Dobbs had uttered on TV was against the law.

Other times, when Trump would call Nielsen and demand she execute one of Dobbs's ideas, she would interrupt the president's yelling to inform him, "Sir, we're already doing that. I briefed you on that the other day."

Nielsen recognized the power Dobbs had over Trump, and saw that his commentary was infecting her relationship with the president. The White House communications shop had tried to book Nielsen on Dobbs's show, but he had declined, saying Nielsen wasn't "my cup of tea." As the volume of border crossings spiked, Dobbs had a show focusing on the administration's failure to enact three ideas to secure the border. Nielsen shook her head as she watched. One proposal was legally shaky, the second had already been discarded by the administration because it was impossible to implement, and the third was something the administration was already doing.

Nielsen called Dobbs from her car to correct him. Her aides listened fearfully, sure she would start yelling at the TV host, but she was gracious. "Lou, we'd be happy to help you with your reporting," Nielsen said. "If you ever need any facts or statistics or one of our experts, we'd really be glad to provide it." She then went over why the three ideas he had outlined on air were not workable. Within hours, Trump called Nielsen. He was excited. "Did you call Lou Dobbs?" he asked. She said she had. "That's great," Trump told her. "Lou says you're very smart!"

One of Nielsen's tactics for when Trump asked her to do something illegal—or something that violated a regulation or a treaty—was to ask him, "Okay, sir, what are you trying to accomplish here?" She would then try to figure out a legally permissible way to achieve the same result and often arranged briefings to try to inform the president what he could and could not do. "Let me bring people in," Nielsen would tell Trump. "You don't have to trust me." But the briefings rarely made an impression on Trump. Just when Nielsen thought an illegal or unfeasible idea had been put to bed, the president would awaken it. Trump did not see the law as an impediment, a mind-set forged as a real estate developer. A developer could always just sue, battle it out in court, and negotiate some middle ground.

"Look, we'll get sued and then we'll work it out," Trump told Nielsen during one such discussion. "Just block people from coming in." Stopping people from seeking asylum was a favorite solution of the president's. But he had many ideas, and they would sometimes feel like a sandblast of suggestions, any one of them violating the international conventions on torture, or U.S. rules requiring the study of environmental harm, or regulations governing competitive contracts. Lawyers from the Department of Homeland Security and the White House rarely pointed this out to Trump. Nobody wanted to get him even angrier. Just as he used to recoil from McGahn's repeatedly telling him he couldn't do some of the things he wanted to do, Trump got frustrated with Nielsen.

"Federal law enforcement doesn't work like that," Nielsen told Trump in one such meeting. "People could get in trouble. These people have taken an oath to uphold the law. Do you really want to tell them to do the opposite?"

"Then we'll pardon them," Trump said.

Nielsen knew that every time she asked her agency heads within the Department of Homeland Security to fully secure the porous U.S.-Mexico border, they would complain that the only solution was for

Congress to close legal loopholes. A migrant seeking asylum had to meet a fairly low bar to gain entry, stating that he or she had a credible fear of retribution or harm back home. The overwhelming majority would later be denied asylum based on their circumstances, but by the time of their hearing they had often already disappeared into the country.

On immigration policy, there were many critics and no sponsors. Many offices had to review policy and legislative changes: the National Security Council, the Domestic Policy Council, the White House counsel's office, the chief of staff's office, and the policy coordinators, as well as Kushner and Stephen Miller. It was rare for an idea to survive that gauntlet, and a near miracle for anyone to actually champion it and do the work required to implement it. Kelly sometimes tried to protect Nielsen's turf, once telling Kushner, "You should stay out of it," because Nielsen was in charge of immigration policy.

"The White House was so broken," one administration official later remarked, looking back on this tense period on immigration policy. "There was no process. Ideas would come to the president in a no-process method. Half-baked ideas come in to him. God knows how. It was totally disorganized. To this day, no one is in charge at the White House. No one."

In late October, with the caravan on the move, Trump badgered Nielsen almost endlessly. He suggested lining up border agents and other officers to form a sort of human wall along the portion of the southern border that lacked fencing, roughly 1,200 miles of the 1,933-mile border. A statistician at Homeland Security figured out it would take hundreds of thousands of people standing arm to arm to create a line that long. The number, a conservative estimate, was immediately discarded because it was so staggering. "We were like, this is absurd," one aide remembered.

Nielsen and her team, including the leaders of Customs and Border Protection and U.S. Citizenship and Immigration Services, met for a brainstorming session in downtown Washington's Ronald Reagan Building. Sitting around a conference room, they discussed how to satisfy

Trump's increasingly difficult demands to deny entry to illegal immigrants. The officials felt as if they had already scraped the bottom of the barrel for new options. They contemplated a number of ideas, including sending U.S. marshals to the border, borrowing personnel from another department, or creating a volunteer army. They figured they had to throw some bodies at it, if only to sate Trump. National Guard units had deployed twenty-one hundred troops to the border since the spring, and some homeland security officials suggested ramping up the presence dramatically to create, as one aide put it, "a huge show of force."

At this moment, the border situation was relatively calm. There was no crush of migrants—the caravan was still a few weeks away from reaching the border—and the humanitarian crisis in overcrowded border stations would not unfold until several months later. One senior agency official interjected to point out that additional personnel at the border was not necessary, at least not yet. "This is ridiculous," the official said.

It was not, however, ridiculous to Trump. He was adamant about sending troops to the border, telling aides that the military had tens of thousands of men and women in uniform and he should be able to use them, as commander in chief, to protect the sovereignty of the United States. Advisers explained to Trump that if he sent troops to the border, they would not be allowed to function as if they were law enforcement officers. They could erect temporary fencing or fix vehicles or conduct surveillance, advisers said, but they could not use deadly force. Firing a single shot into Mexico would be considered an act of war.

In late October, Trump decided to use his authority as commander in chief to deploy military troops to the border to guard against migrants. On October 29, the Pentagon announced that it was sending fifty-two hundred troops, as well as Black Hawk helicopters and giant spools of razor wire. This was the largest mobilization of active-duty troops along the U.S.-Mexico border in decades. The next day, Trump floated the idea of sending fifteen thousand troops to the border, an extraordinarily large number that was roughly the size of the U.S. military presence in Afghanistan.

The move immediately inspired howls that Trump was playing politics, militarizing the border to scare voters and turn out his base in the midterm elections, which were now just a week away. But Secretary of Defense Jim Mattis vouched for the mission and said the military was providing "practical support" to homeland security operations. "We don't do stunts in this department," he said.

Nevertheless, Trump made clear that his rush to put troops at the border was about taking strong action to galvanize his supporters to vote Republican in the elections. "If you don't want America to be overrun by masses of illegal aliens and giant caravans, you better vote Republican," Trump said on November 1 at a rally in Columbia, Missouri.

For Trump, deploying the troops wasn't enough. He wanted images—propaganda—distributed through the media showing the military presence. Trump sent word to the Pentagon that he wanted pictures of troops at the border. The presidential demand landed on the desk of Dana White, Mattis's press secretary. Kevin Sweeney, a retired navy rear admiral who was serving as Mattis's chief of staff, told White that the White House needed to see pictures of troops—and fast. White tried to explain this would be unrealistic. This was the Department of Defense, not Coca-Cola. Troops would not be moving to the border instantaneously, even after they received orders.

"I can't give people pictures of something that's not happening," White told Sweeney.

"That's your problem, Dana," Sweeney said. "Just get the damn pictures."

The pressure wasn't coming from Sweeney, of course. It was coming from the top. Trump had pushed the entire military apparatus to help him illustrate the show of might that he had ordered up, which could convince voters that he was protecting the nation from the dangerous "invasion" of migrants that was getting closer each day to a showdown at the border. Sweeney and every senior agency official knew the fastest way to please the president was to get the message on the station he and his fans power watched. "Get something on Fox immediately," Sweeney told White. Trump just didn't understand that U.S. Armed Forces don't simply hop on a C-17 one night and start patrolling the banks of the Rio Grande the next afternoon. "No one would push you to show that except the one person who doesn't know," a Defense Department official said of the president.

Mattis's aides agreed that to satisfy Trump's wishes they would have to get pictures of National Guard troops and asked state National Guard officials who hadn't yet shipped out if they could snap photographs or shoot video of their reserve troops training at home. The first images they finally got—after more than twenty-four hours of hustling—were of the Texas National Guard, the first to have images of troops in drills. "People were more focused on the pictures rather than what we are allegedly doing," the Defense Department official said of the White House. "The urgency wasn't on the mission. It was on getting the pictures." Trump also wanted to see military generals being interviewed on television news, preferably at the border and in a commanding role. Word came down from the White House that images of National Guard officials were not good enough.

By November 3, the first wave of military troops had arrived at the border and photos emerged of uniformed service members installing razor-wire fencing along the Texas side of the Rio Grande. Trump remarked at a campaign rally in Montana that evening, "We have our military on the border. And I noticed all that beautiful barbed wire going up today. Barbed wire, used properly, can be a beautiful sight."

Trump sought to frighten voters in the final days of midterm campaigning by using the threat of an "invasion" of illegal immigrants to stoke fears of cop killers—or, as Trump called asylum seekers, "bad *hombres*." Nancy Pelosi, the House Democratic leader poised to become Speaker, called Trump's fearmongering a "scare-a-thon." This period amplified Trump's ugliest characteristics as president. "He goes out and says crazy, horrible things, blows race whistles and sits back and watches his topic of craziness dominate cable TV for the next 24 hours," said Mike Murphy, a Republican strategist.

On Election Day, November 6, Democrats seized control of the House and picked up several key governorships in the Midwest and even Kansas, propelled by a rejection of Trump's demagoguery in the nation's suburbs, especially among women voters. But Trump's demonization of immigrants helped Republicans expand their majority in the Senate, where the 2018 map had strongly favored Republicans with most of the competitive contests in such red states as Missouri and Texas.

The Democratic triumph in the House was powered by a record number of women candidates. This would be the most racially and gender-diverse freshman class of representatives in congressional history, and Pelosi was set to reclaim the Speaker's gavel she lost eight years earlier. In her election night speech, Pelosi signaled that House Democrats would use their subpoena power to investigate Trump and hold his administration accountable—as Republicans had not. "Today is about more than Democrats and Republicans," she said. "It is about restoring the Constitution's checks and balances to the Trump administration."

The next day, Trump predicted—presciently, it would turn out—"a warlike posture" should House Democrats use their new power to investigate him. "They can play that game, but we can play it better, because we have a thing called the United States Senate," Trump said at a news conference. "I think I'm better at that game than they are, actually." Trump refused to show any contrition or take responsibility for his party's defeats. After the 2010 midterm elections, President Obama talked about his party's "shellacking." And after the 2006 midterm elections, President Bush spoke of his party's "thumpin'." But Trump didn't even acknowledge the loss. Rather, he claimed "very close to complete victory."

Trump did achieve a victory of another sort that day. Finally, he got rid of Sessions. As election results were still being tallied the night of November 6, Trump told advisers he was eager to ax the attorney general right away. The next day, Sessions was gone.

Everything had seemed so normal the night before. Sessions; his wife, Mary; Rosenstein; and aides Isgur Flores and Stephen Boyd were hanging out in Boyd's Justice Department office watching the election returns on Fox. Sessions knew he was not long for Trump World. Internalizing his own fragility, the attorney general had taken to quoting from *Princess Bride* to staffers as he left the office at night: "Good night, Westley. Good work. Sleep well. I'll most likely kill you in the morning."

On November 7, Kelly called Sessions. The president wanted him to resign. Sessions summoned his aides to his office. "It's happening," the attorney general said. "Come on up." It was surreal. Rosenstein counseled Sessions to try to leave on his own terms. "Pick a date," Rosenstein said. "Make it two weeks [from now]. We'll have a farewell party and an appropriate send-off. It's humiliating for you to just walk out. You've been advancing his agenda here, you've gotten a lot done, you have a lot to be proud of, and you shouldn't have to leave under these circumstances."

It was Wednesday and Sessions asked Kelly if he could have until Friday to resign, but Kelly wasn't the decider. He checked with the president and called right back. "It has to happen today," Kelly informed Sessions. "If it doesn't happen right now, there will be a tweet."

Sessions stood behind his desk as he held up the phone, his suit jacket removed and wearing a white shirt, red tie, and glasses. He had long ago drafted a resignation letter, and Isgur Flores immediately started touching it up on her phone. The team debated what his first line should say, and Sessions decided to begin with "at your request," making it clear he had not resigned voluntarily. In the letter, Sessions highlighted his work at the Justice Department to enforce immigration laws and prosecute gang violence. Notably, he called the rule of law, which Trump had so often tried to override or thwart, "a glorious tradition that each of us has a responsibility to safeguard." An assistant printed a copy on Justice Department letterhead, Sessions signed the bottom, and Boyd and O'Callaghan volunteered to hand deliver it to the White House.

When they arrived in the West Wing, a young staffer asked to take it, but O'Callaghan wasn't about to hand the attorney general's resignation letter to someone who looked as if he had just left college. He and Boyd asked to hand it directly to Kelly. When they came face-to-face with the chief of staff, the Justice Department officials thought he looked stressed and pained, visibly conflicted about what he had just ordered. They were surprised by how complimentary Kelly was of Sessions. "He's done a great service to his country," he told O'Callaghan and Boyd.

The instant O'Callaghan and Boyd handed Kelly the letter, Boyd texted Isgur Flores. Back at the Justice Department, she had already briefed a handful of beat reporters on Sessions's resignation and read them his letter under a strict embargo so they could prepare stories. With Boyd's signal, Isgur Flores lifted the embargo, and the journalists published their stories and pushed out news alerts. About ninety seconds later, Trump tweeted the news. The Sessions team had long prepared for this moment, and they were not about to let the president scoop them.

Ordinarily, the deputy attorney general would have stepped into the void left by Sessions's sudden exit, but Trump bypassed Rosenstein. He named Whitaker acting attorney general. A Trump loyalist, Whitaker had publicly criticized the Mueller investigation as a legal commentator before joining the Justice Department as Sessions's chief of staff. As chief, Whitaker had alienated Sessions loyalists and quickly established himself as a palace fighter, firing some officials and attempting unsuccessfully to cast off others, including Isgur Flores, the attorney general's trusted confidante. Now Sessions's temporary successor, Whitaker seized control of the Russia probe. Finally, Trump felt he had his hands on the wheel.

Later that afternoon, Sessions's staff filed into the attorney general's conference room, where Sessions gave an impromptu farewell speech. His celebratory "walkout" from the department aired on live television. Sessions didn't even have a chance to clean out his office. Papers were still stacked on his desk. Files were still open. His nameplate and family pictures were still displayed. The bag in which he carried classified materials was still sitting on a chair. But Sessions had gone home, relieved of duty.

After nearly two years of cruel harassment from Trump, Sessions was loath to criticize the president, even in the confidence of friends. The president didn't even bother to call the attorney general to demand his resignation; he made Kelly do it. Yet Sessions still admired the man he met at that Senate hearing on the United Nations all those years before. Sessions was still in awe of the passions Trump stirred with his former constituents back home in Alabama. He saw in Trump so much fight, so much moxie.

"You know, this guy just has that dragon energy," Sessions remarked to one of his political friends. "He can't be tamed."

Twenty

AN ORNERY DIPLOMAT

On November 9, President Trump headed to Paris, where he was to join some of his Western counterparts for a weekend of ceremonies honoring the hundredth anniversary of the end of World War I. Instead of being excited about a historic commemoration, Trump was brooding. The size of the Democratic majority in the House kept growing as some tight races were called later in the week, making Trump an all-but-certain target of intense Democratic oversight for his next two years in office. On top of that, Acting Attorney General Matthew Whitaker had predictably sparked controversy in the news, both because of his lack of basic qualifications for the job and sketchy business entanglements and because of his public opposition to Robert Mueller's Russia investigation. Speculation was rife that Whitaker, a partisan loyalist, would be Trump's hammer to whack away at the Mueller probe.

As Trump headed to board Marine One to begin his journey to Paris, he snapped at the CNN correspondent Abby Phillip after she asked the pertinent question of the day: Did Trump want Whitaker to rein in Mueller? "What a stupid question that is," Trump replied. "What a stupid question. But I watch you a lot. You ask a lot of stupid questions." Trump did not answer Phillip's question.

Once Trump boarded Air Force One for the six-and-a-half-hour flight to France, he received a phone call from British prime minister

Theresa May. Trump and May were not exactly chums. In July 2018, he famously bashed her handling of Brexit in an interview with the British tabloid *The Sun* just as May was hosting him for a visit. But May tried much more than other European leaders to be deferential to Trump as part of the British government's long-view strategy of preserving the "special relationship" with the United States. May was calling Trump to congratulate him on his party's successes in the midterm elections. Of course, it was not lost on her that the Republicans lost control of the House, but she nevertheless sought to appeal to Trump's ego.

It did not work. The ornery president blew up at the mannered prime minister. Trump berated May over Brexit and told her she was a lousy negotiator. He lit into her about trade deals with European countries that he considered unfair to the United States. It felt like a one-way conversation, with Trump doing most of the talking. Then, suddenly, he changed the topic and told her she must not have brought up Iran because she was ashamed of Britain's position. In fact, she hadn't raised Iran because it wasn't a scheduled topic of conversation—and besides, she could hardly get a word in. No, May told Trump, she was not ashamed.

May had previously been subjected to Trump's erratic temper, but her aides were shaken by the acrimony of this call. They described it as the worst in May's career. The president was so churlish that a British official told *The Telegraph* that he had acted like "Trump the Grump." The testy conversation set the tone for Trump's forty-three-hour visit to France. Upon arriving in Paris, Trump was whisked to the U.S. ambassador's residence, a handsome nineteenth-century manse in the heart of the city. He hunkered down inside, sulking about press coverage of his midterm losses and brooding about recounts in Florida, where his Republican allies would eventually be declared the winners in hotly contested gubernatorial and Senate races.

The next morning, November 10, Trump woke up early and, at 4:52 Paris time, tweeted a two-part defense of Whitaker. He was slated to attend a series of remembrance services and visit the Aisne-Marne American Cemetery, where 2,289 service members had been laid to rest at the foot of the hill where the Battle of Belleau Wood was waged.

Inscribed on the wall of the memorial chapel are the names of 1,060 persons who were missing in action and whose bodies were not recovered. The cemetery grounds also included a monument to U.S. marines.

Trump would never see the cemetery. He told aides he did not feel like making the trek to Aisne-Marne, which was roughly fifty-five miles from central Paris. The president had been scheduled to travel by helicopter, but it was raining and cloudy, and although the presidential helicopter is equipped to fly in most weather conditions, John Kelly and his deputy, Zach Fuentes, gave Trump an out: he could claim a "weather call" and cancel the cemetery visit. They explained that if they had to travel by motorcade, it would take an hour and a half and snarl traffic in parts of Paris and its surrounding suburbs. Trump leaped at the chance to pass on the cemetery visit. "I don't think I'm going to go," he said. Trump was scheduled to participate in other World War I commemorations over the weekend and figured it wouldn't be a big deal to skip this one.

Kelly and Chairman of the Joint Chiefs of Staff Joseph Dunford, both marines, decided to go in his stead and represent the U.S. delegation. Everything was going to be fine—until Trump turned on the television. That's when he saw other dignitaries, including French president Emmanuel Macron, German chancellor Angela Merkel, and Canadian prime minister Justin Trudeau, arriving in the rain at other memorial sites outside Paris. Back in the United States, cable news and social media were abuzz with commentary about Trump's decision to skip the ceremony because of rain. Democrats accused him of disrespecting fallen veterans.

John Kerry, the former secretary of state and a decorated navy veteran, tweeted, "President @realDonaldTrump a no-show because of raindrops? Those veterans the president didn't bother to honor fought in the rain, in the mud, in the snow—& many died in trenches for the cause of freedom. Rain didn't stop them & it shouldn't have stopped an American president." The criticism of Trump was worldwide and merciless. Nicholas Soames, a grandson of Winston Churchill's and a member of the British Parliament, called Trump "pathetic" and "inadequate" because he "couldn't even defy the weather to pay his respects to The Fallen."

As was often the case with Trump's critics, the commentary got out of hand. There were suggestions from others that the president had skipped the cemetery visit simply because he was afraid to get his hair wet. Kelly and Dunford, meanwhile, appeared dignified and downright presidential as they toured the cemetery with a handful of other Americans and marked the anniversary. They stopped at the marines' monument atop the hill to pay their respects. Kelly made solemn remarks there about his son Robert, a lieutenant in the U.S. Marines who had been killed in Afghanistan at age twenty-nine.

As Trump saw Kelly getting positive attention for visiting the memorial, he erupted. He vented to aides that his absence made him look "terrible" in the media. "I could've fucking gone!" Trump said. "I was willing to go! They're killing me for it!" Trump took out his anger on Fuentes. "Your general should've convinced me to go," the president screamed at the deputy chief of staff, referring to Kelly. He faulted Kelly for not having the political savvy to foresee this public relations nightmare and for not persuading him to take the motorcade to the cemetery. "What a stupid decision," Trump told Fuentes.

"Sir, we made the best decision we could," Fuentes replied, not wanting to stoke the president by pushing back.

Later, talking to other advisers, Trump shirked any responsibility for bailing on the cemetery visit. "It was John Kelly's decision [that] I couldn't go," Trump said. "I would've been happy to go. I don't care about the rain."

On November 11, Trump was still smarting when he attended an Armistice Day ceremony at the foot of the Arc de Triomphe, the Roman-style arch that stands as the grandest war memorial in Paris. More than sixty world leaders attended to celebrate the hundredth anniversary of bugles and church bells sounding throughout France to mark the end of World War I. Before the ceremony began, dozens of the visiting dignitaries marched shoulder to shoulder along the Champs-Élysées toward the arch as military jets left streaks of red, white, and blue smoke in the Parisian sky. But Trump did not participate in the march, nor did Russian president Vladimir Putin. They arrived at the arch instead via individual motorcades. Bundled up in a black overcoat, Trump took his seat next to

Merkel, a few chairs down from Putin. Trump was in the unusual position of not being the center of attention. He was a mere guest; this was Macron's show. The choreography was consistent with the outsized role the French played in World War I relative to the United States, but Trump felt slighted to be given a less prominent role.

Speaking French, Macron delivered a speech that journalists interpreted as a pointed rebuke of Trump, as well as of Putin. In the darkest hours of World War I, Macron said, "that vision of France as a generous nation, of France as a project, of France promoting universal values, was the exact opposite of the egotism of a people who look after only their interests, because patriotism is the exact opposite of nationalism: nationalism is a betrayal of it. In saying 'our interests first and who cares about the rest!' you wipe out what's most valuable about a nation, what brings it alive, what leads it to greatness and what is most important: its moral values." Macron warned that "the old demons are reappearing" and summoned the world's political leaders to "break with the new 'treason of the intellectuals,' which is at work and fuels untruths, accepts the injustice consuming our peoples and sustains extremes and present-day obscurantism."

Trump complained to advisers about Macron's speech but didn't hit back. He attended a luncheon with the other world leaders and then gave a speech of his own at Suresnes American Cemetery and Memorial. Suresnes is closer to Paris than Aisne-Marne and was the resting place of 1,541 U.S. service members. Trump delivered a ten-minute speech in the rain, ditching his umbrella and joking that everyone was "getting drenched," as if he were trying to make amends for the day before.

"The American and French patriots of World War I embody the timeless virtues of our two republics: Honor and courage; strength and valor; love and loyalty; grace and glory," Trump said. "It is our duty to preserve the civilization they defended and to protect the peace they so nobly gave their lives to secure one century ago."

Trump then headed to the airport, where he boarded Air Force One for the flight home to Washington. The next day, November 12, Veterans' Day was observed in the United States, but Trump opted against paying his respects at Arlington National Cemetery, a tradition for presidents—something he later acknowledged he should have done. Instead, Trump spent the holiday inside the White House sulking about the poor media coverage of his Paris trip and tweeting about "the prospect of Presidential Harassment by the Dems" once they take control of the House in January.

On November 13, Trump came out swinging with an early-morning Twitter broadside against Macron. He wrote, in reference to World Wars I and II, "They were starting to learn German in Paris before the U.S. came along." He assailed the French for "not fair" trade policies that make it more difficult to sell U.S. wines in France than to sell French wines in the United States. And he said Macron "suffers from a very low Approval Rating in France."

"By the way, there is no country more Nationalist than France, very proud people—and rightfully so!" Trump added. "MAKE FRANCE GREAT AGAIN!"

Reading Trump's tweets in Paris, Macron was concerned. He immediately called his envoy in Washington, Gérard Araud, and asked what to do. The ambassador called one of his contacts in the White House who advised, "Please do nothing. He'll have this outburst, but afterwards, if you don't answer, it's over. Please tell Macron not to react, not to bother." This adviser explained that Trump had lashed out at Macron because of media coverage of the French president's speech: "Trump doesn't want to lose in the media, especially on Fox. If he appears weak on Fox, that's totally unacceptable." Araud passed this advice on to Paris, and Macron followed it.

The Paris trip proved to be the final straw for Kelly. He would last in the job for less than a month after that. Trump's advisers could not tell how angry the president truly was at Kelly over the Paris debacle. One posited that he was just looking for an excuse to "cut the cord." It felt like a wise time to change course. Fueling the president's feelings throughout the fall was a lobbying campaign from Kelly's internal enemies, including Jared Kushner and Ivanka Trump, to ditch him for a more politically minded chief of staff. The pressures were converging on Trump. He felt vulnerable. Robert Mueller's investigation was nearing an uncertain end. Nancy Pelosi intended to bring investigative heat on the president, if not eventually impeachment charges. More than two dozen Democrats were gearing up to run to unseat him as president. And many of his longest-serving and most trusted staffers were gone or eyeing the exits.

Ever since the gruesome murder on October 2 of Jamal Khashoggi, a Saudi dissident journalist who was a contributing columnist to *The Washington Post*, Trump and his administration had been on the defensive. Audio and video recordings obtained by the Turkish government showed that Khashoggi had walked into the consulate to obtain documents for his upcoming wedding but was detained inside by a Saudi security team, then interrogated, tortured, killed, and dismembered with a bone saw. The operation was likely ordered by Mohammed bin Salman, known as MBS, the crown prince of Saudi Arabia whose government Khashoggi had criticized in his writings, according to U.S. intelligence analysis.

Throughout October and early November, a mountain of evidence surfaced, but Trump and Kushner, who both had close personal relationships with MBS, still refused to hold the Saudis responsible for the murder, with the president even repeating MBS's denials. On November 16, the case against the Saudis became even more definitive when the *Post*'s Shane Harris, Greg Miller, and Josh Dawsey reported that the CIA had concluded with high confidence that MBS had ordered Khashoggi's assassination. The CIA had also determined that Khalid bin Salman, the Saudi ambassador to the United States and the crown prince's brother, had called Khashoggi at MBS's direction to instruct him to go to the consulate in Istanbul to retrieve his wedding documents and to assure him he would be safe doing so.

In response, the Trump administration imposed small economic sanctions on seventeen Saudis who U.S. intelligence operatives believed were responsible for the act, but did not implicate MBS. Many U.S.

lawmakers said the sanctions were woefully insufficient punishment for the crime. Senator Rand Paul, a Republican ally of Trump's, tweeted in response, "We are pretending to do something and doing NOTHING." Meanwhile, Trump cast doubt on the CIA's assessment by telling reporters it was "very premature" and boasting about Saudi Arabia as "a truly spectacular ally."

Throughout the fall, the president's lawyers had had reason to feel they were in the catbird seat. With Mueller's capitulation to take some answers from Trump in writing, they were confident their client wasn't going to be subpoenaed to testify. The agreement—to provide answers only about Russian interference, the central reason for Mueller's appointment, and only pertaining to the time until the November 2016 election—was favorable. However, even within these narrow confines, the possible questions were numerous. Did Trump receive regular briefings from Michael Cohen as he pursued the Moscow Trump Tower deal? When did he first learn about WikiLeaks' having damaging Democratic emails? Did he know anything about Donald Trump Jr.'s being offered a meeting about "dirt" on Hillary Clinton?

Through September and October, Trump's lawyers kept telling the public that they were working with the president to complete the written answers to Mueller, but the reality is they were having significant trouble getting time with their client, even though he spent many hours a day watching television. As his lawyer Rudy Giuliani often told reporters, their client was the president, and he was pretty busy.

On October 24, Trump's lawyers planned to sit down with their client to go over the written answers. They were only about twenty-five minutes into the meeting when their session came to an abrupt end. Trump's national security and federal law enforcement teams needed to give him a briefing about pipe bombs that had been mailed to several prominent Democrats, including former president Obama and Hillary Clinton. Giuliani and Jay Sekulow, along with Jane and Martin Raskin, were drafting

Trump's answers on his behalf based on a rolling series of meetings with him to go over his recollections. They had most of them drafted by Halloween and considered the answers so far pretty uncontroversial.

On the morning of November 1, Sekulow went to the White House for another sit-down with Trump to finalize answers, but the president was interrupted by calls from Turkish president Recep Tayyip Erdogan and Chinese president Xi Jinping. "There goes my meeting," Sekulow said with a sigh.

As eager as Trump's lawyers were to complete the answers, they had not wanted to submit them before the November 6 midterm elections. But after the GOP's crushing loss of its House majority, the lawyers faced a new challenge. Trump was in a sour mood, especially after he returned from Paris on November 12, and seemed to get testy when they brought up the subject of the Mueller questions. Then two things happened the week before Thanksgiving—one right after the other—which spooked them. First, sometime around November 15, Sekulow received a strange email from what looked like a fictitious account. It contained a short note that said something along the lines of "This is very important. You may want to see it." Attached were several documents. Sekulow was afraid to open the attachments, suspicious that it might be a setup. "You're the criminal lawyer, so tell us what to do," he said to Giuliani.

Together with the Raskins, they decided to open the documents. "They were shocking," Giuliani recalled. "Everything we expected." One of the attachments was a copy of a draft plea agreement that Mueller's office had written as part of its ongoing negotiations with Jerome Corsi. Corsi was a longtime Clinton critic and ally of Roger Stone, an off-and-on political adviser to Trump for the previous decade.

Prosecutors wanted to know how Stone correctly predicted that WikiLeaks' Julian Assange would leak damaging emails about Clinton in 2016, and they suspected Corsi might provide the missing link. An email from August 2, 2016, showed that Corsi, who was traveling in Europe at the time, alerted Stone to the planned release by their "friend in embassy"—an apparent reference to Assange, who since 2012 had been living in the Ecuadorian embassy in London. "Word is friend in embassy plans 2 more dumps," Corsi had written. "One shortly after I'm back. 2nd in Oct. Impact planned to be very damaging."

What surprised Sekulow and the president's other lawyers was that Mueller's draft plea agreement—which Corsi was refusing to sign—specifically referred to Trump. Mueller wanted Corsi to acknowledge that Stone had asked him during the campaign to reach out to WikiLeaks—referred to as "Organization 1" in the document—to find out what material they still had to release. The agreement said Corsi understood that Stone was asking because he was "in regular contact with senior members of the Trump Campaign, including with then-candidate Donald J. Trump." Corsi complained, through his lawyer, that he felt railroaded into signing this agreement and that Mueller's investigators told him that they planned to indict him if he didn't admit the truth. Trump's lawyers thought that was playing hardball but also found the reference to Trump in the plea agreement draft worrisome. They told their client, and the president instructed them, "Make sure you give it to the FBI right away."

The second event happened late on the night of November 15. It started with chatter on Twitter that some mysterious documents showed federal prosecutors had indicted Assange under seal, possibly earlier that year. Due to the mistaken filing, the sealed charges had been mentioned in a court document on a public website. In the document, prosecutors wrote that the unexplained charges "would need to remain sealed until Assange is arrested in connection with the charges in the criminal complaint and can therefore no longer evade or avoid arrest and extradition in this matter."

Trump's legal team found these developments unsettling, and they wondered whether Mueller was plotting to expand or extend his investigation into a new untapped vein. They groused about documents being mishandled and concerns about prosecutors leaking damaging material, but their central fear was that Mueller's probe might be ramping up rather than closing down. The lawyers demanded a meeting with Mueller's team and with his supervisor, Rod Rosenstein, to discuss their concerns about the Trump reference in the Corsi document and the in-advertent Assange filing. Giuliani, Sekulow, and Jane Raskin all felt strongly that Mueller should be there, so Giuliani specifically requested Mueller personally explain his office's actions. They also wanted the special counsel's Justice Department overseers to be present. "Somebody had to know how they were behaving," Giuliani said.

A few days before Thanksgiving, Trump's lawyers arrived at Rosenstein's conference room at the Justice Department. In walked James Quarles, Aaron Zebley, and Andrew Goldstein of the special counsel's office. Rosenstein was out of town and was represented by Ed O'Callaghan. But Mueller was a no-show. His deputies said he couldn't attend, but provided no reason. The Trump lawyers were flabbergasted that their concern didn't rate as important enough to command Mueller's presence. They later wondered if Mueller was ill, presuming it was the only reason he would skip an important meeting with opposing counsel.

"We weren't repping some minor player; we were representing the president of the United States," recalled one of Trump's lawyers. "We are meeting with the deputy in his conference room. . . . [Mueller] wouldn't even talk with us."

The meeting got off to a hostile start. "You're not conducting an investigation," Giuliani told the special counsel trio. "You're conducting a complete frame-up focused on one person, Donald Trump. This is an outrage and the Justice Department will be disgraced by this."

At one point, Sekulow said something along the lines of "You're trying to squeeze this old guy to flip another guy against my client."

Quarles led the defense. "You're mischaracterizing it," he responded to Giuliani.

O'Callaghan tried to calm Trump's lawyers. "Rudy, I've been briefed on this," he said. "I know where this is going. It's not about flipping Corsi to open up another avenue of the investigation. It's just not."

Despite Mueller's absence, the meeting ultimately helped to smooth over anxieties. The special counsel lawyers insisted they had nothing to do with the Assange leak and that it had been an electronic filing mistake by the U.S. Attorney's Office in the Eastern District of Virginia.

They said they couldn't get into a lot of details about the Corsi agreement but that there was nothing untoward about making clear this related to the Trump campaign and Trump's candidacy.

As the meeting wrapped up, Giuliani told the special counsel team that they would take "a little interruption right now in deciding on submitting the answers." But on November 20, Trump's lawyers submitted the president's answers to Mueller's questions. They had successfully persuaded Trump to repeatedly use a phrase he had ardently resisted uttering over the years: "I do not recall." In his written submission, drafted by his lawyers but approved by Trump, the president provided twenty-two answers to Mueller questions on four main subjects: the Trump Organization's proposed tower in Moscow; Russia's interference in the 2016 election; the Trump campaign; and contacts by Trump allies with Russians during the campaign. In nineteen of his twenty-two answers, Trump said he couldn't remember enough to answer some or all of the questions.

Regarding the infamous June 2016 Trump Tower meeting between Trump junior, Jared Kushner, Paul Manafort, and a Russian lawyer, Trump said in his answers to Mueller that he didn't recall whether he learned about it before or after it happened; whether he knew about Trump junior's work to set it up; or whether he spoke with Trump junior, Kushner, or Manafort on the day of the meeting. Asked if he was told by anyone during the campaign that Putin supported his candidacy, Trump replied, "I have no recollection of being told."

But in July 2018, Trump had reacted to news reports about the meeting by denying any knowledge of it. He tweeted, "I did NOT know of the meeting with my son, Don jr." One thing Trump told Mueller he could remember from that time was that he was "aware of reports indicating that Putin had made complimentary statements" about him.

Had Mueller secured a face-to-face interview with Trump, he or others on his team might have been able to press the president with follow-up questions or bring evidence to his attention to rejigger his memory and better get the truth out of him. But that was not to be. As Mueller would later write in his report on the investigation, "We viewed the written answers to be inadequate."

Twenty-one

GUT OVER BRAINS

On December 6, 2018, Rex Tillerson made his first extensive public remarks since being ousted as secretary of state that spring. He was remarkably candid. Fielding questions from Bob Schieffer of CBS News at a Houston event, Tillerson described the difference between transitioning from the highly disciplined, process-oriented Exxon Mobil Corporation to the Trump White House. He described Trump as "a man who is pretty undisciplined, doesn't like to read, doesn't read briefing reports, doesn't like to get into the details of a lot of things, but rather just kind of said, 'Look, this is what I believe and you can try to convince me otherwise, but most of the time you're not going to do that.'"

When Schieffer asked how his relationship with Trump went off the rails, Tillerson said, "We are starkly different in our styles. We did not have a common value system. I'll just be blunt about that and so often the president would say, 'Well, here's what I want to do and here's how I want to do it.' And I had to say to him, 'Mr. President, I understand what you want to do, but you can't do it that way. It violates the law. It violates the treaty.'"

Never one to let a slight go unaddressed, Trump slammed Tillerson. He cast the man who rose from civil engineer to chief executive at one of the world's largest companies and who considered himself a student of history as, of all things, unintelligent. Trump tweeted that Tillerson "didn't have the mental capacity needed. He was dumb as a rock and I couldn't get rid of him fast enough. He was lazy as hell."

The insult was a reminder to all who served in the administration that loyalty was a one-way street. An honest reflection like the one Tillerson gave Schieffer after more than a year of service in government could easily be interpreted by the president as a personal betrayal, from which there could be no complete recovery. Tillerson was entirely unbothered, confiding to friends there was nothing to learn or gain by taking Trump's bait. "Don't ask me," he would say to associates with a chuckle months later. "I'm dumb as a rock!"

The first week of December, Trump was focused on selecting a new attorney general. Finally, he could have a loyal foot soldier helming the Justice Department. He considered a range of candidates but kept gravitating toward Bill Barr, sixty-eight, a well-respected Republican lawyer who held the job a quarter century earlier, during the George H. W. Bush administration. Barr was a favorite of Trump's legal team and close to Pat Cipollone, the new White House counsel. Emmet Flood, the White House lawyer dealing with Robert Mueller's investigation, helped sell Barr to the president as "the gold standard." Trump did not really know Barr, but Flood argued that he could be trusted to be a grown-up and, importantly, had the pedigree to make him "totally unimpeachable" on Capitol Hill. Barr at first resisted entreaties to become attorney general again but eventually warmed to the idea.

Trump also considered Chris Christie for the job and had a much greater level of comfort with the former New Jersey governor, who was a ruthless political brawler and had proven his loyalty as Trump's campaign-trail sidekick. As he angled to be attorney general, Christie played up their long relationship and sowed doubts about Barr. "I cannot believe you're going into a reelect with an attorney general you don't know," he told Trump.

Christie assumed that Barr, a fixture in Washington's legal community, would be more loyal to the American Bar Association than to the president. "If he has to choose between the ABA crowd and you in terms of who he's going to make happy, he's picking the ABA crowd every day of the week," Christie told Trump. "It's just who he is. It's where he's from, and it's who he's going back to."

But Barr had already signaled his loyalty to Trump in a nineteen-page unsolicited private memo to the Justice Department on June 8, 2018. He had originally intended to share his thoughts on the Mueller investigation in an opinion column, but Barr was so verbose he figured the better vehicle would be a memo, which he addressed to Rod Rosenstein, who oversaw the Russia probe, and Assistant Attorney General Steven Engel, who ran the Office of Legal Counsel. Barr sent Flood a courtesy copy. Barr authored the memo as a "former official deeply concerned with the institutions of the Presidency and the Department of Justice" and said he hoped that his views "may be useful."

In the memo, Barr denounced Mueller's obstruction of justice inquiry by arguing that in most of the publicly known episodes the president had acted within his broad executive authority and that probing his actions in those cases as possible obstruction was "grossly irresponsible." A student of constitutional law who had once overseen the OLC, the government's premier legal office, Barr believed prosecutors could not question any president's unfettered power to remove his subordinates. Any inquiry into the president's firing of Comey and wish to remove Sessions struck Barr as ridiculous.

"Mueller should not be permitted to demand that the President submit to interrogation about alleged obstruction," Barr wrote. "Apart from whether Mueller [has] a strong enough factual basis for doing so, Mueller's obstruction theory is fatally misconceived. As I understand it, his theory is premised on a novel and legally insupportable reading of the law."

Barr went on to warn about the special counsel's indulging in "the fancies by overly-zealous prosecutors" and wrote that investigating the president's "discretionary actions" would have "potentially disastrous implications" for the executive branch as a whole. "I know you will agree that, if a DOJ investigation is going to take down a democratically-elected President, it is imperative to the health of our system and to our national cohesion that any claim of wrongdoing is solidly based on evidence of a *real* crime—not a debatable one," Barr wrote.

On December 7, Trump called Barr to say he was ready to nominate him as attorney general. Barr's youngest daughter was getting married the next day, so he was preoccupied, but Trump wanted to share the news right away. "I'm going to go out to the helicopter and announce it," Trump told Barr. Shortly thereafter, Trump strode onto the South Lawn and announced his intention to nominate Barr. "He was my first choice since day one," Trump told reporters. Later that day, at a Justice Department event in Kansas City, Trump praised Barr for having "demonstrated an unwavering adherence to the rule of law, which the people in this room like to hear. There is no one more capable or more qualified for this role. He deserves overwhelming bipartisan support."

At the wedding reception the night of December 8, at the Willard hotel, a couple of blocks from the White House, Barr's daughter Meg said in her remarks, "Pop, you're the only guy I know who would upstage his daughter's wedding." When it came time for him to deliver the father-of-the-bride toast, Barr said, "Meg, look at it this way. Just before the name Barr is being dragged through the mud, you are changing yours to McGaughey."

At the same time that Trump was heralding Barr, he was cutting ties with John Kelly. Trump complained more and more to friends about Kelly, arguing the retired Marine Corps general sometimes acted as if he had been elected president. "He didn't have the guts to work for the job like I did," Trump vented to at least one confidant. This kind of mockery by the headstrong president signaled an aide's end was near. Trump also started telling other aides not to bother keeping Kelly abreast of important developments, effectively cutting the chief of staff out of decisions in the White House that he had once commanded with military precision.

This frustrated Kelly, who after his decades of service in the U.S. Marines had little tolerance for being disrespected or marginalized. More dangerous, however, was the fact that Trump was no longer heeding Kelly's advice on matters of national security. In the week after returning from Paris in mid-November, Trump agitated to withdraw U.S. forces from the wars in Afghanistan and Syria, as well as bases in South Korea. He talked openly about pulling out of NATO.

Meanwhile, Ivanka and Jared Kushner, as well as a pair of ambitious aides who were eyeing Kelly's job—Nick Ayers, chief of staff to Vice President Pence, and Mick Mulvaney, director of the Office of Management and Budget—were telling Trump that he needed to change chiefs. Ayers had been open with Kelly, telling him he wanted to succeed him when Kelly decided it was time to go; Mulvaney was less so. They reinforced their own selling points: Kelly had his strengths, but Trump needed a more politically savvy chief of staff as he prepared to run for reelection and deal with a divided Congress.

On December 7, after returning from Kansas City, Trump and Kelly met privately and decided to part ways. The next day, as Trump left the White House to attend the Army v. Navy football game in Philadelphia, he stopped on the South Lawn to tell reporters, "John Kelly will be leaving. I don't know if I can say 'retiring.' But he's a great guy." The announcement was anticlimactic, considering tensions between the two men had long ago spilled into the press. Still, Trump afforded Kelly a graceful exit compared with how he had dismissed Tillerson, Reince Priebus, H. R. McMaster, and other senior advisers.

Trump settled on Ayers as Kelly's replacement. The thirty-six-year-old was a smooth and slick political operative, a wunderkind when he ran the Republican Governors Association in his twenties. Through his position as Pence's chief, Ayers had regular access to Trump and cultivated an easy rapport with the president. He also aligned himself with Ivanka and Kushner, who were enthusiastic boosters of his. But when Trump offered him the job, Ayers shocked the president by turning him down. He was unwilling to commit to Trump's request that he serve for two years, through the 2020 election. A father of triplets, Ayers would agree to do the job only on an interim basis for a few months because he had plans to relocate his family to his home state of Georgia. While family concerns were his stated reason for bowing out, Ayers confided to some in the White House he had been concerned watching how frequently the president bypassed or ignored a person as serious and respected as Kelly. By leaving, Ayers also dodged inquiries into his work as a political consultant, for which he reported amassing a net worth of $12.8 million to $54.8 million, before he had become Pence's chief of staff.

Trump, who for days had been telling friends that Ayers would be his next chief, was suddenly a red-faced groom left at the altar. It was a humiliating blow for a president who loathes humiliations. Trump had no Plan B and would scramble in the days ahead to recruit other candidates.

On December 11, Trump got his first taste of divided government. Two years of operating without a check on his power came to a crashing halt as the combustible president met for the first time since the midterm elections with Nancy Pelosi and Chuck Schumer. The leaders faced a December 22 deadline to pass a government spending bill or face a shutdown, and they were at a stalemate over Trump's demand for it to include $5.7 billion to construct his long-promised border wall. But the meeting was about more than federal appropriations. It would establish the postelection power dynamic in Washington.

White House advisers knew the stakes were high, so they tried to prepare Trump. Kelly, who had stayed on as chief of staff through the end of the month, and legislative affairs director Shahira Knight, among others, implored Trump to strive for a deal but to be guarded with the Democrats, who they warned might try to manipulate him. They cautioned Trump about the politics of a government shutdown and told him, no matter what happens, don't say anything that would make him "own" a government shutdown. "Don't take the bait," the president's aides told him. But Trump seemed to be only half listening to their advice. He wanted a dramatic clash on immigration with the Democrats. In his mind, immigration was his issue—a winning issue. After all, he figured, who wouldn't want a more secure border?

As the Democrats arrived in the Oval, Pelosi tried to set the tone. She led a prayer about King Solomon. She and Schumer took seats on the soft cream couches, while Trump and Pence sat in the yellow wingback chairs. The meeting was scheduled to be closed to the press, but Trump, as he often did, invited the press pool in to record the exchange. What followed were seventeen minutes of raised voices, pointed fingers, and boorish interruptions, with each principal playing for the television audience. At one point, Trump suggested Pelosi couldn't share her true beliefs without hurting her bid to be elected House Speaker. "Nancy's in a situation where it's not easy for her to talk right now," Trump said. "Mr. President," Pelosi said, "please don't characterize the strength that I bring to this meeting as the leader of the House Democrats, who just won a big victory."

Schumer baited Trump by reminding him that he had repeatedly threatened to shut down the government if he did not get his wall funding. Flustered, the president said, "I am proud to shut down the government for border security, Chuck, because the people of this country don't want criminals and people that have lots of problems and drugs pouring into our country. So I will take the mantle. I will be the one to shut it down. I'm not going to blame you for it." There it was. White House aides immediately felt a pit in their stomachs. Their boss had just handed the Democrats an unexpected gift. All that preparation was for naught. Trump got played.

When Pelosi returned to the Capitol later that day, she recounted the highlights to some of her colleagues. She described the Oval Office meeting as being in "a tinkle contest with a skunk." The Speaker in waiting said debating the wall with Trump was "like a manhood thing for him. As if manhood could ever be associated with him."

Yet as acrimonious as the meeting was, Trump was simultaneously on the cusp of a rare bipartisan accomplishment. The First Step Act, which would be signed into law on December 21, represented the biggest overhaul to the nation's criminal justice system in a generation by reducing mandatory minimum sentences for some drug offenses and expanding programs such as job training designed to control the exploding federal prison population.

The quiet force behind the criminal justice reform efforts had been Kushner, for whom the issue was deeply personal considering his father's incarceration. Kushner helped orchestrate a months-long lobbying campaign to unite tough-on-crime Republicans and liberal Democrats to reconsider sentencing laws. He had even invited the rapper Kanye West and the reality-television star Kim Kardashian West, both criminal justice reform advocates, to the White House to help spotlight the issue.

At Trump's Oval Office signing ceremony, Senator Mike Lee reflected on Kushner's persistence. "I speak to Jared Kushner about five times a day," the Utah Republican said. "In the middle of dinner, when my phone rings, my family says to me, 'It's Jared, isn't it?'"

On December 12, Trump called Christie with an urgent request. He asked his old friend if he could come down from New Jersey right away. They made plans to meet on December 13 at 5:30 p.m. in the White House residence. When Christie asked what was going on, Trump wouldn't tell him. But on the train down to Washington the afternoon of December 13, Christie got a call from Rudy Giuliani, the president's lawyer and another old friend.

"Listen," Giuliani told Christie. "He's going to offer you chief of staff tonight.

"He just got off the phone with me," Giuliani added, referring to Trump. "He told me that that's the decision he's made. You're the best person in position for the reelect. You're the smartest politician. You can run the place. He needs you."

"Rudy, is Jared leaving?" Christie asked.

"No," Giuliani said.

"Why the fuck am I going to take this job?" Christie said. "You guys are nuts. I'm not going in there and [having] Jared down the hall."

As the train hurtled toward Union Station, Christie's mind was racing. If Trump really was about to offer him chief of staff, he had to figure out what to say. So he called Jim Baker, a legendary former White House chief of staff under both President Reagan and President George H. W. Bush. Christie knew Baker and relied on his sage advice; when he was Trump's transition chairman, Christie had spent two hours in Houston talking with Baker about staffing administrations. Baker picked up right away. "Governor," he said, "if you're calling me, you're about to be offered the worst fucking job in America."

Christie asked what kinds of things he should request from the president. Baker went through a list of demands, including that he have walk-in privileges to the Oval Office; is able to attend any meeting in the White House that the president is in; chooses all staff and that all staff report to him, other than family members; controls his own media appearances; and gets his own personal lawyer. Christie jotted down notes as he listened.

"If you take this," Baker told Christie, "we have to come up with a new phrase that goes beyond patriot."

Carrying a briefcase with his notes, Christie arrived at the White House and was whisked into the residence through a back entrance so he wouldn't be spotted. He met the president and Melania Trump in the Yellow Oval Room upstairs; downstairs, the staff was preparing for a holiday party later that evening, which the president and first lady were due to attend.

The Trumps and Christie started talking about the chief of staff job right away. The only one of Baker's points that the president objected to was that Christie control his own media appearances. Christie told him, "I'm not here to be your press spokesman. I'm here to be your chief of staff." But Trump insisted upon being the one to decide when Christie went on television. When Melania asked Christie how he intended to deal with Kushner and Ivanka, considering his famous tensions with the presidential son-in-law, the president interjected.

"Don't worry about that," Trump said. "I'll handle that part of it."

"Sir, that is something to be concerned about," Christie said.

"Jared really doesn't have any problem with you," Trump said.

"Mr. President, please, this is ridiculous," Christie said.

"Don't worry about that," Trump insisted.

Christie wanted to avoid giving the president an answer to his offer on the spot. He was looking to buy some time. And as they wrapped up their conversation, Trump told him, "I know you. You're going to want to talk to Mary Pat about this, so go home and talk to Mary Pat and I'll call you in the morning. But I want you here."

Christie went straight to the train station to head home. By the time the Amtrak passed the Wilmington station, about ninety minutes into the ride, Christie saw a breaking news headline on his phone: "Trump meets with Chris Christie to discuss chief of staff role." This was another scoop for Jonathan Swan, a White House reporter for *Axios*. Swan quoted "a source familiar with the president's thinking" as saying of Christie, "He's tough; he's an attorney; he's politically-savvy, and one of Trump's early supporters."

Early the next morning, December 14, Christie's phone rang. It was Kushner. He told Christie something along the lines of "I know the decision the president's made. I'm completely supportive. You and I can work together great. All the things in the past are things in the past. All the things that matter is getting the president reelected, and I know you're the best person to help us do that. I'm excited about you coming." Though Kushner reached out to Christie that morning, and stood ready to work with him in the White House, he told associates that he did not recall this specific conversation.

Later that morning, Ivanka called Mary Pat Christie. "Mother to mother, wife to wife, I know what your concerns must be," the presidential daughter said, pledging that no harm would come to Christie were he to take the job.

"You don't have to worry about me saying, 'Oh, this is bad for the family, you can't go,'" Mary Pat told her. "This is Chris's career. If he wants to do it, I'm not going to stand in the way, but I'll give him the advice I think he needs to hear."

"I hope that advice would be positive towards taking the job," Ivanka said.

Mary Pat ended the call by saying that she would tell her husband what she felt was important for him to hear and that her advice would stay between them. Mary Pat then said to Christie, "Listen, if you're going to take it, take it, but if you're going to say no, you better call him now because these calls didn't happen by accident. With him, you never know. He could just tweet out that you're getting it, and then you're fucked if you don't want to take it."

At his wife's urging, Christie called Trump. "It's just not the right time," he told the president. Christie explained that he had concerns about working with Kushner and that his memoir was set to be published the following month, which the world would soon learn was unsparing in its criticism of Trump's son-in-law.

Trump was already frustrated by Ayers's rejection of the job and the resulting media narrative that no one wanted to be his chief of staff. So Christie proposed a face-saving way to bow out without embarrassing the president. "How about if I just tweet out that I'm withdrawing from consideration, that way I didn't say no to you?" he asked.

Trump liked that idea. "That will be a great story for us, you withdrawing from consideration," Trump said. "Like the *Axios* story last night. Wasn't that a great story?"

"I wondered about that," Christie said. "It was just me, you, and Melania in the room, and I'm pretty sure nobody saw me coming in, so how'd that happen?"

"Oh, I did it," Trump said.

"Who did it for you?" Christie asked.

"No, no, I did it myself," Trump said. "I called Jonathan and told him."

Christie thought to himself, "You're leaking yourself? And to think I came this close to being your chief of staff?" But he held his tongue.

"You're really not supposed to be doing that," Christie told Trump.

"Ahhh," the president said playfully. "Don't worry about it. He's a good kid."

Trump told Christie he would go ahead and name Mulvaney a temporary chief of staff. "He's begging for the job," Trump said of Mulvaney. "So I'll make him the acting. He'll be fine with that. He'll take whatever I offer him. And then you and I, six months from now, you and I will revisit it."

A few hours later, Trump named Mulvaney as his acting chief of staff, replacing a strict disciplinarian with a conservative hard-liner eager to please the president at the dawn of a divided government. Mulvaney, fifty-one, had long ago declared his loyalty to the president's family. He quietly campaigned for the job for months, once even vowing to Trump that if he were chief of staff he would manage the staff but not the president. But he never formally interviewed for the job. Mulvaney came into the Oval Office the afternoon of December 14 for a meeting about the budget showdown, and Trump offered it to him right then and there. The news was announced an hour or two later.

On December 17, Christie returned to the White House with his wife to attend a Christmas party for cabinet members and other administration officials. As soon as he walked in, he locked eyes with Secretary of Defense Jim Mattis.

"Look at this! A ray of sunshine has entered the building," Mattis said.

"To what do I owe that compliment, General?" Christie asked.

They shook hands and Mattis said, "Because you're smart enough not to get into the shitshow."

As he walked away, Christie said to Mary Pat, "There's someone who's not happy in their job."

"*Really* not happy," Mary Pat said.

I n the first week of December, Mattis visited Ottawa for a meeting with a small group of coalition partners in the U.S.-led network to defeat ISIS worldwide, where he assured them the United States had their backs in the ISIS strongholds of Syria. By late 2018, the coalition's multi-pronged effort to liberate vast swaths of Syria from the grip of ISIS had been stunningly successful. America's secret weapon was a unique pairing: small teams of U.S. Special Forces, highly sophisticated in their training and surveillance capabilities, partnered with a comparatively large militia led by General Mazloum Abdi. Coalition forces provided air cover, and since Trump's arrival in 2017 the U.S. military provided the Kurdish forces with weaponry.

In his early December meetings in Canada, Mattis assured his partners the United States would provide financial and military backing at least into 2020, per a policy vetted by the National Security Council and signed by John Bolton. Aboard his plane flying to Ottawa, Mattis told reporters that "this remains a coalition effort" and added, "There's more work to be done. That hardened core means tough fighting there."

Brett McGurk, the special presidential envoy for the Global Coalition to Defeat ISIS, had joined Mattis on the trip to help explain how the coalition needed to adapt to cut off ISIS's spread. On December 11, McGurk gave a press briefing at the State Department to help spread the word of the U.S. commitment and the need to ensure the "enduring defeat" of ISIS. He seemed to dismiss the idea the United States would withdraw from Syria anytime soon.

"We have obviously learned a lot of lessons in the past, so we know that once the physical space is defeated we can't just pick up and leave," McGurk said. "So we're prepared to make sure that we do all we can to ensure this is enduring." He added, "Nobody is saying that [ISIS is] going to disappear. Nobody is that naive."

But on December 14, a single phone call between Trump and Turkish president Recep Tayyip Erdogan undid those plans. On the phone with Trump, Erdogan beat a familiar drum: Why did the United States have to keep arming Kurdish fighters to fight ISIS? And why did Trump need two thousand U.S. military personnel in Syria if they were close to triumphing over the caliphate? Erdogan argued that his forces could ensure ISIS didn't creep back to power—and that they didn't need the Kurds, an enemy of the Turkish regime.

"You know what? It's yours," Trump told Erdogan. "I'm leaving."

One senior administration official summed up the sentiment: "Trump was like: You want that pile of dirt, Erdogan? Fine."

Without thinking it through or conferring with any of his government's many experts on the region, Trump effectively condemned a tireless partner of the U.S. military, the Kurdish general Mazloum Abdi, to death. Kelly called Kevin Sweeney, Mattis's chief of staff, to let him know what Trump had just done.

"He told Erdogan we're pulling out of Syria," Kelly said.

Sweeney knew this spelled disaster. Words failed him at first.

"Phhhhhfffft," he exhaled. "Fuck."

On December 17, Secretary of State Mike Pompeo alerted McGurk and a handful of senior State Department leaders that he needed them to join him in an important call. McGurk was stunned when Pompeo told him "there had been a change of plans" about Syria. Pulling out meant withdrawing the two thousand troops and an estimated two thousand more special forces currently there, as well as turning off the spigot of money and intelligence. The size of the U.S. military footprint in Syria was a pittance compared with the local coalition force, the Syrian Democratic Forces, which had sixty thousand Arab, Kurdish, and other fighters trying to regain towns from ISIS control. In the most active years of their partnership, the SDF estimated it lost eleven thousand fighters in Syria, while the United States had lost fewer than two dozen.

Just before 9:30 a.m. on December 19, Trump announced the U.S. withdrawal from Syria as if it were a triumph. "We have defeated ISIS in Syria, my only reason for being there during the Trump Presidency," he wrote. Trump also posted a short video on Twitter in which he stood in the Rose Garden and looked skyward to the fallen U.S. soldiers and declared that they, too, would want the United States to withdraw from its battle against ISIS. "Our boys, our young women, our men—they're all coming back, and they're coming back now," Trump said.

Trump's announcement drew immediate criticism, from Republicans as well as Democrats. Sarah Sanders called over to Mattis's office asking if the Pentagon would be sending any military brass or spokespeople out for media hits to discuss the value of withdrawing from Syria. Dana White, Mattis's communications chief, checked with Sweeney. "No one is going out," Sweeney told White. "You can go back and tell her that this was a White House decision. So help her, but no one in this department is going out to represent this decision."

White called Sanders back with the bad news. "Sarah, we're not putting anyone out," White explained. "This was a decision that was not made here. I'll send you everything. . . . We'll help you make your case. The caliphate used to be the size of California. Now it's 98 percent gone. That's all I can do. Nobody here is going out."

"No one?" Sanders asked.

"No," White explained. "I'm sorry."

Mattis was genuinely distraught. He believed it was wrong for America to abandon its Kurdish allies. And he worried that the president's sudden tweet announcing the U.S. withdrawal would put troops in greater danger than if they had stayed the course. "He began to feel like he was becoming complicit," recalled one of the secretary's confidants. "Sending the troops to the border was obviously a no-no and inappropriate, especially based on the circumstances at hand. That began to chip away at his feelings of being a patriot. And then the Syria thing. We were six weeks away from annihilating these guys and then he just tweeted it out. That was devastating."

The Pentagon's leaders, still licking their wounds, had more serious work to do than help the White House generate sound bites defending the president. At 2:00 p.m. on December 20, Mattis's assistant secretary for policy, John C. Rood, led a meeting about the practicalities of pulling out. McGurk, the premier expert on the ground, had canceled his trip to Jordan and flown back to the States the previous night to help, gotten up that morning after a few hours of sleep, thrown on a suit without shaving, and arrived at the Pentagon for a slew of meetings. The military officials had so many questions crying out for decisions. How would they withdraw the troops? In what order? What was the time frame for stopping key elements of their work? Did they have to stop air support for fighters on the ground immediately, or could they continue for some time? If other coalition members wanted to continue working with the militia, what should the United States tell them? What advice or help should the United States give other allies that had joined the U.S.-led coalition who might be in harm's way?

A central question nagged at everyone. How would they help protect the SDF and coalition members? Erdogan's Turkish fighters were reported to be massing at the border, waiting for U.S. forces to leave. Rood explained that they were getting some specific operational questions from General Mazloum. He had explained that ISIS was still a threat, but if the United States let the Turks rush into Syria from their northern border, Mazloum would have to redirect his fighters to the north to protect themselves. Around the table at the Pentagon were dejected faces. "We were all resigned to the fact that he was going to massacre the Kurds," one civilian official said of Erdogan.

A question arose about whether the U.S. forces should technically reclaim the weapons they gave the SDF fighters. Some discussed whether the National Security Council should review and decide whether militia members kept or surrendered the weapons. Rood stepped in with a firm no. He said something to the effect of "It's not our priority to take back certain weapons because this is too lethal for them. ISIS is not defeated. We are not taking them back."

At that moment, McGurk had had it. He burst into the discussion with a fury.

"Let's just be real, everybody," McGurk said. "Stop the wishful thinking. The president's ordered us to leave without a plan or any apparent thought. We're not picking up weapons on our way out. We can't get out safely without the Kurds. They protect our supply lines, convoys, and facilities. To say we'll take their weapons as we invite in the Turks is nuts. It will get Americans killed. The Kurds will be slaughtered from all sides."

McGurk warned that because of the president's lack of planning, the odds were high the Kurds would be slaughtered. The SDF might crack apart. ISIS would rush back in to wreak havoc on the villages the United States and its partners had temporarily turned into peaceful havens.

Nobody spoke up to dispute him or to counsel against the derisive way he was speaking about Trump. The miliary officers in the room looked resigned and defeated, as if mourning the loss of something sacred. Before and after the meeting, several talked privately in small clusters about Mattis, their rock. They wondered how he was going to handle this latest assault on a soldier's code, the military's duty to its brothers-in-arms. Trump had effectively forced Mattis to abandon a fellow warrior on the battlefield.

"This is an abandonment of a partner and an ally in such a cavalier fashion," recalled one person who attended the meeting. "He had worked so hard to get us out of Syria, and out of Afghanistan, in a responsible way." This person added, "I remember thinking, 'I don't know how Mattis deals with this.'"

They would all find out how Mattis would handle "this" in a few hours. The afternoon of December 20, an aide showed Sweeney the video that Trump had posted on Twitter about "our boys" coming home and said, "SecDef should see this." It was about 3:30 p.m., and Mattis was fixing his tie in his office, getting ready to go to the White House for a 4:00 p.m. meeting with the president. At Sweeney's direction, he watched the video. He had no obvious facial reaction. "Huh," Mattis said. "Okay."

Mattis had been in a pensive mood that day, with a lot of major events to ponder. He had been to a memorial service for a friend, commander of the Fifth Fleet, who appeared to have killed himself. He left for the White House to meet with the president.

Around 4:30 p.m., Sweeney called an emergency meeting of all of Mattis's senior staff, including Deputy Secretary Patrick Shanahan, Rood, and the other assistant secretaries, Ellen Lord, Robert Hood, and Michael Griffin. He passed out Mattis's resignation letter. There were long faces and expressions of shock.

In the resignation letter, which Mattis had delivered to Trump, he offered no praise for the president, but rather laid out his own core beliefs. He wrote that America's strength "is inextricably linked to the strength of our unique and comprehensive system of alliances and partnerships." And he wrote that "we must be resolute and unambiguous in our approach to those countries whose strategic interests are increasingly in tension with ours," including Russia and China.

"My views on treating allies with respect and also being clear-eyed about both malign actors and strategic competitors are strongly held and informed by over four decades of immersion in these issues," Mattis wrote. He added, "Because you have the right to have a Secretary of Defense whose views are better aligned with yours on these and other subjects, I believe it is right for me to step down from my position."

McGurk also resigned that day, which Trump would later dismiss as a "nothing event!"

Mattis joined his team at the Pentagon conference room. He smiled warmly at them all, folded his arms on the back of his chair at the end of the table, and said, "Come on, guys, it's okay. All things have to come to an end. As long as the sergeants and corporals are on watch, it's fine."

Mattis explained that he and the president had a "good conversation" and that he would stay on as defense secretary until February 28, to ensure a "proper turnover." Mattis was light. He was reassuring. His emphasis was on the people who do the real work and how they would still be doing the real work no matter who the secretary was. Nobody asked any questions. One person who looked the most upset and shocked was Shanahan. He was indeed floored, later telling his deputies, "I always thought Mattis was going to run through the tape. This was his life." Shanahan didn't know at this point that he would succeed Mattis, but some believed they saw the deputy bracing for it.

"There was a whole lot of fear in his eyes," recalled one person who was present. "He was going to have to shepherd this ship until whenever. The rest of us were like, 'The world is about to end!'"

PART
FIVE

Twenty-two

AXIS OF ENABLERS

The deal was done. After days of maneuvering at both ends of Pennsylvania Avenue, the White House announced on December 18 that President Trump planned to sign a spending compromise to keep the government funded for two months. He would punt into the New Year his fight with congressional Democrats over border wall funding.

Convinced that there were not enough votes in the House to secure $5.7 billion for the wall, Trump had bowed to political reality. This was a rare concession from a president accustomed to sparring until he got his way. His retreat averted a government shutdown over Christmas, a prospect Republican leaders universally regarded as a political loser, one easily branded "the Trump shutdown" thanks to the president's eagerness to own it in his earlier meeting with Nancy Pelosi and Chuck Schumer.

As he celebrated the agreement to avoid a shutdown, Senate majority leader Mitch McConnell told reporters, "You remember my favorite country saying: There's no education in the second kick of a mule. We've been down this path before, and I don't believe we'll go down this path again."

When Trump tuned in to conservative media, he faced a full-scale rebellion. Rush Limbaugh told his millions of radio listeners, "Trump gets nothing and the Democrats get everything." Ann Coulter published a column titled "Gutless President in Wall-less Country" and predicted in a podcast that Trump's tenure will go down in history as "a joke presidency." Even on the curved white couch of *Fox & Friends*, a cradle of Trump sycophancy each morning, the host Brian Kilmeade chided him over the compromise spending bill.

Congressman Mark Meadows and other members of the House Freedom Caucus joined in the howls of indignation, warning Trump personally and in media appearances that he was being led astray. They implored the president to reject the terms, demand his proposed $5.7 billion in wall funding, and force a government shutdown if that's what it took.

At the White House, Trump was in a tailspin as he absorbed the convulsions within his political base. On December 20, with just one day until the government funding deadline, Trump threatened to veto the compromise bill unless it included wall funding. The president's sudden shift torpedoed the deal negotiated earlier in the week. At the end of December 21, funding for numerous agencies expired, shutting down large parts of the federal government, halting numerous services, and sending close to 400,000 workers home without pay indefinitely. Trump dug in and vowed not to budge until Democrats agreed to fund wall construction. The president warned that the shutdown could last "a very long time."

"Do we succumb to tyranny of radio talk show hosts? We have two talk radio hosts who influenced the president. That's tyranny, isn't it?" an exasperated Bob Corker, who was retiring from the Senate, told reporters at the Capitol. "This is a juvenile place we find ourselves. The reason we're here is that we have a couple talk radio hosts that get the president spun up."

Plunging into a government shutdown just before Christmas with no plan to reopen it was classic Trump. It was a decision made in duress. "It was a suicide mission," one of Trump's former White House advisers said. "There was no off-ramp. There was no way the Democrats would just back down. There was no way to win. It was done based on impulse and emotion and dogmatism and a visceral reaction rather than a strategic calculation. That's indicative of a lot of the presidency and who he is."

Trump canceled his holiday vacation plans, staying at the White House in light of the government shutdown while Melania and Barron flew to sunny Palm Beach to hang out at Mar-a-Lago. Marooned for the pre-Christmas weekend at the White House, Trump watched hours of cable news and stewed over the coverage—not only of the shutdown, but also of Mattis's resignation. Mattis's letter—distributed to reporters by his aides—was interpreted in the media as a scathing rebuke of Trump's worldview.

Trump's anger reached a boiling point early on the morning of December 23. At 9:00 a.m. in Washington, he called Patrick Shanahan, who was then in Seattle, where it was 6:00 a.m. Shanahan was preparing to depart for a family vacation to Mexico over Christmas. Trump told him he wanted him to be his new defense secretary, starting immediately, and complained about Mattis's "attack" letter. Shanahan defended Mattis but also pleaded with Trump to allow the gargantuan Defense Department a more reasonable transition period. Shanahan often said he had gotten a Ph.D. in foreign policy watching Mattis, and he wanted to ask him more critical questions before he left. Trump grudgingly agreed Mattis could stay, but only until December 31. Shanahan canceled his trip and flew back to Washington. That same morning, Sweeney warned Mattis's staff, "Anticipate the tweet."

Mattis had just received a phone call from Mike Pompeo, who said the president was abruptly forcing him out. Trump was removing the defense secretary two months ahead of schedule, only he was apparently too afraid to tell Mattis himself, so he made the secretary of state call him instead. Administration officials said Trump was retaliating against the negative news coverage, which he baselessly suspected Mattis had helped stoke.

Trump's tweet arrived at 11:46 a.m. announcing that Patrick Shanahan, who was Mattis's No. 2 and for many years prior was an executive at

Boeing, one of the largest defense contractors, would become acting defense secretary.

As happened with just about everybody in Trump's orbit, the invisible clock had run out. Late in 2018, Trump was complaining about Mattis to friends. He told one, "Mad Dog, that's not the perfect nickname for him because he's not aggressive enough. He's not assertive enough. He didn't really earn that nickname."

At the Pentagon that day, a young marine who often worked at the security station guarding the Potomac River entrance, which Mattis and his staff used to enter the building, threw his phone down on the pavement when he read the news that Trump was removing Mattis early.

"Marines don't forget," the guard said.

Marines revered Mattis, and the guard was no exception. The general had earned his reputation the slow and steady way. A bachelor who never married, the commander made it a tradition that he would volunteer to take a junior officer's shift on Christmas Day so his subordinates could spend the holiday with their families.

Trump's treatment of Mattis upset the secretary's staff. They decided to arrange the biggest clap out they could. The event was a tradition for all departing secretaries. They wanted a line of Pentagon personnel that stretched for a mile applauding Mattis as he left the Pentagon for the last time as secretary. It was going to be "yuge," staffers joked, borrowing from Trump's glossary.

But Mattis would not allow it.

"No, we are not doing that," he told his aides. "You don't understand the president. I work with him. You don't know him like I do. He will take it out on Shanahan and Dunford."

On his last day, New Year's Eve, Mattis left the Pentagon without public fanfare. He was hoping to protect the men he left behind, including Chairman of the Joint Chiefs of Staff Joseph Dunford. He did record an audio farewell message to Defense Department employees, which he began by quoting from a telegram President Lincoln sent to General Ulysses Grant in 1865: "Let nothing which is transpiring, change, hinder, or delay your military movements, or plans."

"I am confident that each of you remains undistracted from our sworn mission to support and defend the Constitution while protecting our way of life," Mattis told the employees. "Our department is proven to be at its best when the times are most difficult."

In the weeks that followed, Trump's remaining national security advisers, buttressed by the pleas of foreign leaders and Republican allies on Capitol Hill, engaged in a tug-of-war with the president to reverse or alter his decision to withdraw from Syria. As was often the case with his rash decisions, Trump would ultimately backtrack. A contingency force of U.S. troops would remain in Syria for many months to come.

Christmas Eve was Trump's third straight day holed up inside the White House during the partial federal government shutdown, and his grievances billowed out to form a heavy cloud of Yuletide gloom. All morning on December 24, the president barked out frustrations on Twitter. Democrats are hypocrites! The media make up stories! The Federal Reserve chairman is like a golfer who can't putt! Senators are wrong on foreign policy—and so is Mattis!

Trump's tenth tweet of the day, at 12:32 p.m., was a plaintive complaint that landed like a cry for help. "I am all alone (poor me) in the White House waiting for the Democrats to come back and make a deal on desperately needed Border Security," he wrote.

The night of Christmas Eve, Trump made his first public appearance since the government closed. He and the first lady—who had flown back from Florida for the occasion—participated in an annual presidential tradition: a photo opportunity tracking Santa Claus on military radar. The couple sat in armchairs near a crackling fire in the State Dining Room, which was cleared of furniture, save for two Christmas trees. They talked into separate phones with children calling in as part of the North American Aerospace Defense Command's Santa tracker.

Trump risked blowing Santa's cover when he was patched through to a seven-year-old girl, Collman Lloyd, calling from her home in South Carolina.

"Are you still a believer in Santa?" Trump asked.

"Yes, sir," Lloyd replied.

"Because at 7, that's marginal, right?" the president said.

Lloyd later told *The Post and Courier* that she had never heard the word "marginal" before.

On December 26, at 12:06 a.m., in the dark of night, Trump took off from Joint Base Andrews on a secret mission to Iraq, his first visit to a conflict zone as commander in chief. Rallying U.S. service members at al-Asad Air Base west of Baghdad, Trump amplified his call to draw down America's presence in foreign wars and, at a moment of leadership turmoil at the Pentagon, asserted his personal influence over the military.

"We're no longer the suckers, folks," Trump declared. "The United States cannot continue to be the policeman of the world."

Trump broke norms in his speech to the troops. He criticized their commanders for failing to meet his deadlines to withdraw from Syria and other conflicts. He told a number of falsehoods, including that troops had not received a raise in more than ten years until he recently authorized a 10 percent raise; in fact, troops had received raises every year for decades, and the one Trump authorized was 2.6 percent.

Trump also jeopardized the neutrality Mattis strove to maintain by making his event with troops overtly political. He attacked Pelosi by name for her party's refusal to fund construction of a border wall and signed "Make America Great Again" caps. And he imported the signature stagecraft of his campaign rallies to Iraq, entering to Lee Greenwood's "God Bless the U.S.A." and exiting to the Rolling Stones' "You Can't Always Get What You Want."

Trump enjoyed playing the role of commander in chief—zipping up his bomber jacket, giving orders to generals, saluting officers in uniform. On his visit to Iraq, he sounded awestruck by the stealthy safety requirements of war-zone travel. "I had concerns for the institution of the presidency," he told reporters traveling with him. "Not for myself, personally.

I had concerns for the first lady, I will tell you. But if you would have seen what we had to go through, with the darkened plane, with all windows closed, with no lights on whatsoever, anywhere—pitch black. I've never seen it. I've been in many airplanes—all types and shapes and sizes. I've never seen anything like it."

Trump began the year 2019 as a president unchained. He had replaced a raft of seasoned advisers who sought to enlighten and restrain him with a cast of enablers who executed his orders and engaged his obsessions. Jim Mattis was replaced by Patrick Shanahan. Don McGahn was replaced by Pat Cipollone. Jeff Sessions was replaced by Bill Barr. John Kelly was replaced by Mick Mulvaney. They saw their mission as telling the president yes.

On January 4, Trump showed he was in charge when he dressed down Mulvaney in front of congressional leaders from both parties during a White House meeting to negotiate a budget compromise to reopen the government. Just as Mulvaney was trying to nail down specifics on border wall funding, Trump interrupted his chief of staff. "You just fucked it all up, Mick," Trump said, according to *Axios*. The president rebuffed Mulvaney and hit the reset button. Needless to say, there was no deal.

The episode, later confirmed by attendees, was stunning and, for Mulvaney, humiliating. It illustrated the limited regard with which Trump held the man he had just entrusted with helming his West Wing, and it diminished him in the eyes of the principals in Congress with whom he would need to regularly negotiate.

Mulvaney was no match for Kelly, either in physical presence or in professional experience. Trump liked Mulvaney just fine but did not afford him the same respect he did his predecessor. Mulvaney was named to the job in an acting capacity, although unlike Shanahan he did not require Senate confirmation to hold the position permanently.

If Mulvaney was bothered by the diminished title, he didn't let on. Internally, he fashioned himself as a consensus builder. One of his subordinates explained his approach to the job as basic: "Mick just wants to be liked."

"Mick's inclination is to try to find a way to make the boss's impulses work," no matter how destructive or dangerous Trump's idea might be, a senior administration official said. "He'll enable rather than advise and manage, which in this presidency is a recipe for disaster."

That description belied Mulvaney's opportunism and ambition. A former Tea Party congressman, Mulvaney had his own political ideology, forged years before Trump ran for president. He calculated that by not literally standing guard over the president hour after hour, as Kelly and Priebus had done, and by avoiding palace skirmishes, he could quietly push forward on building a right-wing fiefdom. In the name of "Make America Great Again," Mulvaney would pursue his own conservative agenda on fiscal, labor, health-care, and other domestic policies.

After Pelosi became House Speaker the first week of January, the threat of congressional investigators bearing down on Trump became real. Democratic committee chairmen were readying a vast array of probes, from Trump's efforts to thwart the Russia investigation and his secret communications with Vladimir Putin to the president's tax returns and bank records to alleged abuse in the White House security clearance process and the separation of migrant children from their families at the border.

It fell to Cipollone to captain the administration's defense. The conservative former Kirkland & Ellis partner, who was then working at a boutique plaintiffs' firm, had several "ins" to Trump's orbit. He had gotten to know Trump by privately advising the president's legal strategy since the summer of 2018, and Jay Sekulow found his assistance invaluable. The Fox News host Laura Ingraham, who had been close to Trump for years, also recommended Cipollone; they became close friends when Cipollone helped her through a time of personal struggle over her faith.

Cipollone had another great calling card: he was a genuine fan of

Trump's policies and was determined to help advance his legislative agenda and put more of Trump's aspirations into the "win" column.

Despite Cipollone's conservatism, he had friends and admirers across the aisle, too. His former coworkers said he had a comfortable, genial style and put people around him quickly at ease. In his cases, he tried to find compromises to move forward. Melanie Sloan, a Trump critic and prominent government ethics lawyer, applauded Trump's choice. She noted that Cipollone had a moral code and predicted that he would be unlikely to cross ethical boundaries in service to the president, despite Trump's frequent demands of advisers to do so.

"He will advocate for his client quite zealously, but within the confines of the law," Sloan said. She added, "It's hard for me to imagine Pat doing something that would harm his reputation. He has a pretty strong core."

Cipollone officially joined the office in November and spent the next couple of months repopulating the White House counsel's office with warrior-lawyers in anticipation of a drawn-out battle with House Democrats over investigations. With McGahn's departure in October, four of the five deputy White House counsels had left, and by late that year the number of lawyers on staff had dwindled to fewer than twenty from thirty-five. This shrinkage had eroded the ability of the White House to vet policies and personnel and left the administration ill-prepared for the looming oversight fight, but the silver lining for Cipollone was that he had a clean slate to build from.

By the beginning of January, Cipollone had hired seventeen lawyers, including three new deputies he had handpicked: Patrick Philbin, Kate Comerford Todd, and Mike Purpura. They joined John Eisenberg, a deputy since Trump took office. Each of the three newcomers possessed considerable experience working in the George W. Bush administration, either in the White House counsel's office or in the Justice Department. They were well versed in executive privilege, the legal topic that Cipollone planned to deploy as both a protective tool and a cudgel in fending off the prying demands of Democratic lawmakers.

Cipollone and his team crafted Trump's executive privilege strategy as a means of fending off the expected blizzard of requests from Democratic lawmakers and to protect the confidentiality of the office of the president.

The lawyers were prepared to make a robust argument that White House communications must remain shielded in order for the president to receive full and frank advice from his aides and advisers. They also anticipated blocking congressional subpoenas for testimony from scores of current and former administration officials, citing executive privilege.

Meanwhile, Barr was preparing to assume control of the Mueller investigation. Barr's reputation, forged during his first tour as attorney general under President George H. W. Bush, was that of a devoted institutionalist who cared deeply about protecting Justice Department norms and rising above petty political gamesmanship. The Senate had unanimously approved his nominations for all three of his past Justice Department jobs, a fact Barr quietly reminded friends of. But it was clear to any student of the modern era that his confirmation process to become Trump's attorney general would not be so smooth and that the outcome would not be unanimous.

In early January, as he prepared for his Senate confirmation hearings, Barr spent considerable time thinking through what, at least in the near term, his No. 1 job was: handling the conclusion of Mueller's investigation and the release of his expected report. He closely read the special counsel's stated mission and underlying statutes, as well as the Justice Department opinions that constrained how prosecutors could treat the president in an investigation.

Barr assumed Mueller and his team would write some sort of report at the end of their investigation but had not spoken to the special counsel and did not know what form it would take. The special counsel regulations called for the findings to be delivered to the attorney general but did not require a public report. Rod Rosenstein's plan had long been to keep any such report private; at most, the Justice Department would make a public announcement that a confidential report had been delivered and the special counsel's office was being disbanded. But over time, the idea of keeping the report private seemed impractical. Rosenstein's deputies would joke about the furor it could cause, not only in the media, but also at the Capitol and the White House. "From which side of Pennsylvania Avenue would the pitchforks penetrate the building?" one quipped.

As Barr met privately with dozens of senators, courtesy calls in the run-up to his confirmation hearings, most of them were adamant that Mueller's findings become public. He decided then that he would have to release the report; by withholding it, the Justice Department could look as if it were hiding something. He rationalized that if it documented criminal wrongdoing, the attorney general couldn't sit on it, and if the president didn't do anything wrong, the attorney general ought to tell the American people. More than a year and a half into Mueller's investigation, the body politic needed a cathartic moment. And even if the department didn't release the report, Barr assumed someone would leak it eventually.

At his January 15 confirmation hearing before the Senate Judiciary Committee, Barr testified, "The country needs a credible resolution of these issues. If confirmed, I will not permit partisan politics, personal interests, or any other improper consideration to interfere with this or any other investigation. I will follow the special counsel regulations scrupulously and in good faith, and on my watch, Bob will be allowed to complete his work. Second, I also believe it is very important that the public and Congress be informed of the results of the special counsel's work. For that reason, my goal will be to provide as much transparency as I can consistent with the law."

Though he could not control the timetable for his confirmation, Barr fully expected Mueller's final decisions and report to land in his lap, as opposed to that of the department's interim caretaker, Matt Whitaker. Whitaker's brief tenure as acting attorney general was not kind to his reputation. He had a frosty relationship with some of the most senior officials in the department, leading to paralysis at times. He suspected colleagues were leaking damaging material about him to reporters. Whitaker craved public adoration, and those who worked with him sensed in him a deep insecurity. He was quiet in internal meetings, striking some attendees as more of an observer than a decision maker. A few administration lawyers shared a private joke about Whitaker, saying he reminded them of the character Mongo from the Mel Brooks comedy *Blazing Saddles*.

Barr compared so favorably to Whitaker, on the gravitas measure alone, that many Justice Department lawyers suspected Mueller would try to time his report so that he could hand his baby to Barr, his trusted former boss. Mueller considered Barr not only a peer but also a friend; he had been invited to Barr's daughter's wedding. The Senate would vote on February 14 to confirm Barr, 54 to 45, and he would be sworn in later that day.

Throughout January and into February, the Mueller report was like a mysterious plane, circling the atmosphere undetected by radar but rumored to be landing sometime soon. Inside the special counsel's offices, which had effectively been hermetically sealed for nearly two years, the Mueller opus was taking shape. The special counsel team was divided into two—one group of prosecutors and investigators pursuing Russian interference, the other Trump's obstruction of justice. The teams hashed out drafts of their separate volumes, while Mueller and his senior leadership team worked on the report's summary. There was considerable haggling over nearly every word, but especially so on the issue of the substantial evidence they had gathered suggesting Trump had obstructed justice and the Office of Legal Counsel opinion stating that the special counsel could not charge a sitting president.

"It was vigorously debated. How do we articulate 'obstruction'?" said one person who talked to multiple members of the team. "How do we conclude what his conduct was? It was spirited. They understood the OLC opinion prohibited them from charging him. But the OLC opinion doesn't say you can't recommend charges."

Some prosecutors felt the evidence was substantial and that they had met the requirements for bringing a prosecution if the subject were not the president. Others felt they were missing hard proof of Trump's intent. Because of the legal opinion prohibiting prosecution of a sitting president, they had not reached a formal conclusion about whether they could bring a case. They argued the special counsel should make the gravity of Trump's actions more clear to Congress, which was empowered to pursue impeachment, and ultimately to the public.

"The debate was more spirited," said the person who talked to multiple team members. "Did it ever get angry? Did anyone get short? Yes. But that is business as usual. That does not mean that it is contentious necessarily. This is how these things go when you have nineteen lawyers debating how to handle something."

Inside Trump's camp, meanwhile, Giuliani, Sekulow, and the Raskins were convinced that Mueller could never make a case for conspiracy between the president and any Russians. They had read every document. They had modest readouts of most of the special counsel's witness interviews. And nothing they saw or heard suggested that Trump knew in advance about the illegal hacking of Democratic emails or urged it, despite his public plea—"Russia, if you're listening"—to release Hillary Clinton's deleted emails. The only thing that gnawed at Trump's lawyers was the possibility that there were U.S. intelligence intercepts or foreign intelligence reports that found a link between a Trump campaign aide or associate and a Russian discussing the central crime of hacking Democratic emails.

Trump's lawyers believed the president was more vulnerable on obstruction. The worst-case scenario, they were warned by Flood, was that Mueller's report stated that investigators had enough evidence to prove to a jury beyond a reasonable doubt that the president had committed a certain number of specific federal crimes but that the special counsel did not indict him solely because of the Justice Department policy forbidding prosecution of a sitting president. That would be tantamount to calling Trump a criminal who was walking around scot-free, out on a technicality.

The president's lawyers were drafting their own rebuttal report to issue in the event that Mueller leveled such an accusation. A short version was about ten pages; the longest version ran as high as eighty-five pages. That longer version rebutted all the legal positions that Trump's team figured Mueller would have to take to conclude the president committed the crime of obstruction, ignoring his broad powers to fire subordinates and exert his executive authority over the Justice Department.

The rebuttal report draft also documented what the Trump lawyers argued was political bias in the FBI's handling of the probe. That included what the Justice Department's inspector general found to be a worrisome "willingness to take official action" on the part of some FBI investigators to hurt Trump's chances of election. Exhibit A in the lawyers' trove of evidence were the text messages that the then senior FBI agent Peter Strzok, one of Mueller's original team members, exchanged with the then FBI lawyer Lisa Page. The two were having an affair and, prior to Mueller's appointment, were at the forefront of the FBI's Trump-Russia probe.

"He's not ever going to become president, right? Right?!" Page wrote to Strzok in one message while they were in the middle of deciding on launching an investigation of Trump and his campaign in August 2016.

"No. No he's not. We'll stop it," Strzok responded.

Strzok and Page had by now become lead characters in Trump's "witch hunt" plot, with recurring roles on the president's Twitter feed and on Fox shows. As Trump tweeted on January 12, for instance, "Lyin' James Comey, Andrew McCabe, Peter S and his lover, agent Lisa Page, & more, all disgraced and/or fired and caught in the act. These are just some of the losers that tried to do a number on your President. Part of the Witch Hunt. Remember the 'insurance policy?' This is it!"

Another recurring character of the drama was Giuliani, the public face of Trump's defense. Though never regarded for his eloquence or precision with language on television, Giuliani unspooled a dizzying string of sound bites in mid-January that required substantial cleanup and rankled other Trump advisers.

Giuliani gave divergent accounts of when conversations about developing a Trump Tower project in Moscow occurred. He first said they occurred throughout the 2016 campaign, then said they were hypothetical altogether, then said they might have gone on for the entirety of the campaign, and then said they ended around January 2016, just before the Iowa caucuses.

Then there was the matter of the Michael Cohen tapes. Giuliani claimed to have listened to recordings that showed Trump had not instructed his personal attorney to lie to Congress about the Moscow project, then said he should never have mentioned the tapes at all, then said such a conversation would have been "perfectly normal," then said he wasn't sure whether they had spoken, before claiming, finally, that they definitely had not.

On January 23, Giuliani tried to explain his various statements and clarifications by telling *The Washington Post*'s Josh Dawsey, "There is a strategy. The strategy will become apparent." Then he pleaded with Dawsey, "You have to be patient."

Trump was not a patient man, however. The president—who has made more than his share of whoppers—complained about Giuliani to one of his political advisers. "He's the only guy in the world who's less prepared than I am," Trump said. "Rudy goes on TV and doesn't know what the fuck he's talking about."

For the next several days, Giuliani stopped appearing on TV. Trump temporarily benched his lawyer.

By its thirty-fifth straight day, the government shutdown that Trump had said he would be proud to instigate was wreaking havoc across the country. The nation's air travel was in chaos. Federal workers were lining up at food banks. Some Republican senators were in open revolt. Even Christopher Wray, Trump's handpicked FBI director, was decrying the dysfunction.

"It takes a lot to get me angry, but I'm about as angry as I've been in a long, long time," Wray said in a video message to FBI employees.

"I'm not a loser," the president said. "I'm not going to lose this. I'm not going to look weak. I'm not going to give in."

But on January 25, Trump gave in.

The master deal maker wasn't the wizard he claimed. "It's like Mc-Donald's not being able to make a hamburger," the Republican strategist Mike Murphy said.

Trump cast about for someone to blame and pointed fingers at two staffers who led the negotiations on Capitol Hill, Mulvaney and Jared Kushner. During the shutdown, Kushner claimed his bipartisan victory in reforming criminal sentencing law as evidence that he could execute a grand bargain around wall funding and broader immigration changes. Another senior administration official recalled of Kushner, "He kind of said, this is how we made the donuts last month and this is how we'll make donuts again this month because they were really delicious donuts, we made them well, and it worked, so let's use the same recipe." But it was naive to think Democrats like Senator Dick Durbin, who had been willing to support a bill reducing recidivism, would ever agree to fund Trump's wall.

Trump did not give up on the wall, however. He reopened the government only temporarily, giving Congress three weeks to pass a longer-term budget. During that period, as a seventeen-member bipartisan panel of lawmakers negotiated a spending compromise, Cipollone, Mulvaney, and other officials devised a drastic plan for Trump to build his wall. The president would declare a national emergency at the southern border, which would trigger extraordinary powers to redirect taxpayer money.

On February 15, Trump signed the new budget agreement, which contained $1.375 billion for fencing and other border expenditures—far less than the $5.7 billion Trump had sought—and formally declared the national emergency. He used the word "invasion" seven times to describe the migration patterns at the border. "We're talking about an invasion of our country with drugs, with human traffickers, with all types of criminals and gangs," Trump said.

At the Pentagon around this time, Shanahan considered gradually withdrawing the troops Trump deployed to the border shortly before the November 2018 elections, but he quickly realized he would not last very long if he did. After all, Shanahan was acting, and Trump liked it that way. He was more vulnerable to the president's pressure. "He gets to lord it over them," explained one senior administration official.

Shanahan was left shaky in his interim position. It was clear that Trump would never nominate him as the permanent secretary of defense unless he played ball. So on February 22, the Pentagon announced it would *increase* the number of military personnel on the border by a thousand, bringing the total number of troops to six thousand. Their primary orders were to string concertina wire along the border and install detection systems to secure remote areas between official entry points.

This decision tended to confirm the doubts within the Pentagon that Shanahan would not be able to fill Mattis's shoes. Officials noticed that he liked to bring Dunford or Chief of Staff of the U.S. Army Mark Milley to any substantive meetings, leaning on their expertise as a crutch. Shanahan wasn't trying to pretend he had Mattis's credentials. He knew he was "the Accidental Secretary," thanks to Trump's vicissitudes, and had no problem admitting what he didn't know. Still, he had critics inside who yearned for someone with Mattis's grounding.

"He likes the red carpet," one military official said of Shanahan. "But he can't stand up to Trump. He doesn't have the credibility and experience to say, 'Hey, this is why you shouldn't do that.'"

After two years of being told no by Mattis, Trump considered Shanahan precisely the kind of replacement he had in mind.

Twenty-three

LOYALTY AND TRUTH

On February 27, 2019, Michael Cohen, who had once said he would take a bullet for Trump, gave the most sensational day of congressional testimony of the Trump era. The president watched snippets from half a world away in Vietnam, where he was turning up the charm for Kim Jong Un at their second summit. For him, Cohen's testimony before the House Oversight Committee amounted to the ultimate betrayal. And with the collapse of the Hanoi summit over the murderous North Korean dictator's refusal to abandon his country's nuclear program, Trump was dealt twin disasters.

Cohen's decision to turn on the president—to become "a rat," in Trump's mobster lingo—was set in motion several months earlier. On November 29, 2018, a week after Thanksgiving, Cohen pleaded guilty to lying to Congress about then-candidate Trump's interest in a Trump Tower project in Moscow. Cohen admitted that he told a false story to match Trump's repeated public denials that he had pursued the project deep into the presidential campaign. Cohen also acknowledged repeated contacts with Russian officials to try to secure approvals for the Trump project, and that he kept Trump apprised of his progress.

In Washington, meanwhile, the Democratic congressman Elijah Cummings was preparing to become chairman of the House Oversight Committee. The congressman called an old friend from his days defending the Clintons, Lanny Davis, who had taken on Cohen as a client. Cummings asked Davis whether Trump's estranged fixer might be willing to testify before his committee and reveal to the American people, in more detail than he had in his guilty plea, how Trump directed him to commit crimes.

Davis replied that he didn't think so. Cohen was under a continuing cooperation agreement with federal investigators—both in the Southern District of New York, which was trying the campaign finance case, and in Robert Mueller's special counsel office—as part of his plea deal. SDNY prosecutors still had an open case examining the Trump Organization and Trump's role in the hush-money payments, while Mueller's Russia investigation was ongoing. Prosecutors held a lot of power over Cohen's life, including advising on how much time he should serve in prison. Still, Davis told Cummings, "I'll ask him."

A few days before Christmas, Cohen got on the phone with Cummings and agreed to testify before his committee. Cohen decided he wanted to explain himself fully, in a way he had not yet been able to—certainly not when he was under investigation and trying to sing from Trump's songbook, and not when he was following the strict choreography dictated by the prosecutors who negotiated his plea deal. Working closely with Davis, Cohen cataloged dozens of stories he was ready to share about Trump that would spotlight the president's dishonesty and depravity. Davis believed there were many words that described Trump: "insane," "sociopath," "monster," and "cruel." But he wanted to hear Cohen walk through the characteristics he had witnessed firsthand.

"Name-calling isn't what we do," Davis told Cohen. "You are going to be name-calling with facts you can prove. Because Bob Mueller is going to be listening."

As Cohen studied his anecdotes and memories, he sorted them into three categories that he believed best described Trump: racist, con man, and cheat. In telephone calls and emailed exchanges of drafts, Cohen worked with Davis to structure the opening statement he would deliver before Cummings's committee. Davis had two requirements for his client: Cohen had to acknowledge his regret and shame over what he had done in service to Trump, and he had to state unequivocally that he was not seeking and would not accept a pardon from the president. Together these two assertions would help address the skepticism many lawmakers felt about Cohen, a convicted felon who previously lied before Congress.

Just before his February 27 testimony, a team that Davis had assembled ran Cohen through a murder board, asking him intentionally vicious questions to steel Cohen for what one member of the team called "the nastiest cross-examination Republicans would give him." Cohen was uneasy about admitting to a national audience that he was ashamed about his behavior but ultimately agreed with Davis that it wasn't sufficient to state, "I'm sorry," or, "I take responsibility." Those phrases had become almost trite in modern political theater.

The morning of February 27, Cohen stood in the House Oversight Committee's hearing room, raised his right hand, and swore an oath that his testimony was the whole truth and nothing but the truth. Looking down to read from his prepared statement before a hushed room, Cohen expressed far more than an apology. "I regret the day I said 'yes' to Mr. Trump," he said. "I regret all the help and support I gave him along the way. I am ashamed of my own failings, and I publicly accepted responsibility for them by pleading guilty in the Southern District of New York. I am ashamed of my weakness and misplaced loyalty—of the things I did for Mr. Trump in an effort to protect and promote him. I am ashamed that I chose to take part in concealing Mr. Trump's illicit acts rather than listening to my own conscience.

"I am ashamed because I know what Mr. Trump is," Cohen continued. "He is a racist. He is a conman. He is a cheat."

Cohen laid out a devastating bill of particulars against the president, sharing specific anecdotes and, in some cases, brandishing evidence to support his claims. He presented copies of Trump's financial statements from 2011 to 2013; a copy of a check Trump wrote from his personal bank account after becoming president to reimburse Cohen for hush-money payments to the adult-film star Stormy Daniels; and copies of letters Cohen wrote at Trump's direction threatening civil and criminal action against his high school, colleges, and the College Board if they ever released his grades or SAT scores.

Cohen offered testimony that drove at the heart of Mueller's investigation. He said Trump directed negotiations over the proposed Trump Tower in Moscow, which continued throughout the 2016 campaign, and lied to the public about it. Cohen also alleged that then-candidate Trump knew that Roger Stone had spoken with Julian Assange in advance of WikiLeaks' release of Democratic National Committee emails.

The most chilling part of Cohen's testimony, however, was what he said about Trump's character. Cohen argued that Trump ran for office "to make his brand great, not to make our country great," and that as president he has become "the worst version of himself." Cohen described Trump as far more craven, dishonest, and racist in private than he lets on in public. He said Trump "speaks in code, and I understand the code," as if he were a mob boss giving orders to his henchman.

Cohen said working for Trump was "intoxicating," adding that he became so "mesmerized" by his boss that he routinely did things that he knew were wrong. And he said his experience should be a cautionary tale for Republican members of Congress. "I did the same thing that you're doing now for 10 years. I protected Mr. Trump for 10 years," Cohen said. He added, "People that follow Mr. Trump, as I did blindly, are going to suffer the same consequences that I'm suffering."

Trump's allies on the panel treated Cohen roughly, just as Davis's murder board team had prepared him for. "You're a pathological liar," the Republican congressman Paul Gosar said. "You don't know truth from falsehood."

The well-rehearsed witness didn't flinch. "Are you referring to me or the president?" Cohen shot back.

"When I ask you a question, I'll ask for an answer," Gosar replied, cutting him off.

The Republican congressman Jim Jordan, a fierce Trump defender, sought to portray Cohen as a disgruntled former employee who was left behind in New York when his boss became president. "You wanted to work in the White House," Jordan said. "You didn't get brought to the dance."

"Mr. Jordan, all I wanted was what I got, to be personal attorney to the president," Cohen replied.

Notably, no Republican on the panel tried to defend Trump by engaging with the substance of Cohen's testimony. They only attacked Cohen's credibility as a witness.

Eighty-three hundred miles away from the fireworks in Cummings's hearing room, Trump was cozying up to Kim at the luxurious Sofitel Legend Metropole Hanoi hotel. At the very moment he was conducting diplomacy with the world's most erratic dictator, Trump was being called a con man by his former attorney. At a brief photo opportunity during his one-on-one meeting with Kim, Jonathan Lemire of the Associated Press asked whether he had a response to Cohen's testimony. Trump bristled, shaking his head and declining to answer.

The White House abruptly banned Lemire and three other U.S. journalists from covering Trump's dinner with Kim shortly thereafter, where the leaders tried to bond over grilled sirloin and chocolate lava cake. This was an extraordinary act of retaliation by the U.S. government, which had historically upheld the rights of journalists whenever a president traveled overseas, and especially in the presence of autocrats whose countries do not have a free press. Sarah Sanders cited "sensitivities over shouted questions in the previous sprays." Trump had complained to aides many times before about being embarrassed by the questions reporters ask him in front of other world leaders. Trump had hoped his interactions with Kim would drive news coverage back home, showing him acting as a statesman, just as in Singapore seven months earlier. Instead, television networks aired round-the-clock coverage of Cohen's testimony.

The next day, February 28, Trump made a play for history when he sat for more formal negotiating sessions with Kim and their delegations. He was so certain that he could broker a nuclear disarmament accord of some kind with the North Korean leader that the White House announced a joint signing ceremony at the summit's conclusion that afternoon. But there ended up being nothing to sign. A working luncheon for the two leaders was canceled amid a standoff over Kim's demand that the United States remove economic sanctions against North Korea without a promise to end his nuclear program. The talks were over. "Sometimes you have to walk, and this was just one of those times," a chastened Trump told reporters before flying home to Washington.

Before leaving Hanoi, Trump delivered a stunning defense of Kim's brutality. Early in his presidency, Trump made Otto Warmbier the heart of his maximum-pressure campaign on North Korea. He spotlighted the twenty-two-year-old University of Virginia student's death upon being released by the North Koreans in a coma following seventeen months in captivity, and invited Warmbier's grieving parents as his guests to his first address to a joint session of Congress. Yet when *The Washington Post*'s David Nakamura asked Trump in Hanoi whether he had confronted Kim about Warmbier's death, the president said Kim was not to blame. "I don't believe that he would've allowed that to happen," Trump said. "Just wasn't to his advantage to allow that to happen. Those prisons are rough. They're rough places. And bad things happened. But I really don't believe that he was—I don't believe he knew about it."

Here again Trump accepted the words of a foreign autocrat, just as he had believed Saudi crown prince Mohammed bin Salman did not order the murder of the journalist Jamal Khashoggi and as he had believed Russian president Vladimir Putin did not interfere in the 2016 U.S. election. Trump said that Kim "felt very badly," but claimed to only know about Warmbier's case after the fact. "He tells me that he didn't know about it," Trump said, "and I take him at his word."

Jim Mattis, John Kelly, and Kirstjen Nielsen had once all been wary of Trump's October 2018 decision to deploy troops to the southern border, realizing they provided useful support but uneasy about service members being used as political props. By February 2019, however,

Nielsen realized she desperately needed those troops—and even more of them—at the U.S.-Mexico border to support the overwhelmed customs and immigration officials in Texas and Arizona. Scores of migrant families, as well as some traffickers using children as decoys, were rushing the border claiming asylum. The number of migrants detained in February, seventy-six thousand, marked a twelve-year high for illegal border crossings. The arrivals deluged U.S. border agents.

Now that the midterms were over, Trump and his political advisers cared little about the humanitarian crisis of immigrants. "They said, 'Yeah, yeah, you have a bunch of kids to take care of,'" a senior national security official recalled. "They [just] want the illegals to stop coming in."

Nielsen asked for a meeting with Trump and finally got one in early March. The homeland security secretary hoped that if they met face-to-face she could get the president to focus on this one topic. Trump veered toward discussing the overall immigrant "invasion" but would not acknowledge Nielsen's consistent argument that the only real solution to immigrants seeking asylum was thoughtful legislation to close legal loopholes. But Trump was angry and believed Nielsen and her team should be doing much more. As Nielsen tried to refocus the meeting on the impossibility of her agency's shouldering the crush of migrants entering the country in the last two months, Stephen Miller, who was also in attendance, brought up a side project. He suggested to Trump and Nielsen that they start imposing visa sanctions for countries that had a high number of residents overstay their visas. Miller's visa idea was diverting the president's attention from the crisis at the border and would do nothing to address the current problem.

Nielsen left the meeting cursing under her breath. She couldn't get through to Trump and felt the aides around him were suggesting she could pull some mythical solution out of her hat that she was stubbornly refusing to do. After their meeting, the crisis got worse. That spring, Department of Homeland Security officials counted fourteen hundred immigrant children under their care in a single day.

Fresh from her frustrating meeting with Trump, Nielsen began urging White House chief of staff Mick Mulvaney to convene a cabinet meeting to create a crisis action plan. The border problem was crying out for health-care workers and supplies, food stocks, and emergency response teams—resources that involved other federal departments. Nielsen hounded Mulvaney for two weeks, telling him she urgently needed help from the Pentagon to transport families, and she needed the Department of Health and Human Services to speed up the conveyor belt to take kids into its care.

The Department of Homeland Security wasn't supposed to keep children in its custody longer than seventy-two hours. The border patrol stations—concrete slabs with little jail cells that resembled the inside of a small-town sheriff's department—were never designed to detain kids, but they had crammed four times as many people as the fire code allowed in ten border stations. The department's border effort was on the cusp of disaster: Nielsen had a backlog of a thousand kids who were overdue to get into Health and Human Services facilities, but the agency was moving too slowly to take them in.

"I urgently need a cabinet meeting," Nielsen told Mulvaney. "I'm going to explain to you how bad this is. I'm going to show you photos and [then] you tell me you aren't going to help me." Mulvaney agreed, but when Nielsen arrived, she was shocked to see there were no other cabinet secretaries present. "Well, look, I thought we would talk about it a little more," Mulvaney told her.

Nielsen told Mulvaney what she thought this emergency demanded: a White House czar to coordinate border security steps among agencies. Mulvaney suggested she work through this with the other agencies. She said she had tried that already. The Pentagon, HHS, and other agencies weren't treating the situation like the emergency it was. They needed the boss to tell them this was a priority. Children were in danger. Border stations were in violation of their fire codes. There was no more time for more discussion, she said. They needed an action plan.

Nielsen was used to her close partnership with Kelly, but Mulvaney seemed more interested in managing up—talking to Trump—than in managing down, more like a chief staffer than a chief of staff. After she returned from the White House, Nielsen told her senior leadership team, "Forget it. We're going to pull down our own cabinet meeting." She convened other agency heads on a conference call, and they made a plan to address the emergency together. It was what a normal White House would have taken the lead in doing.

In late February, a week or so after Bill Barr was sworn in as attorney general, he was briefed on the state of the Mueller investigation by Rod Rosenstein and Ed O'Callaghan. As Rosenstein's principal deputy, O'Callaghan had been the point man consulting regularly with the special counsel team. He reported back to Barr that Mueller was nearing the end but needed more time. The special counsel's deputies still had some loose investigative ends to tie up, most of them related to documents and other materials from Roger Stone, whose Florida home the FBI had raided on January 25.

What Barr, Rosenstein, and O'Callaghan did not know was that Mueller and his team were hard at work wrestling over the best way to conclude and summarize their nearly two-year investigation. Prosecutors had been actively drafting their final report in two volumes. The first volume was complicated, with a series of shadowy figures with strange-sounding names, but fairly straightforward to write. It documented the Russian government's effort to interfere in the 2016 presidential election. The second volume was far more controversial and caused internal angst. It documented the evidence the team had gathered on ten episodes when Trump appeared to be seeking to thwart or shutter a criminal investigation of his campaign and himself.

All winter, Mueller and his team had been paying close attention to Barr's words and realized during his confirmation hearings that the ground had shifted. The team had to write a report summarizing their findings; they had always known that was one of their duties under the special counsel regulations. But now they had to write it with an eye toward much or all of their report becoming public. And the team did not agree on how forcefully they should describe the president's efforts to block a criminal investigation.

A few members of Mueller's team wanted to be explicit in the report about the incriminating information they had found about Trump and explain that if he had not been a sitting president, he could likely have faced charges. They understood the Office of Legal Counsel opinion prohibited prosecuting Trump, but they pointed out it did not state that they could not recommend charges.

"There were people in the group who were pushing for a clearer expression of the president's misconduct and why they were not charging it," said one person who talked with members of the team. They believed they "definitely had enough to indict any other human being."

Mueller argued a pure, apolitical view about the impropriety of concluding Trump had engaged in a crime, considering the OLC opinion. Amid an extensive back-and-forth over how they should summarize Trump's actions—and all the indications he had sought to interfere in the probe—Mueller and his team agreed to language stating that Trump could not be exonerated: "If we had confidence after a thorough investigation of the facts that the President clearly did not commit obstruction of justice, we would so state."

But some on the team felt that phrasing was still unsatisfyingly passive. It was "as far as the special counsel was willing to go," this person said, but added, "I don't think that that was the consensus view. I think the boss made a call."

On March 5, Barr got some answers. Mueller and his top deputies, James Quarles and Aaron Zebley, arrived at the Justice Department for a secret meeting. To ensure they would not be spotted, Mueller's security detail snuck them in through the basement and whisked them up a back elevator and into the attorney general's conference room. The trio met Barr for the first time since he had become attorney general, and they were joined by Rosenstein, O'Callaghan, and Barr's chief of staff, Brian Rabbitt. The atmosphere was friendly and jovial. Everyone exchanged pleasantries, and then they got down to business.

Mueller kicked off the meeting by pulling out a piece of paper with some notes. The attorney general and his aides believed they noticed something worrisome. Mueller's hands shook as he held the paper. His voice was shaky, too. This was not the Bob Mueller everyone knew. As he made some perfunctory introductory remarks, Barr, Rosenstein, O'Callaghan, and Rabbitt couldn't help but worry about Mueller's health. They were taken aback. As Barr would later ask his colleagues, "Did he seem off to you?" Later, close friends would say they noticed Mueller had changed dramatically, but a member of Mueller's team would insist he had no medical problems.

Mueller quickly turned the meeting over to his deputies, a notable handoff. Zebley went first, summing up the Russian interference portion of the investigation. He explained that the team had already shared most of its findings in two major indictments in February and July 2018. Though they had virtually no chance of bringing the accused to trial in the United States, Mueller's team had indicted thirteen Russian nationals who led a troll farm to flood U.S. social media with phony stories to sow division and help Trump. They also indicted twelve Russian military intelligence officers who hacked internal Democratic Party emails and leaked them to hurt Hillary Clinton's campaign. The Trump campaign had no known role in either operation.

Zebley explained they had found insufficient evidence to suggest a conspiracy, "no campaign finance [violations], no issues found. . . . We have questions about [Paul] Manafort, but we're very comfortable saying there was no collusion, no conspiracy."

Then Quarles talked about the obstruction of justice portion. "We're going to follow the OLC opinion and conclude it wasn't appropriate for us to make a final determination as to whether or not there was a crime," he said. "We're going to report the facts, the analysis, and leave it there. We are not going to say we would indict but for the OLC opinion."

Quarles said they would lay out the evidence "dispassionately" in volume 2 of their report so as not to leave an impression with readers about any determination of Trump's criminality. "We don't reach a final judgment that any specific conduct equals a crime," he said. "We do not reach the crime or no crime conclusion."

Barr and his team were surprised and entirely confused. Seeking clarity, the attorney general tried to sum up the point Quarles was making: "It's not the case that you could say Bob Mueller would've indicted the president of the United States but for the OLC opinion."

Correct, Quarles agreed.

According to the Justice Department's OLC opinion, federal prosecutors, including the special counsel, could not indict a sitting president, but they could investigate him. Nothing in the OLC opinion said prosecutors could not decide whether or not a president committed crimes. In fact, the special counsel statute explicitly stated Mueller had one central job: to investigate and then report to the attorney general on his decision to prosecute or not to prosecute.

Yet Quarles was saying they would not go down that road of deciding one way or another. Barr thought, why not? You're the special counsel. Your job was to investigate and make charging decisions.

Mueller spoke up to reiterate the position Quarles presented. "We determined we should not try to decide if the conduct constitutes a crime due to the reasoning of the OLC memo," he said. "It would be possible for somebody else later on to decide."

Barr wanted to be sure. He asked specifically whether someone could review the report and make an independent decision about criminality. The special counsel's team told him yes. Later, another Barr aide asked whether the attorney general could decide whether there was enough evidence to constitute a crime. Again, the Mueller team said they assumed the attorney general had that power. Of course, Barr was in charge of the probe and could have said to Mueller, "I want you to make a recommendation," but he didn't. Mueller's team thought they were discussing legal authority in the abstract. They gave the answers never contemplating Barr might actually exercise that power within days.

The meeting then turned to the logistics and technicalities of the report itself. Mueller said the report would be lengthy and written in two volumes: the first, covering Russian interference, would clock in at about 140 pages, while the second, on obstruction, would be about 120 pages. Mueller and his deputies explained that the report would contain an executive summary. "We tried to take the facts as we saw them," Mueller said.

Mueller said the report would contain "6(e)" material, meaning sensitive evidence and testimony gathered through grand jury subpoenas that by law could not be released publicly, and the special counsel's office offered to help the Justice Department think through what would have to be redacted.

"My intent is to put as much out as possible, but I'm very concerned about the gap between when I get it and when I can put it out," Barr said. "My goal is to put as much out as I can as quickly as I can, but I need your help with that." He asked the special counsel's team to identify as they finished drafting the report any 6(e) material in advance so it could be redacted in a timely fashion. The special counsel's team agreed, and the meeting soon wrapped up.

In the days that followed, Barr, Rosenstein, and O'Callaghan chewed over Mueller's decision not to decide. They could hardly understand Mueller and Quarles's reasoning, and they thought, this is going to be a big mess. Barr concluded that he would decide whether the president criminally obstructed justice. The special counsel was under the auspices of the Justice Department, using the criminal process to obtain evidence, and Barr, Rosenstein, and O'Callaghan all believed firmly that the department must make the decision. There was no hesitation. The attorney general would make the call.

On Friday, March 15, at 7:41 a.m., Trump began a three-day Twitter spree in which he would post sixty-three missives by the end of the weekend. The Justice Department chiefs kept Trump and his lawyers in the dark, and in a series of tweets Trump wrote that Mueller "should never have been appointed and there should be no Mueller Report. This was an illegal & conflicted investigation in search of a crime. Russian Collusion was nothing more than an excuse by the Democrats for losing an Election that they thought they were going to win."

Then came his conclusion: "THIS SHOULD NEVER HAPPEN TO A PRESIDENT AGAIN!"

Trump spent the weekend marooned at the White House rather than making his typical winter and spring weekend jaunt to Mar-a-Lago, and he stayed off the golf course, meaning he had little to keep himself occupied. He was triggered, at least in part, by a *Politico* article reporting that his advisers were building an early reelection strategy around "dignified settings like the Oval Office and the Rose Garden" rather than his "rambunctious rallies," in part to make Trump appear more traditionally presidential. The story, written by Gabby Orr, was published on March 8, but Trump didn't read it until an aide handed him a printout of it just before the March 15 weekend and provocatively inquired, "Sir, you are now going to be more presidential?"

Few media narratives got under Trump's skin more than the impression that his staff was managing him, and whenever this happened, Trump found a way to prove that he could not be managed. He vented about it to Corey Lewandowski, one of his trusted outside political advisers. "These guys are going to tell me how to communicate?" Trump said. "They're going to tell me when I'm going to do a rally and when I'm not?"

Twenty-four

THE REPORT

Around noon on March 22, an otherwise quiet Friday in spring, Ed O'Callaghan got a special delivery at his Justice Department office. He was handed a heavy ream of paper bound by a clear plastic sheet on top and a durable black backing. The title: "Report on the Investigation into Russian Interference in the 2016 Presidential Election." Robert Mueller had completed his probe, and here were his long-awaited findings, all 448 pages of them.

O'Callaghan, Bill Barr, Rod Rosenstein, and Brian Rabbitt, Barr's chief of staff, dropped their plans for the day, walled themselves off from others in the office, and started reading. Their first thought was that there were more than four hundred pages and Mueller's team had not redacted anything. They instead used footnotes to mark sensitive material learned in the grand jury, but it wasn't clear precisely what Mueller's team felt should be kept secret. The special counsel's team had indicated in the March 5 meeting that they would identify that sensitive information, known as 6(e) material, which could be a cumbersome process. But Mueller's investigators did not feel it was their role to redact, only to identify the material. Justice Department officials saw this as a failure by Mueller's team to redact as promised, and this critical missing step would make it difficult to release the report quickly to the public.

The Barr team's immediate priority was to wrap their heads around what Mueller wrote, so they skipped around the two volumes looking for his conclusions and summaries. Midafternoon they decided they should notify the public that the special counsel had transmitted his report to the attorney general, so the team drafted a letter to Congress. Barr wrote, "I am reviewing the report and anticipate that I may be in a position to advise you of the Special Counsel's principal conclusions as soon as this weekend." He also reiterated his intention to make the findings public, adding, "I remain committed to as much transparency as possible."

Between four and five o'clock that afternoon, Rabbitt called White House lawyer Emmet Flood to let him know that the Justice Department had the report. He read Flood a draft of Barr's letter to congressional leaders but did not tell Flood what Mueller's report said or what his bottom-line conclusions were. He telegraphed one bit of good news: Mueller was not recommending any additional indictments. Flood relayed the news to Trump. A few minutes later, Stephen Boyd, the assistant attorney general for legislative affairs, hand delivered Barr's letter to Capitol Hill, and it was almost immediately distributed to the news media. The world now knew that Mueller's nearly two-year investigation was over, and his findings were in the hands of Barr.

Trump had already left for Florida that morning to spend the weekend at Mar-a-Lago. Flood and Pat Cipollone, believing that delivery of the Mueller report was imminent, accompanied him in case he needed lawyers close at hand and were added at the last minute to the Air Force One manifest for the 10:00 a.m. flight. But that Friday afternoon, the Trump team could do little but wait on Barr.

The president restrained himself from calling his attorney general to find out more, for once following his lawyers' guidance about not communicating with Barr so as not to compromise the independence of the investigation. Trump's team felt confident Mueller could not accuse Trump of any conspiracy to collude with Russians and was on shaky ground to accuse him of obstruction, based on the evidence they knew Mueller had compiled. They knew Mueller did not plan to indict Trump, a sitting president, and did not want to risk the negative political implications of preventing the Justice Department from making fully independent decisions. They knew the Democrats would want nothing more than to catch the president interfering with the end stage of the Mueller investigation.

In the weeks leading up to this moment, Barr had tried to maintain a healthy distance from Trump. He avoided too many visits to the White House for fear of appearing too chummy with the boss. But although Barr was new on the job, Trump and his team had full confidence in his judgment, in no small part because of Barr's expansive view of presidential power and his June 2018 memo arguing that the obstruction of justice investigation into the president had been "fatally misconceived." They also believed Barr had the will to fight to protect the president and his executive authority. Inside the White House, some aides nicknamed Barr "the Honey Badger," a reference to a viral video in which a fearless badger climbs a tree to kill a snake, gets bitten by the snake, passes out, and then starts eating the slithering creature.

"It was always going to be Barr's show," one Trump legal adviser said. "Even if we wanted to be a puppeteer, why would we risk it? Emmet was not going to let stupid decisions be made at the end of this game. We were not going to snatch defeat from the jaws of victory."

On March 22, Rudy Giuliani, Jay Sekulow, and Jane and Martin Raskin were scattered around the country, from New York to Nashville, and scrambled to get back to Washington. They gathered the next day in the oversized conference room in Sekulow's law offices on Capitol Hill, an 1880s pharmacy that had been converted into office space. The Maryland Avenue building featured a conference room with a massive mural of Washington. There, Sekulow, Giuliani, and the Raskins prepared for what could come. "We felt confident, but until you have it, you don't have it," one team member recalled.

All of them agreed there could be no finding that the president had engaged in collusion with the Russians. But they remained concerned about the other half of the probe. They thought it was possible the report might claim that Trump had broken the law and that the president would have been charged with crimes but for the Justice Department's Office of

Legal Counsel policy prohibiting prosecution of the president. The team did not like that scenario, but if Mueller were to accuse Trump of crimes, the president's team had planned a counter-narrative. "We didn't know how obstruction would happen," the team member said. "We thought they might lay out the facts. . . . We just didn't know how."

Inside the special counsel's office, Mueller and his prosecutors eagerly awaited the debut of their investigative findings and the breaking of a sacred silence the team had maintained for the past two years. Finally, the copious evidence they had combed the globe to gather would be released in some form to the public. But the prosecutors on the team didn't know how much Barr would ultimately decide to share right away, and they anxiously discussed what he might do.

In preparation for this moment, the two main teams—one working on Russian interference, the other working on obstruction of justice—had written the report with overarching summaries, which they hoped would give Barr something easy to share with the public before releasing the full report. They felt at a bare minimum he would release those.

The 448-page report was a breathtaking catalog of presidential scheming and misconduct. Volume 2 detailed ten events that the special counsel scrutinized for possible obstruction of justice by Trump. It was not just a historical record. It also provided a dense legal analysis of the evidence, the kind of assessment prosecutors would ordinarily make to determine whether to bring criminal charges. Mueller laid bare in granular detail a presidency plagued by paranoia and insecurity, depicting Trump's inner circle as gripped by fear of the president's spasms as he frantically pressured his aides to lie to the public and fabricate false records. Some of the episodes had previously been highlighted in news reports, but Mueller's report was singular for its definitive examination and revelatory details of the events, with the main actors under oath and on the record.

Just as James Quarles had previewed to Barr on March 5, the special counsel decided not to decide whether Trump committed a crime, based on his interpretation of the OLC opinion prohibiting the prosecution of a sitting president. Though it did not state so explicitly, the report suggested that Congress should assume the role of prosecutor. "The conclusion that Congress may apply the obstruction laws to the President's corrupt exercise of the powers of office accords with our constitutional system of checks and balances and the principle that no person is above the law," the report stated.

The report was classic Mueller: brimming with damning facts, but stripped of advocacy or judgment, and devoid of a final conclusion. Many of the deeply investigated moments, retold almost as scenes in a movie, were engrossing. But the analysis of what to make of the president's conduct was written in overly legalistic prose, complete with double negatives. It was not clear what the facts added up to, nor did it provide a road map for Congress to pursue impeachment proceedings. For instance, the report stated, "If we had confidence after a thorough investigation of the facts that the President clearly did not commit obstruction of justice, we would so state. Based on the facts and the applicable legal standards, we are unable to reach that judgment."

Mueller figured the American people and their elected representatives in Congress would read the report and decide whether and how to act.

Thanks to Barr's notification to Congress, the media were on standby for breaking news. Cameras staked out the attorney general outside his home in Virginia and the Justice Department's Washington headquarters. Barr and Rosenstein set a deadline for themselves of Sunday evening to report back to Congress with Mueller's principal conclusions, in part because they did not want the financial markets to open on Monday morning with only rumors in the media and the specter of criminal indictment hanging over the president. So they dug in to devour the report, staying up into the wee hours on Saturday morning to read.

On Saturday, March 23, Barr, Rosenstein, and O'Callaghan reconvened at the office to hash out the report. They tried to weigh the evidence in volume 2 and assumed, for the sake of argument, that each of the ten episodes constituted obstruction of justice and first considered each one alone. They found the evidence truly disturbing but felt they couldn't prove the president had corrupt intent. They asked themselves, could we get a criminal conviction on this evidence and survive an appeal? Their conclusion was unanimous: no.

Their decision made, Barr, Rosenstein, and O'Callaghan had to decide how to announce it to the public. Ordinarily a decision not to prosecute would remain confidential, but this was no ordinary case. The top Justice Department officials considered it an abomination that the Mueller investigation had become so public, but realized that because of the public scrutiny they had to explain in detail what had happened, even though Trump was not being charged with or accused of a crime.

Barr decided to write a second letter to Congress, which would detail the special counsel's principal conclusions. He and his team scanned the Mueller report looking for sentences that they could quote in the letter that summarized the special counsel's findings or reflected the bottom line. They found the report to be a garbled mess and struggled to find something worth quoting. At one point, O'Callaghan homed in on this line: "While this report does not conclude that the President committed a crime, it also does not exonerate him."

"If we don't include that, people are going to criticize us," O'Callaghan said.

Barr agreed. "You know what, Ed? That's a good point. Let's put that in there," he said.

As they finalized the draft of the letter, O'Callaghan called Aaron Zebley, Mueller's chief of staff. He told Zebley that Barr would be laying out Mueller's bottom-line conclusions and asked if he would want to read the draft before it was released. Zebley responded no, telling O'Callaghan that they did not need to see it. Zebley was hoping and assuming that Barr's letter would quote the summaries the team had spent so much time on. But he didn't say that to O'Callaghan. Yet again, the Mueller team declined an opportunity to weigh in on how their investigation's findings would be presented to the public.

At Mar-a-Lago, Trump awoke early on the morning of Sunday, March 24. He got dressed in his golf shirt and khaki pants and headed out at about nine o'clock to the Trump International Golf Club. He played a round of golf, ate lunch at the clubhouse, and chatted with friends.

Giuliani was in Washington with the rest of Trump's personal legal team but spoke by phone with the president regularly all weekend. He told *The Washington Post*'s Robert Costa that Trump was in a "watch and wait" mode of cautious optimism. "However, until you read the report, you don't know exactly what it entails, so you should keep your powder dry," Giuliani added.

Trump told friends that weekend, "From everything I hear, it's good," but refrained from celebrating prematurely. As Kellyanne Conway remarked to Vice President Pence, "That's the businessman. That's somebody in real estate who knows the deal is not the deal until after it's notarized."

Trump's team had prepared responses to a range of eventualities, with a worst-case scenario that the Mueller report could leak to the public unexpectedly and be so damaging, with surprise evidence, that it triggered an immediate impeachment inquiry in the House. The drafted response was exceedingly hard-hitting, a take-no-prisoners, blood-in-the-water jeremiad against Mueller, the FBI, and their methods.

The president's personal lawyers gathered again on Sunday at Sekulow's office, wearing casual work clothes, with both Sekulow and Giuliani in bulky sweaters because it was chilly. A little after 3:15 p.m., Rabbitt alerted Flood in Mar-a-Lago that within the hour Barr would release the key takeaways from the report. He gave Flood the bottom line but read aloud some key conclusory sections from Barr's letter. Flood and Cipollone then told Trump what to expect, and the president reached out to his personal legal team back in Washington.

That afternoon, Barr made an announcement that would define how the world would interpret Mueller's findings. Barr submitted a four-page letter to congressional leaders to, as he wrote, "summarize the principal conclusions set out in the Special Counsel's report." The document was immediately released online.

At Sekulow's office, Trump's lawyers sat in front of open laptops, impatiently waiting for the Barr letter to download. It was taking forever. The letter was already circulating among members of the press, who were texting and calling Trump's lawyers for reaction. John Santucci of ABC News was on one line asking for comment, and Sekulow, flustered by the slowness of his computer, admitted he hadn't been able to read a copy yet. "John, will you just send it to me?" he asked the journalist.

Finally, the lawyers read it around the table.

Barr wrote that the investigation found no evidence that any Trump campaign members or associates conspired or coordinated with the Russians to tilt the election—in essence, "no collusion." On obstruction, he wrote that the special counsel had chosen not to reach a normal prosecutor's decision on whether Trump had committed a crime. "The Special Counsel therefore did not draw a conclusion—one way or the other—as to whether the examined conduct constituted obstruction," Barr wrote. "Instead, for each of the relevant actions investigated, the report sets out evidence on both sides of the question and leaves unresolved what the Special Counsel views as 'difficult issues' of law and fact concerning whether the President's actions and intent could be viewed as obstruction."

Barr explained he therefore concluded the evidence of obstruction was insufficient. "In cataloguing the President's actions, many of which took place in public view, the report identifies no actions that, in our judgment, constitute obstructive conduct, had a nexus to a pending or contemplated criminal proceeding, and were done with corrupt intent," Barr wrote.

Barr's letter included the key line from Mueller's report that O'Callaghan had suggested adding in good faith that the report "does not exonerate him." Nonetheless, Barr's letter laid the groundwork for Trump to declare otherwise.

Barr had served his boss an unmistakable political victory, and a feeling of euphoria swept over Trump and his team. Jane Raskin snapped a picture on her phone that forever captures the moment they read Barr's summary of the report. Sitting at the conference table side by side, Giuliani grabbed Sekulow by the neck to give him a hug. They looked tired and relieved.

Sekulow talked to Trump by phone. He was elated but also very practical, asking about the team's media strategy. Of paramount importance to the president was the TV spin wars. "This is great," Trump said. "How are you all responding? Are you going out?"

Trump wanted every television network to trumpet the news of his victory. Sekulow assured him that they had a detailed media plan. "This is very good news," Trump replied. "I'll see you tonight."

Shortly before 5:00 p.m., Trump arrived by motorcade at Palm Beach International Airport for the two-hour flight home to Washington. He stood under the wing of Air Force One and offered his first reaction to the press corps: "There was no collusion with Russia. There was no obstruction—none whatsoever. And it was a complete and total exoneration."

That night was a special memory for Trump's lawyers, who freshened up and assembled around dusk at the Yellow Oval Room in the second-floor residential quarters of the White House to give the president a homecoming. At 7:04 p.m., they watched Marine One land on the South Lawn. Trump stepped off the helicopter, dressed in a suit and red tie, and greeted the assembled press with a hearty wave. "This is a great country," he said.

Inside the residence, Trump's defenders felt pride in their work during a tumultuous time when so many were rooting against them. Watching the ebullience of their client strolling across the South Lawn, they felt a swell of relief. Trump walked upstairs and grinned as he saw his lawyers gathered around the room. He had two words for them: "Great job!" Trump, who is not a hugger, heartily shook every hand in the room.

Sarah Sanders joined them for a moment of celebration and posed for a photo with Trump and his legal team, along with Flood and Cipollone, all of them beaming. Sekulow, the conductor and the heart of the operation, offered thanks to his partners. A year earlier, the president's legal team had endured a devastating stretch after John Dowd quit and the president had no lead lawyer other than Sekulow. The team had to be re-created from scratch, and here they now all stood.

"Thank you to you all," Sekulow told the group. "This was the best example of a team effort, where everybody brought their ideas to the table. It was a tremendous team effort and I am grateful that our paths have crossed."

Trump was well aware that there was more to come that would not be so flattering, when some larger portion of the report would be released. But he was glad to have this phase behind him. He felt in the clear. He had won. The president offered his thanks, repeatedly saying, "Great job." The team knew that was the highest praise. "You're in good shape when he says, 'Great job.' You're not so good when he says, 'Let's see,'" one team member joked.

The celebration ended with Trump's gentle good night.

"All right, kids. Thanks," he said.

What Barr included in his summary of principal conclusions, what he left out, and how he framed the special counsel's findings were the first and only words the public received that month about the probe's long-awaited conclusion. Inside the bunker of Mueller's lawyers, Barr's letter stung. Members of the special counsel team would later describe Mueller's reaction: He looked as if he'd been slapped.

Some team members were livid at what they considered Barr's calculated and selective word choices that sidestepped the unpleasant evidence the team had uncovered about Trump himself and his campaign's encouragement of the Russians. The team had made groundbreaking discoveries about Russian bots and intelligence officers rushing to hack Clinton's personal emails hours after Trump's "Russia, if you're listening" remarks, yet that work was reduced to less than a sentence in Barr's letter. Even the portion of the dependent clause in that sentence that Barr chose to make public put Trump in the most flattering light.

Quoting from the report, Barr wrote that "the investigation did not establish that members of the Trump Campaign conspired or coordinated with the Russian government in its election interference activities." He left out the thirty-nine preceding words from that passage, which confirmed the very facts Trump hated to acknowledge and refused to hear: "Although the investigation established that the Russian government perceived it would benefit from a Trump presidency and worked to secure that outcome, and that the Campaign expected it would benefit electorally from information stolen and released through Russian efforts."

The authors of volume 2, who struggled to reveal every detail of Trump's moves to shut down or curtail the criminal investigation, practically had steam coming out of their ears. Barr's letter appeared to the uninformed reader to say the opposite of what they painstakingly laid out in their report. For example, Barr wrote that none of Trump's actions, "in our judgment," were done with corrupt intent. Actually, the report's authors had detailed four episodes in which they identified substantial evidence of Trump's intent to thwart the probe.

What had once been Trump's defiant mantra of "No collusion! No obstruction!" instantly became a rallying cry for his reelection, lines he and his surrogates repeated on every media platform. Never mind what the Mueller team actually had found. Trump was winning the spin war.

Mueller had himself to blame for the misrepresentation of his work, in that he was a by-the-books creature of bureaucratic norms miscast for the Trump era, a period of profound polarization, fraying institutions, and news delivered like an IV to the public in fits and spurts.

"We're the Twitter society," said Frank Figliuzzi, a former Mueller colleague at the FBI. "We're the digital streaming society. We're the scan-the-headlines-to-get-some-news society. That's not Mueller. That's not a four-hundred-page report. Somebody's got to show their face on a TV screen and scream and yell. What many of us have asked is, in the age of Trump, as steadfast as Mueller's been to the principles of democracy that got us here, has Mueller served us well with this style? The answer is no."

On the morning of March 25, less than twenty-four hours after Barr sent his summary letter, Zebley contacted O'Callaghan. He asked that the Justice Department release the executive summaries from each volume of Mueller's report. O'Callaghan was noncommittal and said he, Barr, and Rosenstein would think about it. O'Callaghan asked Zebley to mark up the summaries for all necessary redactions of sensitive grand jury material and send them back.

Later that day, Zebley called O'Callaghan with a complaint. He said there was "public confusion" in the media reporting about Barr's letter. When O'Callaghan briefed Barr on the call, the attorney general was taken aback and a bit peeved. As Barr saw it, he had written the letter to be intentionally brief and include only Mueller's baseline conclusions, and as an act of good faith he quoted Mueller's language about not being able to "exonerate" the president. What's more, Barr told his team, they had given Mueller and his deputies an opportunity to review a draft of the letter and Zebley declined. How could Zebley now be upset about it?

On March 27, Mueller signed a letter to Barr from the special counsel's office objecting strongly to the attorney general's handling of the principal conclusions: "The summary letter the Department sent to Congress and released to the public late in the afternoon of March 24 did not fully capture the context, nature, and substance of this Office's work and its conclusions. We communicated that concern to the Department on the morning of March 25. There is now public confusion about critical aspects of the results of our investigation. This threatens to undermine a central purpose for which the Department appointed the Special Counsel: to assure full public confidence in the outcome of the investigations."

The letter said that the introductions and executive summaries of the report "accurately summarize this Office's work and conclusions," and included those redacted documents as attachments. "Release at this time would alleviate the misunderstandings that have arisen and would answer congressional and public questions about the nature and outcome of our investigation."

Barr's office did not receive the letter until March 28. When they first read it, the attorney general and his team thought, "Holy shit! What is this? Give us a break." To them, it was an uncharacteristically passive-aggressive move by Mueller. On April 30, the eve of Barr's Senate testimony, the correspondence was reported by Devlin Barrett and Matt Zapotosky of *The Washington Post*. At his hearing the next day, Barr characterized the letter's tone as "snitty" and speculated that it was written by one of Mueller's underlings.

As he first absorbed the letter in private on March 28, Barr was pissed. He thought the letter was nasty. And he felt betrayed by his friend. "I'm calling Bob," Barr told his staff. "We'll work this out." Mueller was out of the office getting a haircut that morning, but they connected later, shortly before lunchtime. Listening in from the Justice Department were Rosenstein, O'Callaghan, and Rabbitt.

"What the hell, Bob?" Barr asked. "What's up with this letter? Why didn't you pick up the phone and call me?"

Mueller replied by saying something along the lines of "We have concerns that certain issues were not given their full context. The executive summaries are the precise information necessary to reach the conclusion. There's not something that's absolutely wrong with your letter. The problem is misrepresentations in the media. We need to get something out soon that is more accurate, to clarify things."

Despite his well-established lack of interest in public relations, Mueller zeroed in on the media coverage of his report. He said something along the lines of "We have concerns that our report is losing its impact because the full story's not out there and the media's not covering it the way we want them to."

"This is supposed to be confidential," Barr told Mueller.

Barr said the department was moving quickly to prepare the report for public release, but explained that there would be an unwanted gap of time as a consequence of the report's being 448 pages and not containing the necessary redactions.

"To be clear, we're not trying to summarize the work; we're just giving the principal conclusions," Barr told Mueller. "We offered you the opportunity to look at the letter and you said no. We're flabbergasted here."

"Your summary letter fails to put into context the decisions we made," Mueller said.

At this point, Zebley jumped in. He had no problems with Barr's description of their Russian interference work and said nothing about it. "It's all about obstruction. Your letter doesn't give enough context as to our thinking about the OLC opinion and the media coverage is misleading about that."

Barr again defended his letter. "We weren't trying to summarize. We weren't trying to put in context. We were just trying to state your conclusions," he told Mueller and Zebley.

The temperature started to come down. Mueller asked how long it would be until the report was released in full, and Barr said they were aiming for mid-April. Mueller then made another pitch for issuing the executive summaries. "We've had a really good relationship with you so far, and we're asking you to do this, and we'd like it to happen sooner rather than later," Mueller said.

Barr replied, "I'd prefer to push forward and get it all done. I don't think putting it out piecemeal is good." The attorney general said he thought issuing the summaries would cause even more confusion than was already in the body politic.

"Thanks for entertaining the request," Mueller said. "I appreciate it. We really just want full disclosure."

The call ended on an uplifting note.

"At the end of the day, you're part of the Department of Justice," Barr said.

"I agree," Mueller replied.

"We're all in the department together," Barr said. "We'll get back to you."

That night, Mueller's team considered putting out a press statement of their own explaining their objections to Barr's four-page letter but decided against it.

For the rest of the day and into the next morning, Barr, together with Rosenstein, O'Callaghan, and Rabbitt, debated Mueller's request. They nearly decided to release the executive summaries but opted against it for the reasons Barr articulated on the call with Mueller. The report was lengthy, nuanced, and confusing, and Barr worried that people would pick apart the summaries and draw misleading conclusions.

Barr and his team regretted having used the word "summarize" in the March 24 letter. They also lamented that Trump was claiming that Mueller had "totally exonerated" him. That was false, but Barr decided not to publicly correct his boss. The president's lawyers understood the truth, too: a lot of iceberg remained under the water, but they could do little to wean their client off his talking points.

On March 29, Barr decided to write another letter to congressional leaders to clear up his intentions. "My March 24 letter was not, and did not purport to be, an exhaustive recounting of the Special Counsel's investigation or report." He added, "Everyone will soon be able to read it on their own. I do not believe it would be in the public's interest for me to attempt to summarize the full report or to release it in serial or piecemeal fashion."

Barr intended this letter to be a warning shot—to Congress and the media, but also to Mueller's angry prosecutors—to calm down, stop jumping to conclusions, and be patient. There was a lot more still to see.

Twenty-five

THE SHOW GOES ON

On Sunday, March 31, 2019, Kirstjen Nielsen was fast asleep in a London hotel when a call came through from the White House. It was the middle of the night London time. A military aide traveling with the homeland security secretary answered, and the White House operator said President Trump wanted to speak to the secretary. "Is it an emergency?" the aide asked. "The secretary is asleep. Do you want to wake her up?" They decided no, the call was not urgent and could wait.

When Nielsen woke up Monday morning, she learned of Trump's call and called him back later when it was morning on the East Coast. The president was peeved.

"Why the hell are you out of the country?" he asked Nielsen. "What are you doing over there?"

Nielsen reminded Trump that she was meeting with her counterparts in the United Kingdom to discuss a series of threats they were partnering to thwart, including cyberattacks and child trafficking. It was a trip she had previously mentioned to him and White House officials. She had been planning to head from London to meetings in Sweden later that week with security ministers from the Group of Seven, the elite club of the world's most powerful industrial nations.

On the call, Trump asked her questions about border enforcement. Nielsen could tell he was angry she hadn't taken his call the night before. The president didn't seem to understand the obstacles the time difference presented. He kept homing in on Nielsen's being out of the country at a critical time for security at the U.S.-Mexico border. The Department of Homeland Security was set to announce that apprehensions at the southern border had soared to nearly 100,000 arrests in March, many of them Central American families seeking asylum. Trump had again been threatening to close off the border, although he would stop short of doing so because of stark warnings of economic ruin from the business community.

As the president and his White House aides scrambled to come up with actions to take to stem the flow of migrants, Nielsen was across the Atlantic. She was adamant that Trump's obsession with the border not distract her and her team from other areas of her department's mission, especially global cybersecurity, considering the attacks from Russia, China, and other countries. Still, the president did not seem to comprehend that her job entailed more than border security and enforcement.

"I'm sorry, sir," she told him over the phone.

By the time they hung up, Nielsen had the sense that something was up back home. She began to suspect her own job security hung in the balance. In the back of her mind, she was thinking about all the complaints Stephen Miller had lobbed behind her back. He hated when she focused on other missions of her department, whose central reason for being was to prevent another terrorist attack like 9/11. "Why is she doing this?" Miller would ask. "All the president cares about is the border."

Later on Monday, April 1, Nielsen called Mick Mulvaney, the acting White House chief of staff, to check in.

"I don't know why you're away," Mulvaney told Nielsen as he mentioned the high volume of migrant crossings, a reaction that only exacerbated her concern. When she told him there were many things the Department of Homeland Security did besides border enforcement, Mulvaney replied, "Right now, all we're doing here at the White House is the border."

Nielsen also spoke with Vice President Pence, who offered his support but whose comments revealed her overseas trip had been the subject of much internal discussion. "I'm glad you're doing that," Pence told her, then mentioned she could stay or return. "I'll support you either way."

Nielsen knew something wasn't right. When her aides visited in her hotel suite, she told them, "Guys, I think we've got to get back." She left her deputy to be her proxy in the G7 meetings and hastily conferred with Sajid Javid, the United Kingdom's home secretary, to let him know the U.S. position on a few key issues.

In the days that followed, Nielsen returned stateside to become the public face of U.S. border enforcement amid a record-setting surge of migrants. She sped up the deployment of 750 Customs and Border Protection officers to support U.S. Border Patrol agents and arranged a series of emergency calls with other cabinet secretaries to engage their departments in support. Back in Washington the night of April 2, Nielsen appeared on set for an interview with Tucker Carlson, whose 9:00 p.m. Fox News show Trump watched religiously, to detail what her department was doing to address the crisis at the border—as well as to praise her boss.

"The president predicted this as a candidate," Nielsen told Carlson. "He predicted this before he was a candidate. He continues to show leadership and to raise the alarm bells."

Nielsen also said that Trump was prepared to close down the U.S.-Mexico border. "We have to stop the drugs, we have to stop the smuggling and trafficking," she said. "I don't think the president could be any clearer in his position. He will take every action within his authority to stop this flow."

On April 3, Nielsen traveled to the border to inspect the situation firsthand and continue her media tour. In an April 4 interview with Chris Cuomo on his 9:00 p.m. CNN show, Nielsen said she had instituted an "emergency response posture" across the federal government to address the surge of migrants. She said she was treating the situation as if the United States had been hit by a "Cat 5 hurricane."

The next day, April 5, Nielsen met up with Trump on the president's tour of a section of new border wall in Calexico, California. Shortly before a pair of media appearances there, Trump told Nielsen, "Go tell them we're full. We can't take any more [migrants]."

Nielsen declined. "That's not a legal reason," she told the president. Being "full" didn't justify denying people legal asylum.

Trump then pulled aside Kevin McAleenan, the commissioner of Customs and Border Protection, for a chat out of Nielsen's earshot. At a roundtable session with border security officials, Trump said himself what he had asked Nielsen to say: "The system is full. Can't take you anymore. Whether it's asylum, whether it's anything you want, it's illegal immigration. We can't take you anymore. We can't take you. Our country is full. Our area is full. The sector is full. Can't take you anymore, I'm sorry. Can't happen. So turn around. That's the way it is."

When Trump toured the border wall in Calexico for his second media appearance, he did not praise Nielsen.

Nielsen and McAleenan flew back to Washington that afternoon aboard a small Coast Guard jet. The two got along pretty well, and Nielsen had even talked Trump out of firing McAleenan when the president randomly threatened it a time or two. Nielsen didn't fully realize it then, but something big was up. One of her senior staffers called her on the plane, and through the din of noise she heard him say that on April 4, while Nielsen had been at the border, Trump had vented frustration about her and the border situation in an Oval Office meeting. She would later learn that McAleenan had attended it.

Later the night of April 5, Nielsen called Trump, who had stayed in California to attend a political fund-raiser. "I know you're frustrated," she said. "Can I come in this weekend?"

Nielsen wanted to brief Trump on the new agreements she had just brokered with Northern Triangle countries designed to slow the flow of migrants into the United States by setting penalties for kidnappers, imposing blockades on travelers without visas, and establishing border checkpoints in southern Mexico. "I have seven or eight other ideas for what we can do," she told him.

"It's not your fault," Trump said, adding something like "I know you're doing your best." Then he agreed to meet. "Sure, come to the residence this Sunday," he told her.

When Nielsen showed up at the White House on April 7 to meet with Trump in the Yellow Oval Room, Mulvaney was there with the president. She started to explain a major agreement she had secured in private negotiations with Mexican authorities the previous week. Mexico had promised to stop 50 percent of the migrants flowing through its internal border checkpoints as they headed north. But Trump cut her off. Looking at Mulvaney, he said, "See, this is what's wrong with her. It should be 100 percent."

Things were off to a very bad start.

"Mr. President, *we* can't stop 100 percent," Nielsen said.

They went back and forth. Trump didn't listen to Nielsen's explanations about the Northern Triangle agreement, how important it was to have partners in those regions to discourage the migration from within.

"Sir, can we agree on what we are trying to accomplish?" she asked. But they couldn't. He was tuning her out. The conversation escalated. Trump made it clear he wanted her gone.

"Sir, why don't I give you my resignation," Nielsen asked the president.

Trump accepted. He wanted a change. "But I want you to be in my administration elsewhere," he added.

Nielsen didn't respond to that offer, but returned to the substance. "Okay, but can I explain how you can fix this, whoever does it?" she asked.

Trump didn't want to hear it.

"Why don't we do a week of transition?" Nielsen offered.

Trump agreed and the meeting was over. Within minutes, as Nielsen was being driven home a few miles away in Alexandria, the president tweeted, "Secretary of Homeland Security Kirstjen Nielsen will be leaving her position, and I would like to thank her for her service. . . . I am pleased to announce that Kevin McAleenan, the current U.S. Customs and Border Protection Commissioner, will become Acting Secretary for @DHSgov. I have confidence that Kevin will do a great job!"

So much for that week of transition, Nielsen figured. Trump's announcement made it sound immediate. She finalized her resignation letter and made it effective that date, April 7. Just like some other secretaries who had departed before her, Nielsen did not directly thank Trump or celebrate his leadership in her letter. Rather, she singled out the men and women of her department. "I could not be prouder of and more humbled by their service, dedication, and commitment to keep our country safe from all threats and hazards," she wrote.

Mulvaney called Nielsen later that evening, after getting her letter. "Why are you resigning today?" he asked.

Nielsen was surprised by the question. "I'm not the one who changed the date," she said.

Mulvaney explained they weren't trying to force her to leave immediately. But the president was in a rush, wanting to announce that he was the one making the decision for her to leave and trying to control the story. Mulvaney invoked Jim Mattis, reminding her of the umbrage the president had taken at the defense secretary's resignation letter. It turned out Trump feared Nielsen might criticize him or reveal damaging information about him on her way out the door, but the president thought if he made the first announcement, he could dismiss anything she might say later as sour grapes from a disgruntled former employee.

Mulvaney asked her to stay on until April 10 to ensure a smooth transition and explained that Trump intended to keep McAleenan as an acting secretary instead of nominating him for Senate confirmation. "You know the president," Mulvaney said. "He likes actings."

Nielsen would soon learn that the White House had one main goal for her three days of transition: to get her to sign off on changing the legal succession plan so the White House could install the people they wanted in the department's top jobs without following the civil service regulations that would place Nielsen's deputy in charge.

In her sixteen months as homeland security secretary, Nielsen had become the face of Trump's immigration policies, arguably the most controversial aspect of his presidency. As such, she had received threats against her life, including on the day she resigned. Nielsen had a heavy security detail as secretary. Packages that were delivered to her home were first scanned and searched at a secure facility. But she was told that once she left the administration, she would be losing her protection.

Some other high-profile national security officials maintained protective details for a period of time after leaving the government, but only if requested by the White House chief of staff and authorized by the president. No such accommodation had been prearranged for Nielsen. As she left government service, Nielsen's security team was preparing to remove the alarms and cameras from her home. If she wanted protection, she would have to hire it herself, and unlike her über-wealthy colleagues in Trump's cabinet she did not necessarily have those kinds of resources.

When some of her international counterparts visited Washington, they offered to hire personal security for Nielsen to protect her, but she declined. "That would look horrible," Nielsen told them. "Can you imagine the story? Foreign governments provide security because the U.S. won't."

Nielsen called Trump. She appealed to him to keep her security detail for another few weeks until she had time to install her own system. "Just say I say it's fine," Trump told her.

The evening of April 3, amid the border crisis and Nielsen's scramble to save her job, Trump gathered his most senior military brass for an annual White House tradition: a dinner hosted by the commander in chief. It was partly a gesture of gratitude, partly an informal session to share ideas.

The atmosphere inside the Pentagon was rather unsteady, with officials still adjusting to the sudden exit of Mattis and the interim leadership of Patrick Shanahan, who had been the acting secretary for three months but still not nominated for the permanent post. Administration officials read Trump's unwillingness so far to formally nominate Shanahan for what it was: a clever ploy to try to turn Shanahan into a yes-man and to keep him on his toes. By June, however, he would withdraw from consideration to be the permanent secretary amid reports of domestic troubles.

Several of the generals and admirals gathered for dinner at the White House had grave concerns about whether Shanahan, a former Boeing executive with little experience on the global stage, had the knowledge, experience, and gravitas to lead the department, with a budget of roughly $700 billion a year. Some of them had been quietly grousing to one another that Shanahan didn't seem able to stand up to Trump, and noted that he had acquiesced earlier that year to the president's demands to claim a national "emergency" and tap Pentagon funds for construction of the border wall.

At dinner in the State Dining Room, many of the faces gathered around the room would be retiring or moving to other posts in the coming months. One chose to use this opportunity to stand up to the president's casual disregard for boundaries and the sacred rules of military justice.

Trump had been obsessed with the prosecution of the Navy SEAL Edward Gallagher, forty, a special forces operator accused of the savage murder of an Iraqi teen. Military prosecutors said Gallagher stabbed to death a seriously wounded Islamic State prisoner of war in May 2017 in a SEALs compound near Mosul and posed for pictures with the corpse. Trump had been watching the case closely, in part because of the sympathetic, pro-Gallagher coverage by the *Fox & Friends* host Pete Hegseth, a Trump booster and informal adviser to the president on veterans' issues.

In addition, one of Trump's biggest defenders throughout the Russia investigation, Congressman Devin Nunes, had been appealing to the president for leniency in Gallagher's case. Trump had announced March 30 that he had intervened to have Gallagher moved to "less restrictive confinement" while he awaited trial, tweeting that he did so "in honor of his past service to our Country."

Now at dinner with the nation's senior military leaders, Trump asked whether they believed Gallagher had been unfairly persecuted. Wasn't it pretty awful, the president asked, for a Navy SEAL to be accused of the crime of just doing his job, killing the enemy?

Trump turned to the army general Richard Clarke, who had just taken over as commander of the U.S. Special Operations Command, leading the elite teams whose members included Gallagher and others under investigation for misconduct on the battlefield. "What about Gallagher?" Trump asked.

The Uniform Code of Military Justice required Gallagher's peers to serve as his judge and jury, with impartiality and without fear of pressure from above. It was improper for the commander in chief to talk about any case in a way that could appear to apply pressure to the military judge far lower down in the military's chain of command. For a president to attempt to tilt the result of the proceedings would be like a Supreme Court justice discussing how he or she would decide a case to the lower-level judge presiding over the trial.

Clarke stammered a bit, looking for the right words to answer. Then Admiral John Richardson, the chief of naval operations, stepped in. He decided to be the one to take a bullet because he was just four months away from ending his four-year term. He didn't have to worry about the president's wrath, at least not as much as Shanahan or some of the others around the table.

"Sir, this is not the appropriate forum to talk about that," Richardson told the president.

Trump was visibly annoyed and folded his arms across his chest.

"Okay," the president said, leaving no doubt to those around the dinner table that he was pissed.

The dinner-table discussion of Gallagher ended awkwardly, with a lull of silence before someone brought up a new topic. But Trump remained fixated on the case. In May, *The New York Times* would report that he was seriously considering pardons for Gallagher and several other U.S. military members accused of war crimes, a rare presidential intervention that experts warned could undermine military law.

In June, Gallagher would stand trial in a military courtroom in San Diego and on July 2 would be found not guilty of murdering the ISIS captive, although the military jury would convict him of posing for photos with the dead fighter's body. The next day, Trump would celebrate the ruling and claim partial credit for the outcome with a Twitter message directed at the Gallagher family: "You have been through much together. Glad I could help!"

Trump would intercede once more on Gallagher's behalf, ordering the navy to penalize the military lawyers who prosecuted the war crimes case against him. "The Prosecutors who lost the case against SEAL Eddie Gallagher (who I released from solitary confinement so he could fight his case properly), were ridiculously given a Navy Achievement Medal," Trump would write July 31 on Twitter, adding that he had directed Richardson and Secretary of the Navy Richard Spencer to "immediately withdraw and rescind the awards."

The law permitted Trump to order the prosecutors be stripped of their medals, but there was little precedent for the move. Unlike the Medal of Honor, achievement medals are determined within the military and do not require a president's endorsement. The presidential decree—made on Twitter no less—was yet another reminder for the Pentagon brass that Trump had no qualms about maximizing his power and intervening whenever he saw fit.

The week of April 8, Washington was in a state of panicky anticipation for the release of Robert Mueller's report. For the past couple of weeks, Justice Department officials had been carefully redacting portions of the 448-page document, but the public version was expected to drop imminently. Reporters were being told by their sources to be on standby.

Trump and his lawyers were being told the same. They had been wrestling with a major decision—whether to read the report before it became public. The normal answer for any attorney representing a client was a resounding yes. But Trump had to consider his lawyers' fear that his critics could accuse him of getting the attorney general to redact portions that were particularly embarrassing to him before the document was publicly released.

"He could have said at any time, 'I want to see the report.' He didn't do that," one of the team members recalled about the president. "Everybody involved in that process was very concerned that Mueller's report and the attorney general's review and summary or release was viewed as being allowed to proceed without intervention. We wanted it to be clean. We didn't want to give anyone an excuse to say we are sticking our fingers in."

On the other hand, Trump's legal team knew Mueller had delivered a monster of a document, which they jokingly called "a son of Starr report," a reference to the 211-page document on Clinton investigations released in 1998 by independent counsel Kenneth Starr. The size of Mueller's report made the Trump team anxious. The lawyers were expected to be prepared to respond to the report whenever it was released.

On April 11, Jane Raskin wrote a letter to Bill Barr explaining the Trump legal team's belief that they had a right to read the report ahead of time. She cited the Justice Department's policy that third parties who are not charged with a crime are entitled to ensure that their privacy and reputational interests are respected in Justice Department releases. She made clear that they merely wanted to read the document and did not intend to suggest any changes to it or request further redactions.

Barr agreed and told Jay Sekulow that his team should get ready to come over and read the report on April 15. But because the Justice Department's final review took longer than expected, the Trump team's review was pushed back a day. On the afternoon of April 16, Barr welcomed Sekulow, Rudy Giuliani, and Jane and Marty Raskin to his secure conference room on the sixth floor of the Justice Department's headquarters to read Mueller's work product.

The Trump team had developed a habit of reading their memos and correspondence aloud to one another to edit and refine the copy. So they decided they would try to read the Mueller report aloud. The scene became slightly comical. Marty Raskin was designated to read the first few pages of volume 1. But after reading a page, the team ditched the oral history reading.

"We're like, 'Forget it,'" recalled one team member. "It's like you haven't eaten for a week. Here's a huge buffet in front of you. They give you *amuse-bouche*."

The voracious lawyers began reading volume 1 but soon put it down.

It didn't implicate Trump. They quickly turned their focus to volume 2, which was a damning collection of evidence about Trump's attempts to thwart the investigation. Though the scenes were unspooled in a gripping narrative, the legal analysis and explanations were difficult to follow.

"I had trouble getting through the first four pages," said the team member. "It's where they lay out why they aren't going to reach a conclusion. The first dealt with the [Office of Legal Counsel] opinion. They recognized it was there and they were bound by it. They do an analysis of the opinion and whether they should even investigate this."

The lawyers were stuck on the fourth page, reading it over and over again. This part dealt with Mueller's justification for investigating Trump for two years even if he couldn't prosecute him. It was a window into the special counsel's strategy and legal reasoning. Mueller's team explained that even reaching a decision about whether Trump had engaged in criminal conduct that would normally warrant prosecution would be as unfair as charging him, something they were prohibited from doing. The only fair solution, Mueller's team wrote, was to document the evidence in a report that could be shared with the Justice Department and ultimately Congress.

But the president's lawyers grew angry as they let this sink in. In their opinion, the report showed there was never any evidence that Trump engaged in an underlying crime, such as conspiring with Russians to interfere in the election, and so it was nearly impossible to conceive that he could be accused of obstructing a criminal probe. They thought, what was fair about investigating a president for the entirety of his presidency so far and then deciding not to determine whether the evidence amounted to a crime? The Trump lawyers firmly believed their client was innocent. His only "crime" was being a politician who felt shackled and slandered by being under investigation. As she read Mueller's report, Jane Raskin thought, "This should never happen again."

Mueller's day of reckoning for the public turned out to be April 18. That morning, Barr, flanked by Rod Rosenstein and Ed O'Callaghan, strode to a lectern at the Justice Department's press briefing room to hold a news conference moments before his office released the Mueller report to Congress and to the public. In his half an hour before the cameras, the attorney general said exactly what the president wanted to hear.

Barr reinforced Trump's talking points that the report had found "no collusion," even though, as the report stated, "collusion" was not a term in federal criminal law. He also tried to spin volume 2 as less damaging for the president than many other readers of the evidence would argue, and he even offered a defense, or at least a sympathetic explanation, for Trump's potentially obstructive acts.

"President Trump faced an unprecedented situation," Barr told reporters. "As he entered into office, and sought to perform his responsibilities as President, federal agents and prosecutors were scrutinizing his conduct before and after taking office, and the conduct of some of his associates. At the same time, there was relentless speculation in the news media about the President's personal culpability. Yet, as he said from the beginning, there was in fact no collusion. And as the Special Counsel's report acknowledges, there is substantial evidence to show that the President was frustrated and angered by a sincere belief that the investigation was undermining his presidency, propelled by his political opponents, and fueled by illegal leaks."

An array of former federal prosecutors and Democratic lawmakers denounced Barr's performance as a partisan farce and castigated him as a henchman. He was accused of serving as Trump's defense counsel, not as the nation's attorney general. But one person cheering him on was the president.

"I love this guy," Trump told Chris Christie about Barr's handling of the Mueller report. "He's a warrior."

Trump was thrilled with the report's conclusions and with Barr's protective moves but was furious with the news coverage of the report's most derogatory scenes. Many of them were attributed in the footnotes to Don McGahn or to the notes kept by the then White House counsel's chief of staff, Annie Donaldson.

Donaldson's notes, scribbled rapidly on a legal pad, were the closest thing the Trump White House had to the Nixon tapes: a sort of diary guiding Mueller's prosecutors through months of West Wing chaos and chronicling Trump's attempts to blunt the investigation. Her words were unflinching and even humorous. "Just in the middle of another Russia Fiasco," she wrote on March 2, 2017. In another entry, on March 21, 2017, Donaldson wrote of Trump, "beside himself" and "getting hotter and hotter."

The morning of April 19, Trump was at Mar-a-Lago for the Easter weekend and was stewing over media coverage. Trump, who had long been suspicious of paper trails, tweeted, "Statements are made about me by certain people in the Crazy Mueller Report, in itself written by 18 Angry Democrat Trump Haters, which are fabricated & totally untrue. Watch out for people that take so-called 'notes,' when the notes never existed until needed."

Trump seethed in particular over McGahn's extensive cooperation with Mueller, which was clear given his ubiquity in the report's sourcing. Giuliani attacked McGahn in a series of media interviews and argued that the White House counsel should have resigned if he thought what Trump was doing violated the law.

Other Trump advisers said they believed McGahn was being singled out unfairly by some in Trump's orbit because of his past tensions with key figures, including Jared Kushner and Ivanka Trump. One of these advisers told Robert Costa of *The Washington Post*, "If anything, Don saved this presidency from the president. If Don had actually gone through with what the president wanted, you would have had a constitutional crisis. The president's ego is hurt, but he's still here."

Trump escaped, at least for now, the justice so many legal professionals believed he deserved. In May, more than a thousand former federal prosecutors who served under both Republican and Democratic administrations signed an open letter stating that Trump's conduct as documented in Mueller's report "would, in the case of any other person not covered by the Office of Legal Counsel policy against indicting a sitting President, result in multiple felony charges for obstruction of justice."

Yet in the summer months that followed, Democrats in the House would fail to generate sufficient momentum to begin impeachment proceedings based on the Russia probe. The White House counsel's office would block their requests for records and testimony from scores of current and former Trump advisers under claims of executive privilege. More Democratic legislators would slowly speak out in favor of impeachment, but the fall would arrive without any meaningful congressional action in response to the devastating evidence the special counsel uncovered.

If Mueller believed Congress ought to pursue impeachment, he did almost nothing to help achieve that outcome. By refusing to answer questions about his findings until his July 24 House testimony, by offering up a 448-page report and expecting the public or even members of Congress would have the attention span to absorb its lawyerly analysis, Mueller fumbled the moment. He was too pure and too invested in the norms of an institution of yore, the Justice Department, whose core values and the public servants who upheld them had been under assault for two straight years.

"His silence, his telling people to just read the report, has allowed a guy like Trump and a disappointing guy like Barr to come in, and Barr knows Mueller and he knows that Mueller won't fight back," said Frank Figliuzzi, the former Mueller FBI colleague. The special counsel, he concluded, "ended up getting played. But I don't mean that he should've done something different because it might turn out that history will look at Mueller and say the guy brought faith and credibility back to institutions and Barr and Trump could be dismissed by history. We don't know where this is going. But in the moment, it looks like he was suckered and he lost the fight."

On June 18, it was ninety degrees, humid, and hazy in Orlando. Just sixteen miles down the road from Disney World, citizens of MAGA nation converged at the Amway Center early in the morning to obtain spots in the security line. People adorned themselves with "Make America Great Again" caps and red, white, and blue boas. They parked themselves under the shade of camping tents or in folding chairs, wheeled up coolers with beverages, and waited patiently for the superstar to arrive.

That night, Trump swooped in to officially launch his reelection campaign. As he was aboard Air Force One en route to central Florida, the capacity crowd of roughly twenty thousand inside the Amway Center was rapturous. Paula White, a pastor and televangelist who said she had a nearly two-decade relationship with the Trump family, delivered the opening prayer.

"I come to you in the name of Jesus," White told the crowd. Quoting from scripture, she said, "We're not wrestling against flesh and blood, but against principalities, powers, against rulers of darkness of this world, against spiritual wickedness in high places. So right now let every demonic network that has aligned itself against the purpose, against the calling of President Trump, let it be broken, let it be torn down in the name of Jesus, let the counsel of the wicked be spoiled right now. According to Job 12:17, I declare that President Trump will overcome every strategy from hell and every strategy from the enemy—every strategy—and he will fulfill his calling and his destiny."

In White's telling, naturally, Trump's calling was to win reelection. And in interviews with people in the crowd, it became clear that Trump's followers took his word as gospel.

The Democrats? Liars and sore losers.

The Russia investigation? A witch hunt.

Mueller's conclusion? No collusion. No obstruction. Total and complete exoneration.

"The whole thing was based on rumors—unsubstantiated, made-up facts," said Karen Osborne, a sixty-two-year-old retired realtor from Vero Beach, Florida. She made air quotes with her fingers as she said "made-up facts."

"The so-called obstruction of justice is no different than a kid being bullied at school and complains to his parents about it," Osborne added. What Trump's critics saw as paranoia, Osborne called "righteous anger."

"He was pissed off and complained to his trusted advisers," she said. "He could've stopped it, but he didn't."

Trump strode onto the stage with his wife, Melania, to Lee Greenwood's "God Bless the U.S.A." The cheers were so loud that the arena's concrete floors pulsated. People craned their necks and raised their phones in the air to snap photos and record videos. For the sweaty masses who had waited all day to see the president, this was the moment.

"Thank you, Orlando!" Trump said. "What a turnout! What a turnout!"

Trump declared himself the victor in "the greatest witch hunt in political history." He called the Justice Department's Russia investigation "an illegal attempt to overturn the results of the election" and to "subvert our democracy."

Never mind that the Russians actually did subvert America's democracy by interfering in the 2016 election to help Trump win, a brazen act of subterfuge that got the FBI investigation started in the first place.

"We call it the Russian hoax," Trump said, still refusing two and a half years later to accept the conclusions of his own intelligence agencies.

Invoking the "18 very angry Democrats," as he inaccurately described the special counsel team, Trump added, "They went after my family, my business, my finances, my employees, almost everyone that I've ever known or worked with, but they are really going after you. They tried to erase your vote, erase your legacy of the greatest campaign and the greatest election, probably in the history of our country. And they wanted to deny you the future that you demanded and the future that America deserves."

Trump framed the 2020 election as a referendum not merely on his performance in office but also on "the un-American conduct" of investigators. "This election is a verdict on whether we want to live in a country where the people who lose an election refuse to concede and spend the next two years trying to shred our Constitution and rip your country apart."

The crowd roared in approval.

EPILOGUE

On July 25, 2019, as the sun rose on a hot, humid Thursday morning, President Trump declared the witch hunt over. He had triumphed over Robert Mueller, who a day before gave Congress a halting, inconclusive summary of his investigation of the president—a painful capstone to the special counsel probe. Finally, the Russia cloud had lifted. Trump no longer had to obey his cautious advisers. He was invincible, or so he thought. And then the unfettered president walked himself right over the edge of a legal precipice and into a politically treacherous crevasse. At 9:03 a.m., he picked up the phone in the White House residence and was connected to his newly elected Ukrainian counterpart, Volodymyr Zelensky. What Trump did next would stun national security officials, trigger impeachment proceedings, and culminate in the gravest test yet of whether America's rule of law could survive its rogue president.

So many of Trump's impulsive and reckless decisions had shocked the conscience. His aides and advisers had long ago grown accustomed to mad scrambles to avert dangerous plans or to repair the damage he had caused to international alliances out of pique or ignorance. But what Trump said to Zelensky on July 25 set off alarm bells with an entirely new and ear-piercing peal.

Trump's call was supposed to be the clincher of a dodgy diplomatic effort that he had initiated that spring to help convince the Ukrainian government to announce it was investigating former vice president Joe

Biden, a leading 2020 Democratic challenger, and lucrative fees his son, Hunter, collected from a Ukrainian energy firm. Speaking in the language of crime bosses, Trump reminded Zelensky that the United States had been "very, very good to Ukraine," a reference to years of military aid that helped Ukraine protect itself from its aggressive neighbor, Russia. Trump didn't mention that he had personally blocked the most recently approved U.S. aid package, nearly $400 million. He didn't have to; a U.S. diplomat had warned Zelensky's government that Trump wanted something before releasing the funds.

"I would like you to do us a favor though," Trump added. He asked Zelensky to work with Rudy Giuliani as well as Attorney General Bill Barr to investigate the Bidens and look into an unproven conspiracy theory—which Trump embraced—that his perceived enemies had fabricated evidence of Russian interference in the 2016 election. "I would like you to get to the bottom of it," Trump said.

Just like that, Trump effectively asked the Ukrainian government to interfere in the 2020 U.S. presidential election. The brazen request—an apparent attempt to leverage taxpayer dollars to extort Ukraine for opposition research on a domestic political opponent—revealed what little Trump had learned from the Mueller investigation and the exhaustive national conversation about the illegality of seeking political assistance from a foreign government.

Pressuring the leader of a far smaller and more vulnerable nation to help him smear Biden in hopes of boosting his own reelection chances came naturally to Trump. As a developer, he had bullied casino regulators and manipulated contractors. This was, to borrow the Trumpian phrase, the art of the deal.

As he ended the call, a handful of the nearly dozen U.S. officials who had been listening in fretted about what they had just witnessed. If they believed their ears and their gut, Trump had tried to use his public office for personal gain. The next day, July 26, one of the White House aides who had listened to the call confided in a CIA official that Trump's comments to Zelensky had been "crazy," "frightening," and "completely lacking in substance related to national security." The aide added that "the President had clearly committed a criminal act."

That fear led the CIA official to blow the whistle in a formal complaint that triggered House Speaker Nancy Pelosi to formally open an impeachment inquiry on September 24.

The Ukraine episode revealed some essential and worrisome truths about Trump, two and a half years into his term. He was a president entirely unrestrained, free from the shackles of seasoned advisers who sought to teach him to put duty to country above self and to follow protocols. He had concluded he was above the law, after dodging accountability for flouting rules and withstanding the Mueller investigation. He had grown so confident of his own power, and cocksure that Republicans in Congress would never dare break with him, that he thought he could do almost anything.

The result was a historic test for America's institutions and the very durability of its democracy.

Trump came into office uncertain about how to operate the machinery of government and tolerated to some degree the efforts of his top advisers to influence him. John Kelly, Jim Mattis, Don McGahn, Rex Tillerson, and others tried to tutor him about the three branches of government and the constitutional balance of powers. They tried to temper his rash impulses. They tried to coach him about his sacred duty as leader of the world's most powerful nation to always put country first.

Over time, however, Trump had systematically dispensed with these human guardrails. And by the time Trump deputized Giuliani to be his political avenger by running a shadow foreign policy with the Ukrainians, the adults were no longer there to stop or even to warn the president about the dangers of doing so, for they had been replaced by willing enablers. Trump had grown increasingly emboldened to make his own decisions and to enforce them. "It's very easy actually to work with me. You know why it's easy? Because I make all the decisions," Trump quipped on September 12, reflecting on John Bolton's abrupt exit as national security adviser.

Trump appeared to head into a tailspin of volatility as the impeachment probe gained traction. In early October, he suddenly decided, against the counsel of his national security team, to withdraw U.S. troops from Syria, abandoning America's Kurdish allies. The commander in chief's decision may have distracted the public from his conduct, but it was calamitous. It eased the way for Turkey to launch a deadly offensive that empowered Bashar al-Assad's regime, thrust the Middle East into turmoil, and raised grave new doubts about America's leadership around the world.

Former senior administration officials and many Republican lawmakers watched with horror. Earlier in Trump's term, one of these officials explained, "There was more of an ethos in the place of trying to help the institution and to help enlighten him rather than simply to execute his marching orders." Now, this official said, "I'm not sure there are many, if any, left who view as their responsibility trying to help educate, moderate, enlighten and persuade—or even advise in many cases.

"There's a new ethos: This is a presidency of one," this official added. "It's Trump unleashed, unchained, unhinged."

Indeed, Trump seemed unmoored at the bipartisan revolt over his callous abandonment of Kurdish allies in Syria and the U.S. military's strategic presence in the region. He spoke illogically and inconsistently, calling Syria a place where warring factions could "play with a lot of sand," threatening to torpedo Turkey's economy if he so chose, and boasting of his "great and unmatched wisdom."

Trump's solipsism threatened to become his undoing. In Ukraine, the president's determination to pursue his personal benefit even at the expense of the nation, coupled with his egocentric obsession with winning and exacting revenge on his enemies, led him into trouble.

By the fall of 2019, Trump was acting as if he were convinced of his own invincibility, believing that he could wield the vast powers of his office in pursuit of his personal and political goals without accountability. He genuinely believed that his interests came first and that, as president, he was above the law. Trump had good reason to think so, having sidestepped any legal punishment after the Mueller investigation produced extensive evidence that he had worked to block and thwart the Russia probe. Trump skirted penalties for a battery of other offenses, ranging from past racist, misogynistic, or otherwise bigoted comments to accusations of self-dealing in violation of the emoluments provision of the Constitution to blocking Congress's ability to conduct oversight.

As the legislative branch scrutinized his actions, Trump looked in the mirror and saw no wrongdoing. Rather, he nursed a deep and inescapable sense of persecution and self-pity, casting himself as a victim in a warped reality and alleging that Democrats and the media were conspiring to perpetuate hoaxes, defraud the public, and stage a coup. This mind-set followed the historical pattern of authoritarian leaders creating a cult of victimization to hold on to power and to justify their repressive agendas.

"We haven't seen anything like this in my lifetime. He appears to be daring the rest of the political system to stop him—and if it doesn't, he'll go further," William A. Galston, a senior fellow in governance at the Brookings Institution, told *The Washington Post*'s Robert Costa.

"What we're discovering is that the Constitution is not a mechanism that runs by itself," Galston added. "Ultimately, we are a government of men and not law. The law has no force without people who are willing to enforce it."

As autumn bore on, the question facing the Congress and indeed the country was not whether Trump had done anything wrong. The emerging fact pattern plainly showed a quid pro quo with Ukraine and a White House scheme to cover it up. The question was who might enforce the Constitution.

When Alexander Hamilton wrote the two essays in *The Federalist* devoted to the idea of impeachment, Trump was the kind of president he had in mind—a populist demagogue who would foment frenzy, pander to prejudices, feed off chaos, and secretly betray the American people in the accumulation of power—according to Hamilton's biographer Ron Chernow.

Two hundred thirty-two years after Hamilton put pen to paper, Trump's pressure campaign on Ukraine forced a reckoning. Would the system the Founding Fathers imagined withstand the pressures of this moment? Or would Trump prevail yet again, another pursuit of justice stymied by his sheer political force and the fealty of his followers?

As Congress considered impeaching President Richard Nixon in 1974, most Republicans defended their president's claim that he was the victim of a political witch hunt. But the decision of one Republican congressman marked a turning point. Maryland's Lawrence J. Hogan became the first Republican to side with the Democrats and vote for all three articles of impeachment against Nixon. He said he wished "with all my heart" he could say the president had not committed impeachable offenses, but he knew the truth was that Nixon had. He was chastened by history.

Republicans now faced the same choice Hogan did forty-five years before. They had held their tongues in fear after so many Trump transgressions. They, too, had called the investigations into the president witch hunts. They had made quiet calculations about when, if ever, they might take a stand. Yet the time was nearing to consider not merely the judgment of their party or the punishment from their president, but the fate of history.

Acknowledgments

We first acknowledge the people who were willing to share their experiences from this period. We cannot name them here, but each aided us immeasurably in telling the full story of this presidency. We thank them. Some struggled with a difficult choice: to honor the duty they felt from government service to keep confidences and show respect for a sitting president, or to follow an internal compass urging them to help document these episodes to the public for the benefit of history.

This project would not have been possible without the generous support and commitment of our editors at *The Washington Post*—first and foremost Marty Baron, whose leadership, judgment, and commitment to unearthing truths has not only guided our newsroom but also helped shield and bolster a free press during this extraordinary period. Steven Ginsberg, who has expertly and gracefully directed the *Post*'s coverage of the Trump administration, was an enthusiastic and essential advocate of our partnership and of this deeper examination. We also are indebted to Cameron Barr, Dave Clarke, Dan Eggen, Matea Gold, Tracy Grant, Lori Montgomery, and Peter Wallsten for the faith they put in us and the energy they gave to our project. They made it possible for us to be absent during periods when news was furiously breaking and granted us the time and flexibility to see this book to completion.

Our work has been lifted and inspired by the very best journalists in America, our colleagues at the *Post* whose coverage of President Trump has lit the way. We thank profusely Devlin Barrett, Bob Costa, Alice Crites, Josh Dawsey, Karoun Demirjian, Karen DeYoung, Peter Finn, Anne Gearan, Tom Hamburger, Shane Harris, Rosalind Helderman, Sari Horwitz, John Hudson, Greg Jaffe, Michael Kranish, Greg Miller, Nick Miroff, Carol Morello, Ellen Nakashima, Ashley Parker, Paul Sonne, Julie Tate, and Craig Timberg. They lent us their wisdom and kindness and then took on more work when we temporarily stepped aside.

During a generation of turmoil for media companies, we have had the good fortune to find stability and success at the *Post*. Carol came to the paper in 2000 and Philip in 2005, and we consider ourselves lucky to work in a newsroom that seeds excellence in its journalism and nurtures collegiality in its journalists. The *Post*'s mission flourishes because of an unbroken chain of leaders committed to the public good and our democracy. These values were first enshrined by Katharine Graham and protected by Don Graham and Katharine Weymouth. Jeff Bezos and Fred Ryan have championed and built upon the Graham family legacy with their determination to uphold the highest journalistic principles, hold the powerful to account, and expand the *Post*'s reach.

We also are fortunate at the *Post* to work with a diligent group of public relations professionals, led by Kris Coratti, Molly Gannon, and Shani George, who dedicate themselves to ensuring our journalism finds a broad audience on many platforms. We also are indebted to Alma Gill, Brooke Lorenz, Sam Martin, Elliot Postell, and Liz Whyte for giving us the tools to do our best work.

Ann Godoff's reputation as a peerless book editor precedes her. When she decided to take a chance on us, we were equal parts thrilled and terrified. Ann brilliantly nourished this project, pushing us out of our comfort zone and helping us bring our reporting into the round. She schooled us in teleology and was our lodestar in this work. Ann and her superlative team at Penguin Press, including Matthew Boyd, Colleen Boyle, Casey Denis, Bruce Giffords, William Heyward, Sarah Hutson,

Do Mi Stauber, and Ingrid Sterner, ensured these pages would sparkle and reach many readers. We are also grateful to Alexis Kirschbaum and the team at Bloomsbury London—including Jasmine Horsey, Lauren Whybrow, Emma Bal, Anna Massardi, Hannah Paget, Nicola Hill and Jonathon Leech—for skillfully helping to expand the global reach of this book.

Elyse Cheney is the most committed agent, counselor, and advocate any author could ask for, and a force of nature. Elyse recognized the potential for this book before we did, and she remained intimately involved throughout. When we doubted whether we had what it took to craft this historic narrative, she dug deep and helped show us that we could. We are grateful for Elyse and her team, including Allison Devereux, Natasha Fairweather, Claire Gillespie, and Alex Jacobs.

A number of other people played essential roles in this project. Julie Tate, our longtime collaborator and friend, trained her scrupulous eye for detail to stress test our manuscript. There is a reason Julie has been a part of so many winning Pulitzer Prize entries. Grace Barnes conducted valuable research. Cynthia Colonna transcribed many of our interviews. Melina Mara, our friend and *Post* photojournalist, shot our author portraits, and Alicia Majeed made us look great.

We have spent three years in the trenches with scores of journalists at the top of their game, each striving to bring light to darkness and to explain the sometimes incomprehensible. This has been the most challenging and exhilarating period in American journalism during our lifetimes, of which the citizens of our country are the beneficiaries. Our competitors, of which there are too many to list here, have enlivened and inspired our work.

Leonnig

I want to thank the people who have lifted, inspired, and cheered me, including when this project seemed insurmountable. First, I give endless love and thanks to my husband, John Reeder, who somehow bounces back each day, happy and encouraging. He unfailingly carried me, as well as our children, on so many days when I was going to fall down. I am ridiculously lucky to have him as my partner and center in this life. Our literal and figurative house is still standing because of him.

Next, I give buckets of gratitude and love to my wonderful girls, Elise and Molly. You gave me smiles and hugs when I had only a furrowed brow. During this project, you handled major responsibilities on your own, beautifully. You make me so proud. Both of you, along with your father, gave me the reason to keep going when I needed it most.

I will be forever grateful to my work partner, Phil Rucker, who injected our project with an amazing drive and rigor that was stunning to witness in progress. He is a colleague par excellence who never lets up, who demands so much of himself, and who never asks of you what he has not already delivered and cross-checked. The skills and energy he brought to this work left me in awe. I couldn't imagine a more precise, caring, and gifted collaborator in any narrative project, in this moment, and at any time.

Words fail in expressing my gratitude for the treasure of family and friends who have been critical cheerleaders, in spirit and in deed. Thanks always to my mother, Dolly, who wordlessly did so much for me; to my sister, Brooke, and brother, Henry, for constant support and understanding; to my late father, Harry, who instilled in me a joy for a hard job done well. Major thanks to every member of my extended Reeder clan, too long to list, and to Maureen Reeder and Glenn Kelley for their graceful help throughout.

I am forever indebted to a group of friends—including Michelle Dolge, Julie Maner, Lisa Rosenberg, Kristianne Teems, Liz Wieser, and Kristin Willsey—for giving me the gifts one cannot buy: their ear, laughter, and time. Thank you for the soul-restoring breaks, sometimes running through Rock Creek Park or talking over wine. Caitrine Callison, I couldn't have made it without your every gracious deed and welcoming hug. Thanks also to people who were encouraging listeners from the earliest days, including Cynthia Baker, Kitson Jazynka, Juliana Reno, Laura Scalzo, and Elizabeth Shreve.

Thanks to the people in the craft who were my early guides. I'm grateful to Steve Coll, Anne Hull, Carlos Lozada, David Maraniss, Dana Priest, Karen Tumulty, Joby Warrick, Paige Williams, Bob Woodward, and many more, who generously offered their advice on book writing over lunches and long talks. Thank you, Paige, for hopping on the phone at any hour.

I have a wealth of fabulous collaborators at the *Post*, where teamwork is a hallmark and the reason I love the place. Rachael Bade, Bob Barnes, Bob Costa, Aaron Davis, Josh Dawsey, David Fahrenthold, Anne Gearan, Tom Hamburger, Shane Harris, Rosalind Helderman, Greg Jaffe, Michelle Lee, Ashley Parker, Beth Reinhard, Mike Semel, Ian Shapira, Craig Timberg, and so many others make the work invigorating—and fun. I'm indebted to the magical poise and instincts of Matea Gold, who leads our political enterprise team, along with John Drescher and Sandhya Somashekhar. Finally, thank you to the amazing team at NBC and MSNBC, where smart, savvy pros including Chris Hayes, Dafna Linzer, Rachel Maddow, Andrea Mitchell, Nicolle Wallace, Brian Williams, and many others shine a light day in and day out on the best breaking journalism and bring our reporting to a broader audience.

Rucker

To my mother, Naomi, who brought me into this world with bravery and unconditional love, thank you. You afforded me every opportunity a shy boy curious about the world could ever need or want, sometimes at great personal sacrifice. You gave me the courage to walk through open doors and taught me to live a life of honor, to think critically, and, importantly, to write. There could never be a book without you.

Clara, my brilliant, loving, and free-spirited sister, and Karen have proven that there is more to living than hustle. My nephew, Lee, has brightened my life and makes me hopeful about the future. My late grandparents, Helen and Bunny, were trailblazers for equality and justice and endowed me with the resolve to question authority.

I could not have partnered with a more faithful and indefatigable co-author than Carol Leonnig. Her prowess as a reporter is beyond compare. To watch Carol follow a lead and reconstruct a scene in exacting detail was breathtaking. She imbued this project with shrewd intuition and intellectual integrity, and her persistence expanded our ambitions. The readers are the richer for it. Carol's warm spirit and optimism kept me moving forward, no matter my apprehensions, for which I will forever be in her debt.

I have had the great fortune to cover the Trump presidency as part of the strongest White House reporting squad in the news business: Josh Dawsey, Anne Gearan, Seung Min Kim, David Nakamura, Tolu Olorunnipa, and Ashley Parker, led by the steadfast and sharp Dan Eggen and Dave Clarke. Jacqueline Alemany, Rachael Bade, Jabin Botsford, Bob Costa, Colby Itkowitz, Jenna Johnson, Paul Kane, Damian Paletta, Felicia Sonmez, and John Wagner have lent their smarts and firepower to our team. You all have elevated my craft and still given me reasons to laugh. You are simply the best.

Three reporting partners have shaped my past decade covering politics at the *Post*. Dan Balz took me under his wing when I was a rookie on the trail and taught me to be rigorous and fair and to explore the country with an open notebook, imparting the simple truth that campaigns are about more than what candidates say. They are about how voters feel. Bob Costa, who took Trump's aspirations seriously before anyone else in the media, showed me the power of reporting to challenge conventional wisdom. And Ashley Parker, my rival as a Romney Rambler in 2012, became my indispensable collaborator during the Trump presidency, coaching me in the art of language and counseling me through trials large and small.

I am privileged to have found a second professional home at NBC News and MSNBC. Thank you to Peter Alexander, Phil Griffin, Kasie Hunt, Hallie Jackson, Andy Lack, Dafna Linzer, Chris Matthews, Craig Melvin, Andrea Mitchell, Elena Nachmanoff, Kelly O'Donnell, Jesse Rodriguez, Stephanie Ruhle, Katy Tur, Nicolle Wallace, Kristen Welker, Brian Williams, and so many others. I am indebted to the inimitable Alan Berger and his crack team at Creative Artists Agency for making it all possible.

Al Kamen graciously opened his home on Lake Michigan in Pentwater for me to write with a change of scenery. Holly Bailey, Mary Jordan, Ruth Marcus, Eli Saslow, Mike Shear, and Karen Tumulty shared book-writing tips and offered encouragement. Ann Gerhart and Maralee Schwartz buoyed me with wisdom and warmth. Tammy Haddad offered generous counsel. The cheerful staff at Philz in Adams Morgan kept me caffeinated.

To Luis Gabriel Cuervo, Elizabeth Dooghan, Borja Gracia, Anna Gregory, Mari Fer Merino, Justin Mills, Ryan Ozimek, John Petersen, Sarah Strom, and April Warren, who have been my D.C. family at Sunday night "Noche" dinners, thank you for your love and nourishment. To Mike Bender, Andrew and Liz Cedar, Matt Lachman, Elyse Layton, Tom Lee, Will and Addar Levi, Rebecca Livengood, Leslie Pope, Adam and Rachel Presser, Julia Pudlin, Maeve Reston, Matt Rivera, Tim Runfola, Eli Stokols, Rachel Streitfeld, Keith and Kristen Urbahn, Burden Walker, Nate Wenstrup, and David Wishnick, thank you for always being there. And to Evelyn Kramer, Michelle Kwan, the Wieners, Christine Brennan, and the rest of the Ice Castle diaspora, you knew me when.

Notes

Chapter One: Building Blocks

13 **Nor of his attendance:** Greg Miller, "Trump's Pick for National Security Adviser Brings Experience and Controversy," *Washington Post*, Nov. 17, 2016, www.washingtonpost.com /world/national-security/trumps-pick-for-national-security-adviser-brings-experience -and-controversy/2016/11/17/0962eb88-ad08-11e6-8b45-f8e493f06fcd_story.html.

13 **Flynn called for the United States:** Michael T. Flynn, "Our Ally Turkey Is in Crisis and Needs Our Support," *Hill*, Nov. 8, 2016, thehill.com/blogs/pundits-blog/foreign-policy /305021-our-ally-turkey-is-in-crisis-and-needs-our-support.

16 **During the March 5 Kansas caucuses:** Susan B. Glasser, "Mike Pompeo, the Secretary of Trump," *New Yorker*, Aug. 19, 2019, www.newyorker.com/magazine/2019/08/26/mike -pompeo-the-secretary-of-trump.

17 **"Don't forget, he's a showbiz guy":** Philip Rucker and Karen Tumulty, "Donald Trump Is Holding a Government Casting Call. He's Seeking 'the Look,'" *Washington Post*, Dec. 22, 2016, www.washingtonpost.com/politics/donald-trump-is-holding-a-government-casting -call-hes-seeking-the-look/2016/12/21/703ae8a4-c795-11e6-bf4b-2c064d32a4bf_story .html.

24 **But Trump dug in:** Greg Miller, Greg Jaffe, and Philip Rucker, "Doubting the Intelligence, Trump Pursues Putin and Leaves a Russian Threat Unchecked," *Washington Post*, Dec. 14, 2017, www.washingtonpost.com/graphics/2017/world/national-security/donald -trump-pursues-vladimir-putin-russian-election-hacking/.

Chapter Two: Paranoia and Pandemonium

27 **"You know, I won":** Max Greenwood, "Trump Told Pelosi: You Know I Won the Popular Vote," *Hill*, June 9, 2017, thehill.com/blogs/blog-briefing-room/news/337117-trump-told -pelosi-you-know-i-won-the-popular-vote.

31–32 **Chris Christie and his wife:** Special Counsel Robert S. Mueller, "Report on the Investigation into Russian Interference in the 2016 Presidential Election," U.S. Department of Justice, March 2019.

Chapter Three: The Road to Obstruction

43 **McGahn's mind raced:** Mueller, "Report on the Investigation into Russian Interference in the 2016 Presidential Election."

48 **He discovered an unexpected ally:** Meghan Clyne, "Trump Scoffs at U.N.'s Plan for New H.Q.," *New York Sun*, Feb. 4, 2005, www.nysun.com/new-york/trump-scoffs-at-uns -plan-for-new-hq/8727/.

48 **He told the other senators:** "U.S. Financial Involvement in Renovation of U.N.

Headquarters," Committee on Homeland Security and Governmental Affairs Hearing, July 21, 2005, www.govinfo.gov/content/pkg/CHRG-109shrg23164/pdf/CHRG-109shrg 23164.pdf.

51 **But that didn't seem to bother Trump:** Philip Rucker, Robert Costa, and Ashley Parker, "Inside Trump's Fury: The President Rages at Leaks, Setbacks, and Accusations," *Washington Post*, March 5, 2017, www.washingtonpost.com/politics/inside-trumps-fury-the -president-rages-at-leaks-setbacks-and-accusations/2017/03/05/40713af4-01df -11e7-ad5b-d22680e18d10_story.html.

Chapter Four: A Fateful Firing

53 **"This is terrible, Jeff":** Mueller, "Report on the Investigation into Russian Interference in the 2016 Presidential Election."

54 **"While I greatly appreciate":** Mueller, "Report on the Investigation into Russian Interference in the 2016 Presidential Election."

61 **The straitlaced Rosenstein:** Ruben Castaneda, "Profile of Rod Rosenstein, U.S. Attorney for Maryland," *Washington Post*, Oct. 9, 2011, www.washingtonpost.com/local/profile-of -rod-rosenstein-us-attorney-for-maryland/2011/09/29/gIQAfOTWYL_story.html?utm _term=.4055254b7e1e.

62 **"This was a tumultuous time":** Testimony of James A. Baker, Executive Session, October 18, 2018. Committee on the Judiciary, Joint with the Committee on Government Reform and Oversight, U.S. House of Representatives.

62 **"We need to open the case":** Catherine Herridge, "Strzok-Page Calling to 'Open' Case in 'Chargeable Way' under Fresh Scrutiny," Fox News, September 17, 2018, https://www .foxnews.com/politics/strzok-page-texts-calling-to-open-case-in-chargeable-way-under -fresh-scrutiny.

63 **Then the president told them:** Matt Apuzzo, Maggie Haberman, and Matthew Rosenberg, "Trump Told Russians That Firing 'Nut Job' Comey Eased Pressure from Investigation," *New York Times*, May 19, 2017, www.nytimes.com/2017/05/19/us/politics/trump-russia -comey.html.

65 **On May 16, Michael Schmidt:** Michael S. Schmidt, "Comey Memo Says Trump Asked Him to End Flynn Investigation," *New York Times*, May 16, 2017, www.nytimes.com /2017/05/16/us/politics/james-comey-trump-flynn-russia-investigation.html.

Chapter Six: Suiting Up for Battle

84 **He was particularly incensed:** Ellen Nakashima, Adam Entous, and Greg Miller, "Russian Ambassador Told Moscow That Kushner Wanted Secret Communications Channel with Kremlin," *Washington Post*, May 26, 2017, www.washingtonpost.com/world/national -security/russian-ambassador-told-moscow-that-kushner-wanted-secret-communications -channel-with-kremlin/2017/05/26/520a14b4-422d-11e7-9869-bac8b446820a_story .html?tid=sm_fb&utm_term=.7fb4395f2b1a.

89 **All of them followed Sullivan's lead:** Robert Costa and Ashley Parker, "Trump Close to Choosing Outside Counsel for Russia Investigation," *Washington Post*, May 22, 2017, https://www.washingtonpost.com/politics/trump-close-to-choosing-outside -counsel-for-russia-investigation/2017/05/22/8709f62e-3f22-11e7-9869 -bac8b446820a_story.html.

Chapter Seven: Impeding Justice

96 **Testifying June 13 before:** Miles Park, "Rosenstein Says He Wouldn't Fire Special Counsel Mueller Without Good Cause," NPR, June 13, 2017.

99 **McGahn drove from his home:** Mueller, "Report on the Investigation into Russian Interference in the 2016 Presidential Election."

106 **On June 21, *The Wall Street Journal*:** Eli Stokols and Michael C. Bender, "White House Looks to Chart Steadier Course amid Turmoil over Russia Probes," *Wall Street Journal*,

June 21, 2017, www.wsj.com/articles/white-house-looks-to-chart-steadier-course-amid -turmoil-over-russia-probes-1498088253.

Chapter Eight: A Cover-Up

110 Yet Trump, who harbored deep: Greg Miller, "Trump Has Concealed Details of His Face-to-Face Encounters with Putin from Senior Officials in Administration," *Washington Post*, Jan. 12, 2019, www.washingtonpost.com/world/national-security/trump-has-concealed -details-of-his-face-to-face-encounters-with-putin-from-senior-officials-in -administration/2019/01/12/65f6686c-1434-11e9-b6ad-9cfd62dbb0a8_story.html.

116 As she later told the special counsel: Mueller, "Report on the Investigation into Russian Interference in the 2016 Presidential Election."

120 Once Trump boarded Air Force One, however: Ashley Parker et al., "Trump Dictated Son's Misleading Statement on Meeting with Russian Lawyer," *Washington Post*, July 31, 2017, www.washingtonpost.com/politics/trump-dictated-sons-misleading-statement-on-meeting -with-russian-lawyer/2017/07/31/04c94f96-73ae-11e7-8f39-eeb7d3a2d304_story.html.

121 At the last minute, Trump: Mueller, "Report on the Investigation into Russian Interference in the 2016 Presidential Election."

121 "It was a short introductory meeting": Jo Becker, Matt Apuzzo, and Adam Goldman, "Trump Team Met with Lawyer Linked to Kremlin During Campaign," *New York Times*, July 8, 2017, www.nytimes.com/2017/07/08/us/politics/trump-russia-kushner-manafort .html.

125 "After pleasantries were exchanged": Jo Becker, Adam Goldman, and Matt Apuzzo, "Russian Dirt on Clinton? 'I Love It,' Donald Trump Jr. Said," *New York Times*, July 11, 2017, www.nytimes.com/2017/07/11/us/politics/trump-russia-email-clinton.html.

127 Trump junior, meanwhile: Becker, Goldman, and Apuzzo, "Russian Dirt on Clinton?"

127 Trump ripped into Attorney General: Peter Baker, Maggie Haberman, and Michael S. Schmidt, "Citing Recusal, Trump Says He Wouldn't Have Hired Sessions," *New York Times*, July 19, 2017, www.nytimes.com/2017/07/19/us/politics/trump-interview-sessions -russia.html.

Chapter Nine: Shocking the Conscience

132 "That's our task, right?": Philip Rucker and Ashley Parker, "How President Trump Consumes—or Does Not Consume—Top-Secret Intelligence," *Washington Post*, May 29, 2017, www.washingtonpost.com/politics/how-president-trump-consumes—or-does -not-consume—top-secret-intelligence/2017/05/29/1caaca3e-39ae-11e7-a058 -ddbb23c75d82_story.html.

133 Trump said U.S. troops: Bob Woodward, *Fear: Trump in the White House* (New York: Simon & Schuster, 2018).

139 The secretary of state came: Carol E. Lee et al., "Tillerson's Fury at Trump Required an Intervention from Pence," NBC News, Oct. 4, 2017, www.nbcnews.com/politics/white -house/tillerson-s-fury-trump-required-intervention-pence-n806451.

140 Over the next few days: Philip Rucker et al., "Trump Names Homeland Security Secretary John Kelly as White House Chief of Staff, Ousting Reince Priebus," *Washington Post*, July 27, 2017, www.washingtonpost.com/news/post-politics/wp/2017/07/28/trump-names -homeland-security-secretary-john-kelly-as-white-house-chief-of-staff-ousting-reince -priebus/.

Chapter Ten: Unhinged

147 Scaramucci unloaded on Priebus : Ryan Lizza, "Anthony Scaramucci Called Me to Unload About White House Leakers, Reince Priebus, and Steven Bannon," *New Yorker*, July 27, 2017, www.newyorker.com/news/ryan-lizza/anthony-scaramucci-called-me-to-unload -about-white-house-leakers-reince-priebus-and-steve-bannon.

154 This abdication of moral leadership: Demetri Sevastopulo and Gillian Tett, "Gary Cohn

Urges Trump Team to Do More to Condemn Neo-Nazis," *Financial Times*, Aug. 25, 2017, www.ft.com/content/b85beea2-8924-11e7-bf50-e1c239b45787.

Chapter Eleven: Winging It

165 In March, McMaster was: Greg Miller, Greg Jaffe, and Philip Rucker, "Doubting the Intelligence, Trump Pursues Putin and Leaves a Russian Threat Unchecked," *Washington Post*, Dec. 14, 2017, www.washingtonpost.com/graphics/2017/world/national-security /donald-trump-pursues-vladimir-putin-russian-election-hacking/.

168 U.S. ambassador to the United Nations Nikki Haley: Greg Jaffe and Philip Rucker, "National Security Adviser Attempts to Reconcile Trump's Competing Impulses on Afghanistan," *Washington Post*, Aug. 4, 2017, www.washingtonpost.com/world/national-security/the -fight-over-trumps-afghan-policy-has-become-an-argument-over-the-meaning-of -america-first/2017/08/04/f2790c80-785f-11e7-8f39-eeb7d3a2d304_story.html.

172 "Remember what we've always said": Mueller, "Report on the Investigation into Russian Interference in the 2016 Presidential Election."

174 unnamed senior officials: Carol D. Leonnig, Adam Entous, Devlin Barrett, and Matt Zapotosky, "Michael Flynn Pleads Guilty to Lying to FBI on Contacts with Russian Ambassador," *Washington Post*, Dec. 1, 2017, www.washingtonpost.com/politics/michael -flynn-charged-with-making-false-statement-to-the-fbi/2017/12/01/e03a6c48-d6a2 -11e7-9461-ba77d604373d_story.html.

176 "What the president has to say": Miller, Jaffe, and Rucker, "Doubting the Intelligence, Trump Pursues Putin and Leaves a Russian Threat Unchecked."

Chapter Twelve: Spygate

183 "Television is often": Ashley Parker and Robert Costa, "'Everyone Tunes In': Inside Trump's Obsession with Cable TV," *Washington Post*, April 23, 2017, www.washingtonpost .com/politics/everyone-tunes-in-inside-trumps-obsession-with-cable-tv/2017/04/23 /3c52bd6c-25e3-11e7-a1b3-faff0034e2de_story.html.

185 When a CNN reporter: Dan Merica, "John Kelly Likes to Pretend Trump's Tweets Don't Matter. But They Do," CNN, Jan. 11, 2018, www.cnn.com/2018/01/11/politics/john-kelly -donald-trump-tweets/index.html.

187 Trump's comment in the closed-door meeting: Josh Dawsey, "Trump Derides Protections for Immigrants from 'Shithole' Countries," *Washington Post*, Jan. 12, 2018, www.washing tonpost.com/politics/trump-attacks-protections-for-immigrants-from-shithole -countries-in-oval-office-meeting/2018/01/11/bfc0725c-f711-11e7-91af-31ac729add94 _story.html?utm_term=.51cd945b8204.

195 "My counsel to him is": "Trey Gowdy Full Interview with Erin Burnett," CNN, Jan. 24, 2018, YouTube, www.youtube.com/watch?v=mpjva6xa-Nc.

Chapter Thirteen: Breakdown

198 In a White House staff notable: Katie Rogers, "Rob Porter's Charisma and Ambition Disguised Flare-Ups of Anger," *New York Times*, Feb. 19, 2018, www.nytimes.com/2018 /02/19/us/politics/rob-porter-white-house-resigned.html.

200 In addition, the Porter case coincided: Michael Rothfeld and Joe Palazzolo, "Trump Lawyer Arranged $130,000 Payment for Adult-Film Star's Silence," *Wall Street Journal*, Jan. 12, 2018, www.wsj.com/articles/trump-lawyer-arranged-130-000-payment-for-adult -film-stars-silence-1515787678.

201 Amid the media scrutiny: Carol D. Leonnig, Robert Costa, and Josh Dawsey, "Top Justice Dept. Official Alerted White House 2 Weeks Ago to Ongoing Issues in Kushner's Security Clearance," *Washington Post*, Feb. 23, 2018, www.washingtonpost.com/politics /top-justice-dept-official-alerted-white-house-2-weeks-ago-to-ongoing-issues-in -kushners-security-clearance/2018/02/23/aa9b37c8-17f4-11e8-92c9-376b4fe57ff7_story .html.

201 Bill Daley, a former White House: Philip Rucker, Ashley Parker, and Josh Dawsey, "'Jared Has Faded': Inside the 28 Days of Tumult That Left Kushner Badly Diminished," *Washington Post*, March 2, 2018, www.washingtonpost.com/politics/jared-has-faded-inside-the-28-days-of-tumult-that-left-kushner-badly-diminished/2018/03/02/62acb9ce-1ca8-11e8-9de1-147dd2df3829_story.html.

202 An aide briefed on: Shane Harris et al., "New White House Security Clearance Policy Could Put 'Bull's Eye' on Kushner," *Washington Post*, Feb. 16, 2018, www.washingtonpost.com/politics/overhaul-of-white-house-security-clearance-process-could-threaten-kushners-access/2018/02/16/09f2dc9e-11b5-11e8-9065-e55346f6de81_story.html.

202 "This is a man who": Philip Rucker, "John Kelly's Credibility Is at Risk After Defending Aide Accused of Domestic Violence," *Washington Post*, Feb. 8, 2018, www.washingtonpost.com/politics/john-kellys-credibility-is-at-risk-after-defending-aide-accused-of-domestic-violence/2018/02/08/e8e1ff06-0ccf-11e8-8890-372e2047c935_story.html.

203 Kelly said he would: Sophie Tatum, "Kelly Says He'll 'Never' Apologize for Comments About Rep. Frederica Wilson," CNN, Oct. 31, 2017, www.cnn.com/2017/10/30/politics/john-kelly-frederica-wilson-apologize/index.html.

204 "When you lose that power": Ashley Parker, Josh Dawsey, and Philip Rucker, "'When You Lose That Power': How John Kelly Faded as White House Disciplinarian," *Washington Post*, April 7, 2018, www.washingtonpost.com/politics/when-you-lose-that-power-how-john-kelly-faded-as-white-house-disciplinarian/2018/04/07/5e5b8b42-39be-11e8-acd5-35eac230e514_story.html.

206 The two men argued so loudly: Maggie Haberman and Katie Rogers, "The Day John Kelly and Corey Lewandowski Squared Off Outside the Oval Office," *New York Times*, Oct. 22, 2018, www.nytimes.com/2018/10/22/us/politics/john-kelly-lewandowski-fight-secret-service.html.

207 The intelligence agencies were on guard: Shane Harris et al., "Kushner's Overseas Contacts Raise Concerns as Foreign Officials Seek Leverage," *Washington Post*, Feb. 27, 2018, www.washingtonpost.com/world/national-security/kushners-overseas-contacts-raise-concerns-as-foreign-officials-seek-leverage/2018/02/27/16bbc052-18c3-11e8-942d-16a950029788_story.html.

208 Kushner and Ivanka disputed: Jonathan Swan, "Kushner, for First Time, Claims He Never Discussed Security Clearance with Trump," *Axios*, June 3, 2019, www.axios.com/jared-kushner-security-clearance-donald-trump-f7706db1-a978-42ec-90db-c2787f19cef3.html.

210 Observers registered a new level: Philip Rucker, Ashley Parker, and Josh Dawsey, "'Pure Madness': Dark Days Inside the White House as Trump Shocks and Rages," *Washington Post*, March 3, 2018, www.washingtonpost.com/politics/pure-madness-dark-days-inside-the-white-house-as-trump-shocks-and-rages/2018/03/03/9849867c-1e72-11e8-9de1-147dd2df3829_story.html.

Chapter Fourteen: One-Man Firing Squad

214 Paul Rosenzweig, who worked: Carol D. Leonnig and Robert Costa, "Mueller Raised Possibility of Presidential Subpoena in Meeting with Trump's Legal Team," *Washington Post*, May 1, 2018, www.washingtonpost.com/politics/mueller-raised-possibility-of-presidential-subpoena-in-meeting-with-trumps-legal-team/2018/05/01/2bdec08e-4d51-11e8-af46-b1d6dc0d9bfe_story.html?utm_term=.6c6e572f2b4a.

220 At the same time, some of Trump's top: Ashley Parker et al., "'It Was a Different Mind-Set': How Trump Soured on Tillerson as His Top Diplomat," *Washington Post*, March 13, 2018, www.washingtonpost.com/politics/it-was-a-different-mind-set-how-trump-soured-on-tillerson-as-his-top-diplomat/2018/03/13/899b1fba-26d7-11e8-b79d-f3d931db7f68_story.html?utm_term=.976cb15f60a2.

222 As a twenty-year veteran: Matt Zapotosky, "Andrew McCabe, Trump's Foil at the FBI, Is Fired Hours Before He Could Retire," *Washington Post*, March 16, 2018, www.washington

post.com/world/national-security/fbis-andrew-mccabe-is-fired-a-little-more-than-24
-hours-before-he-could-retire/2018/03/16/e055a22a-2895-11e8-bc72-077aa4dab9ef
_story.html?utm_term=.e7f6d060ca6d.

223 **Dowd got twisted in knots:** Betsy Woodruff, "Trump's Lawyer: It's Time to End the
Mueller Probe," *Daily Beast*, March 17, 2018, www.thedailybeast.com/trumps-lawyer-its
-time-to-fire-robert-mueller.

223 **A few hours later:** Carol D. Leonnig and Philip Rucker, "Trump's Lawyer Calls On Justice
Department to Immediately End Russia Probe," *Washington Post*, March 17, 2018, www
.washingtonpost.com/politics/trumps-lawyer-calls-on-justice-department-to
-immediately-end-russia-probe/2018/03/17/c7c58ac8-29f2-11e8-874b-d517e912f125
_story.html.

223 **"That is certainly an unconventional way":** Ashley Parker et al., "Trump Shakes Up
Team of Lawyers as Legal Threats Mount," *Washington Post*, March 19, 2018, www.wash
ingtonpost.com/politics/trump-shakes-up-team-of-lawyers-as-legal-threats-mount/2018
/03/19/fad71bb0-2ba1-11e8-b0b0-f706877db618_story.html?utm_term=.05c099cf1ed8.

224 **Dowd issued a short, simple statement:** Carol D. Leonnig, Josh Dawsey, and Ashley
Parker, "Trump Has Trouble Finding Attorneys as Top Russia Lawyer Leaves Legal Team,"
Washington Post, March 22, 2018, www.washingtonpost.com/politics/trump-attorney-john
-dowd-resigns-amid-shake-up-in-presidents-legal-team/2018/03/22/0472ce74-2de3
-11e8-8688-e053ba58f1e4_story.html.

Chapter Fifteen: Congratulating Putin

225 **"Everybody fears the perp walk":** Ashley Parker et al., "Trump Decides to Remove National Security Adviser, and Others May Follow," *Washington Post*, March 15, 2018, www
.washingtonpost.com/politics/trump-decides-to-remove-national-security-adviser-and
-others-may-follow/2018/03/15/fea2ebae-285c-11e8-bc72-077aa4dab9ef_story.html
?utm_term=.0dd538b03dd0.

226 **It was, as the BBC:** Sarah Rainsford, "Russia Election: Putin Basks in Election He Could
Not Lose," BBC News, March 19, 2018, www.bbc.com/news/world-europe-43454830.

228 **"It's not us":** Greg Jaffe, Josh Dawsey, and Carol D. Leonnig, "Ahead of NATO and Putin
Summits, Trump's Unorthodox Diplomacy Rattles Allies," *Washington Post*, July 6, 2018,
www.washingtonpost.com/politics/ahead-of-nato-and-putin-summits-trumps
-unorthodox-diplomacy-rattles-allies/2018/07/06/16c7aa4e-7006-11e8-bd50
-b80389a4e569_story.html.

230 **For her part, British prime minister:** Adam Taylor, "Trump Congratulated Putin on His
Victory. Other World Leaders Stopped Short of That," *Washington Post*, March 21, 2018,
www.washingtonpost.com/news/worldviews/wp/2018/03/21/trump-congratulated-putin
-on-his-victory-other-world-leaders-stopped-short-of-that/.

230 *The Washington Post* **first reported:** Carol D. Leonnig, David Nakamura, and Josh
Dawsey, "Trump's National Security Advisers Warned Him Not to Congratulate Putin.
He Did It Anyway," *Washington Post*, March 20, 2018, www.washingtonpost.com/politics
/trumps-national-security-advisers-warned-him-not-to-congratulate-putin-he-did-it
-anyway/2018/03/20/22738ebc-2c68-11e8-8ad6-fbc50284fce8_story.html?utm
_term=.8e5b5df5699a.

235 **Jay Sekulow announced:** Josh Dawsey, Carol D. Leonnig, and Rosalind S. Helderman,
"Trump's Legal Team Remains in Disarray as New Lawyer Will No Longer Represent
Him in Russia Probe," *Washington Post*, March 25, 2018. https://www.washingtonpost.com
/politics/in-another-blow-to-trumps-efforts-to-combat-russia-probe-digenova-will-no
-longer-join-legal-team/2018/03/25/8ac8c8d2-3038-11e8-94fa-32d48460b955_story.html.

Chapter Sixteen: A Chilling Raid

236 **"He was treated like":** Marc Perrusguia, "Power Broker," *Daily Memphian*, May 17, 2018,
dailymemphian.com/article/1174/POWER-BROKER.

237 "This search warrant is like": Philip Rucker, Josh Dawsey, and Robert Costa, "'A Bomb on Trump's Front Porch': FBI's Cohen Raids Hit Home for the President," *Washington Post*, April 9, 2018, www.washingtonpost.com/politics/a-bomb-on-trumps-front-porch-fbis -cohen-raids-hit-home-for-the-president/2018/04/09/6abb816e-3c37-11e8-974f -aacd97698cef_story.html.

237 The sections of the U.S. criminal codes: Carol D. Leonnig, Tom Hamburger, and Devlin Barrett, "Trump Attorney Cohen Is Being Investigated for Possible Bank Fraud, Campaign Finance Violations," *Washington Post*, April 9, 2018, www.washingtonpost.com /politics/fbi-seizes-records-related-to-stormy-daniels-in-raid-of-trump-attorney -michael-cohens-office/2018/04/09/e3e43cf4-3c30-11e8-974f-aacd97698cef_story.html.

242 Syrian leader Bashar al-Assad: Anne Gearan and Carol Morello, "Trump Says U.S. Will Decide on Response to 'Atrocious' Attack in Syria in 24 to 48 Hours," *Washington Post*, April 9, 2018, www.washingtonpost.com/politics/trump-says-us-to-decide-on-response-to -atrocious-syria-chemical-attack-in-24-to-48-hours/2018/04/09/1398c5aa-3bfa-11e8 -a7d1-e4efec6389f0_story.html?utm_term=.880adbc397bd.

252 testified to Congress: Katie Rogers, Maggie Haberman, and Nicholas Fandos, "Ex-White House Official Says No One Pressured Him to Overturn Security Clearance Recommendations," *New York Times*, May 2, 2019, https://www.nytimes.com/2019/05/02/us/politics /carl-kline-security-clearance.html.

253 tell ABC News: Allison Pecorin, "Ivanka Trump Says She and Jared Kushner Got No Special Treatment for Security Clearances," ABC News, Feb. 8, 2019, abcnews.go.com /Politics/ivanka-trump-jared-kushner-special-treatment-security-clearances/story?id =60940398.

Chapter Seventeen: Hand Grenade Diplomacy

259 "Here, Angela. Don't say I never": Aris Folley, "Ian Bremmer: Trump Tossed Candy to Merkel at G-7, Said 'Don't Say I Never Give You Anything,'" *Hill*, June 20, 2018, thehill .com/blogs/blog-briefing-room/news/393311-ian-bremmer-trump-tossed-candy -to-merkel-during-g-7-said-don't.

261 The president, this adviser added: Philip Rucker, "The 'Dotard' Meets 'Little Rocket Man': Trump and Kim Are Adversaries with Many Similarities," *Washington Post*, June 10, 2018, www.washingtonpost.com/politics/the-dotard-meets-little-rocket-man-trump-and -kim-are-adversaries-with-many-similarities/2018/06/09/583b9ddc-6a89-11e8-bea7 -c8eb28bc52b1_story.html.

261 Trump was restless: Ashley Parker et al., "'Why Can't We Just Do It?': Trump Nearly Upended Summit with Abrupt Changes," *Washington Post*, June 14, 2018, www.washing tonpost.com/politics/why-cant-we-just-do-it-trump-nearly-upends-summit-with-abrupt -changes/2018/06/14/36e9cb2e-6fe6-11e8-bd50-b80389a4e569_story.html?noredirect =on&utm_term=.74425ec3cf5d.

262 The summit was carefully staged: Philip Rucker and Anne Gearan, "'A Great Honor': In a Bid for History, Trump Flatters North Korea's Totalitarian Leader," *Washington Post*, June 11, 2018, www.washingtonpost.com/politics/a-great-honor-in-a-bid-for-history-trump -flatters-north-koreas-totalitarian-leader/2018/06/11/22a4411c-6d8e-11e8-bf86 -a2351b5ece99_story.html?utm_term=.c1b5a6c9597c.

262 Trump's nearly nine-hour day: Philip Rucker, "'Getting a Good Picture, Everybody?': Inside the Trump Production in Singapore," *Washington Post*, June 12, 2018, www.wash ingtonpost.com/politics/getting-a-good-picture-everybody-inside-the-trump-production -in-singapore/2018/06/12/27d44bfc-6e4a-11e8-afd5-778aca903bbe_story.html.

263 "classic traits of the authoritarian leader": Philip Rucker, "'Dictator Envy': Trump's Praise of Kim Jong Un Widens His Embrace of Totalitarian Leaders," *Washington Post*, June 15, 2018, www.washingtonpost.com/politics/dictator-envy-trumps-praise-of-kim-jong -un-marks-embrace-of-totalitarian-leaders/2018/06/15/b9a8bbc8-70af-11e8-afd5 -778aca903bbe_story.html?utm_term=.46df06790611.

263 Trump's courtship and flattery: Karen DeYoung, "John Bolton, Famously Abrasive, Is an Experienced Operator in the 'Swamp,'" *Washington Post*, March 23, 2018, www.washington post.com/world/national-security/john-bolton-famously-abrasive-is-an-experienced -operator-in-the-swamp/2018/03/23/b9b72000-2eab-11e8-8ad6-fbc50284fce8_story.html.

264 In February 2018, just before joining: John Bolton, "The Legal Case for Striking North Korea First," *Wall Street Journal*, Feb. 28, 2018, www.wsj.com/articles/the-legal-case-for -striking-north-korea-first-1519862374.

267 As Nielsen answered questions: Margaret Sullivan, "A Reporter at the White House Decided to Play the Audio of Children Sobbing. Somebody Had To," *Washington Post*, June 19, 2018, www.washingtonpost.com/lifestyle/style/a-reporter-at-the-white-house-decided -to-play-the-audio-of-children-sobbing-somebody-had-to/2018/06/19/bbb8d814-73aa -11e8-805c-4b67019fcfe4_story.html.

267 In addition to the sounds of sniffling: Ginger Thompson, "Listen to Children Who've Just Been Separated from Their Parents at the Border," ProPublica, June 18, 2018, www .propublica.org/article/children-separated-from-parents-border-patrol-cbp-trump -immigration-policy?utm_campaign=sprout&utm_medium=social&utm_source=twit ter&utm_content=1529351580.

273 The indictment, which Rosenstein publicly announced: Devlin Barrett and Matt Zapotosky, "Mueller Probe Indicts 12 Russians with Hacking of Democrats in 2016," *Washington Post*, July 13, 2018, www.washingtonpost.com/world/national-security/rod-rosenstein -expected-to-announce-new-indictment-by-mueller/2018/07/13/bc565582-86a9-11e8 -8553-a3ce89036c78_story.html.

274 Earlier, when the CBS anchor: "Trump on Putin Meeting: 'I Go In with Low Expectations,'" CBS News, July 15, 2018, www.cbsnews.com/news/trump-russia-low-expectations -putin-meeting/.

275 "nothing short of treasonous": John O. Brennan (@John Brennan), Twitter, July 16, 2018, 8:52 a.m., twitter.com/johnbrennan/status/1018885971104985093?lang=en.

275 After consulting with Sanders: Ashley Parker et al., "Trump's Putin Fallout: Inside the White House's Tumultuous Week of Walk-Backs," *Washington Post*, July 20, 2018, www .washingtonpost.com/politics/trumps-putin-fallout-inside-the-white-houses-tumultuous -week-of-walk-backs/2018/07/20/7cfdfc34-8c3d-11e8-8b20-60521f27434e_story.html.

277 Bolton sprang into action: Parker et al., "Trump's Putin Fallout."

277 At this very moment, Coats: "A Look over My Shoulder: The DNI Reflects and Foreshadows," Aspen Security Forum, July 19, 2018, aspensecurityforum.org/wp-content/up loads/2018/07/ASF-2018-A-Look-Over-My-Shoulder-The-DNI-Reflects-and -Foreshadows-3.pdf.

Chapter Eighteen: The Resistance Within

278 On the sidelines of the NATO meetings: Carol D. Leonnig et al., "A Fist Bump, Then a Rancorous Call: How Trump's Deal to Free an American Pastor in Turkey Fell Apart," *Washington Post*, July 26, 2018, www.washingtonpost.com/politics/trump-says-us-will -impose-large-sanctions-on-turkey-for-detaining-american-pastor-for-nearly-two-years /2018/07/26/75dcde32-90e5-11e8-bcd5-9d911c784c38_story.html?utm_term=.817c4cf0.

280 On July 25, the court convened: Kareem Fahim and Karen DeYoung, "American Pastor Freed from Prison in Turkey but Remains Under House Arrest," *Washington Post*, July 25, 2018, www.washingtonpost.com/world/turkish-court-orders-american-pastor-freed-from -prison-and-placed-under-house-arrest/2018/07/25/7b3f9382-900a-11e8-ae59 -01880eac5f1d_story.html?utm_term=.409dfb3da338.

281 "They want to hold": Anne Gearan and Felicia Sonmez, "In Trump's Standoff with Turkey, Two Tough-Guy Leaders and a Deal Gone Wrong," *Washington Post*, Aug. 16, 2018, www.washingtonpost.com/politics/in-trumps-standoff-with-turkey-two-tough-guy -leaders-and-a-deal-gone-wrong/2018/08/16/d9b6c728-a162-11e8-8e87-c869fe70a721 _story.html?utm_term=.dd2ad3d4526c.

283 Earlier in 2018: Ryan Duffy, "McRaven, Castro, Brennan, and Inman Talk Leadership at LBJ School," *Alcalde*, Feb. 28, 2018, alcalde.texasexes.org/2018/02/mcraven-castro-brennan -and-inman-talk-leadership-at-lbj-school/.

285 As Tumulty sat: William H. McRaven, "Revoke My Security Clearance, Too, Mr. President," *Washington Post*, Aug. 16, 2018, www.washingtonpost.com/opinions/revoke-my -security-clearance-too-mr-president/2018/08/16/8b149b02-a178-11e8-93e3 -24d1703d2a7a_story.html?utm_term=.da3e667e7996.

286 Just after four o'clock: Devlin Barrett et al., "Michael Cohen Says He Worked to Silence Two Women 'in Coordination' with Trump to Influence 2016 Election," *Washington Post*, Aug. 21, 2018, www.washingtonpost.com/world/national-security/trumps-longtime-lawyer -michael-cohen-is-in-plea-discussions-with-federal-prosecutors-according-to-a-person -familiar-with-the-matter/2018/08/21/5fbd7f34-8510-11e8-8553-a3ce89036c78_story .html?utm_term=.e3fcf13076b1.

287 On August 27: David Nakamura, "'Hellooo … Hellooo?': An Awkward Phone Call Becomes Part of the Trump Spectacle," *Washington Post*, Aug. 27, 2018, www.washington post.com/politics/hellooo--hellooo-an-awkward-phone-call-becomes-part-of-the -trump-spectacle/2018/08/27/9e698d1a-aa16-11e8-8a0c-70b618c98d3c_story.html ?utm_term=.e214b40f8dba.

289 On September 1: Greg Jaffe and Philip Rucker, "McCain's Funeral Was a Melancholy Last Hurrah for What's Been Lost in the Trump Era," *Washington Post*, Sept. 1, 2018, www.washingtonpost.com/politics/mccains-funeral-was-a-melancholy-last-hurrah-for -whats-been-lost-in-trump-era/2018/09/01/156784c6-ad46-11e8-b1da-ff7faa680710 _story.html.

289 Ivanka Trump and Jared Kushner attended: Katie Rogers, "Washington Mourned John McCain. President Trump Played Golf," *New York Times*, Sept. 1, 2018, www.nytimes.com /2018/09/01/us/politics/trump-john-mccain.html.

290 On September 5: Anonymous, "I Am Part of the Resistance Inside the Trump Administration," *New York Times*, Sept. 5, 2018, www.nytimes.com/2018/09/05/opinion/trump -white-house-anonymous-resistance.html.

290 Administration aides were so alarmed: Philip Rucker, Ashley Parker, and Josh Dawsey, "'The Sleeper Cells Have Awoken': Trump and Aides Shaken by 'Resistance' Op-Ed," *Washington Post*, Sept. 5, 2018, www.washingtonpost.com/politics/the-sleeper-cells-have -awoken-trump-and-aides-shaken-by-resistance-op-ed/2018/09/05/ecdf423c-b14b-11e8 -a20b-5f4f84429666_story.html.

Chapter Nineteen: Scare-a-Thon

295 By the time he finished: Glenn Kessler, "Anatomy of a Trump Rally: 70 Percent of Claims Are False, Misleading, or Lacking Evidence," *Washington Post*, Sept. 12, 2018, www.wash ingtonpost.com/politics/2018/09/12/anatomy-trump-rally-percent-claims-are-false -misleading-or-lacking-evidence/.

295 On September 21: Ivana Hrynkiw, "AG Jeff Sessions Visits Auburn University, Tailgates Ahead of Saturday's Game," AL.com, Sept. 22, 2018, www.al.com/news/birmingham /2018/09/ag_jeff_sessions_visits_auburn.html.

296 Later that day: Adam Goldman and Michael S. Schmidt, "Rod Rosenstein Suggested Secretly Recording Trump and Discussed 25th Amendment," *New York Times*, Sept. 21, 2018, www.nytimes.com/2018/09/21/us/politics/rod-rosenstein-wear-wire-25th -amendment.html?module=inline.

298 Then *Axios* reported: Jonathan Swan, "Rod Rosenstein Offered to Resign," *Axios*, Sept. 24, 2018, www.axios.com/rod-rosenstein-resign-justice-department-trump-cf761f4c-fca3 -4794-92d4-a56c9e32ff43.html.

299 "I think it pleases him": Ashley Parker and Philip Rucker, "Resign, Fire, or Stay? Rosenstein Is the Latest Contestant in Trump's Favorite Game," *Washington Post*, Sept. 26, 2018, www.washingtonpost.com/politics/resign-fire-or-stay-rosenstein-is-the-latest

-contestant-in-trumps-favorite-game/2018/09/25/b59c6924-c0f2-11e8-90c9
-23f963eea204_story.html.

299 Some of Trump's attorneys: Devlin Barrett et al., "Rod Rosenstein to Stay in Job for Now, Will Meet with Trump on Thursday, White House Says," *Washington Post*, Sept. 24, 2018, www.washingtonpost.com/world/national-security/rod-rosenstein-who-had-been
-overseeing-russia-probe-has-offered-to-resign/2018/09/24/d350477c-aad8-11e8-8a0c
-70b618c98d3c_story.html.

299 Christine Blasey Ford alleged: Emma Brown, "California Professor, Writer of Confidential Brett Kavanaugh Letter, Speaks Out About Her Allegation of Sexual Assault," *Washington Post*, Sept. 16, 2018, www.washingtonpost.com/investigations/california-professor-writer
-of-confidential-brett-kavanaugh-letter-speaks-out-about-her-allegation-of-sexual
-assault/2018/09/16/46982194-b846-11e8-94eb-3bd52dfe917b_story.html?utm_term
=.e206d29eeaf7.

301 "I've had a lot of false charges": Philip Rucker et al., "Defending Kavanaugh, Trump Laments #MeToo as 'Very Dangerous' for Powerful Men," *Washington Post*, Sept. 26, 2018, www.washingtonpost.com/politics/defending-kavanaugh-trump-laments-metoo-as-very
-dangerous-for-powerful-men/2018/09/26/e9116536-c1a4-11e8-97a5-ab1e46bb3bc7
_story.html.

301 The next day: Ashley Parker, Josh Dawsey, and Philip Rucker, "For Trump and White House, Kavanaugh Hearing Was a Suspenseful Drama in Two Acts," *Washington Post*, Sept. 27, 2018, www.washingtonpost.com/politics/for-trump-and-white-house-kavanaugh
-hearing-was-a-drama-in-two-acts/2018/09/27/6b82f8c8-c276-11e8-a1f0
-a4051b6ad114_story.html?utm_term=.171a47be64c2.

303 On August 18: Michael S. Schmidt and Maggie Haberman, "White House Counsel, Don McGahn, Has Cooperated Extensively in Mueller Inquiry," *New York Times*, Aug. 18, 2018, www.nytimes.com/2018/08/18/us/politics/don-mcgahn-mueller-investigation.html.

304 At a cabinet meeting: Josh Dawsey and Nick Miroff, "Trump Unloads on Homeland Security Secretary in Lengthy Immigration Tirade," *Washington Post*, May 10, 2018, www
.washingtonpost.com/world/national-security/trump-unloads-on-homeland-security
-secretary-in-lengthy-immigration-tirade/2018/05/10/f0ded152-54a0-11e8-9c91
-7dab596e8252_story.html?utm_term=.cdd691914581.

308 In late October: Paul Sonne and Missy Ryan, "Trump Says He May Send 15,000 Troops to U.S.-Mexico Border," *Washington Post*, Oct. 31, 2018, www.washingtonpost.com/world
/national-security/ahead-of-midterm-elections-trump-says-he-may-send-15000
-troops-to-us-mexico-border/2018/10/31/9e7740ec-dd4a-11e8-aa33-53bad9a881e8
_story.html?utm_term=.f5bd0c483703.

310 The move immediately inspired: Aaron Blake, "Mattis Vouched for Trump's Decision to Send Troops to the Border. Trump Seems Bent on Making Him Regret It," *Washington Post*, Nov. 2, 2018, www.washingtonpost.com/politics/2018/11/02/trump-is-doing-his-best
-make-fool-jim-mattis/?utm_term=.89c4f7679128.

311 Trump sought to frighten: Philip Rucker, "'Full Trumpism': The President's Apocalyptic Attacks Reach a New Level of Falsity," *Washington Post*, Nov. 4, 2018, www.washington
post.com/politics/full-trumpism-the-presidents-apocalyptic-attacks-reach-a-new
-level-of-falsity/2018/11/04/8e4fb87e-e043-11e8-b759-3d88a5ce9e19_story.html.

Chapter Twenty: An Ornery Diplomat

317 It did not work: Josh Dawsey and Philip Rucker, "Five Days of Fury: Inside Trump's Paris Temper, Election Woes, and Staff Upheaval," *Washington Post*, Nov. 13, 2018, www.wash
ingtonpost.com/politics/five-days-of-fury-inside-trumps-paris-temper-election-woes
-and-staff-upheaval/2018/11/13/e90b7cba-e69e-11e8-a939-9469f1166f9d_story.html
?utm_term=.9e2d15ddad5b.

317 The president was so churlish: Ben Riley-Smith, "'Trump the Grump': Moody US

President Challenged Theresa May over Brexit During Phone Call," *Telegraph*, Nov. 14, 2018, www.telegraph.co.uk/news/2018/11/14/donald-trump-berated-theresa-may-air-force -one-phone-call/.

318 **Nicholas Soames, a grandson:** Nicholas Soames (@NSoames), Twitter, Nov. 10, 2018, 6:51 a.m., twitter.com/NSoames/status/1061270124404113408.

319 **On November 11:** David Nakamura, Seung Min Kim, and James McAuley, "Macron Denounces Nationalism as a 'Betrayal of Patriotism' in Rebuke to Trump at WWI Remembrance," *Washington Post*, Nov. 11, 2018, www.washingtonpost.com/world/europe/to-mark -end-of-world-war-i-frances-macron-denounces-nationalism-as-a-betrayal-of-patriotism /2018/11/11/aab65aa4-e1ec-11e8-ba30-a7ded04d8fac_story.html?utm_term =.f7ed6b6c15f5.

320 **Speaking French, Macron delivered:** "Emmanuel Macron's Speech at Commemoration of the Centenary of the Armistice," Nov. 11, 2018, onu.delegfrance.org/Emmanuel-Macron -s-speech-at-Commemoration-of-the-centenary-of-the-Armistice.

322 **On November 16:** Shane Harris, Greg Miller, and Josh Dawsey, "CIA Concludes Saudi Crown Prince Ordered Jamal Khashoggi's Assassination," *Washington Post*, Nov. 16, 2018, www.washingtonpost.com/world/national-security/cia-concludes-saudi-crown-prince -ordered-jamal-khashoggis-assassination/2018/11/16/98c89fe6-e9b2-11e8-a939 -9469f1166f9d_story.html?noredirect=on&utm_term=.4097ecac0008.

324 **Corsi was a longtime Clinton critic:** Carol D. Leonnig et al., "Mueller Seeks Roger Stone's Testimony to House Intelligence Panel, Suggesting Special Counsel Is near End of Probe of Trump Adviser," *Washington Post*, Dec. 19, 2018, www.washingtonpost.com /politics/mueller-seeks-roger-stones-testimony-to-house-intelligence-panel-suggesting -special-counsel-is-near-end-of-probe-of-trump-adviser/2018/12/19/ac5c3ee6-0226 -11e9-b5df-5d3874f1ac36_story.html?utm_term=.ab1560413c06.

324 **An email from August 2:** Rosalind Helderman, Manuel Roig-Franzia, and Carol D. Leonnig, "Conservative Author and Stone Associate Jerome Corsi Said He Expects to Be Indicted by Special Counsel for Allegedly Lying," *Washington Post*, Nov. 12, 2018, www .washingtonpost.com/politics/conservative-author-and-stone-associate-jerome-corsi -said-special-prosecutors-plan-to-indict-him-for-allegedly-lying/2018/11/12/773e6722 -e6c7-11e8-a939-9469f1166f9d_story.html?utm_term=.945366b72865.

325 **The agreement said Corsi understood:** "Draft Jerome Corsi Statement of Offense," *Washington Post*, apps.washingtonpost.com/g/documents/politics/draft-jerome-corsi-statement -of-offense/3324/.

325 **The second event happened:** Devlin Barrett and Matt Zapotosky, "Julian Assange Has Been Charged, Prosecutors Reveal Inadvertently in Court Filing," *Washington Post*, Nov. 15, 2018, www.washingtonpost.com/world/national-security/julian-assange-has-been -charged-prosecutors-reveal-in-inadvertent-court-filing/2018/11/15/9902e6ba-98bd -48df-b447-3e2a4638f05a_story.html?utm_term=.6b2ea45e42a5.

325 **"would need to remain sealed":** Charlie Savage, Adam Goldman, and Michael S. Schmidt, "Assange Is Secretly Charged in U.S., Prosecutors Mistakenly Reveal," *New York Times*, Nov. 2018, www.nytimes.com/2018/11/16/us/politics/julian-assange-indictment-wikileaks .html.

327 **But on November 20:** Carol D. Leonnig and Robert Costa, "Trump Submits Answers to Special Counsel Questions About Russian Interference," *Washington Post*, Nov. 20, 2018, www.washingtonpost.com/politics/trump-submits-answers-to-special-counsel-questions -about-russian-interference/2018/11/20/3b5a18d4-ed0f-11e8-baac-2a674e91502b_story .html?utm_term=.ff71fff698ae.

327 **Regarding the infamous June 2016:** David A. Fahrenthold, "'I Have No Recollection': Trump Turned to Familiar Refrain in Response to Mueller Questions," *Washington Post*, April 19, 2019, www.washingtonpost.com/politics/i-have-no-recollection-trump-turned -to-familiar-refrain-in-response-to-mueller-questions/2019/04/19/7230817c-62bc-11e9 -9ff2-abc984dc9eec_story.html?utm_term=.1adeca216183.

327 **Trump said in his answers:** Jim Sciutto, Carl Bernstein, and Marshall Cohen, "Cohen Claims Trump Knew in Advance of 2016 Trump Tower Meeting," CNN, July 27, 2018, www.cnn.com/2018/07/26/politics/michael-cohen-donald-trump-june-2016-meeting -knowledge/index.html.

Chapter Twenty-one: Gut over Brains

331 **At the wedding reception:** Jacquie Kubin, "The Story Behind AG Barr, His Bagpipes, and the NYPD Pipes and Drums," *Communities Digital News*, June 27, 2019, www.commdigi news.com/politics-2/willam-barr-plays-the-bagpipes-with-nypd-pipes-and-drums -120463/.

333 **By leaving, Ayers:** Maggie Haberman, "Nick Ayers, Aide to Pence, Declines Offer to Be Trump's Chief of Staff," *New York Times*, Dec. 9, 2018, www.nytimes.com/2018/12/09/us /politics/nick-ayers-trump-chief-of-staff.html.

333 **Trump, who for days:** Philip Rucker, Josh Dawsey, and Robert Costa, "'There Was No Plan B': Trump Scrambles to Find Chief of Staff After Top Candidate Turns Him Down," *Washington Post*, Dec. 10, 2018, www.washingtonpost.com/politics/there-was-no-plan-b -trump-scrambles-to-find-chief-of-staff-after-top-candidate-turns-him-down/2018/12 /10/9b6d0424-fc9c-11e8-862a-b6a6f3ce8199_story.html.

334 **As the Democrats arrived in the Oval:** Philip Rucker, Josh Dawsey, and Robert Costa, "'This Has Spiraled Downward': Democrats Introduce Trump to Divided Government," *Washington Post*, Dec. 11, 2018, www.washingtonpost.com/politics/this-has-spiraled -downward-democrats-introduce-trump-to-divided-government/2018/12/11/f832b92e -fd6e-11e8-862a-b6a6f3ce8199_story.html?utm_term=.ee2306da300a.

335 **Kushner helped orchestrate:** Annie Karni, "The Senate Passed the Criminal Justice Bill. For Jared Kushner, It's a Personal Issue and a Rare Victory," *New York Times*, Dec. 14, 2018, www.nytimes.com/2018/12/14/us/politics/jared-kushner-criminal-justice-bill.html.

335 **He had even invited:** Helena Andrews-Dyer, "Here's What Happened at Kanye West's Incredibly Bizarre Meeting with Donald Trump," *Washington Post*, Oct. 11, 2018, www .washingtonpost.com/news/reliable-source/wp/2018/10/11/that-was-quite-something -kanye-wests-meeting-with-president-trump-covers-everything-from-mental-health -to-male-energy/.

337 **Christie saw a breaking news headline:** Jonathan Swan, "Trump Meets with Chris Christie to Discuss Chief of Staff Role," *Axios*, Dec. 13, 2018, www.axios.com/trump-met-with -chris-christie-to-discuss-chief-of-staff-role-684f9465-a6ea-4a80-9df3-2d91ba67cf35 .html.

340 **"We have obviously learned":** Kyle Rempfer, "Troops to Immediately Withdraw from Syria as Trump Declares Victory over ISIS," *Army Times*, Dec. 19, 2018, www.armytimes .com/news/your-army/2018/12/19/troops-may-immediately-withdrawal-from-syria-as -trump-declares-victory-over-isis/.

341 **McGurk was stunned:** Annalisa Merelli, "Another Leader in the US Fight Against ISIS Resigned to Protest Trump's Syria Decision," *Quartz*, Dec. 22, 2018, qz.com/1505835/top -syria-envoy-brian-mcgurk-resigned/.

341 **In the most active years:** Liz Sly and Louisa Loveluck, "The 'Caliphate' Is No More. But the Islamic State Isn't Finished Yet," *Washington Post*, March 23, 2019, www.washington post.com/world/the-islamic-states-caliphate-has-been-defeated-us-backed-forces-say /2019/03/23/04263d74-36f8-11e9-8375-e3dcf6b68558_story.html.

Chapter Twenty-two: Axis of Enablers

349 **As he celebrated the agreement:** Erica Werner, Damian Paletta, and Seung Min Kim, "Trump Backs Off Demand for $5 Billion for Border Wall, but Budget Impasse Remains Ahead of Shutdown Deadline," *Washington Post*, Dec. 18, 2018, www.washingtonpost.com /business/economy/white-house-signals-its-backing-down-in-shutdown-dispute-will

-find-other-ways-to-fund-border-wall/2018/12/18/159994dc-02d9-11e9-9122
-82e98f91ee6f_story.html?utm_term=.9472e6deb7d0.

350 **Congressman Mark Meadows:** Philip Rucker, Robert Costa, and Josh Dawsey, "'A Tailspin': Under Siege, Trump Propels the Government and Markets into Crisis," *Washington Post*, Dec. 20, 2018, www.washingtonpost.com/politics/a-tailspin-under-siege-trump -propels-the-government-and-markets-into-crisis/2018/12/20/e30347e0-046b-11e9 -b6a9-0aa5c2fcc9e4_story.html?utm_term=.961668fb2900.

350 **At the end of December 21:** Erica Werner, Damian Paletta, and John Wagner, "Major Parts of the Federal Government Begin Shutting Down for an Indefinite Closure," *Washington Post*, Dec. 21, 2018, www.washingtonpost.com/politics/trump-leans-on -mcconnell-to-pass-spending-bill-with-border-funding-in-senate/2018/12/21/31bb453a -0517-11e9-b5df-5d3874f1ac36_story.html.

350 **"Do we succumb":** Andrew Blake, "Donald Trump Succumbed to 'Tyranny of Radio Hosts' over Government Shutdown: GOP Senator," *Washington Times*, Dec. 22, 2018, www.apnews.com/0ca586c8ad6c3f7f73a0cfa33e74be39.

353 **In the weeks that followed:** Anne Gearan, Josh Dawsey, and John Hudson, "'They Screwed This Whole Thing Up': Inside the Attempt to Derail Trump's Erratic Syria Withdrawal," *Washington Post*, Jan. 13, 2019, www.washingtonpost.com/politics/they-screwed -the-whole-thing-up-inside-the-attempt-to-derail-trumps-erratic-syria-withdrawal/2019 /01/13/0ae1149c-1365-11e9-803c-4ef28312c8b9_story.html?utm_term=.a1dcbf520820.

353 **The night of Christmas Eve:** Eric Levenson, "Trump Asks 7-Year-Old, 'Are You Still a Believer in Santa?,'" CNN, Dec. 26, 2018, www.cnn.com/2018/12/25/politics/trump-santa -phone-call/index.html.

354 **"Because at 7":** Hannah Alani, "Do a 'Marginal' Number of 7-Year-Olds Believe in Santa? That's What Trump Told a SC Girl," *Post and Courier*, Dec. 25, 2018, www.postandcourier .com/news/do-a-marginal-number-of--year-olds-believe-in/article_2c86d3ec-0876 -11e9-a470-87234a04ef7e.html.

354 **Trump also jeopardized:** Paul Sonne and Philip Rucker, "Trump's Visit to Iraq Prompts Concerns About Politicization of Military," *Washington Post*, Dec. 27, 2018, www.wash ingtonpost.com/world/national-security/trumps-visit-to-iraq-prompts-concerns-about -politicization-of-military/2018/12/27/42aa20fe-0a13-11e9-892d-3373d7422f60_story .html?utm_term=.15f6c712a1df.

355 **"You just fucked it all up":** Jonathan Swan, "Scoop: Trump Dressed Down Mulvaney in Front of Congressional Leaders," *Axios*, Jan. 13, 2019, www.axios.com/donald-trump-mick -mulvaney-government-shutdown-meeting-7d84ea72-5aaf-45e0-a707-5f955836070e .html.

357 **By the beginning of January:** Carol D. Leonnig, "A Beefed-Up White House Legal Team Prepares Aggressive Defense of Trump's Executive Privilege as Investigations Loom Large," *Washington Post*, Jan. 9, 2019, www.washingtonpost.com/politics/a-beefed-up-white -house-legal-team-prepares-aggressive-defense-of-trumps-executive-privilege-as -investigations-loom-large/2019/01/09/066b8618-1045-11e9-84fc-d58c33d6c8c7_story .html.

363 **On January 23:** Josh Dawsey, "Giuliani's Missteps Frustrate Trump but Underscore the Unique Role He Plays for the President," *Washington Post*, Jan. 23, 2019, www.washington post.com/politics/giulianis-missteps-frustrate-trump-but-underscore-the-unique -role-he-plays-for-the-president/2019/01/23/447ec0a4-1f23-11e9-bda9-d6efefc397e8 _story.html?utm_term=.9250633bd190.

364 **"not being able to make a hamburger":** Philip Rucker and Josh Dawsey, "Trump Two Years in: The Dealmaker Who Can't Seem to Make a Deal," *Washington Post*, January 20, 2019, https://www.washingtonpost.com/politics/trump-two-years-in-the-dealmaker-who -cant-seem-to-make-a-deal/2019/01/20/ecdede96-1bf9-11e9-88fe-f9f77a3bcb6c_story .html.

364 **On February 15:** Damian Paletta, Mike DeBonis, and John Wagner, "Trump Declares

National Emergency on Southern Border in Bid to Build Wall," *Washington Post*, Feb. 15, 2019, www.washingtonpost.com/politics/trumps-border-emergency-the-president-plans-a -10-am-announcement-in-the-rose-garden/2019/02/15/f0310e62-3110-11e9-86ab -5d02109aeb01_story.html?utm_term=.516e628ecdb8.

365 So on February 22: Paul Sonne, "Pentagon Sending 1,000 More Troops to the Mexican Border," *Washington Post*, Feb. 22, 2019, www.washingtonpost.com/world/national-security /pentagon-sending-another-1000-troops-to-the-mexico-border/2019/02/22/c4e06998 -36e6-11e9-946a-115a5932c45b_story.html.

Chapter Twenty-three: Loyalty and Truth

366 Cohen pleaded guilty: Devlin Barrett, Matt Zapotosky, and Rosalind S. Helderman, "Michael Cohen, Trump's Former Lawyer, Pleads Guilty to Lying to Congress About Moscow Project," *Washington Post*, Nov. 29, 2018, www.washingtonpost.com/politics/michael-cohen -trumps-former-lawyer-pleads-guilty-to-lying-to-congress/2018/11/29/5fac986a-f3e0 -11e8-bc79-68604ed88993_story.html?utm_term=.b029279bf91e.

368 The morning of February 27: "Michael Cohen's Prepared Statement to the House Committee on Oversight and Reform," *Washington Post*, Feb. 27, 2019, www.washingtonpost .com/michael-cohen-s-prepared-statement-to-the-house-committee-on-oversight-and -reform/d2cdc193-2f0c-44bb-b2f8-e7dadddf545e_note.html?questionId=a194ac05 -9c53-4be2-868d-777713d7c30e&utm_term=.9c1a0f6342e8.

371 Before leaving Hanoi: David Nakamura, "Trump Whipped Up Public Emotion over Warmbier's Death. Now It's Boomeranging Back on Him," *Washington Post*, March 2, 2019, www.washingtonpost.com/politics/trump-whipped-up-public-emotion-over-otto -warmbiers-death-now-its-boomeranging-back-on-him/2019/03/02/ef426ff4-3d23-11e9 -a2cd-307b06d0257b_story.html?utm_term=.c17b49404ae2.

379 "dignified settings like the Oval Office": Gabby Orr, "Advisers Urge Trump to Defer 2020 Rallies," *Politico*, March 8, 2019, www.politico.com/story/2019/03/08/trump-2020 -rallies-1211799.

Chapter Twenty-four: The Report

380 The Barr team's immediate priority: "DOJ Notification to Congress Regarding the Conclusion of the Mueller Investigation," *Washington Post*, March 22, 2019, www.washington post.com/context/doj-notification-to-congress-regarding-the-conclusion-of-the-mueller -investigation/?noteId=501d8d23-1823-4140-9b29-daaee164275e&questionId =111ad2f8-d378-4dd6-a39a-a3241842594d.

383 The 448-page report was a breathtaking catalog: Devlin Barrett and Matt Zapotosky, "Mueller Report Lays Out Obstruction Evidence Against the President," *Washington Post*, April 17, 2019, www.washingtonpost.com/world/national-security/attorney-general -to-provide-overview-of-mueller-report-at-news-conference-before-its-release/2019/04 /17/8dcc9440-54b9-11e9-814f-e2f46684196e_story.html.

383 Some of the episodes: Philip Rucker and Robert Costa, "Paranoia, Lies, and Fear: Trump's Presidency Laid Bare by Mueller Report," *Washington Post*, April 18, 2019, www.washing tonpost.com/politics/paranoia-lies-and-fear-trumps-presidency-laid-bare-by-mueller -report/2019/04/18/3379c49a-571b-11e9-814f-e2f46684196e_story.html.

386 Giuliani was in Washington: Rucker et al., "The Battle over the Mueller Report Begins as Trump Allies Claim Victory."

391 The letter said that the introductions: "Special Counsel Mueller's Letter to Attorney General Barr," *Washington Post*, March 27, 2019, www.washingtonpost.com/context/special -counsel-mueller-s-letter-to-attorney-general-barr/e32695eb-c379-4696-845a -1b45ad32fff1/.

392 On April 30: Devlin Barrett and Matt Zapotosky, "Mueller Complained That Barr's Letter Did Not Capture 'Context' of Trump Probe," *Washington Post*, April 30, 2019, www .washingtonpost.com/world/national-security/mueller-complained-that-barrs

-letter-did-not-capture-context-of-trump-probe/2019/04/30/d3c8fdb6-6b7b-11e9-a66d
-a82d3f3d96d5_story.html.

Chapter Twenty-five: The Show Goes On

397 Back in Washington the night of April 2: Nielsen interview on *Tucker Carlson Tonight*, YouTube, April 2, 2019, www.youtube.com/watch?v=rEfma2hj2sU.

397 Nielsen also said that Trump: Dan Cancian, "DHS Chief Kirstjen Nielsen Hints Donald Trump May Close Border: 'He's Very Serious About It,'" *Newsweek*, April 3, 2019, www.newsweek.com/donald-trump-us-mexico-wall-kirstjen-nielsen-border-wall -1384455.

397 In an April 4 interview: Priscilla Alvarez and Geneva Sands, "Homeland Security Secretary on Border Situation: 'We Have an Emergency on Our Hands,'" CNN, April 4, 2019, www.cnn.com/2019/04/04/politics/nielsen-border-cnntv/index.html.

400 "I could not be prouder": "Kirstjen Nielsen's Resignation Letter," *Washington Post*, April 8, 2019, www.washingtonpost.com/context/kirstjen-nielsen-s-resignation-letter/ ?noteId=db93edc2-df04-49ed-b0a4-6a64d7d5d765&questionId=e4834bfe-8b59-4d74 -9cb0-a261d6c4857e.

401 By June, however: Aaron C. Davis and Shawn Boburg, "As Trump's Defense Pick Withdraws, He Addresses Violent Domestic Incidents," *Washington Post*, June 18, 2019, www .washingtonpost.com/investigations/trumps-defense-nominee-addresses-violent -incident-between-ex-wife-son-amid-fbi-vetting-process/2019/06/18/e46009de-190b -11e9-a804-c35766b9f234_story.html.

402 Some of them had been: Paul Sonne, "Seeking to Sell Military Budget, Pentagon Chief Faces Political Fire over Wall," *Washington Post*, March 14, 2019, www.washingtonpost .com/world/national-security/pentagon-chief-rules-outcost-plus-50-approach-with -allies/2019/03/14/d49c676c-4666-11e9-9726-50f151ab44b9_story.html.

403 In May, *The New York Times*: Dave Philipps, "Trump May Be Preparing Pardons for Servicemen Accused of War Crimes," *New York Times*, May 18, 2019, www.nytimes.com /2019/05/18/us/trump-pardons-war-crimes.html.

405 On the afternoon of April 16: Matt Zapotosky et al., "Mueller Report Will Be Lightly Redacted, Revealing Detailed Look at Obstruction of Justice Investigation," *Washington Post*, April 17, 2019, www.washingtonpost.com/world/national-security/attorney-general -plans-news-conference-to-discuss-mueller-report/2019/04/17/f5ca1cc6-6138-11e9-9ff2 -abc984dc9eec_story.html.

407 Donaldson's notes: Carol D. Leonnig, "Watergate Had the Nixon Tapes. Mueller Had Annie Donaldson's Notes," *Washington Post*, May 3, 2019, www.washingtonpost.com /politics/watergate-had-the-nixon-tapes-mueller-had-annie-donaldsons-notes/2019/05 /03/d2b1bc62-66b5-11e9-8985-4cf30147bdca_story.html.

408 One of these advisers: Philip Rucker, Josh Dawsey, and Robert Costa, "Trump Blames McGahn After Mueller Paints Damning Portrait with Notes from White House Aides," *Washington Post*, April 19, 2019, www.washingtonpost.com/politics/trump-blames-mcgahn -after-mueller-paints-damning-portrait-with-notes-from-white-house-aides/2019/04/19 /ea0f153a-62b4-11e9-9412-daf3d2e67c6d_story.html.

408 In May, more than a thousand: "Statement by Former Federal Prosecutors," *Medium*, May 6, 2019, medium.com/@dojalumni/statement-by-former-federal-prosecutors-8ab76 91c2aa1.

409 That night, Trump swooped in: "Pastor Paula White Delivers Opening Prayer at President Trump's Reelection Rally," YouTube, www.youtube.com/watch?v=MY4MYPCzAfk.

Epilogue

412 Trump's call was supposed: Craig Timberg, Drew Harwell, and Ellen Nakashima, "In Call to Ukraine's President, Trump Revived a Favorite Conspiracy Theory About the DNC Hack," *Washington Post*, September 25, 2019, www.washingtonpost.com/technology

/2019/09/25/trumps-mention-crowdstrike-call-with-ukraines-president-recalls-russian
-hack-dnc/.

413 Trump reminded Zelensky: Karoun Demirjian, Josh Dawsey, Ellen Nakashima, and
Carol D. Leonnig, "Trump Ordered Hold on Military Aid Days Before Calling Ukrainian
President, Officials Say," *Washington Post*, September 23, 2019, www.washingtonpost.com
/national-security/trump-ordered-hold-on-military-aid-days-before-calling-ukrainian
-president-officials-say/2019/09/23/df93a6ca-de38-11e9-8dc8-498eabc129a0_story.html.

413 "I would like you to do us a favor though": Memorandum of Telephone Conversation,
Subject: Telephone Conversation with President Zelenskyy (*sic*) of Ukraine, White House,
declassified by order of the president, September 24, 2019, www.whitehouse.gov/wp-content
/uploads/2019/09/Unclassified09.2019.pdf?fbclid=IwAR2NRvNaYh-nrFMBa2SSG1
bumdyNoJhXVCDNtBYugM-klXGctnWce6qDjD0.

413 The next day, July 26: Arden Farhi, "Read the Whistleblower's Memo About Trump's
Ukraine Call, as Described to CBS News," CBS News, October 9, 2019, www.cbsnews.com
/news/the-whistleblower-complaint-read-full-text-whistleblower-memo-trump-ukraine
-call-described-cbs-news-exclusive/.

415 "There was more of an ethos in the place": Philip Rucker and Robert Costa, "'A Presidency
of One': Key Federal Agencies Increasingly Compelled to Benefit Trump," *Washington
Post*, October 2, 2019, www.washingtonpost.com/politics/a-presidency-of-one-key-federal
-agencies-increasingly-compelled-to-benefit-trump/2019/10/01/f80740ec-e453-11e9
-a331-2df12d56a80b_story.html.

416 "We haven't seen anything like this": Philip Rucker, Robert Costa, and Rachael Bade,
"Trump's Ukraine Call Reveals a President Convinced of His Own Invincibility," *Washington Post*, September 21, 2019, www.washingtonpost.com/politics/trumps-ukraine-call
-reveals-a-president-convinced-of-his-own-invincibility/2019/09/21/1a56466c-dc6a
-11e9-ac63-3016711543fe_story.html.

416 When Alexander Hamilton wrote the two essays: Ron Chernow, "Hamilton Pushed for
Impeachment Powers. Trump Is What He Had in Mind," *Washington Post*, October 18, 2019,
www.washingtonpost.com/outlook/2019/10/18/hamilton-pushed-impeachment-powers
-trump-is-what-he-had-mind/?arc404=true.

417 He said he wished "with all my heart": Michael S. Rosenwald. "'A very bad blow': The
GOP Lawmaker Who Turned on Nixon Paid a Price for It," *Washington Post*, September
29, 2019, www.washingtonpost.com/history/2019/09/29/a-very-bad-blow-gop-lawmaker
-who-turned-nixon-paid-price-it/.

Index